Dining Room
and
Banquet Management

FOURTH EDITION

Join us on the web at

www.hospitality-tourism.delmar.com

Dining Room and Banquet Management

FOURTH EDITION

Anthony J. Strianese
Pamela P. Strianese

THOMSON

DELMAR LEARNING ™

Australia Canada Mexico Singapore Spain United Kingdom United States

THOMSON

DELMAR LEARNING ™

Dining Room and Banquet Management, Fourth Edition
Anthony J. Strianese and Pamela P. Strianese

Vice President, Career Education Strategic Business Unit:
Dawn Gerrain

Director of Learning Solutions:
John Fedor

Senior Acquisitions Editor:
Matthew Hart

Developmental Editor:
Patricia Osborn

Editorial Assistant:
Patrick Horn

Director of Content and Media Production:
Wendy Troeger

Production Manager:
Mark Bernard

Senior Content Project Manager:
Glenn Castle

Director of Marketing:
Wendy E. Mapstone

Channel Manager:
Kristin McNary

Cover Design:
Bernadette Skok

Cover Image:
Francesco Lagnese/The Image Bank/© Getty Images

Printed in Canada
1 2 3 4 5 XXX 11 10 09 08 07

For more information contact Delmar Learning, 5 Maxwell Drive, Clifton Park, NY 12065-8007.

Or you can visit our Internet site at
http://www.delmarlearning.com or
http://www.hospitality-tourism.delmar.com

For permission to use material from this text or product,
contact us by
Tel (800) 730-2214
Fax (800) 730-2215
www.thomsonrights.com

Library of Congress Cataloging-in-Publication Data

Strianese, Anthony J.
  Dining room and banquet management /
Anthony J. Strianese, Pamela P. Strianese. -- 4th ed.
    p. cm.
  Includes bibliographical references and index.
  ISBN-10: 1-4180-5369-4
  ISBN-13: 978-1-4180-5369-7
  1. Food service management. I. Strianese, Pamela P.
II. Title.
  TX911.3.M27S76 2007
  647.95--dc22
                                        2007026790

NOTICE TO THE READER

Publisher does not warrant or guarantee any of the products described herein or perform any independent analysis in connection with any of the product information contained herein. Publisher does not assume, and expressly disclaims, any obligation to obtain and include information other than that provided to it by the manufacturer.

The reader is expressly warned to consider and adopt all safety precautions that might be indicated by the activities herein and to avoid all potential hazards. By following the instructions contained herein, the reader willingly assumes all risks in connection with such instructions.

The Publisher makes no representation or warranties of any kind, including but not limited to, the warranties of fitness for particular purpose or merchantability, nor are any such representations implied with respect to the material set forth herein, and the publisher takes no responsibility with respect to such material. The publisher shall not be liable for any special, consequential, or exemplary damages resulting, in whole or part, from the readers' use of, or reliance upon, this material.

Contents

Foreword

I was five years old. My parents were having one of their 100-person, holiday cocktail parties at our house in Ballston Lake, New York. They knew that it would be amusing to have their children passing hors d'oeuvres and drinks. They told my sister and me to smile, introduce ourselves to the guests, and offer them something to drink and eat. When we finished, my father said, "Georgie, you did well." That was the greatest praise I have ever received. Reflecting back on my memories of my parents' parties and their direction for service, I realized, the incredibly uncomplicated and simple message they gave to us is enduring at any level. "Smile, introduce yourself, and bring your guests something to drink and eat."

Previously I was Executive Director of Food and Beverage at the Bellagio Hotel in Las Vegas, Nevada. My position entailed the responsibilities of joyfully serving over 17,000 people each day. Our team accomplishes this through the professional efforts of approximately 3,000 employees divided equally between front and back of the house over 18 restaurants, 16 front bars, room service, 120,000 square feet of banquet space, and an employee dining room. Bellagio executive team, prior to opening this 3,005-room resort, partnered with brand recognized restaurateurs and chefs from across the country to assemble the most respected culinary and food and beverage management team available. Sirio Maccioni, known as one of the most charismatic restaurateurs, was the first to become partners with Bellagio by bringing his family's tradition for excellence with both Le Cirque and Circo, New York-based haute cuisine. Our restaurant Picasso features the memorable cooking of Julian Serrano, while boasting a large collection of Pablo Picasso original artwork. Picasso was awarded the prestigious Mobil 5-star award in January 2000, just 14 months after opening. Aqua restaurant from San Francisco features the James Beard award-winning Chef Michael Mina. Designer Tony Chi created a dynamic environment incorporating rare woods, terrazzo tiles, and sumptuous fabrics. Aqua also showcases two Robert Rauschenberg paintings. Todd English brought his renowned casual Mediterranean restaurant Olives from Boston. Our steakhouse Prime partnered with award-winning four-star chef and restaurateur Jean-George Vongerichten. Along with our chef/partners we also operate Jasmine, our contemporary gourmet Chinese restaurant, which is designed with European influences and is flanked on three sides by our spectacular lake and garden views. Shintaro, our Japanese restaurant, prepares sushi, teppanyaki, and multicourse Pacific Rim Kaiseki menus prepared by Bellagio's Chef O'Connell. Bellagio's other restaurants include Noodles, a Hong Kong noodle shop, designed by Tony Chi; Cafe Bellagio, our 450-seat 24-hour restaurant; Buffet Bellagio, which serves 4,500 people daily; the Pool Cafe; Palio, our coffee shop; and Gelato, our Italian ice cream shop, along with additional snack bars.

In my current position as the Vice President of Food and Beverage at Beau Rivage Resort and Casino in Biloxi, I am intensely engaged in the operations, marketing, and human resource development of 14 restaurants, 6 bars, room service and a banquet facility in this AAA Four Diamond Resort. Since finishing with the rebuilding efforts after Hurricane Katrina devastated our business in August 2005, my team and I enjoy 22 newly designed kitchen and world-class designed dining areas. I even resurrected my friendship with celebrity chef Todd English and convinced him to place his Olives concept at Beau Rivage. We are well on our way to becoming the South's premier resort.

The hospitality industry has changed dramatically over the past 35 years since my first venture into service, but the principles remain the same. *Service is an experience, as opposed to a tangible product.* It is fleeting, and, therefore, difficult to describe, measure, and in some cases, standardize. Service must be anticipatory, professional, friendly, and leavened with good humor. Every detail must be carefully considered and thought through. This encompasses the temperature of the room, the softness of the lighting, the height of the table, the cushion on the chair, the pattern on the china, the crispness of the linen, the sound of the music, the firmness of the butter, the sense of arrival at the entrance, and the greeting of your host. As well, guests will not accept service that is not joyfully given. Guests want to be served, not fed. Does this sound like something that can be measured and standardized? In all cases, a successful restaurant, hotel, club, or pub has created this environment of great service through a common set of values for their management and staff.

The method is not only to have meaningful training material, presented in an organized fashion and consistently followed, but most importantly to have the resources and experience to hire the absolute most caring candidates. The theory meets practice each time an employee has the opportunity to enhance a guest's experience through service. Thus, the practice needs to be trained and reinforced on a daily basis throughout the division by means of formal and informal meetings, memos, e-mails, training sessions, and pre-shift talks. Regardless of the format of the meetings, certain words should continually be repeated like drumbeats: *service, commitment, improvement, pride, consistency, and training.*

Because service is heterogeneous and the quality of the service experiences is measured by the perception of the guest, it can never be the same for two individuals. Consequently, it is nearly impossible to standardize each guest transaction or experience. What can be standardized are the values instilled into each employee. For example, the Ritz Carlton has a philosophy for their staff of "ladies and gentlemen serving ladies and gentlemen." Hyatt describes their hotels as having the "Hyatt Touch." And in the words of the late Joe Baum, restaurateur of the century, "Values and standards are those you make for yourself. You don't have to be as good as the other guy. You have to be better—a lot better." In each one of the above-mentioned cases, each management team has made an effort to establish a set of values that offers certain tangibility to the guest's complete experience.

The concept of service will continue to be the most important and necessary ingredient in the successful management of any hospitality endeavor. In the mature environment of the industry today, it will be even more important that management be able to communicate their vision and values of service to their frontline employees.

Oh yes, and remember to smile!

George Goldoff
Vice President Food and Beverage
Beau Rivage Resort and Casino
Biloxi, Mississippi

Mr. Goldoff is Vice President of Food and Beverage for the Beau Rivage Resort and Casino located in Biloxi on the Mississippi Gulf Coast. This luxury resort blends the charm and character of the Mediterranean with the elegance of Southern hospitality. After hurricane Katrina devastated the original 1780-room hotel. Mr. Goldoff had to assist in the planning, design, and overseeing the construction of the restaurants, bars, and banquet facilities in AAA Four Diamond resort. The resort features exciting entertainment, a retail promenade and distinctive restaurants with renowned chefs and varied cuisine. Beau Rivage originally opened in March 1999, and brought Mirage Resorts' standard of excellence to the Mississippi Gulf Coast. The resort was completely rebuilt after the Katrina and reopened in 2006.

Preface

Dining Room Service!! Unfortunately, that is what is missing from much of the dining experience in the United States. During the decade of the 1990s, food preparation and celebrity chefs received the accolades from the American public. Now it is time for *service* to take center stage. Dining room and banquet managers should train their waitstaffs to make their guests raving fans by providing them with superb *service*. As we gathered information for this fourth edition of *Dining Room and Banquet Management*, we conducted both primary and secondary research to promote our theory. For example, Elissa Elan writing in the May 23, 2005 issue of Nation's Restaurant News quotes Ed Korry, the chairman of Johnson & Wales University's Beverage and Dining Service Department, at the school's Providence, R.I. Campus states "An insufficient number of front-of-the-house mangers…have been trained in service technique and therefore cannot train others to emulate them." She also quoted Tim Zagat, the publisher of the New York-based Zagat survey dining guides who stated "Service is the weak link in the industry. In survey after survey, we ask people what irritates them most, what should be worked on. And every time service wins— big time." He further states that, "falling service scores are a direct result of servers who are not properly educated in the rudiments of their profession. The industry has not paid the same amount of attention to front-of-the-house operations as it has to other concerns. There needs to be more education for the front."[1] In reading *Setting the Table*, the CEO of the Union Square Hospitality Group Danny Meyer writes and explains how his philosophy of enlightened hospitality that has made his business a success. Much of his book relates how his guests and, yes, employees are treated to provide enlightened hospitality of which excellent service is a key component.

---

[1] Elan, Elissa. "Industry Vets, Educators Say Training an Answer to Poor-Service Problem." *Nation's Restaurant News* (May 23, 2005), Vol. 39, No. 21: 6, 36.

Our travels have allowed us to research dining room service first hand and observe the effect it has on guests and ourselves in a restaurant setting. We have been fortunate to discuss with owners of restaurants how they train their staff to give great service; restaurant professionals like Drew Nieporent and Marty Shapiro of Myriad Restaurants; Bert Cutino of The Sardine Factory; and Daniel Boulud of Restaurant Daniel.

Dining out has been a passion of ours. Each dining experience brings a new challenge. That challenge is to find a restaurant that offers excellent service to the guest. Whether we are dining at a restaurant in our own region, vacationing, or participating in professional activities, we are constantly searching to discover the perfect restaurant that has outstanding service. Each wedding, bar mitzvah, or banquet attended is also a research trip. To discover perfect service at restaurants and banquets is our goal.

Our research has taken place in restaurants as diverse as large chain restaurants like TGIFridays, mom-and-pop operations such as The Bears, and haute cuisine restaurants like Restaurant Daniel in New York City. Banquets have been attended at Elks Clubs, VFW posts, church halls, four-star resorts, and elegant country clubs. The service has ranged from awful to outstanding.

The first job coauthor Toby held was as a banquet manager at a hotel in the middle of a decaying inner city. The secret of success was quickly learned in the banquet business. The secret—*service*. Service was of utmost importance to all guests regardless of their socioeconomic status or any other classification with which society labels individuals. Day after day this fact was confirmed by letters and thank-you notes; but most convincing was the fact that the banquet business increased, when by all other indicators it should have been declining or nonexistent.

Toby's next job was as a food and beverage manager at a brand-new hotel. Again the importance of service was taught to the staff. The restaurant and banquet rooms were filled to capacity nightly. Unfortunately, the food was not consistently excellent; in fact, at times it was embarrassingly bad. The conclusion: Excellent service will make up for mediocre food.

We (Toby and Pam) then entered into the catering business. Business grew because of the excellent service provided to our clients. We had many clients who would plan their parties only after discovering when we were available to serve their parties!

The techniques presented in this book are used by students to provide excellent service at Schenectady County Community College in serving both banquets and à la carte patrons. Both banquets and the à la carte restaurant, The Casola Dining Room, are filled to capacity each semester by patrons wanting to experience great food and service. Service has made the restaurant and banquets stand out. The demand created for the Casola Dining Room is such that the 60-seat dining room is booked in less than 10 minutes.

Throughout our careers, we have realized and recognized the importance of great service, which we define as competency and friendliness. To any patron, it should not matter whether the menu item costs $6.00 or $60.00; nor if it is a chain (e.g., Red Lobster), a hotel (e.g., Marriott), or an independent restaurant. Great service, as great food, should be provided consistently to all guests. When we dined at The Old Dock in Essex, New York, we spent $6.95 each on our menu item. We received the excellent service that we hope will become standard for our industry. Our personable, friendly waitperson, upon approaching our table, realized that our table was not level. In the middle of her busy lunch hour, she took the time to obtain equipment to make the table level. Her service skills were excellent and flawless.

We have been fortunate to travel extensively throughout the United States and Canada. We have dined at both independent and chain restaurants. During our travels, we discovered six other exceptional restaurants that provided us with superb service, service that should be emulated by all restaurant operators: The Beaver Club in the Queen Elizabeth Hotel in Montreal, Canada; The White Barn Inn in Kennebunkport, Maine; Le Bernardin in New York City; TRU in Chicago, Illinois; AlpenGlow Stube in Keystone, Colorado. Canoe in Toronto, Canada; The Sardine Factory in Monterey, California; Victoria and Albert's in the Grand Floridian Resort and Spa at Walt Disney World; and Tribecca Grill in New York city.

This excellent service was experienced during a single visit. Restaurant managers should remember and abide by the Head and Shoulders commercial that states, "You only have one chance to make a second impression." This is because most of your guests will base their experience about your restaurant on a single visit. Our goal and vision in writing this book is for the service profession to become as respected as the culinary profession in the United States.

SYSTEMATIC SEQUENCE OF BOOK

The fourth edition of *Dining Room and Banquet Management* has been revised by the authors. We have read and reread the third edition and have added new objectives and factual material to the text. All chapter summaries have been rewritten to match the objectives of each chapter. Throughout the book, the authors have added a series of Sweet or Sour vignettes to assist the reader in solving problems and understanding concepts of dining room and banquet service. We have duplicated our popular "Chef Sez" from our *Math Principles for Food Service Occupations* by adding a "Manager's Message or Chef's Choice" in each chapter. This is a quote from a manager, chef, or food editor about the importance of service in their own particular operation. Chapter 1 has been revised to reflect the current state of dining operations in the United States. In all of the chapters we have added a series of thought provoking discussion questions that will challenge the reader's ability to solve the stated problem from material discussed in the chapter. For this edition, the authors discovered the answer to the age-old question of where the term "in the weeds" came from. We have added key words at the beginning of each chapter and Appendix B, Place Settings has been also added. Terminology in the chapters on Banquet Management has been completely revised to reflect current trends in the industry.

The content of the text has been divided into three coordinated parts to demonstrate subject association and simplify learning.

Part One, "The Food Service Industry," consists of five chapters. The authors believe that the readers must have an understanding of the history and current state of the industry to assist them in providing excellent service. We have completely revised the first chapter to reflect the current state of dining room service in the industry. The importance of proper sanitation is reemphasized in the second chapter by giving examples of positive and negative sanitation practices and citing new legislation. Chapter 5 has major additions about wine and wine service. More emphasis is placed upon wine and wine service to reflect the surge in popularity of wine in America.

Part Two, "Dining Room Management," consists of four chapters that focus on procedures to manage a dining room and proper dining room service. Chapter 6 reflects major changes and updating to reflect current practices in the industry. The importance of knowledge of menu items concerning food allergies has been added. New diagrams concerning table and station assignments have been added. The biggest changes provide the reader with step-by-step instructions of how to serve a typical meal by an individual waitperson and how to enter orders and close out checks using a MICROS Point of Sale Computer system. Information about reservations, priority seating, and reservations systems have been updated in Chapter 8. Using electronic devices to manage the dining room has been added to Chapter 9, along with describing a true "scam" that was attempted on a restaurant owner.

Part Three, "Banquet Management," consists of four chapters that focus on how to run a banquet or catered event successfully. In Chapter 10, we have added sections to include new methods that banquet establishments utilize to set guarantees for an event and the use of grazing stations to feed guests at an event. In Chapter 11, information has been added about audio visual equipment. Chapters 12 and 13 include new methods on how to plate and serve banquets, including combination meal plates instead of offering entree choices at banquets.

The material contained in this text will provide the student with excellent dining room and banquet service knowledge to demonstrate confidence and utilize skills that will lead to rapid job advancement in their career. Service skills, along with math and culinary skills, are an essential part of the equation that makes a food service operation a success. Many talented food service professionals have succeeded in business, others have failed. The authors want to emphasize that there is more to operating a successful food service operation than putting quality food before the guest. This book is a "keeper." We know that the reader who trains his or her staff using the techniques detailed in this book and continues monitoring these techniques in dining room and banquet service will provide excellent service to their guests. This book will be a valuable reference tool as you climb the career ladder.

Acknowledgments

When we were asked to write this fourth edition of *Dining Room and Banquet Management*, we knew that we would need help acquiring examples, information, and illustrations. We were fortunate that our travels have taken us to many locations where we could interview chefs and managers. Because of our many interests and participation at conventions and conferences, we have made important and meaningful contacts with influential leaders in the American Culinary Federation, New York State Hospitality and Tourism Association, New York State Restaurant Association, the Albany County Convention and Visitors Bureau, and graduates of the Hotel, Culinary Arts and Tourism program at Schenectady County Community College. Our experiences in writing the fifth edition of *Math Principles for Food Service Occupations* and *The Food Service Industry Video Series*, and numerous articles for local business publications has allowed us research opportunities. We have been guest speakers at numerous industry shows giving speeches about service. At the New York State Restaurant Show held in New York City, we spoke to a standing room only crowd of over 120 on "Whining and Dining: An Amusing and Not So Amusing Look at Service in the Restaurant Industry." Both of us have Master degrees: Pam in Education and Toby in Educational Psychology. Toby also is certified by the American Culinary Federation as a Certified Culinary Educator.

When undertaking this fourth edition, we asked ourselves what would make this book stand out from other service books in our field. We knew we could bring a positive perspective about dining room service to the student because of our combined 53 years teaching experience at the elementary and college level. That coupled with our love of dining and the experience of over 40 years of patronizing restaurants gives us great experience to draw upon. Also, we knew that we could call upon our hospitality experience throughout our careers as cook, chef, bookkeeper, waitperson, food and beverage manager, butler, bartender, and banquet manager to reflect the importance of dining room service in the food service industry to the reader. But we wanted more . . . we wanted to make dining room service meaningful. So in each chapter we added a section called Manager's Message and/or Chef's Choice in which the leaders in this industry explain to the reader why service is important. In alphabetical order we list the contributors and their titles:

Jackie Appeldorn, General Manager, Mohonk Mountain House, A National Historic Landmark, New Paltz, New York

Ted Balestreri, cofounder and owner of Sardine Factory Restaurant, Monterey, California

Barry Correia, Executive Chef/Executive Director, Canyon Ranch in the Berkshires Health Resort, Lenox, Massachusetts

Bert P. Cutino, Certified Executive Chef, American Academy of Chefs, cofounder and Chef of Sardine Factory Restaurant, Monterey, California

Gale Gand, Chef/Partner, TRU, 676 N. St. Clair Street, Chicago, Illinois

George R. Goldoff, Vice President of Food and Beverage, Mirage Resorts, Beau Rivage Resort and Casino, Biloxi, Mississippi

Glenn Gray, Director of Food and Beverage, Renaissance Austin Hotel, Austin, Texas

Kate Harrigan, managing editor of *Chef* magazine, Chicago, Illinois

Chris Littis, chef de Cuisine, The Martini House, St. Helena, California

Aram Mardigian, Executive Chef, Spago Restaurant, Pato Alto, California

Angelo Mazzone, Owner, Mazzone Management Group, Scotia, New York

Brian Palazzolo, President, Classe Catering, Albany, New York

Joyce Slater, Dining Room Manager, Canyon Ranch in the Berkshires Health Resort, Lenox, Massachusetts

Carmine Sprio, Chef/Owner and television personality, Carmine's Restaurant, Albany, New York

Denise Volpicello, General Manager, East Hampton Point (Restaurant), East Hampton, New York

Paul Wixted, Food and Beverage Operations Manager, Disney's Grand Floridian Resort and Spa Convention Center, Walt Disney World, Lake Buena Vista, Florida

Some other individuals also gave us assistance in obtaining quotes, providing facts about their businesses, and supplying us with information that has been used in this book. They are:

Heather Bigley, Dining Room Manager, Eiffel Tower Restaurant in the Paris Resort, Las Vegas, Nevada

Angela Dugan, Beverage Store Coordinator, Decresente Distributing Company in Mechanicville, New York

Kevin Gadreault, General Manager of Dakota Steak, Seafood & Smiles in Latham, New York

Guy Sementilli, Chef/Owner of Scotti's Restaurant in Schenectady, New York

Don Yurkonis, General Manager of the Desmond in Albany, New York

We were fortunate to have several editors at Delmar who assisted us with this project: our Acquisitions Editors, Matthew Hart; Patricia Osborn, our previous Product Manager who started us on this fourth edition project; and our current Product Manager Patrick Horn, who guided us through our final drafts. The authors also wish to thank the reviewers of this book:

Victor Bagan	James W. Paul II
Hibbing Community College	The Art Institute of Atlanta
Hibbing, MN	Atlanta, GA
Lawrence D. Stalcup	Walter Wright
Georgia Southern University	Coastal Georgia Community College
Statesboro, GA	Brunswick, GA

We also would like to thank these individuals from Schenectady County Community College in the Department of Hotel, Culinary Arts and Tourism: Robert Payne and Kim Williams, who assisted us with new and updated information about Dining Room procedures and MICROS operation; and Terry Treis, the duplicating machine operator who assisted and advised us with the duplication process of our copies.

Special thanks must be given to two individuals who have introduced us to and provided us with the opportunity to interview restaurant icons over the years. Risk Sampson, the President and CEO of the New York State Restaurant Association and Harold Qualters, the

Executive Director of the New York State Restaurant Association Educational Foundation. They have made it possible for us to meet with Julia Child, Bobby Flay, Daniel Boulud, Nick Valenti, John Fellin, Drew Nieporent and Marty Shapiro.

Another industry icon that we must thank is Bert P. Cutino, the chief operating officer of The Sardine Factory Restaurant in Monterey, California. This gentleman has won almost every industry award, including the IFMA Silver Plate Award for Independent Restaurants. He has been inducted in the Nation's Restaurant News MenuMasters Hall of Fame. Most importantly, he gives his knowledge back to the Industry to individuals who want to enter and to those that are already in the hospitality industry. The knowledge he has shared with us has been invaluable.

Finally, we would like to thank our employers for the support and encouragement they have given us to undertake this project: The North Colonie Central School District in Loudonville, New York, and Schenectady County Community College in Schenectady, New York. A special thanks goes to our sons Mike and Larry and to our family.

If you would like to contact us with a question, comments, or suggestions or any other pertinent information, contact either Delmar Learning, a division of Thomson Learning, or us by e-mail at strianaj@gw.sunysccc.edu.

Part One

The Food Service Industry

1

The Importance of Service

OBJECTIVES   At the completion of this chapter, the student should be able to:

1. Verbally define service as it relates to the hospitality industry.
2. Give examples of excellent service based upon your experience.
3. List Maslow's hierarchy and explain its importance in the hospitality industry.
4. Name the different types of service the dining room manager and banquet manager may provide.
5. Write a definition for the word *ubiquitous* and give an example of it as it relates to the hospitality industry.
6. List and explain the qualifications that managers must possess to provide excellent service.
7. List and explain the five categories of customers.

KEY WORDS

busy bees	dependent needs	impulsives
cater-to-me's	80/20 rule	love and belonging
celebrators	esteem	Maslow's hierarchy
coaching	friendliness	MBWA
competence	front of the house	physiological need

safety	service person	ubiquitous
self–actualization	shadowing	word of mouth
service	socializers	

Service for the Present and Future

The beginning of the twenty-first century has brought with it a lifestyle change that has affected western society and has had an impact on the restaurant business. This change is most apparent in the fact that eating in a restaurant is no longer a special occasion; it is a way of life. The Zagat 2006 survey of America's Top Restaurants reported that the national average for consuming meals outside the home has reached a rate of 53 percent and is continuing to grow. New York City residents lead the nation in consuming meals outside of the home at a 60 percent rate, while Los Angeles residents are a close second at 55 percent. Most encouraging is the fact that the national average has reached a rate of 53 percent and continues to grow.[1]

The authors have observed other favorable trends that bode well for the restaurant industry. In many homes, two individuals are working full-time and overtime. If they have children, they are taking them to after-school or evening events. An increasing market for restaurants is working single parents, who value the time they can spend with their children. They often choose a restaurant because they can share more time with their children, instead of being isolated from them while they prepare a meal. In addition to this market, the advent of television's Food Network has created a more sophisticated public who take a serious interest in cooking. They are becoming experts on raw food products, recipe preparation, and unique food products. More Americans are retiring with increased disposable income. These lifestyle changes will continue to cause the restaurant industry to grow. Experts predict that by year 2016, the restaurant industry will have 14.5 million employers, making our industry the largest private-sector employer in our nation.[2] Today, guests have more choices and styles of restaurants to patronize than ever before!

The professional chef and fabulous food were the stars of the 1980s and 1990s. The turn of the century has added a new star for the restaurant owner and manager: providing excellent, friendly service to guests.

William Grimes, writing about "The New American Service" in the *New York Times*, reported on restaurant patron Daniel Swee, who eats out up to five nights a week. Mr. Grimes stated that Mr. Swee "has felt a change in restaurant service that's a little like a change in the weather. It's nothing specific, it's hard to put your finger on, but it's there, and it has made him happy." He quotes Mr. Swee as saying, "There's a trend toward restaurants where the food is really fantastic, but the atmosphere is casual, and you are made to feel welcome. In the past, you felt that dining in a top restaurant was a rare privilege, and you'd better behave. Now, there's a warmth and an interaction that wasn't there before."[3]

The formal white tablecloth restaurants that were almost exclusive in the 1960s are being joined by expensive steak restaurants. In addition, the children of the 1980s and 1990s who patronized McDonald's, Wendy's, and Burger King are trading up to the casual, less formal adult fast food of TGI Friday's, Applebee's, and other establishments that provide waitstaff table service in an informal setting.

T I P $

TO INSURE PROPER SERVICE

Patronize restaurants and observe the job that the waitstaff does. Determine if the restaurant has provided great service. If it has, determine what made the service great. In the preface of this book the authors have identified great restaurants where they experienced superb service.

Fortunately, there is a demand for all types of restaurants. The white tablecloth restaurant will never become obsolete. It will always be the place where a guest will bring a date, celebrate a relative's birthday or anniversary, or entertain business clients. More and more of our guests, who have the income to patronize restaurants, do not have the time to cook because of the demands of their job or family activities.

Guests in the twenty-first century will be no different from guests throughout the ages. All guests want to be and appreciate being pampered. When leaving their homes for an evening out to spend their hard-earned money, they want an enjoyable, entertaining evening. More and more individuals are choosing a restaurant not only for their special evening out but also for regular family meals. After a hard day's work, the choice for many two-income families is to dine at a restaurant rather than cook a meal. As competition becomes more intense between restaurants, the one difference that will make a restaurant stand out is the **service** it offers to its guests. Many businesspeople choose a banquet facility or restaurant in which to conduct important business meetings. It is up to you, the restaurant and banquet manager, to make their experience enjoyable.

The purpose of this textbook is to emphasize and illustrate the importance of great guest service. It will not contain recipes on preparation or cooking. It will train individuals in methods and attitudes to provide guests with superb service, from both a management and **service person's** point of view.

Reasons to Provide Good Service

Guests enjoy talking about their experiences at a restaurant. They *like* to talk to their friends about good service, and they *love* to tell their friends about poor service. Consider this scenario: Ms. Smith invites Ms. Jones to dine with her at your restaurant. Their check total is $100.00. Ms. Jones is pleased with the service, food, and price value of the dining experience and is thrilled to have found a new restaurant to recommend to her friends. Ms. Jones recommends your restaurant to Mr. Feldman and Ms. Glock. They each dine at your restaurant and introduce your restaurant to a guest who has never dined there. Both Mr. Feldman and Ms. Glock are impressed with your restaurant. For his next business dinner meeting, Mr. Feldman invites Mr. Zorn and spends $100.00. For Ms. Glock's date night, she invites Mr. Malary and the bill is $100.00.

The initial amount of money—$100—that Ms. Smith and Ms. Jones spent has resulted in increased revenue from the Feldman and Glock parties of $200.00, for a total of $300.00 in revenue. If this pattern of repeat business continues, with Mr. Zorn and Mr. Malary also bringing in new guests, the revenue will continue to multiply. When Mr. Zorn and Mr. Malary choose to dine at your restaurant, bringing in two new guests, the amount of revenue generated, along with Mr. Feldman and Ms. Glock returning to the restaurant, results in four more dining experiences, totaling an additional $400.00. The repeat business from the recommendation of Ms. Jones is now up to $700.00 (see Figure 1–1). The restaurant and restaurant manager that provide excellent, friendly service, along with great food, will continue to see their business prosper. If this pattern is repeated for 10 years, think how valuable that first guest was to the restaurant. This fact, called **positive word of mouth,** is extremely effective in generating business. For example, the late Michael Hurst, once owner of the 15th Street Fisheries in Fort Lauderdale, Florida, stated that the value of a party of four guests spending $150.00 can result in sales of over $2,000,000 dollars over 10 years. In business, there is a rule called the **80/20 rule**. This means that 80 percent of your business will come from 20 percent of your guests. Managers, owners, and all employees should realize that the guests who patronize the restaurant have a major economic

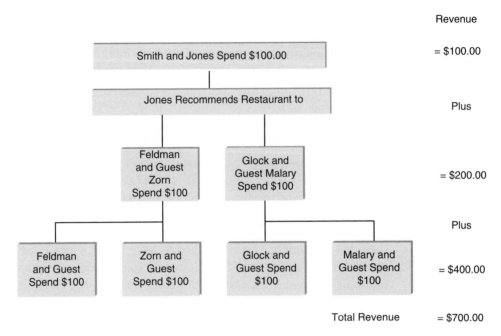

FIGURE 1–1

Repeat business goes on and on

influence on the success or failure of a business. Even though the authors have pointed out the economic benefit of word of mouth, bear in mind the words of Michael Hurst (who was also a past president of the National Restaurant Association). He stated that managers should "think customers, not dollars!"

T I P $

TO INSURE PROPER SERVICE
A restaurant where we experienced great service was Canoe in Toronto, Canada. Our wine glasses were never too full or too empty.

On the other hand, negative word of mouth is devastating to a business. Writing in *The National Culinary Review*, which is the official magazine of the American Culinary Federation, past President Dr. Noel Cullen stated, "Guest service and guest retention is vital. Operators who focus on end-user satisfaction are acutely aware of data that indicate that for every guest who complains, there are 26 others who remain silent. The average displeased guest will tell 8 to 16 people, and 91 percent of unhappy guests will never return. It costs about five times as much to get a new guest as it costs to keep a current one. It has been determined that one of the major reasons why guests stop patronizing a restaurant is employee indifference to guest service (68 percent)."[4] With a little simple math, the reader can see that a negative experience can affect that restaurant's business substantially (see Figure 1–2). As positive as word of mouth can be, negative word of mouth is devastating. Word of mouth is both the best and worst type of promotion for a business. It has more effect on business at a restaurant or banquet house than any other factor. Why? Because people like to ask other people where to find a great place for dining or holding banquets. They trust recommendations from a friend rather than advertising.

T I P $

TO INSURE PROPER SERVICE

The two restaurant reviewers for the Albany *Times Union*, Bill Dowd and Ruth Fantasia, have addressed the issue of service. Mr. Dowd says, "Excellent service can make up for faults or inconsistencies. Poor service only exacerbates them."[5] Ms. Fantasia, speaking to the Capital District Chapter of the New York State Restaurant Association told the group that "bad service rarely compensates for good food."[6]

FIGURE 1–2

This is what occurs when a restaurant has 90 unhappy guests: to avoid repeat of below. 1,070 people will believe that your restaurant is poor. This is the impact of negative word-of-mouth publicity.

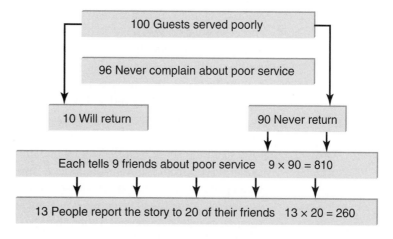

THE IMPACT OF NEGATIVE WORD-OF-MOUTH PUBLICITY

100 Guests served poorly

96 Never complain about poor service

10 Will return

90 Never return

Each tells 9 friends about poor service   9 × 90 = 810

13 People report the story to 20 of their friends   13 × 20 = 260

90 Negative guests create 1,070 negative word-of-mouth publicity

Guests who patronize restaurants and banquet houses love to tell their friends about the service they received from those establishments. Therefore, it is imperative that restaurant and banquet managers strive to provide excellent service and make **word of mouth** work positively for them and make their business successful.

What Guests Think of Service

Historically, poor service has been the biggest complaint about restaurants. A MasterCard dining out study highlighted rude and slow table service as the two biggest problems identified by a study group of 400 national consumers, 50 restaurateurs, and 50 restaurant critics.[7] Conversely, they stated that friendly service is the number one reason why families will eat away from home. Parents stated that the key criteria for choosing a restaurant are service, value, and family atmosphere.

T I P $　　**TO INSURE PROPER SERVICE**

Waitstaff must be shown the direct correlation between giving guests poor service and receiving a poor tip.

Sweet or Sour?　The following vignette illustrates how bad service contributes to negative word of mouth.

Three guests went to one of New York City's highest rated French restaurants that was well known for excellent service. Their Saturday luncheon reservation was for 2:30 P.M. When the reservation was made, the individual who made the reservation asked whether there would be any problem with a reservation so late in the day. She was assured by the person on the phone that they would not be rushed and there should be no problems. The guests arrived and were seated in a beautiful dining room. To their left was a party of 14 guests. These 14 guests were being given excellent service. The three guests ordered their bottle of wine and their food from the set price (prix fixe) menu. They also experienced professional service from the waitstaff. Indeed they were not rushed through their appetizer, main course, and dessert. Their wine was poured throughout the meal, and the three guests congratulated themselves on choosing such an excellent restaurant. When the guest check was presented, the guests looked over the check and discovered that the waitperson had only charged them for two meals, instead of three! By this time, it was close to

(continues)

(continued)

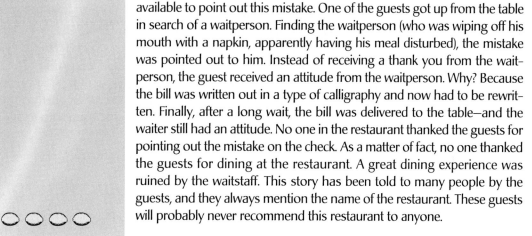

4:00 P.M.; all of the waitstaff had left the dining room. There was no one available to point out this mistake. One of the guests got up from the table in search of a waitperson. Finding the waitperson (who was wiping off his mouth with a napkin, apparently having his meal disturbed), the mistake was pointed out to him. Instead of receiving a thank you from the waitperson, the guest received an attitude from the waitperson. Why? Because the bill was written out in a type of calligraphy and now had to be rewritten. Finally, after a long wait, the bill was delivered to the table—and the waiter still had an attitude. No one in the restaurant thanked the guests for pointing out the mistake on the check. As a matter of fact, no one thanked the guests for dining at the restaurant. A great dining experience was ruined by the waitstaff. This story has been told to many people by the guests, and they always mention the name of the restaurant. These guests will probably never recommend this restaurant to anyone.

The restaurant industry was and is based upon excellent food and service. The dictionary definition for *service* is "the act or manner of serving food and drink."[8] There are many ways to serve food and beverages. Unfortunately many of these ways are poor. Year after year, survey after survey, the number one reason why guests would not return to a restaurant is always poor service!

Nation's Restaurant News (NRN) devoted an entire section of its magazine/newspaper to customer service satisfaction.[9] The periodical's staff researched and reported on the question of what brings guests back to restaurants.

Since authoring the first edition of *Dining Room and Banquet Management* in 1990, one constant remains concerning the research done for this textbook. It is that guest service has always and continues to be more of a problem than the quality of food in restaurants. As publisher Tim Zagat, the founder of the New York-based Zagat survey dining guides, said "Year after year, our surveys show that service is the weak link in the restaurant industry."[10] Zagat pointed to his contributing critics' ratings of service as lagging at least two points behind food quality, a conclusion reached by fully 72 percent of the respondents. "In survey after survey, we ask people what irritates them most, what should be worked on," Zagat said "And every time service wins—big time."

Zagat asserted that falling service scores are a direct result of servers who are not properly educated in the rudiments of their profession. The industry, he opined, has not paid the same amount of attention to front-of-the-house operations as it has to other concerns.

There needs to be more education for the front.[11] Most alarming to the authors of this book is this fact. In our 2003 edition, we reported that the Zagat survey stated that 62 percent of all complaints related to service. This illustrates that service is not improving. Restaurant, banquet, and catering operations have an opportunity to differentiate themselves from their competition by providing great service! Surveys previously reported on problems that encompassed everything from servers not telling the guests what the specials cost, to individuals who answer the phone acting apathetic or giving an impression that the guests are bothering them. The reservationists give the guests a feeling that they do not want their business.

What the Hospitality Industry Thinks about Service

Jim Sullivan, writing in *Nation's Restaurant News,* said, "Customers will forgive mistakes in the kitchen more than mistakes in bad service."[12] Another story, written by Paul Frumkin in the same publication, had editors ask dozens of professionals for their views on what customers want and the demands that operators should be addressing. Dennis Lombardi, the executive vice president of Foodservice Strategies in Columbus, Ohio, wants restaurants to "enhance the service experience. Anticipate my mood and what I want from the service. Fundamentally, there is already so much focus on food that restaurants need to bring the service and the environment up to par with the energy placed on the food." Fred Thimm, president of The Palm in Washington, DC, said, "More customer recognition, like the GM's taking the time to come by your table and then greeting you by name when you come back."[13]

"Being able to take care of people is a noble thing," says Charlie Trotter, whose Charlie Trotter's Restaurant rated highest for service in the Chicago Zagat survey. "Excellent service even supercedes the food in the dining experience," he said.[14]

TIP$

TO INSURE PROPER SERVICE

Michael Hurst once said, "Good service is what differentiates restaurants in today's saturated marketplace. We are not selling food in my restaurants; we are selling a pleasant experience."[15]

At an NRN-sponsored meeting of restaurant operators held in Atlanta, Georgia, a panel of industry leaders stated that "customer service has become the number one issue in the food service industry today, and finding first-rate employees to fill this need is the number one challenge."[16] In today's society, which continues to move toward more computers and impersonal service, the customer wants smiles and human interaction in place of cold, nonthinking, unemotional computers. It becomes essential that the restaurant and banquet managers of the twenty-first century know how to train their employees to provide excellent service to their guests.

Who Is Responsible for Great Service?

Too many times, the service person is blamed for good or poor service. It appears to the guest that the service person should take the credit or blame. However, the blame or credit falls on the manager. It is up to the manager to set the tone of the business. If the manager cares about his guests, then the message will be loud and clear to the service staff. If the manager gives the impression that he is only there because he has to be or that the guests are an imposition on his time, the service staff will get that message also. Over and over again, the one common thread in all restaurants judged to be outstanding is the care and concern of the owner or manager toward the guests and staff.

Rich Rosenthal, president of the four-unit Max Restaurant Group in Hartford, Connecticut, feels that service is their most important element. "And service obviously goes past the waiter, the waitress, or the bartender. It starts at the telephone and ends when the guest walks out of the restaurant with the valet. . . . Service takes place in the kitchen with special requests and adding or deleting an item. It's not limited to carrying food out to the table and smiling. Service is the way you do everything."[9]

Kevin O'Donnell, vice president and innkeeper of The Old Tavern in Grafton, Vermont, states that guests are experts concerning the cost of food. He asks his staff, "Why should someone pay ten times more in a restaurant for a Chicken Kiev than buying it already prepared at a gourmet section in a supermarket and eating it at their kitchen table?" The answer is the service that is provided to guests.

Who makes the best manager? The authors of *A Passion for Excellence* state that "the best bosses are neither exclusively tough nor exclusively tender." They are both: tough on the values, tender in support of people who would dare to take a risk and try something new in support of those values.[17] One of the authors' most valuable points is that successful managers "pay an obsessive attention to detail."[18] In the highly demanding restaurant business, the restaurants that succeed and prosper are the ones whose owners take the time to pay attention

FIGURE 1–3

A restaurant manager making the guests feel important.

to details and make their guests feel welcome in their establishment (see Figure 1–3).

MBWA

The authors of *A Passion for Excellence* detail a method to create superior performance. This method is to take exceptional care of your customers via superior service. One of their techniques is called **MBWA**, or "management by wandering around." They claim that an effective manager must be where the action is. In a restaurant, the manager should be walking around talking to the guests. In a banquet, the banquet manager should make certain that the guests are happy. By wandering around, the manager can observe all situations and solve problems before they occur.

Service Defined

In the restaurant industry, service is defined by two words—competence and friendliness. **Competence** can be defined as serving food and drinks in the correct manner to the guest: The service person knows who gets the shrimp scampi and who gets the prime rib without asking

Manager's Message

(Courtesy of
CARMINE SPRIO,
CHEF–OWNER,
CARMINE'S
RESTAURANT,
ALBANY, NEW YORK
AND
SAN ANTONIO,
TEXAS)

Carmine Sprio is the chef-owner of the 150-seat Carmine's Restaurant in Albany, New York, which he has owned and operated since 1996. He is a veteran of television appearances, hosting *Carmine's Table* on the Time Warner cable system and has appeared on numerous shows on The Food Network. Additionally, he has hosted a daily one-hour television show on a local NBC station called *Carmine's Table*. But, he considers himself a restaurateur first. In September of 2006, he opened up his second 150-seat restaurant in San Antonio, Texas.

He states, "Restaurants are about the total guest experience. A great dining experience has as much to do with the service they receive as the food they eat. It is hospitality. I say to my staff that part of hospitality is being a guest in my home. Restaurants are all about making the guest feel welcome."

"It starts with the phone call from the guest asking for information, directions to the restaurant, or a reservation. My staff is trained to welcome the guest. I want to immediately create an emotional positive bond between the caller and the restaurant."

"In my restaurant service is the how to. It should be unnoticed. I ask my staff 'what can you do to help our guests enjoy their dining experience.' When I hire service people, I look for individuals that are PASSIONATE, CARING, and PERCEPTIVE."

"My staff must be focused on their guests enjoyment. Hospitality is the passion and caring that drives the performance of the staff. I can teach them how to set a table, serve a guest, etc., but I must have employees that are passionate about the restaurant, both in the front and back of the house. Great hospitality can only be achieved with great staff. Individuals who are not only passionate and caring but hard working and intelligent. Intelligent enough to deduce what guests at a table are at Carmine's for. Is it business, fun, romance? Restaurants are about the package. We must welcome, connect with, exceed their expectations and ultimately feed our guests. It is the feel of price to value. No one likes to feel that they are being ripped off."

"A chef-owner must appreciate the front-of-the-house staff. He or she must convey the message to all employees that each person's job is just as important as their own."

"To me, passionate people create hospitality. They also create a buzz in the room. And hospitality is what the restaurant business is all about: Making your guests feel welcome."

the guests; the service person serves all food to women first; and removes one course before serving the next. Competent service often is not noticed, but it results in a good feeling about the restaurant. After the meal is complete, the guests know that they had a pleasant experience, but they do not necessarily realize why. The service person paid attention to the details. However, competence alone does not make a good service person.

A service person must also have the other attribute—friendliness. It is much more important than competence. The service person should make the guests feel as though they are guests in a private home. When someone comes to your house, you ask them if they want a drink. You pay attention to them. You are nice to them. However, the service person must be realistic and not act overly friendly to the guest. If possible, a service person should address the guest by name (not first name, of course) and be able to make the guest feel welcome in the restaurant. But—a word of caution—do not be phony. In the past, too many establishments had their waitstaff run up to the table with a canned speech: "Hi, I'm Gary and I'll be your waiter tonight. Our specials for the evening are. . . ." and then they went on with what seemed like a five-minute speech outlining specials, pushing drinks and food, and in general boring the customer. A service person should be a professional combining **competency** with **friendliness**.

Wolfgang Puck was once asked, "When you think of restaurant service what word comes to mind?" He replied, "Friendly and professional. Just professional is not enough." He has a service pet peeve: "When I have a nice bottle of wine and the server fills the glass up to the rim. And then if there are four of us, as soon as the server has poured the four glasses, he asks—'Do you want another bottle of wine?' I haven't even had time to taste it." He was asked what makes him happiest when he dines out. He stated, "When I feel the waiter is on my side and suggests good things."[19]

T I P $ **To Insure Proper Service**
When greeting a guest, always make eye contact and smile.

What Is Excellent Service?

Excellent service occurs when guests in a restaurant never have to ask for anything. Many times guests do not realize they have received excellent service until they have left the establishment. The service person does everything correctly without the guests' knowing it. When guests reach for the coffee cup, the handle is right where their thumbs and fingers naturally go. The water and wine glasses are always filled. It is never necessary to ask for the ketchup, butter, or more bread. A second cup of tea or coffee is poured before the guests request it. In the United States, the correctly added check is presented to the guest without having to be requested (in some countries and some restaurants with European cultures, especially French restaurants, the guest must request the check); and the service person and host thank the guest for patronizing the restaurant. It bears repeating: Excellent service is friendliness combined with competency.

Shadowing and Training the Service Staff

A method that some companies have used to train their staff combines shadowing an employee who is an approved trainer and then having the new employee serve the guest under the supervision of the approved trainer.

To make this system succeed, a restaurant or banquet facility must train current employees in the correct manner to serve their guests. Then the company selects competent employees to become approved trainers. Before the new employees are assigned to team up with the approved trainer, they should first attend orientation classes to learn about the history, philosophy, and style of the company.

On the first day at the job, the new employees follow and observe their trainers for half a day. This procedure is called **shadowing**. During this time, the trainers explain how to present the menu and serve the food.

In the second half of the day, the new employees carry out the trays for the trainers. The trainers, because they are regular service people, have their own station in the restaurant. All the training in this phase is accomplished on the job, and new employees have to meet and follow all standards set down by the company. For example, policy may state that every item that comes from the kitchen to the dining room must be carried on a tray. The trainer observes and compliments or corrects the trainee on this part of the training. This immediate feedback is important in reinforcing positive performance and reinstructing as needed.

On the second day of training, the new employees have contact with the guests. They approach the guests, present the menu, and take the order. The trainers now shadow the new employees. Throughout the day, the new employees are encouraged, reminded, and taught the correct ways to serve guests.

On the third day, each new employee begins the day by being assigned two or three of the trainer's tables. By the end of the day, the new employee is waiting on and serving all five tables in the station.

The key to this system is follow-up and **coaching**. The new waitperson is learning from an experienced, approved trainer. This trainer is correcting mistakes and coaching the new waitperson in proper service techniques.

After new employees have completed the three-day training period, they are given their own station. Management must constantly monitor the waitperson's performance. One way to do this is MBWA. Another method is to employ mystery shoppers. These shoppers patronize the restaurants for the sole purpose of observing the operation. Included in their observations is a report on the quality of service by their waitperson. Therefore, the management of the restaurant receives an unbiased report on its operation and can take steps to correct service or problems in other areas.

Follow-up is the key to making the shadowing and training system work. When a new waitperson does something incorrectly, the trainer must take that server aside as soon as possible and explain what the mistake had been so the employee can correct the mistake. In this way, proper service concepts are reinforced.

What Is Poor Service?

Poor service is easy to recognize. Ineffective service can be frustrating, costly, and embarrassing for a restaurant. For instance, you, as a guest, are served your meal and a few minutes later your dining companion is served. Or, how many times have you had to wait for a check when you needed to get to a show on time? And how many times have you been met and upset by rude servers with an "I-don't-care" attitude?

Charles Bernstein, writing in *NRN*, reports on a survey by *U.S. News & World Report*. The survey reported on why guests stop patronizing a particular restaurant or store or cease to buy certain products. "Sixty-eight percent quit because of an attitude of indifference toward customers by a dealer or some employee." Bernstein went on to say, "One unfriendly or nonsmiling reaction to a customer is enough to turn off that person and send him or her scurrying to the nearest competitor next time." Guests tend to remember their last experience in a restaurant. He further states that a lack of friendly service rates as a leading cause for poor sales. Guests often try five different restaurants before encountering some sort of satisfactory experience.[20]

Dr. Chistopher C. Muller from the University of Central Florida observes that "if you look at companies in the most distress, they tend to fall down on the service component. Customers expect food to be good, and they expect service to be good as well."[9]

The Reason for Poor Service

Statistics indicate that 93 percent of restaurant failures stem from poor management. People who manage restaurants very often have no concept of how to please their guests. Many managers prefer operational tasks to the actual running of a restaurant.

During the first 30 days after being hired, employees will establish their work pattern, often based on their manager's style. If a manager fails to conduct formal training sessions, and fails to express the restaurant's philosophy on guest service, the results will be poor service from the employees. After all, the manager does not seem to care about the guests.

On the other hand, if you have a manager or owner who cares and trains the staff properly, the business will prosper. The Union Square Hospitality Group (USHG), which includes the Union Square Cafe, Gramercy Tavern, Eleven Madison Park, Tabala, Blue Smoke, Jazz Standard, Shake Shack, The Modern, Café 2, Terrace 5—all at the Museum of Modern Art—and Hudson Yards Catering, has tackled the tough, New York City market and prospered. Two of the restaurants have been awarded the Ivy Award from *Restaurants & Institutions* magazine, which honors exceptional hospitality. The Union Square Cafe was recognized in 1994 and Gramercy Tavern in 1999. Owner Danny Meyer, who won the prestigious 2000 Gold Plate Award from the International Foodservice Manufacturers Association, did it by providing good value, friendliness, and warm comfort—to please people and really make them happy. Larry Levy, another Gold Plate winner, said that "he brought Midwestern hospitality to New York."[21] Mr. Meyer believes that a happy and knowledgeable staff will insure a pleasant dining experience for his guests. Each month, staff members with at least three months' tenure are given a dining voucher that allows them to dine at any of the USHG group restaurants.[22] They must submit a critique of their dining experience, pointing out the positive and negative aspects.

The intention is to develop a great **front of the house** so that people will feel good while they are eating in the restaurant. In a sense, the core is honesty in hosting, while providing really great, high-quality, interesting food and wine in a nonthreatening atmosphere.

T I P $ | **To Insure Proper Service**
Never let your guests' water or wine glasses become less than one-quarter full.

For example, a bottle of wine ordered at Gramercy Tavern is never placed near the guests; however, their glasses are never empty.

The hiring process is highly structured at Gramercy Tavern. References are checked, and a final interview is held with the general manager. After passing the general manager's interview, the prospective service person has as many as four nights of trial performances. The waitstaff then report on the applicant. (Michael Hurst also used this strategy at 15th St. Fisheries.) The applicant then has to pass a 6-page test based on a 25-page manual that covers food, wine, and service. Training, attention to detail, and a follow-up system pay dividends for the restaurant.

The Psychology of Service

Every person who considers a career in the restaurant field must realize that most guests do not come to a restaurant or banquet facility merely to eat. In the field of psychology, there is a well-known theory formulated by A. H. Maslow called **Maslow's hierarchy** (see Figure 1–4). This hierarchy deals with human needs. Maslow cites five basic needs that an average person possesses. These are the **physiological need** and the needs for **safety**, **love and belonging**, **esteem**, and **self-actualization**. The first four are referred to as **dependent needs** because they are obtained from other people. Self-actualization comes from within. Restaurant managers should know and understand how these needs affect their guests.

The theory states that a person must significantly satisfy one need before moving on to the next. However, it has been demonstrated that it is possible to satisfy portions of two needs simultaneously. Let us relate Maslow's hierarchy to the restaurant business and understand why this theory is important to a restaurant or banquet manager.

A restaurant and/or banquet manager should realize that two of the needs—the physiological and the need for love—most often will

FIGURE 1–4

Maslow's Hierarchy of Human Needs. Every individual has to satisfy the lower need before moving on to the higher one. The physiological, safety, love and belonging, and esteem needs are dependent needs— they occur with the help of the restaurant employees or outside factors. Self-actualization occurs internally when the dependent (external) needs have been met.

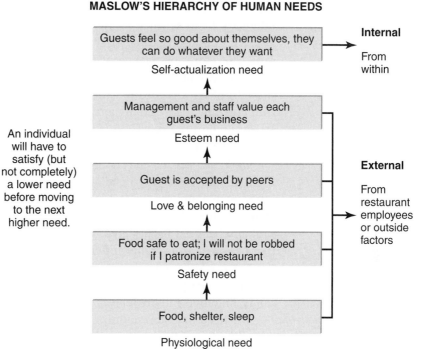

MASLOW'S HIERARCHY OF HUMAN NEEDS

have been met before the guest enters the hospitality establishment. The final need, self-actualization, is an internal need that the manager deals with indirectly. The major needs that the manager and the employees must deal with are those for safety and esteem.

The physiological need means that if we do not have enough money to provide food for ourselves or our family, we will spend the greatest portion of our time trying to earn enough money or to obtain food to satisfy this need. Most restaurant guests have satisfied this need because they are not starving.

Once the physiological need is satisfied, the person moves on to the next need—the safety need. The safety need can play an important part in the success or failure of a restaurant or banquet facility.

Restaurant guests generally have satisfied the safety need, because they probably live in a community that makes them feel comfortable and unafraid. However, some restaurants may have a problem in satisfying the safety need. Problems will arise with an establishment located in a dangerous section of town or one that disruptive customers are allowed to patronize. Guests in these establishments will not be able to enjoy their meals because they will be concerned about their safety after they leave the restaurant. Thus, even though their safety need was satisfied in their own neighborhood, it is not satisfied at the restaurant. Because of this, they will not patronize the restaurant. Therefore, management must make certain that to the guests' safety need will be satisfied. Another part of the safety need can be thought of with regard to sanitation. If the establishment has been shut down by the health department because of unsanitary conditions at any time in the past, guests will most likely not want to patronize the restaurant.

Once the safety need has been satisfied, the guests now move to the love and belonging need. This need refers to being accepted by other people and groups. Most guests have made friends and formed associations with their peers. At times, this need benefits the restaurant and banquet facility greatly, because the guests belong to groups that patronize restaurants and banquet facilities.

For the most part, guests received in restaurants and banquet facilities have significantly satisfied the first three needs: physiological, safety, and love and belonging.

The need that all restaurant managers, banquet managers, and service staff can satisfy is the fourth need—the esteem need. This need centers on self-respect and is generally thought of as ego need. It means that someone—namely, you, the manager or service person—gives the people respect and makes them feel important. For example, addressing the guest by name or inquiring about the guest's family or job are ways to satisfy the ego need. This esteem need is not a new theory. Even back when our country was founded, Ben Franklin is reported to have said, "The taste of the roast is determined by the handshake of the host." This esteem need should almost always be positive.

What Factors Determine Why Guests Go Out to Eat

There are many reasons for guests to dine at a restaurant. Most individuals when asked why guests go out to eat, would state the obvious, they go out because they need food. But that is not necessarily the case. Determining what motivates a guest to go out for breakfast, lunch, or dinner is essential to the success of any restaurant or banquet manager. An in-depth study was conducted by Strategic Food-service Solutions of Tampa, Florida, to find out why guests go out to eat. The study scientifically and randomly selected and questioned 1,026 participants from a U.S. consumer database, and extensive phone interviews were structured to determine the reasons why these participants choose to eat where they did. Statisticians then calculated the demographics—such as age, income, lifestyle, location, and other factors—and integrated those figures with what respondents revealed about how they made decisions.

The results determined that there are five categories of customers. As Food Trends 2000 reported, they are the *cater-to-me's, socializers, celebrators, impulsives,* and *busy bees.*[23] The **cater-to-me's** are defined as guests who patronize the restaurant because they are not in the mood to cook. They feel that they work hard and they deserve a break. An example of the cater-to-me's are the people who work long hours. The next group are the **socializers**. They represent exactly what their name implies. The socializers want to spend time with their family and friends. They either are the host for the meal and will pay the check, or they are invited to have a meal by someone else. The next group are called **celebrators**. These are guests who are on vacation or are celebrating a birthday, wedding anniversary, graduation, or some other special occasion. Guests who fall into the category called **impulsives** are those who crave a menu item or are not in the mood to plan a meal. If you have ever wanted a special meal that only one restaurant prepares, you have fallen into the impulsive category. The final group are the **busy bees**. These guests are the time-crunched people. They work long hours and are busy with their stressful jobs. Their children also may be driving them crazy. For all of these reasons, they fall into the busy bee category. Regardless of the category that the guests fell into, all five categories had one thing in common: Each group identified as their top need the need to be pampered.

Ego Gratification

More and more smart managers are marketing their restaurants by recognizing and playing off of the ego gratification stage of Maslow's theory to their guests. Think of the tremendous ego boost for the guest who patronizes a restaurant and the following scenario occurs. The guests are greeted by name by the host when they enter the restaurant. "Good evening Mr. and Mrs. Suarez, welcome to TRU." As they are being brought to their table by the host, she is having a friendly conversation with them, talking to them about the restaurant and their jobs. Once Mr. and Mrs. Suarez are seated, they are handed individual menus. When the Suarez's open up their menus to look at the dinner selections, the first item at the top of the menu catches their attention. In bold letters, at the top of the menu they see: "Mr. and Mrs. Suarez, welcome to TRU." Wow, what a feeling!

With today's computer technology and printers, it is possible for restaurant owners or managers to welcome their guests by putting the guests' names on the menu. If restaurants have a preprinted menu, this technique can be used on the daily specials.

The fifth need is the self-actualization, which comes from within the person. This is when the person develops his or her maximum potential. Restaurant managers indirectly contribute to the development of this need because they have helped to satisfy the esteem need that preceded it.

All restaurant and banquet managers should know how and when to use Maslow's Hierarchy to understand their guests. Of course, many restaurant owners have no idea why they should know or even use this theory. The following story illustrates how *not* to treat guests.

Mistaken Identity

A recent college graduate invited two fraternity brothers up for a day of watching thoroughbred racing. After a very successful day of playing the horses, his friends asked him where they should go for dinner. Because his father went to a particular restaurant all the time and was a friend of the owner, he suggested they go there.

As they walked into the restaurant, he could see the line of people waiting for tables. This did not bother any of them. They went in, asked for a table, and went to the bar for a few drinks.

Proud of himself for recommending an obviously fine restaurant, he marched up to the hostess desk and, to his delight, saw the owner.

The owner looked up, not recognizing the young man, and said "Yes?"

"Hi, I'd like a table for three," he said. And then he added, "I'm Spenser Marchetta, Art's son."

In a loud voice the owner replied, "I don't care who you are, you will have to wait your turn just like anyone else!"

As Spenser walked back to the end of the line, his face flushed with embarrassment. His friends could not wait to tell him what great influence he had.

A few years later the restaurant closed its doors. However, every time Spenser sees his fraternity brothers, they remind him about that restaurant.

Being Ubiquitous

All individuals who work in a restaurant must be **ubiquitous**. It is one of the most important qualities for restaurant business employees. Ubiquitous means being everywhere at the same time. The restaurant manager must know what is going on at all times. A ubiquitous manager will appear to have eyes in the back of his or her head. If the manager, host, or hostess is talking to a guest at the guest's table, he or she must also be aware of what is occurring in the entire dining room. If a new party enters the restaurant, the host must excuse himself or herself and greet the new guests.

The same is true of the service staff. An example of a ubiquitous service person is one who fills your water glass without you having to ask. The service person knows what you want without you having to request it.

FIGURE 1–5

The banquet manager must take care of all the minute details to insure that the banquet is a success. (© PhotoDisc/ Getty Images)

The banquet manager must be ubiquitous also. The main job of the banquet manager is not to serve or cook food, but to take responsibility of the party off the host's shoulders and put it on his or her own shoulders. People hosting parties want to be able to spend time with their guests. Therefore, a banquet manager must take care of all the minute details to make the banquet a success. He or she must be able to handle all problems for the host of the party.

If the flowers are wrong at a wedding, the banquet manager soothes the bride and her parents and corrects the problems. The banquet manager is ubiquitous and ensures that the party runs smoothly. The job of a banquet or catering manager is one of the most exciting and rewarding but stressful positions in the hospitality industry (see Figure 1–5).

Successful Management

The successful manager, whether of banquets or of à la carte dining, must have the following qualifications:

1. He or she must know the different types of service, when to use them, and how to serve properly. There are two main types of banquet service: Russian and American. À la carte service is American, French, Russian, or a combination of all three.

2. The manager must know the proper methods of beverage service, as well as how to organize, plan, and implement beverage service for banquets and à la carte dining. Included are open and cash bars and proper wine service. The manager must have a knowledge of wines and the proper pairing of food with wine.

3. The manager must be personable and have a genuine fondness for people. Managers must realize the importance of talking to guests and making them feel important. Knowledge of Maslow's Hierarchy must be used in recognizing guests. There is nothing as powerful as addressing a guest by his or her name. Both the dining room manager and the banquet manager must be visible in the dining room so they can talk to the guests.

4. Organization is a key skill for a successful dining room or banquet manager.

5. The manager must possess the ability to stay calm under pressure. This is especially necessary for catering and banquet managers. One factor can be guaranteed at a banquet: No matter how rich or poor, how influential, or how educated the hosts of the party may be, they are always under a tremendous strain. They want the party to be a success. The banquet manager is the person who must keep them calm.

6. The manager must be in good physical condition to withstand the long, unusual hours and stressful conditions. The job involves much physical labor, because the manager often helps move tables, transport food to catering events, and lift heavy items that are needed either in the restaurant or at the banquet.

7. The manager must be able to resist temptation. Because there is so much food and liquor available, managers may find it easy to drink and eat too much.

8. The manager must be able to deal effectively with both employees and guests. Any person considering the restaurant business as a career is advised to take as many psychology courses as possible so that he can manage all the idiosyncrasies of his guests and employees.

9. The manager must know how to train employees. In this industry, most of the training is done on the job. The successful manager will have a training plan, implement it, and have a follow-through system.

Successful managers have many other qualifications; this is not a complete list. However, there is one more important qualification a manager must have. It is the ability to deal with and handle complaints (see Figure 1–6).

FIGURE 1–6

A condensed list of the most important managerial qualifications.

QUALIFICATIONS FOR SUCCESSFUL MANAGEMENT

1. Knowledge of food service
2. Knowledge of beverage service
3. Friendly, outgoing personality
4. Organizational skills
5. Ability to stay calm under pressure
6. Good physical condition
7. Ability to resist temptation
8. Diplomacy
9. Knowledge of training employees
10. Ability to handle complaints

TIP$

TO INSURE PROPER SERVICE

Your bottom line will hit bottom if you reduce service.

Sweet or Sour?

January 11

Mr. John Beier
General Manager, Sheraton Hotel
811 Seventh Avenue
New York, NY 10019

Dear Mr. Beier,

It is my pleasure to recount a wonderful event which occurred at Russo's restaurant on Friday, December 10. My mother, two aunts, mother-in-law, and five of their friends took their annual trip to New York for the Radio City Christmas Show. My sister, a New York City resident, joined them for a 3:30 reservation. The food was enjoyable and the meal a success. When my sister received the check from the very personable 5'9" waiter (she thinks his name is Wil), she read "gratuity not included" printed on the bottom of the check. She calculated the bill, added a 20 percent tip, collected each guest's share and paid cash. When the waiter returned, he said to my sister that there was a problem with the tip. He then pointed out that a gratuity of 20 percent had already been added to the check. It was underlined and clearly noted on the check, and he suggested to her that they may want to reevaluate the tip of 40 percent. They thanked him and

(continues)

(continued)

re-adjusted their gratuity. What GREAT SERVICE!!!!! Now they relate the story to everyone they see.

Service this exceptional must be complimented and recognized. We will do that and we hope that you will compliment your food and beverage director, Atif Youseff; food and beverage manager Bert Miller; and waiter, Wil, for this outstanding service.

Sincerely,

Toby Strianese

Sweet or Sour?

May 28

Ms. Lori Smith, Manager
The Restaurant
Anywhere, USA

Dear Ms. Smith:

At approximately 6:30 P.M. on Sunday, May 20, my family and another family of four had dinner at your restaurant. This letter is to inform you about our dining experience.

Our first impression of the restaurant was excellent. The hostess greeted and seated us at the round 8-top on station or table 35, on the second level. Anne (I believe that is the name she wrote on the check) was asked for two separate checks for the two families. She did not appear to be too pleased about the request, but reluctantly complied (check number 614176). Three glasses of Parducci Chardonnay were ordered along with other beverages. Upon receiving and smelling the wine, the three of us knew it was not Chardonnay. I went to the main bar and asked the bartender to smell the wine and tell me its variety. He informed me that he could not and if I had a problem, I should tell my waitress. Doing this, my waitress said she ordered Chardonnay. We stated it was not, so she took the glass back to the service bar to check. She returned and said, "We are out of the Chardonnay, so the bartender gave you Chenin Blanc." I asked if this was the house white wine and she replied, "Yes." We told her we would drink the wine.

(continues)

(continued)

Why would a bartender and a waitress substitute Chenin Blanc for Chardonnay? It would be like a cook substituting a hamburger for the Philly steak sandwich because they are both beef, which I doubt has ever happened. The waitress should have been informed by the cook that they were out of the menu item, and she should inform the customer.

If this was the only problem, I could have overlooked it. Another problem was Anne's attitude. If she said she made a mistake that would have been okay. But she made us feel like the wine mix-up was our fault. The final straw that prompted me to write occurred when we got our bill. The Chardonnay read $2.45 per glass. When we pointed out the mistake on the bill, she said she charged us the right price for the Chenin Blanc, even though the check read Chardonnay. Since we thought we drank the house white wine (as she said before) at $1.75 per glass, we felt overcharged. Then to insult us more, she brought the menu to prove she was right and we were wrong. On the check, I wrote "very poor service, letter will follow." In addition to the above, she never checked back with us to see if everything was okay nor did she follow any proper guidelines of service. She served the drinks from one spot, just placing them on the table, not asking anyone to pass the drinks, not a friendly word. She avoided the table as much as she could.

On our way out the hostess did an excellent job. She asked if everything was all right. When I told her it was not, she asked what happened. I stated, "A lot!" and kept walking. The hostess continued to ask all members of my party what the problem was. Finally, my wife, the last person out, explained the problem. The hostess tried to get my wife to talk to the manager on duty, but since we were on our way home, we did not want to take the time. The hostess is to be commended for reacting to the situation the way she did.

In summary, the food and hostess were great, but the waitress and bar people should be trained properly and change their attitudes. Remember the customer is not always right but is never wrong!

Very truly yours,

Wayne Bruno

cc: Mr. John Jones
President of the Restaurant Corporation

SUMMARY

1. Excellent service is defined as competence plus friendliness.
2. Excellent service occurs when the guest never has to ask for any item. The waitperson anticipates the needs and wants of the guests.
3. Maslow's Hierarchy of Human Needs plays an important part in the restaurant and banquet business. Most guests at a restaurant or banquet have filled the physiological need. The restaurant and/or banquet manager can fulfill the other three dependent needs of the guest. A manager who understands the hierarchy and how to use it will make the guests feel important.
4. The restaurant manager has the choice of giving guests either American, French, or Russian service. The banquet manager can offer the guests American or Russian banquet service.
5. Managers must know and give the appearance that they know everything that is occurring in the restaurant or banquet at all times. This is called being ubiquitous.
6. To qualify as a manager of a restaurant or banquet, an individual must possess the ten qualifications listed in Figure 1–6.
7. The five categories of customers that patronize a restaurant are: cater-to-me's, socializers, celebrators, impulsives, and busy bees. The cater-to-me's go out to a restaurant because they are not in the mood to cook. The socializers want to spend time with their family and friends. Celebrators are guests who are on vacation or celebrating a birthday, wedding anniversary, graduation, or some other special occasion. Impulsive guests are those who crave a menu item or they are not in the mood to plan a meal. Busy bees are the time-crunched people.

REVIEW QUESTIONS

1. Define service as it relates to the hospitality industry.
2. Give five examples of excellent service you have experienced at a hospitality establishment.
3. List the five stages of Maslow's hierarchy and explain its importance in the hospitality industry.
4. List and explain the different types of service that the dining room and banquet manager must provide to the guests.
5. Write a definition for the word *ubiquitous* and give an example of it as it relates to the hospitality industry.
6. List and explain the qualifications that managers must possess to provide excellent service in the hospitality industry.

7. List the three types of à la carte service a restaurant manager can offer to guests and the two types of banquet service that are available to guests.
8. Give five examples of bad service you have experienced in a restaurant and explain why the service was poor.
9. Explain word-of-mouth publicity. Why is it the most potent form of publicity?
10. What is the key to making training successful? Explain your answer.
11. List the five categories of customers and explain a characteristic of each one.

DISCUSSION QUESTIONS

1. Referring to the incident at the French restaurant in Sweet or Sour what would your response have been to the guests and how would you have handled the situation if you were the waitperson? What would your response be if you were the manager?
2. What actions should John Beier take after receiving the complimentary letter from Toby Strianese?
3. What actions should Lori Smith take after receiving the letter of complaint from Wayne Bruno?
4. Describe your worst restaurant experience. What could have been done to make it better?
5. Describe your best restaurant experience. Tell why it was the best.
6. Explain how a manager would provide Maslow's esteem need to the guest. Give examples.

REFERENCES

1. http://chicago.about.com, retrieved 11/23/06, from Zagat 2006—America's Top Restaurants.
2. Tinsley III, Edward R. FMP "NRA offers opportunities for restaurateurs to become engaged in the political process," *Nation's Restaurant News* (August 21, 2006) Vol. 40, No. 34: 26, 58.
3. William Grimes, "Easygoing, Not French and Formal," *New York Times*, February 1, 1999: F1, F6.
4. Noel Cullen, Ed.D, CMC, AAC, "Opening a Successful Restaurant," *The National Culinary Review* (July 1999): 4, 6.
5. William M. Dowd, "Dorato's Missing Just One Ingredient," *Times Union*, Albany, New York, May 21, 2000, p. 15.

6. Ruth Fantasia, Speech given to the Capital District Chapter of the National Restaurant Association, May 2000, Saratoga Springs, New York.

7. "Survey Points to Restaurants as Growing Magnet for Family Time," *Nation's Restaurant News* (March 11, 1996) Vol. 30, No. 10: 72.

8. *The Random House Dictionary*, s.v. "service." (New York: Ballantine Books, 1978), p. 815.

9. "Operators Fine-tune Fundamentals, Forge Stronger Links to Loyalty", *Nation's Restaurant News* (September 13, 1999) Vol. 33, No. 37: 85; Robin Lee Allen, "Customer Satisfaction: Service," *Nation's Restaurant News* (September 13, 1999) Vol. 33, No. 37: 86–88; Paul Frumkin, "Customer Satisfaction: Customer vs. Customer," *Nation's Restaurant News* (September 13, 1999) Vol. 33, No. 37: 122–124.

10. http://chicago.about.com, 11/23/06.

11. Elan, Elissa. "Industry vets, educators say training an answer to poor-service problem". *Nation's Restaurant News* (May 23, 2005) Vol. 39, No. 21: 6.

12. Sullivan, Jim. "People, Performance and Profit Everything I know I learned in the Restaurant Business" *Nation's Restaurant News* (February 13, 2006): 16.

13. Consumer Trends What do they want (and why) Frumkin, Paul. Thimm, Fred, President, The Palm, Washington, DC. "Consumer Trends: What do they want (and why)." *Nation's Restaurant News* (May 23, 2005) Vol. 39, No. 21: 36, 60.

14. Walkup, Carolyn. "Forum: Service with a smile will keep customers coming back." *Nation's Restaurant News* (July 29, 2002) Vol. 36, No. 30: 8, 56.

15. Michael Hurst, "Wise Words for the Operator: Share Secrets, Generate Talk," *Nation's Restaurant News* (April 17, 1989): F6.

16. "Customer Service As Primary Challenge," *Nation's Restaurant News* (May 1987): 25.

17. T. Peters and Nancy Austin, *A Passion for Excellence, The Leadership Difference* (New York: Warner Books, 1985), xviii.

18. Ibid.

19. Spector, Amy. Turning the Tables. "Puck wants waiters on my side," *Nation's Restaurant News* (September 22, 2003) Vol. 37, No. 38: 26.

20. Charles Bernstein, "The Two Restaurant Kings: Customers, Managers," *Nation's Restaurant News* (May 7, 1990): 41.

21. Gregg Cebrzynski, "Meyer Wins 2000 Gold Plate Award," *Nation's Restaurant News* (June 5, 2000) Vol. 34, No. 23: 1, 71.

22. Meyer, Danny. "Setting the Table", HarperCollins Publisher, c2006, New York: 242.

23. Food Trends 2000. "Consumer Study Reveals What Drives Dining Decisions," Supplement to *Nation's Restaurant News* (December 1999): 4–5.

2

The Importance of Sanitation and Appearance

OBJECTIVES   At the completion of this chapter, the student should be able to:

1. Define sanitation and explain its importance to management in a dining room facility.
2. Determine where and how health regulations can be obtained for a restaurant, catering, or banquet establishment.
3. Describe acceptable cleanliness and appearance standards for employees.
4. List reasons for handling utensils, glasses, and plates by their bases or rims.
5. Explain why tables cannot be set with silverware in advance.
6. Identify the "freedoms from soil."
7. Explain the importance of a clean-looking establishment as it relates to the hospitality industry.
8. Define and explain the importance of using the Hazard Analysis Critical Control Point (HACCP).
9. Define cross-contamination and explain how it can be prevented.

KEY WORDS

consumer orientation   HACCP   QSC
cross-contamination   health department   sanitation

Sanitation

Sanitation is "the development and application of sanitary measures for public health."[1] This simply means that when customers enter a restaurant to eat, the food and the conditions of the restaurant are clean enough so that people will not get sick from eating there. The National Institute for the Food Service Industry (NIFI) defines sanitation this way: "In the food service situation, sanitation means wholesome food handled in a hygienic environment by healthy food handlers in such a way that the food is not contaminated with disease-causing or otherwise harmful agents."[2] Sanitation refers to visual as well as physical conditions. Guests will perceive a restaurant to be dirty if the restrooms are dirty. Any positive impression a customer might have about a restaurant can be ruined by a trip to a dirty or bad smelling restroom. Countertops and other restroom surfaces breed germs that can be transferred to food or utensils by restaurant personnel. It is the responsibility of the manager to keep the restrooms spotlessly clean.

TIP$

To Insure Proper Service
Make sanitation proactive, not reactive!

To the guests, the service person is the restaurant. If they are waited on by a person who looks dirty and unkempt, they may think that the kitchen staff is dirty and the food may not be safe to eat. The guests may be right, or they may be wrong, but their perception determines if the restaurant is clean. They are the customers, and the customers are always right. Often, if the front of the house—the physical area in which the employees serve the guests—appears to be dirty, customers believe the kitchen is dirty even though it is not. They are scared to eat at the restaurant for fear that they may get sick as the result of a dirty kitchen.

Some of the illnesses that guests pick up at restaurants are not worse than getting the flu, but others can be fatal. A simple rule to prevent foodborne illness is to teach and enforce handwashing for all employees. Hands that have touched products that may be contaminated—raw chicken or beef, for example—must be washed thoroughly before handling a glass or a plate. If not, the bacteria may be transferred by the employee to that glass or plate. This can result in infecting the guest with illnesses that cause abdominal pain, diarrhea, vomiting, and chills. *Salmonella* and *shigella* are two examples of food-borne illnesses that cause these symptoms. Both of these illnesses can be prevented by good personal hygiene, which includes proper hand-washing.

Who Monitors the Cleanliness of the Restaurant?

In each community in the United States, there are stringent health rules to protect the public. They have been established because, for many years, businesses lacked concern for both the cleanliness of their establishments and the safety of the food that they served to their guests. Because of this, each state has health laws that restaurant managers must abide by if they are serving the public. In many communities the restaurant must have a permit to operate, which is issued by the local **health department**. Once the restaurant is awarded a permit to operate, management has the obligation and responsibility to know correct sanitation practices—and to make sure all employees know and use them. In addition, the health department of the community in which a restaurant is located will conduct surprise inspections of the establishment. If the health department, when inspecting a restaurant, discovers health code violations, the restaurant could be fined and shut down.

TIP$

TO INSURE PROPER SERVICE
Ask the health department for information about sanitation.

Poor sanitation practices continue to be highlighted by the media. Television shows, newspapers, and magazine articles marketed to the consuming public use their sensational reporting style to drive home the point that restaurants are not safe. The negative publicity will seriously harm the business.

Because health inspections are a matter of public record, any news organization may obtain them and publish or broadcast the results of the inspections. In many communities, the local newspapers publish the name of the food establishment, date of inspection, results of the inspection, and what steps were taken to correct any problems. Greater media attention has resulted since the heightened awareness of foodborne illnesses traced to *E. coli*. In New York City, the city's health department posts restaurant inspection results on the Internet. The date of the inspection along with critical violations are posted.

This media attention, in turn, has resulted in more and tougher restaurant inspections and increased public awareness. Patrons want to know how safe it is to eat in a food service establishment.

Some communities in the United States require restaurants to post the results of their most recent health inspection. The restaurants are graded with either an *A, B,* or *C* rating. Los Angeles County in California, Josephine County in Oregon, and the state of Alaska all list numerical grades on their respective Web sites, and restaurants have to post their grades either at their front doors or inside their establishments.[3]

Canada has also been affected by the public's desire to know about the cleanliness of restaurants. A proposal for a rating system in Toronto would require color-coded inspection signs to be posted at the entrance of the restaurants. A restaurant that passed inspection would post a green sign; yellow would be for conditional passage; and red for failure.

How Improper Sanitation Practices Can Devastate Your Business

For a special party, the host ordered pastries from a specialty restaurant. The pastries were cream-filled. When the host got home, the pastries were placed out in direct contact with the sun, instead of being refrigerated. Sixty-three people became ill from eating the pastries. Negative word-of-mouth publicity spread through the community about the products from the specialty store. The belief among the general public was that it was the store's fault for serving the tainted cream pastries. That facility is but a memory today!

Who is responsible for the sanitation of the establishment? Ultimately the banquet and restaurant managers are responsible, and they must have a plan to clean the restaurant and enforce the highest standards of sanitation. Many food service companies (Centerplate, Walt Disney World, for instance) have a specific person to monitor and be responsible for the sanitation practices of the food-service establishment.

First Appearance

A first impression is a lasting one. This has been stressed throughout our lives. Little things mean a lot to guests. The way the restaurant appears to the guests will influence them in determining if the restaurant is clean. If it is, they will feel safe, have their meals and banquets, and spend their money at your establishment.

Good sanitation begins with how a building appears. Guests perceive the whole restaurant based on the appearance of the building, parking lot, and signage. Hotels must be concerned with the way their lobbies and public areas appear.

TIP$

TO INSURE PROPER SERVICE
Check bathrooms for cleanliness before, during, and after meal periods.

Chef's Choice

At the Martini House, our cooks prepare food in an open kitchen, which means that our guests watch our every move while we prepare their meals. It is essential that my staff and I practice superb sanitation habits when we are working. Since we have lots of eyes watching us, if we sneeze or cough, we must wash our hands immediately!

Chris Litts
Chef de Cuisine
The Martini House
St. Helena, California

The Martini House is an elegant restaurant located in the beautiful Napa Valley of California. Chef Litts works with chef-owner Todd Humphries to prepare a menu described as *Napa cuisine*, based on the best local foods from the wine country. The menus incorporate locally sourced herbs and vegetables, farm raised meats, and wild game.

The Influence of the Manager

Attention to detail is the key to running a great business. Two of the most influential people in the hospitality industry, Ray Kroc of McDonald's and Walt Disney of the Walt Disney Company, were sticklers on cleanliness. (A little trivia: Both were in the same ambulance company in World War I, both served as drivers, and were underage.) People in the hospitality industry should take their lead from the companies these two men founded when it comes to cleanliness and sanitation. In *McDonald's behind the Arches*, author John Love states that "the characteristic that was possibly most responsible for creating the

Manager's Message

(*Courtesy of* STEPHEN JAGIELLO, CERTIFIED EXECUTIVE CHEF/OWNER, EVEN STEPHENS, KENSINGTON, CONNECTICUT)

"Sanitation and safety are much more important now because of the rapid growth of our industry. Keeping your establishment in a safe and clean atmosphere will keep your guests coming back. My previous employer, the Salisbury School, was extremely concerned with the proper cooking of ground beef products because of the *E. coli* outbreaks. They requested that we prepare a minimum amount of menu items from ground beef to serve to the students. Now as an owner, I am concerned about the possibility of an outbreak of foodborne illness, which would be catastrophic to my establishment as well as my career."

—*Stephen Jagiello*

Chef Jagiello owns Even Stephens, a 46-seat restaurant that serves both breakfast and lunch. In addition, he uses Even Stephens as his home base for catering. Before opening up his restaurant, Chef Jagiello was the chef for the Salisbury School in Salisbury, Connecticut, a private boys prep school. He was responsible for the meal service for over 300 meals at each meal period, for a total of 900 per day. Stephen is the secretary for the Connecticut Chefs Association (CCA) and was named Chef of the Year in 2001 by that association.

A Little Assignment

(TO BE DONE ON A REGULAR SCHEDULE)

Make this an everyday habit. Approach your restaurant as a guest would approach it. Vary your approach daily, so you can view your building from different angles (not all guests enter your establishment from the same direction). Notice the condition of the parking lot; are there any potholes? Look to see if there are any papers on the ground. How do the landscaping and the condition of the building appear? Is the front door dirty? Are there cigarette butts outside the entranceway? Do this assignment during the daylight and evening hours.

You are viewing your business from the guests' perspective. This is called **consumer orientation**. Make notes about what is good and bad, compliment those responsible, or devise a plan to correct the problems, and most importantly, follow through on the implementation of the plan.

family image Kroc was looking for was the cleanliness that McDonald's built into its operating system."[4] He further states that "even competitors concede that McDonald's uncommon dedication to running a clean restaurant set a standard in the industry that others aimed for but seldom hit."[5] Ray Kroc used to say, "If you've got time to lean, you've got time to clean."[6] He wanted his stores to be spotless. Any person with a free moment was taught to clean. Whenever Kroc would visit one of his units, he would pick up any papers on the ground before entering the store. This demonstrated to the managers and employees that if the owner of the company can pick up papers, then everyone can pick them up. This is how managers set examples. If your employees observe you stooping over to pick up papers, then they will too. This is also done by the managers at Walt Disney World. The effect is lasting. One alumna of the Walt Disney World College Program remarked that she cannot walk by a piece of paper without picking it up.

Detail Is the Key

Ask parents what factors influence them in choosing a restaurant for their families. Every one of them will rate cleanliness as a high priority item—especially the cleanliness of the high chairs. Parents know what a mess little kids can make. Restaurants that have clean high chairs can make quite a positive impression on parents with young children. Employees should be instructed to clean all high chairs thoroughly after each use. Make certain employees are instructed to clean all those little nooks and crannies where the young toddler throws food. After the

---

Kroc's Zeal for Cleanliness

The difference between a good place and a great place is attention to detail. One of the reasons that McDonald's is the most successful food service company is illustrated by the following story.

One Saturday morning at the original McDonald's, in Des Plains, Illinois, employee Fred Turner—who eventually became president of the company—saw Ray cleaning out the holes in the mop ringer with a toothbrush. No one else had really paid any attention to the mop ringer. But when Ray Kroc looked at the mop ringer, he saw built-up crud in the holes. He wanted to clean the holes so that the wringer would work better.

Ray Kroc built McDonald's on the letters **QSC**, which stands for Quality, Service, and Cleanliness. Cleanliness was made a key part of the strategy to make and keep McDonald's number one in the restaurant business. Half of the 1958 operator's manual was devoted to describing recommended procedures on cleaning. Today, McDonald's has the reputation for being the cleanest operation in the hospitality business.

high chair has been cleaned thoroughly, the tray should be wrapped in a clear plastic wrap. Training employees to do this will increase business, not only when the children are young, but as they grow up.

Appearance of the Employees

Ray Kroc was not the only one who knew that cleanliness would create the atmosphere families were looking for; Walt Disney did too. Disneyland was founded because there was no amusement park where Walt could take his family to have a good time together. The generally recognized concept of an amusement park was unacceptable to Walt Disney's way of doing things. Almost all had dirty looking employees, too many people pressuring the guests to buy things, and too many barkers (salespeople).

When Walt founded Disneyland, he knew that the presentation of the park and its employees had to achieve standards that would earn the respect of the guests. Walt instituted "The Disney Look." It is a major part of the Disney theme parks. The Disney Company stresses to all its employees—called cast members—that "the 'Disney Look' is a tremendously important part of the overall show at both Disneyland and Walt Disney World. This employee excellence has brought more than two decades of compliments and recognition from people the world over."[7]

G. Jack Parisi, director of environmental health for Schenectady County Public Health Services in Schenectady, New York, states that the appearance of the waitstaff is important. When he enters a restaurant, he looks at the length and style of a waitperson's hair. No longer does the health department stress that hair nets must be used. Instead, says Parisi, the hairstyle should be fixed so that if a waitperson is carrying a tray, his or her hair would not be able to fall into the plates on the tray.

The Service Persons' Appearance

In an issue of *Restaurants and Institutions* magazine, the perfect waiter is described. Burt Hixson, owner of the Warehouse Restaurant in Marina del Ray, California, states that good grooming is the most important trait of service persons. Owner Benjamin Bernstein of Mike Fink's in Lexington, Kentucky, says, "Their appearance reflects their regard for themselves. Somebody who doesn't have regard for himself can't make the type of appearance that we want."[8]

Each restaurant should set grooming guidelines for its employees. These grooming guidelines should be explained to the employee when they are hired. Supervisors have the obligation to refuse to allow people to work if they do not adhere to the standards. For example, all Disney employees when hired know they have to adhere to a strict grooming guideline. Male employees cannot have their hair so long that it touches their costume collar. Females cannot wear long, dangling earrings and the acceptable size of earrings is stated. Nail polish is limited to a clear color. All new employees have the policy explained to them before they accept the job. It is up to management to set the standards, explain, and enforce them.

Dining Out: A Pleasant Experience?

A couple invited their neighbors to dinner at a nice, upscale restaurant. The couple had been telling their neighbors for weeks about the good food at this restaurant, the reasonable prices, and the enjoyable evening they would have.

Once the couples were seated, their waiter approached the table. He had on a white shirt with the sleeves rolled up and hair almost to his shoulders that looked as if he hadn't washed it in a week. The neighbor's wife said, "He should have a hair net."

How was the meal? For all four of them it was disappointing, mainly because of the dirty-looking appearance of the waiter. That was the first turnoff. From that point on, all of the guests felt his service was as poor as his appearance. Whether it was or not, in the minds of the four his appearance had ruined their evening out. Do you think the guests will ever return to this restaurant?

Managers should learn from history. Not long ago, it was common practice for a waiter to be clean and well groomed when he reported for work. In the late 1800s and early 1900s, at places like the fashionable Belmont Hotel in New York, the waiters had to pass an inspection every morning by the headwaiter. If they were not dressed properly, they were not allowed to work. Later on, during the Great Depression, if they could not pass inspection by the headwaiter, they were fired immediately. Unemployment was so high that people waited outside the backdoors of restaurants every morning at lineup time. They knew that if they could get a job in a restaurant, they could at least get a good meal. Waiters were clean, well groomed, and had immaculate uniforms.

TIP$

To Insure Proper Service
Before your staff enter the dining room, insist that they have on clean uniforms and are well groomed.

Each business and manager has to set guidelines appropriate for the particular staff and establishment. The uniform and appearance of the staff have to fit the restaurant. A place like TGI, Fridays, or an independent, local mom-and-pop pizza place has a different concept than Disney. Their uniforms are different from one another's. They are less structured than places like McDonald's or Disney, which is fine, as long as they are clean and comply with the standards set by management.

Managers must set guidelines for appearance and cleanliness. A checklist—either mental or written—must be developed. Managers must follow this checklist and not let anyone work who deviates from the standards of the checklist. Appearance codes are rarely a problem for those managers who are clear about appropriate dress during the interview process. The appearance of your waitstaff should reflect your target market. If your restaurant caters to individuals who have multiple body piercings, then it is probably appropriate for your waitstaff to also have them. On the other hand, if your target market is conservative, a waitperson with multiple body piercings, a safety pin in the eyebrow, and black-painted fingernails will negatively affect the image of the restaurant. The National Restaurant Association states that whatever dress policies the restaurant adapts for the waitstaff must apply to both male and female employees, except where reasonable differentiation is needed. For example, gender specific rules are based on "accepted community standards"—long hair and earrings allowed for women but not men; crew socks allowed for men; but not women.[9]

To reemphasize, the manager must set the standards of grooming, inform the employees, and enforce the policy.

In *The Best of Gottlieb's Bottom Line*, Leon Gottlieb writes about the problems with dress codes. "Most importantly, do you enforce your dress code? We suggest you do not—not entirely or consistently. Too many houses have allowed their crews to become sloppy, to everyone's disadvantage. You are not a good boss if you allow your personnel to be out of uniform."[10] For example, Gottlieb states, "Grooming: Clean shaven, mustaches trimmed above the lip line, clean fingernails, haircut above the collar or worn in a net, should be the type of professional appearance required in your house."[11]

Cleanliness During the Shift

Being a service person is a demanding job. It requires much physical labor. In addition, the service person can get sweaty and dirty and look disheveled during the shift. As a manager, be aware of this. If an employee looks messy, the supervisor should have that person immediately change into a clean uniform.

In many restaurants, both employees and guests use the same restrooms. After working a few hours on a shift, a kitchen worker may not make a good appearance. The kitchen whites have turned brown, covered with grease and gravy. The manager should insist that when employees leave the kitchen, they are dressed cleanly and neatly. It is recommended that cooks and chefs have an extra uniform jacket available so that they may change into a clean uniform when they have to appear in the front of the house.

The authors and Certified Master Chef Fritz Sonnenschmidt were judging the New York State Restaurant Association Pro-Start competition. We discussed the importance of the appearance of the culinary staff. Chef Sonnenschmidt said, "I tell everyone it takes a lifetime to learn to cook; it only takes a few minutes to look like a chef. When a chef leaves the kitchen and walks into the dining room, the chef should have changed into a clean chef's jacket."

How Do My Employees Smell?

Employees should smell clean. However, some employees may have a strong aroma that will turn off your guests during their dining experience. Do not allow service people to work wearing perfume or cologne. Guests may become annoyed if all they smell is perfume or cologne. The chef will not be too pleased if the aroma of the food is ruined. At one restaurant, the service person's first customer ordered a glass of wine. When the guest lifted the glass of wine to smell the aroma, all that she smelled was the perfume of the waitress, who had just doused herself with perfume liberally, putting it on with her right hand. When she served the guest the glass of wine, the perfume was transmitted to the glass. Because taste is 85 percent aroma, the guest tasted only the perfume.

As bad or worse is the problem of body odor. It is a must that all service staff use deodorant.

All employees should smell clean. Supply the restrooms with extra soap and deodorant, if needed. Make certain the guests can enjoy the aroma of the food. Do not let other aromas mask the flavor of the food.

The Handling and Storing of Utensils, Glasses, and Plates

Sanitation is extremely important in handling and storing utensils, glasses, and plates. The service staff must be trained to pick up the silverware by the handle, not by the part of the utensil that goes into the guest's mouth (Figure 2–1). The same is true of plates and glasses. Train service staff not to touch the part of the glass or plate that the guest will drink or eat from. (See Figure 2–2.)

FIGURE 2–1

The correct way to hold silverware. Service staff should be trained to pick up the silverware by the handle, not by the part of the utensil that goes into the guest's mouth.

FIGURE 2–2

The incorrect way to hold a glass. Service staff should never handle the glass on the part that will go into the guest's mouth. (Photograph by Randall Perry)

T I P $ **TO INSURE PROPER SERVICE**

Both clean and dirty silverware should be held by the handle, not the food area.

There is an important reason for this. Disease can be transmitted from one person to another by improper handling of serving items. Not only can a disease be transmitted, but guests get upset when they see this type of carelessness on the part of the service staff.

As has already been noted, the lack of sanitation in a food service establishment has more serious consequences than the negative impression given the public by unclean conditions. Unsanitary conditions and careless handling of utensils can result in the spread of disease, food poisoning, and even death.

The story of Typhoid Mary should be known by all workers in the food service industry. A lot of people know the name but do not know that she became famous because of the havoc she wreaked in New York City, where she was a cook. Wherever she worked, an outbreak of typhoid followed her. Typhoid was an easily transmitted disease. It spread in various ways. One of the surest ways was for the carrier to touch something that could transmit the disease.

Mary probably did not wash her hands with extreme care. Unless extreme care is used in washing hands, bacteria may remain on the hands and contaminate anything the carrier touches. This is the reason that you see the signs in all rest rooms that read "All employees must wash their hands before returning to work."

To stop disease from spreading, many municipalities have passed laws stating that food service employees must use a barrier (gloves, utensils, etc.) if they have to touch any food or solid—ice cubes for drinks—that a guest will consume. These laws refer to finished products. For instance, raw carrots that will be cooked could be handled by bare hands. However, raw carrots served with a dip and not cooked must be prepared using the barrier method.

T I P $ **TO INSURE PROPER SERVICE**

To emphasize the importance of using a barrier, do what the health department does when they see a person in violation. Take the product from the person preparing it and throw it in the garbage! Word of mouth among your workers will be more effective than many memos.

The less frequently dishes and silverware are handled, the less chance of contamination. Train employees to keep their fingers out of cups, bowls, and glassware. The eating end of silverware should never be touched after the silver comes out of the dishwashing machine. Sterile dishes and utensils can be recontaminated by contact with a careless hand. The authors recommend that when the dining room or banquet staff set up plates and silverware in advance that they wear gloves. This is to prevent the waitstaff from transmitting diseases from their bare hands to the plates, glasses, and/or silverware.

Setting Up Tables in Advance

Health departments have various rules for presetting tables with utensils. Each manager is advised to check the local health agency to determine how many hours or minutes a table can be set up in advance of guests' arrival. In some localities, silverware must not be preset. It is given to the guests wrapped in a paper or linen napkin when they sit at the table. This is to prevent any germs from contaminating the silverware, cups, or saucers. It is possible that germs can be transmitted from people walking through the restaurant if they cough or sneeze.

For a banquet, most health agencies allow the banquet facility to set up from one to two hours before the event is to take place. However, all health agencies agree that tables cannot be preset with silverware or dishes overnight. The reason is that a lot of disease-carrying rodents and insects are nocturnal. It is possible that cockroaches and mice could contaminate the table settings at night.

In addition, it is of utmost importance that the manager sees to it that utensils, plates, and glasses are stored properly when not in use. This means keeping them in a place that is free from insects and any possibility of contamination.

TIP$

TO INSURE PROPER SERVICE
Turn plates over and check the undersides for cleanliness.

Cleanliness of Eating Items (Freedom from Soil)

It is generally accepted that unclean utensils do constitute potential health hazards. Each service person must inspect all utensils before using them to make sure they are clean. Food cannot be considered safe if permitted to come in contact with dishes, glasses, and utensils that have not been properly washed.

Guests are concerned with the appearance of the utensils. If they see any food left over on the plate or knife from a previous meal, they may become upset. Before waitstaff serve an item or set a table, they should look for certain items. If they find any of the following examples of visible soil, the utensils should not be used:

1. *Adhering foodstuffs*, such as dried-on eggs remaining from the previous meal. Employees should check both the bottom and the top of plates. Sometimes, when dirty plates sit on top of each other, foodstuffs remain dried on the bottom of the plate.
2. *Stains*, such as coffee, tea, or vegetable stains that classify the utensils as rejects.
3. *Physical damage*, such as cracks or chips. A chipped or cracked dish is one that can never be completely cleaned because soils penetrate these areas. The crack or chip harbors bacteria and renders the dish unfit for use. The dish should be discarded.

If guests see any of the problems above, they will interpret the restaurant to be dirty. Visible soil indicates a lack of cleanliness.

T I P $

To Insure Proper Service

The proper way to wipe water spots off silverware is with paper coffee filters, not with cloth napkins, which can carry disease.

Cleanliness of Banquet Rooms

Management must make certain that the banquet rooms are attractive and beautiful (see Figure 2–3). There should be a maintenance program of regular cleaning, just as in the dining room. In addition, there are certain peculiarities regarding banquet rooms that the banquet manager must attend to in order to give the appearance of a clean and spotless establishment.

Details are extremely important in a banquet room. The banquet room guests sometimes have to circulate around the room, setting their drinks on window ledges and running their hands over these ledges. Before every banquet, an employee should be assigned to wipe down window ledges with a damp cloth to remove the dust. Another place where dust is always found is on the lectern. Guest speakers place their hands on the lectern. If it is dusty or feels dirty, they may perceive that the banquet facility is dirty. That cleaning job should also be assigned to the employee. To check on the cleanliness of the banquet room, do

FIGURE 2–3

Making sure the banquet room is clean and beautiful makes a favorable impression on guests. (Photograph by Randall Perry)

what Ellsworth M. Statler used to do whenever he visited one of his hotels. He would enter one of the guest rooms, walk into the bathroom, and lie down in the bathtub. The reason? He wanted to see exactly what a guest would see when the guest took a bath. Was the ceiling paint peeling? Were there any cobwebs on the ceiling? Do the same with the banquet room. Sit in a seat. Look around the room for cobwebs on the light fixtures or for any lights that are burnt out. Taking care of details makes a favorable impression on the guests.

Extra Tables and Chairs

In the regular, à la carte dining room, extra tables and chairs are not a problem. They should always be set with the type of cover and place setting that the establishment uses for its business. However, the banquet rooms are different: extra chairs and tables in view while parties are in progress are not appealing to the eye; in fact, they detract from the appearance of the room. Some banquet houses stack the chairs and put them in the corner of the room with the unused tables. Put yourself in your guests' shoes; you probably would not like to see extra tables and chairs in the room if you were paying for a banquet. Any extra tables and chairs should be stored in another room, or, if there is no other room available, a partition should be purchased to put in front of them.

Keys to Sanitation

Responsibilities of Management

The key to having a sanitary food-service operation is *education*. All employees have to become knowledgeable about sanitation. For instance, did you know that 90 percent of insect problems are caused by poor sanitation practices? The training of new and current employees has to include proper sanitation techniques. Just like all other forms of training, for sanitation techniques to be effective, the training must be ongoing, monitored, and enforced. The rules, the reasons for the rules, and the regulations of the local health department must be explained to the staff.

T I P $

TO INSURE PROPER SERVICE

Pouring old catsup from an old bottle into a new bottle could contaminate the new bottle. Do not do it!

If Your Restaurant Has a Foodborne Illness, What Happens?

Schenectady County Director of Environmental Health, G. Jack Parisi was asked, "If something happened in your business and someone got sick or your restaurant had a serious outbreak, what happens?"[12]

He explained that there is a law in New York State that states if a person calls a food service operator and reports that he or she has gotten sick at your restaurant, your establishment has to report it to the State Health Department. If that is not done, it becomes a violation. Regardless of the law in New York state or any municipality, the manager should inform the health department of the incident so that they can work with you, not against you.

Many times the individuals who complain are suffering from viruses; the symptoms of foodborne illnesses are similar to viruses. Mr. Parisi stated that many food-related illnesses go undetected or are unreported because of the symptoms. He also states that the health department sees a large increase of complaint calls after the media reports a story concerning poor health practices in the food service industry.

The health department must get more than one complaint for an investigation to take place, except for an outbreak of botulism. If more than one person reports contracting a foodborne illness, the process is quite involved to determine why the patrons became ill.

The health department builds a history of the case. They investigate the incident. If possible, food samples from the meal, vomit, and stool samples are collected. Information about previous meals is collected. Questions about symptoms and how long before the onset of those symptoms are researched.

Once all that information is determined, the health department can determine what kind of organism it is looking for. This is done by sending collected samples to a lab for analysis.

The Value of Using Your Local Health Authority

The health department can be a valuable partner in the food service industry. Restaurants and banquet facilities should get into the habit of contacting their local health department before a problem develops. Use the health department as an educational tool. It is important that managers do not see them as adversaries. The health department inspectors realize that operators are trying to make money, but as G. Jack Parisi stated, "Money will come if you have a sanitary place and a professionally run operation." He further added that he has a handful of operators who call him constantly to inquire about regulations. When his inspectors visit these establishments, they rarely find a problem because of the proactive stance taken by the operators.

T I P $

TO INSURE PROPER SERVICE
Restaurant managers should prepare for health inspections. How? By conducting suprise internal inspections.

The Importance of Using HACCP

Restaurant and banquet managers, and any person who prepares food for guest consumption should know the purpose of and how to use the Hazard Analysis Critical Control Point (HACCP). The **HACCP** system enables an operation to identify the foods and procedures most likely to cause illness. It also establishes procedures to reduce the risk of food-borne illness outbreaks and allows management to monitor and insure food safety. To be successful, an HACCP system needs involvement and commitment from all staff members. Effective day-to-day implementation involves all employees who receive, store, cook, and serve food.

The key to using HACCP effectively is to train the staff to use an HACCP Monitoring Procedure Report. Figure 2–4 is a form that the New York State Department of Health uses for monitoring. (CCP abbreviated in the left-hand column refers to Critical Control Points.) For example, the staff cooks a top round of beef for a banquet. The title *cooking* would be circled. The key person would write that the beef must be cooked at 350 degrees Fahrenheit for 2½ to 3 hours. The temperature of 130 degrees would be filled in where it reads "Food temperature at thickest part more than or equal to _____" in the blank where it states "temperature to kill pathogens." At each step in the HACCP process, CCPs are circled and identified. Having the staff use these forms and methods will prevent many foodborne illness outbreaks and other food safety problems.

Hazard Analysis Critical Control Point Monitoring Procedure Report

NEW YORK STATE DEPARTMENT OF HEALTH
Bureau of Community Sanitation and Food Protection

HACCP Page 1

COUNTY	DIST.	EST. NO.	MONTH	DAY	YEAR

THIS FORM CONSISTS OF TWO PAGES AND BOTH MUST BE COMPLETED.

Establishment Name_____Operator's Name_____

Address_____

(T)(C)(V)_____County_____

Food_____

PROCESS (STEP) CIRCLE CCPs	CRITERIA FOR CONTROL	MONITORING PROCEDURE OR WHAT TO LOOK FOR	ACTIONS TO TAKE WHEN CRITERIA NOT MET
RECEIVING/ STORING	☐ Approved source (inspected) ☐ Shellfish tag ☐ Raw/Cooked/Separated in storage ☐ Refrigerate at less than or equal to 45°F	☐ Shellfish tags available ☐ Shellfish tags complete ☐ Measure food temperature ☐ No raw foods stored above cooked or ready to eat foods	☐ Discard food ☐ Return food ☐ Separate raw and cooked food ☐ Discard cooked food contaminated by raw food ☐ Food temperature: More than 45°F more than 2 hours, discard food More than 70°F, discard food
THAWING	☐ Under refrigeration ☐ Under running water less than 70°F ☐ Microwave ☐ Less than 3 lbs., cooked frozen ☐ More than 3 lbs., do not cook until thawed	Observe method Measure food temperature	Food temperature: More than or equal to 70°F, discard More than 45°F more than 2 hours, discard
PROCESSING PRIOR TO COOKING	Food temperature less than or equal to 45°F	Observe quantity of food at room temperature Observe time food held at room temperature	Food temperature: More than 45°F more than 2 hours, discard food More than 70°F, discard food
COOKING	Temperature to kill pathogens Food temperature at thickest part more than or equal to _____°F	Measure food temperature at thickest part	Continue cooking until food temperature at thickest part is more than or equal to _____°F
HOT HOLDING	Food temperature at thickest part more than or equal to _____°F	Measure food temperature at thickest part during hot holding every _____ minutes	Food temperature: 140°F - 120°F: More than or equal to 2 hours, discard; less than 2 hours, reheat to 165°F and hold at 140°F 120°F - 45°F: More than or equal to 2 hours, discard; less than 2 hours, reheat to 165°F and hold at 140°F

FIGURE 2–4

The Hazard Analysis Critical Control Point form used by the New York State Department of Health for monitoring food preparation. (continues)

NEW YORK STATE DEPARTMENT OF HEALTH
Bureau of Community Sanitation and Food Protection

HACCP Monitoring Procedure Report (Page 2)

Food _____ Establishment Name _____ Date _____

PROCESS (STEP) CIRCLE CCPs	CRITERIA FOR CONTROL	MONITORING PROCEDURE or What To Look For	ACTIONS TO TAKE WHEN CRITERIA NOT MET
COOLING	Food 120°F to 70°F in 2 hours: 70°F to 45°F in 4 additional hours by the following methods: (check all that apply) ☐ Product depth less than or equal to 4" ☐ Ice water bath and stirring ☐ Solid piece less than or equal to 6 lbs. ☐ Rapid chill refrigeration ☐ No covers until cold	Measure temperature during cooling every _____ minutes ☐ Food depth ☐ Food iced ☐ Food stirred ☐ Food size ☐ Food placed in rapid chill refrigeration unit ☐ Food uncovered	Food temperature: 120°F - 70°F more than 2 hours, discard food 70°F - 45°F more than 4 hours, discard food 45°F or less but cooled too slowly, discard food
PROCESSING SLICING DEBONING MIXING DICING ASSEMBLING SERVING	Prevent contamination by: Ill workers not working Worker hands not touching ready to eat foods Worker hands washed Cold potentially hazardous food at temperature less than or equal to 45°F Hot potentially hazardous food at temperature more than or equal to 140°F Equipment and utensils clean and sanitized	Observe: Workers' health Use of gloves, utensils Handwashing technique Wash & sanitize equipment & utensils Use prechilled ingredients for cold foods Minimize quantity of food at room temperature Measure food temperature	If yes to following, discard: Ill worker is working Direct hand contact with ready to eat food observed Cold potentially hazardous food: More than 45°F more than or equal to 2 hours, discard; More than 70°F, discard Hot potentially hazardous food 140°F - 120°F More than or equal to 2 hours, discard; less than 2 hours, reheat to 165°F and hold at 140°F 120°F - 45°F More than or equal to 2 hours, discard; less than 2 hours, reheat to 165°F and hold at 140°F If yes to following, discard or reheat to 165°F: Raw food contaminated other foods Equipment/utensils are contaminated
REHEATING	Food temperature at thickest part more than or equal to 165°F	Measure food temperature during reheating	Food temperature less than 165°F, continue reheating
HOLDING FOOD, HOT/COLD TRANSPORTING FOOD	Food temperature ☐ More than or equal to 140°F at thickest part ☐ Less than or equal to 45°F at thickest part	Measure food temperature during holding every _____ minutes	☐ Hot holding potentially hazardous food: 140°F - 120°F More than or equal to 2 hours, discard; less than 2 hours, reheat to 165°F and hold at 140°F 120°F - 45°F More than or equal to 2 hours, discard; less than 2 hours, reheat to 165°F and hold at 140°F ☐ Cold holding potentially hazardous food temperature: 45°F - 70°F More than or equal to 2 hours, discard; less than 2 hours, serve or refrigerate More than or equal to 70°F, discard

I have read the above food preparation procedures and agree to follow and monitor the critical control points and to take appropriate corrective action when needed. If I want to make any changes, I will notify the Health Department prior to such a change.

Signature of person in charge_____

Signature of inspector_____

FIGURE 2–4

(continued)

The importance of using HACCP is especially critical for food-service operations that are serving buffets. The waitstaff can monitor the time that food has been left on the buffet line and the manager can check the holding temperature of the food. Cold foods have to be kept at less than 41 degrees Fahrenheit (4.4 degrees Celsius) and hot food warmer than 140 degrees Fahrenheit (60 degrees Celsius). Any foods that fall within the danger zone from 41 to 140 degrees Fahrenheit should be discarded.

Cross-Contamination

One of the major ways in which foodborne illness can be transmitted is through **cross-contamination**. The Educational Foundation of the National Restaurant Association defines cross-contamination as "the transfer of harmful micro-organisms from one item of food to another by means of a nonfood contact surface (human hands, utensils, equipment), or directly from a raw food to a cooked one."[13] There are many instances where cross-contamination may occur by a waitperson. For instance, a restaurant that serves a slice of lemon with water or tea has to make certain that the knife or slicer is clean before the lemon is cut. If the waitperson slices the lemon on a piece of equipment that was previously used to slice meat and has not been cleaned, cross-contamination may occur. Another example is the waitperson who cuts the lemon on a cutting board where raw chicken was previously cut up without the board being washed. Or how about the cook who has brought raw steaks to cook on a grill on a plate. Once the steaks are cooked, they are put back on the original plate, which may result in the cross-contamination of the cooked steaks. Another example can be of the waitperson who touches cooked food with his/her bare hand. There are many opportunities for cross-contamination to occur. A restaurant or banquet manager has to be vigilant in preventing cross-contamination and take steps to stop it from occurring.

Proper sanitation is not only good for business; a lack of sanitation will put a restaurant out of business.

SUMMARY

1. Sanitation means keeping the restaurant free from dirt. A clean establishment is important in order to have a successful business.
2. Health regulations for a restaurant, catering, or banquet establishment should be obtained from the local health regulator, whether it be municipal, county, or state.

3. Managers should set acceptable appearance standards for grooming for their particular operation.
4. Employees should be taught both the method and the reason for handling utensils correctly.
5. If a banquet establishment or a dining room sets up place settings in advance (like the night, before a morning banquet or morning breakfast), rodents and bugs may contaminate the place settings overnight, while no one is in the establishment.
6. Freedom from soil refers to adhering foodstuffs, stains, or physical damage to plates or utensils. If any are observed by the waitperson, the plates or utensils should not be used.
7. A clean establishment adds to the comfort and security of the guest.
8. Hazard Analysis Critical Control Point (HACCP) is a method to monitor food products, from delivery of the product to when it is served to the guest.
9. Cross-contamination occurs when hands, utensils, knives, or cutting boards are used on a product and not washed before using the same piece of equipment. It can be prevented by washing both the piece of equipment and hands after each use.

REVIEW QUESTIONS

1. Define the term *sanitation*. Explain its importance as it relates to you, the manager of the restaurant.
2. How would you discover the correct sanitation procedures for your establishment?
3. What makes the appearance of an employee acceptable? Describe the acceptable standards for your establishment and your reasons for them.
4. Why should utensils, glasses, and plates be handled by their bases or rims?
5. What are the three "freedoms from soil?" How should a manager address each one?
6. What are the reasons tables cannot be set in advance? Is there any exception to this rule?
7. Why is it important to have a clean-looking establishment in the hospitality business? Include information about extra tables and chairs, light fixtures, and dirty ledges.
8. Where should extra chairs and tables be stored during a banquet? Why should they not be stored in the same room that is having a function? Would there ever be an exception to this rule?

9. Should all restaurants have the same grooming guidelines? Explain your answer, giving examples to support your ideas.
10. What are the minimum standards that all service people must meet in order to serve guests?

DISCUSSION QUESTIONS

1. A waitperson reports for work not properly dressed on a night when the restaurant has been booked to capacity. In addition, two waitstaff have called in sick and will not be reporting to work. As manager, what would you do to handle the situation?
2. You are the manager of a casual restaurant that serves breakfast and lunch to guests of all ages. In the middle of lunch service, you are shocked when you see a mother place her one-year-old on the floor and begin to change her child's diaper. How would you handle this situation?
3. As a manager of a restaurant, you receive a call from a customer who states that when he was in the men's room at your restaurant a cook used the facilities and left without washing his hands. How do you respond to the guest and how do you handle the situation with your staff?
4. A staff member reports to work and has body odor. Another staff member has an overpowering smell of cologne. Describe the actions you would take and the words you would use to handle both situations.
5. What would happen at your restaurant if the health department closed your business because of a health outbreak?
6. A check of the temperature of your refrigerator shows the temperature to be 52 degrees Fahrenheit. In the refrigerator are 200 pieces of salmon prepped for a banquet later that afternoon. What do you do?

REFERENCES

1. *The Random House Dictionary*, s. v. "sanitation." (New York: Ballantine Books, 1978): pp. 793.
2. National Institute for the Foodservice Industry, *Applied Food Service Sanitation*, 2nd ed. (Dubuque, Iowa: WCB, 1978): p. 7.
3. Paul Frumkin, "NYC Mandates Web Posting of Health Inspection Results," *Nation's Restaurant News* (May 29, 2000), Vol. 34, No. 22: pp. 4, 29.
4. John Love, *McDonald's behind the Arches* (Toronto: Bantam Books, 1986): p. 142.

5. Ibid.
6. Ibid, 143.
7. Walt Disney Company, *The Disney Look* (Burbank, California: 1987): p. 3.
8. "Owners Define Perfect Waiter," *Restaurants and Institutions* (October 28, 1987): 26.
9. Rita Rousseau, "Cracking the Code," *Restaurants and Institutions* (June 15, 1997): 1–4. http://www.rimag.com.
10. Leon Gottlieb, *The Best of Gottlieb's Bottom Line* (New York: Lebhar-Friedman, 1980): p. 117.
11. Ibid, 123.
12. G. Jack Parisi, Director of Environmental Public Health Service, County of Schenectady, Schenectady, New York. Interview with author (November 18, 1995).
13. The Educational Foundation of the National Restaurant Association, *Applied Foodservice Sanitation*, 4th ed. (1995).

3

Styles of Service and Place Settings

OBJECTIVES At the completion of this chapter, the student should be able to:

1. Explain how service evolved historically.
2. Describe the characteristics of French, Russian, and American à la carte services.
3. Identify the advantages and disadvantages of the three à la carte services.
4. Lay the correct place settings for French, Russian, and American à la carte service.
5. Describe American, Russian, and buffet banquet styles.
6. Identify the advantages and disadvantages of the three banquet services.
7. Lay the place settings for American, Russian, and buffet banquet services.
8. Give the definition of *cover* and the history of eating utensils.
9. Explain the uses of tablecloths and how to change them during busy times.

KEY WORDS

À la Carte service	buffet	guéridon
American À la Carte service	simple buffet	réchaud
French À la Carte service	modified deluxe buffet	chef de rang
Russian À la Carte service	deluxe buffet	commis de rang
American banquet service	maître d'hôtel	flambé
Russian banquet service	table d'hote	silver service
	place setting	cover
	sub rosa	grazing service
	utensils	station

Confusion over Names of Service

Throughout the United States and Canada, there is no definitive type of service. Each restaurant has its own style of service. There are three basic kinds of service used in **à la carte** restaurants. These are **American**, **French**, and **Russian**. Most restaurants use a combination of all three to serve their guests. Many restaurant personnel have a basic understanding of the three types of service; however, they are not certain about the advantages and disadvantages of each particular service. Likewise, many people are confused concerning the difference between Russian banquet service and French service. Buffet service includes three additional types of service, which adds to the confusion. Overall, there is a lot of misinformation about the origins and the exact definition of the different types of service. (See Figure 3–1.)

Why the Confusion?

For many years service just happened. Only a few textbooks teaching proper service were published before 1950. Service was taught through a "pass it down" system. It was learned only by men, who participated in apprentice programs at the great hotels and restaurants of the time. Little was ever written or recorded about proper service methods. The great hotels and restaurants that had excellent maîtres d'hôtel demanded proper service and had strict rules concerning service. Waiters learned

FIGURE 3–1

The different names of service types. À la carte can be French, American, or Russian. Banquets can be either American or Russian. Buffets can be simple, modified deluxe, or deluxe.

TYPES OF SERVICE COMMONLY USED IN AMERICAN ESTABLISHMENTS		
À la Carte	**Banquet**	**Buffet**
American	American	Simple
French	Russian	Modified Deluxe
Russian		Deluxe

how to serve guests properly, and service remained consistent. Once waiters stopped working at the restaurants where they were trained and became transient, styles of service began to blend together.

Everyone took the best parts of each service and adapted it to his restaurant. Many ideas about service were passed down correctly, but others were passed down incorrectly.

Only in the past few years have textbooks and articles been written concerning service. Service is now beginning to be as important as cooking.

First Textbook for Waitresses

The first textbooks for waitresses and hostesses were written in the late 1800s and early 1900s. These books were not written for the hostesses and waitresses of today, but for the wife who entertained her husband's guests and the female who worked as a domestic in a private home. The preface of *The Up-to-Date Waitress*, written in 1906 by Janet M. Hill, states: "The manner in which we advocate that the duties of a waitress should be carried out has been evolved from a study and comparison of the methods of many housekeepers."[1] The book concentrates on the duties of the waitress serving her employer on a daily basis in his home, as opposed to working in a restaurant. Another book, entitled *The Modern Hostess*, written in 1904, concentrated on the duties of the woman serving at home. However, the beginning of the book does have a description and illustrations of a formal 10-course hotel dinner. Oscar, the great **maître d'hôtel** of the Waldorf Astoria in New York City, described how service should occur throughout the 10 courses. But Oscar did not explain from what side to serve or clear dirty dishes. The author, R. J. Bodmer, did say that serving the formal dinner would be the hardest part of entertaining, and it would be advised to obtain a professional butler "who understands service" and another waiter to serve the meal.[2]

T I P $ **TO INSURE PROPER SERVICE**
Remember: Your most important assets are your employees!

The Beginnings of Service

The job of waiting on people evolved from early times, when individuals owned slaves. These slaves or servants had to serve their masters food and drink. Unfortunately, many people still perceive the service person of today as a servant rather than as a professional. The first jobs were not as demanding as they are today. Most meals were eaten at home. The only meals a wealthy person ate outside the home were at other wealthy individuals' homes. The servants accompanied their masters to serve them their meals.

The first banquets took place in classical Rome. These banquets were attended by wealthy Romans and were restricted to men. At this time, there were no restaurants or banquet houses, but these wealthy Romans did have banquet halls in their houses. The service given was not the type of service we think of today. The servant did not have to set the table with forks, spoons, or knives because the only utensils put on the table were spoons. There were no napkins to fold and put on the table, because each guest was required to bring his own cloth to wipe his hands.

The servants' job was not without danger. In addition to obtaining food and drink for their masters and peeling their grapes, they tasted the food and drink to make certain it had not been poisoned. If the taster ate the food and lived, then the master ate it.

Early Superstitions and Facts

The Roman people were very superstitious. Guests were seated at a single couch with as few as three or as many as thirty people. The key was to have a multiple of three because that number held divine significance. All guests made certain to enter the banquet hall with their right foot first. This assured them that favorable things would happen to them.

Emperor Augustus, the founder of the Roman Empire, gave women official status in Roman society around 27 B.C. He allowed women to accompany their husbands to banquets. Because there was a great amount of gossip at banquets, anything said at the table was not to be repeated if the host put a rose on the table. This led to the term **sub rosa**, which means "under the rose" or confidentially.

The First Commercial Establishments

In the years 1000 to 1500 A.D. travelers would stop for food and lodging at inns and taverns in France and England. Everyone had the same meal served to them. This one choice, a complete meal, was and is still called **table d'hôte**.

In 1533, La Tour d'Argent opened in Paris, France. This was the first restaurant open to the public in the western world. Guests at La Tour could order their own, individual meals from a menu for the first time.

French Service

The first meals served in France were done so with considerable flourish and show. The meal was divided into three separate services. Hors d'oeuvres were served first. Then came the first service. Everything that the guests ate was placed in the dining room on tables and warmers, much like today's buffet. Each guest was waited on by a server called a valet or two. The valet assisted the guests by obtaining the food for them. Guests, while seated, could serve themselves from the offered dish, but more often the valet would serve them. This sounds very similar to the buffet style of today and was called *served buffet service* in ancient France. Food and cooking became the rage in France. Any French person who wanted to be considered knowledgeable in the ways of the world learned about cooking. The French palate was becoming sophisticated. Under the reigns of King Louis XIV and Louis XV, it became stylish to employ a famous chef. Families, like the Béchamels, were proud to have a new sauce named after them. French people started to entertain more, and service became an important element of the meal. Because so many people were becoming knowledgeable about food, service had to become creative to keep up with the new foods. Instead of being prepared solely in the kitchen, food was prepared in front of the guests with a flourish. As the guests were now civilized, they had **utensils** to eat their food with besides their fingers.

The Basic Place Setting

In homes and restaurants, the standard placement of flatware—spoons, forks, knives—generally follows the same pattern. It has not changed substantially from the original **place setting** begun in the homes and restaurants of France. To the left side of the guest are placed the bread and butter dish, and forks. The knives, spoons, glasses, and cups are to the right. A napkin is placed in the center of the place setting. A diagram of the basic place setting is illustrated in Figure 3–2.

T I P $

TO INSURE PROPER SERVICE
Use an assembly-line procedure to set up guests' place settings.

The Correct Way to Set the Table

Needless to say, both the managers and staff must know how to set the table. Then the manager must be a stickler for detail by inspecting all tables and correcting mistakes before the banquet begins or the dining room opens. A manager will be able to walk into any room and know immediately what is correct and incorrect about the place settings. In time, setting the table properly will become second nature to the service staff. Figure 3–3 illustrates the proper way to set the table.

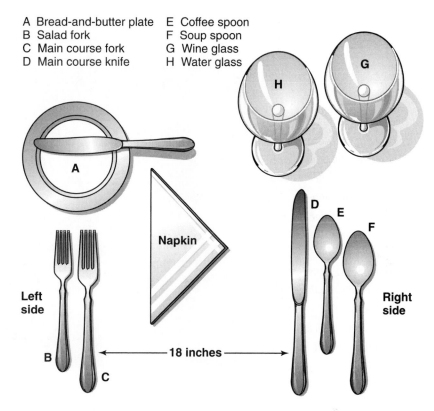

A Bread-and-butter plate
B Salad fork
C Main course fork
D Main course knife
E Coffee spoon
F Soup spoon
G Wine glass
H Water glass

FIGURE 3–2

The traditional American place setting includes a soup and salad course. Forks are on the left side of the guest; knives and spoons are on the right. Water and wine glasses are placed at the tips of the knife and spoon.

T I P$

To Insure Proper Service

For an American Place Setting

Hold your left hand up and make a circle with your thumb and index finger. That looks like a letter b.

B means that the *bread* and *butter* dish go on the left side of the place setting.

There are four letters in the words *left* and *fork*.

The *fork(s)* goes on the *left* side of the place setting.

Hold your right hand up and make a circle with your thumb and index finger. That looks like a d.

Any item a person *drinks* from—wine or water glasses, coffee cups—goes on the right side of the place setting.

There are five letters in *right*, *knife* and *spoon*.

These go on the *right* side of the place setting.

Right has 5 letters, so does *knife* and *spoon* indicating that they go on the right.

FIGURE 3–3

A table set up in the proper manner for a banquet. Forks are on the left side of the napkin, a knife and spoon to the right of the napkin. The bread-and-butter plate is above the forks. Water glass is above the knife, and coffee cup is turned upright (because it is for American banquet service).

History of Knives

In the medieval times, knives were used for hunting and protection. Every man carried a knife with him. One of the uses for the knife, discovered by early man, was to spear his food with the pointed end. He could then transport the food to his mouth without using his hands. The inns and taverns in Europe that served food and drink did not provide their guests with any utensils, because they had their own. In addition, medieval times were dangerous; the patron of the inn was in a strange place, never knowing who might attack him. When the patron ate, if he had to lay his knife down on the table, he would put it on his right-hand side. According to Sandy Rose, former senior vice president of Harry M. Stevens Corporation, this was in case he was attacked. The knife was in a perfect position, ready to be grabbed for protection. Because most people were right-handed, the knife went on the right side of the guest.

By the 1600s, knives were being placed on the tables at restaurants. These knives were still pointed at the end. A French statesman, Cardinal Richelieu, a very powerful figure in the time of King Louis XIV, was eating at one of these restaurants. As he was eating his meal, he looked over at another table and saw an individual sitting there picking his teeth with his pointed knife! He immediately ordered that all knives be rounded off at the edges instead of pointed.

FIGURE 3–4

The proper diagram for a basic à la carte place setting. On the left side of the napkin is the bread-and-butter plate, the salad fork, and the main-course fork. In the center of the place setting is the napkin. To the right of the napkin is the dinner knife (with the edge pointed toward the napkin), coffee spoon, and water glass above the tip of the knife. Notice there is no cup and saucer in this basic setting. However, there is a wine glass that is placed right next to the water glass.

A bread-and-butter plate
B salad fork
C main course fork
D dinner knife

E teaspoon
F soup spoon
G wine glass
H water glass

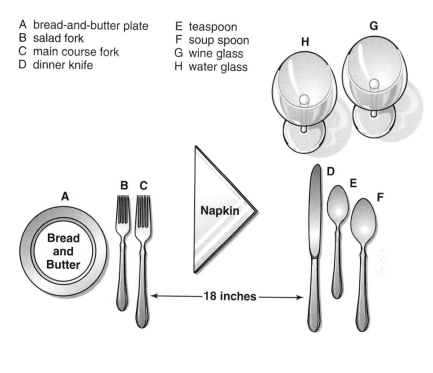

Generally, the utensil that will be used to eat the first course is placed the farthest from the guest. If soup were served first, the soup spoon would be the farthest spoon away from the guest's right hand. Next to the spoons are the knives. All blades are pointed toward the forks or center of the place setting. Figure 3–4 illustrates the basic place setting.

Reason for Location of Utensils

Europeans cut their food with their knife held in their right hand. They eat their food holding the fork in their left hand. Americans have the habit of cutting the food the same way and then transferring the fork to their right hand before eating the food. Because of this European tradition, place settings continue to follow this general pattern.

Above the tip of the dinner knife is the water glass. Next to the water glass is the wine glass. Wine is considered a food in Europe because it complements the meal. In some countries water was not fit for human consumption, it was an important part of the meal. Because guests drank more wine than water—if it was served—the placement of the wine glass made it easy for the service person to pour the wine.

On the left side of the place setting are the dinner and salad forks. Immediately above or to the left of the forks is the bread-and-butter plate.

The distance between the forks and knives should be 12 inches at a banquet, 18 inches at an à la carte establishment. Most service staff, after setting a table for a few days, are able to place the utensils perfectly on the table. There is an easy way for a service person to determine this distance at banquets. The service person should stand facing the table, with a knife in the right hand and a fork in the left hand. These utensils should be placed on the table in direct line with the shoulders. Most adults have shoulders approximately 12 inches wide. The utensils should be placed one inch from the edge of the table. Whether they are put in a straight line or in a staggered up-and-down pattern, as shown in Figure 3–5, is up to the individual management of the restaurant.

Each restaurant can adapt its place settings to its menu, adding or subtracting utensils. For instance, if all guests are served soup with their meal, then a soup spoon is added to the place setting. Notice that there is no coffee cup or saucer at the place setting. These are brought with the dessert course or when the guest orders coffee and placed to the right of the spoons.

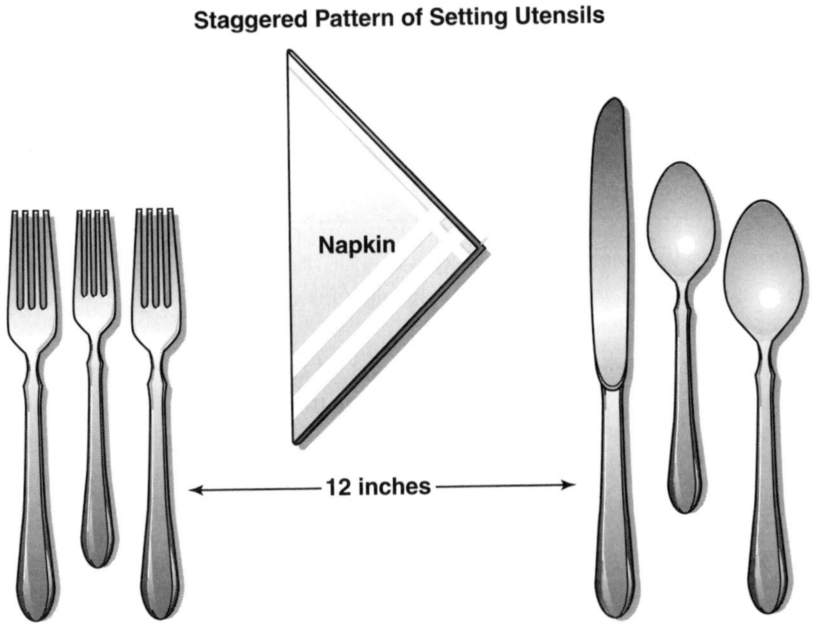

Staggered Pattern of Setting Utensils

FIGURE 3–5

Flatware placed in a staggered pattern makes for a more attractive place setting.

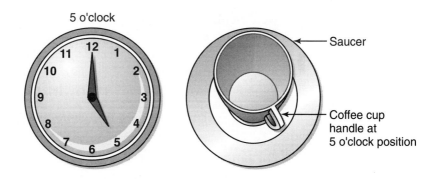

FIGURE 3–6

The handle on a coffee cup should be placed at a position that corresponds to five o'clock on a watch.

The handle on the coffee cup should be located in a position that would be the same as the hour hand on a clock pointing to the number five. This position is called "cup at five o'clock." This is strictly for guest comfort. When the guest reaches for the coffee cup, the handle of the cup will not have to be moved. The guest's fingers will fit perfectly into the handle (see Figure 3–6). This is just another detail that will make a restaurant stand out from its competitors. Everything in the restaurant should be for the benefit and comfort of the guest. Unfortunately, if the guests are left-handed, they will be inconvenienced, because the placement of the utensils is a direct result of a right-handed society and European etiquette. When a service person notices (being ubiquitous) that the guest has moved the beverage glass to the left side, the coffee cup should be placed to the guest's left, with the handle at seven o'clock. These are details that make a guest leave a restaurant satisfied, even though nothing exceptional appeared to have happened. All that the restaurant did was to take care of the smallest details to make the guest's dining experience complete.

T I P $

TO INSURE PROPER SERVICE
If a guest wears a watch on his or her right arm, he or she is most likely left-handed. Ask if you can place beverage glasses on his or her left side above the forks. Watch your tips increase!

French Service Today

During the period when kings were in power and the wealthy aristocrats were influential in France, all the skilled cooks, chefs, and valets were employed by these individuals. In 1789, a revolution took place; the royalty was overthrown and removed.

As Napoleon gained power, it appeared that France's great culinary development would stop. This was a blessing in disguise for service. Because there was no more royalty, there was very little employment for the great cooks in the homes of wealthy people. The cooks had to find a new place to earn a living. Restaurants gave these cooks an opportunity for employment. Either the cooks worked for someone else or opened up their own establishments. From 1765 until 1800, the number of restaurants increased, from 1 to 500 in Paris, France. The cooks introduced a new type of service to the French people, using their culinary skills to prepare meals in front of the guest. **French service** as we know it today was born.

Today's French service is characterized by a service person's finishing off—cooking, carving, flaming, and so on—the food in front of the guest. The food is partially prepared in the kitchen and brought to the table on a cart called a **guéridon**. On the guéridon is a small heating utensil called a **réchaud**. The food will be prepared on this guéridon, using the réchaud for last-minute cooking in full view of the guests.

Because the people doing the cooking at the table after the French Revolution were called chefs, the job title of this service person is **chef de rang**. This person might be highly skilled in order to prepare foods in front of the guest. The French looked upon food service as a profession; therefore, many talented individuals made a career as a chef de rang. Soon, going out to a restaurant became part of the culture of France. A career in the dining room or front of the house became a proud and acceptable profession. Having the skill to prepare a meal in front of the guests was soon expected by the French public. Even today, food that is not prepared at the table but served from the kitchen on a plate is looked down upon. The person who assists the chef de rang is called the **commis de rang**. The main jobs of the commis are to place the food orders in the kitchen, bring the food to the chef de rang, and clear the dirty dishes from the guest's table.

TIP$

TO INSURE PROPER SERVICE

To understand French service, dine at a restaurant that serves food using this style of service.

See Figure 3–7 for a condensed list of advantages and disadvantages of French service.

ADVANTAGES AND DISADVANTAGES OF FRENCH SERVICE
Advantages
1. Guest obtains high degree of personal attention.
2. Service is showy and elegant.
3. Food is prepared with flourish and showmanship.
4. It may be possible to decrease kitchen labor cost.
Disadvantages
1. Highly skilled waitstaff is required.
2. Quality standards are difficult to enforce.
3. Dining room fills with the smell of cooked food.
4. Much more physical space is required than in American Service.
5. More and costlier equipment is needed.
6. Residence time is greatly increased, resulting in less turnover.
7. Menu prices are highest in restaurants that use French service.

FIGURE 3–7

Advantages and disadvantages of French service.

French service has some excellent advantages:

1. The main advantage is for the guest, who gets a high degree of personal attention.
2. The service is showy and elegant.
3. Food is prepared with showmanship.
4. It may be possible to decrease the labor cost, because the chef and commis de rang are partially compensated with gratuities. Therefore fully staffed, highly paid kitchen crew may not be needed.

However, there are more disadvantages than advantages for a restaurant in using French service:

1. The restaurant must employ highly skilled service staff, knowledgeable in both cooking and service. They must know how to bone fish and poultry, carve meats, dress salads, and prepare **flambé** items. The chef de rang must be knowledgeable about ingredients and must have the personality to perform constantly. These individuals might be impossible to find in some areas of the country. Therefore, a well-planned training program must be instituted and maintained.
2. If a restaurant does not have a good training program—and even if it does—there could be a problem with consistent quality of food prepared by all the chefs de rangs at all the tables. It becomes difficult to enforce standardized recipes and to correct mistakes. Thus, the guests may get different quality food at different visits.
3. Because cooking is done in the dining room, the air may become stale with the odor of cooking unless the dining room has a good ventilation system.

4. Because guéridons must be used, a restaurant using French service will have less space for tables. French service requires 18 square feet per guest, whereas other services only require 15.

5. It costs more to buy and maintain the guéridons and réchauds. Other equipment must also be purchased that may not have to be purchased using American or Russian service.

6. It takes longer to serve guests using French service. A restaurant cannot serve as many guests in an evening. Generally, restaurants with this type of service have only one sitting a night, or they have an early and late sitting, if the demand is great.

7. The price of the meal must be high enough to cover all these costs involved. Therefore, restaurants that use French service have to charge considerably more for a meal than those that use any other type of service.

Russian Service

The cuisine of Russia was greatly influenced by the French. Catherine the Great of Russia (1762–1796) imported French chefs and corresponded regularly with Voltaire. She was a great Francophile. In turn, the service in French restaurants was influenced by the Russians.

Because the Russians did not have many skilled chefs, the food served to wealthy aristocrats was prepared in the kitchen, rather than in front of the guests. To make the food look as appealing as possible, it was served on royalty's best serving pieces: silver trays. As the rulers of the two countries became allies (Peter II, Catherine's son, and Napoleon planned to invade Egypt together), each country influenced the other. When the French returned home from Russia, they brought with them an idea for a new type of service to be used in restaurants. This new style of service in France was referred to as **silver service**.

When this new type of service was introduced to French restaurants, it revolutionized the industry. It became popular in the mid-1800s. No longer did restaurants have to find talented chefs to prepare food at the table—nor did they need guéridons. Now food could be served more quickly to more guests. **Russian service** is characterized by food being cooked and preportioned in the kitchen. All the food for a table is presented to the guests on silver trays. The service person then serves the food to the guests' plate from the tray. In the United States and Germany this service is called Russian. A more casual example would be family style service. In France, because it originated in French restaurants, it is called French or silver service.

FIGURE 3–8

Advantages and dis-advantages of Russian service.

ADVANTAGES AND DISADVANTAGES OF RUSSIAN SERVICE

Advantages
1. Food looks impressive when served.
2. Less floor space is required per table.
3. Guests have more space for comfort.
4. Russian is faster than French service.
5. Waitstaff does not have to be as skilled as French service waitstaff.
6. Quality control of food is maintained.

Disadvantages
1. Service person has to be skilled in serving from platter to plate.
2. Tables must be positioned so that they are easy to serve.
3. Different entrees require different silver platters, resulting in cold food for the first guest.
4. High initial cost for purchasing equipment. Theft of silver is a possibility.
5. Last guest to be served is presented with an unappetizing platter.

See Figure 3–8 for a condensed list of advantages and disadvantages of Russian service.

Russian service has many advantages over French service for a restaurant owner or manager. It is best used for banquets rather than for à la carte service.

1. Food portioned and arranged on a silver platter looks appealing and impressive.
2. Less space is required than for French service, because guéridons are not needed; therefore, more tables can be placed in the dining room, resulting in more meals served.
3. Guests will be more comfortable at the table, because 30 inches of linear space are needed for Russian service, as opposed to 24 inches for other services.
4. Guests can be served more quickly, which allows for more turnover than does French service.
5. The service staff do not have to be skilled in food preparation.
6. The quality control can be better maintained than with French service, because all food is cooked and put on platters in the kitchen.

Russian service does have some disadvantages:

1. A service person has to be skillful in manipulating a fork and spoon to transfer food from the platter to the guest's plate.
2. All tables must be located so that they can be easily served. If a table is located too close to a wall, it becomes impossible to serve a guest.

3. When guests order different entrees it requires bringing different platters to the table. This is time consuming. The first guest served will end up with cold food to eat if he or she waits for all the guests to be served.

4. There is a high initial cost for purchasing the silver platters. A larger problem is controlling the inventory of silver and preventing theft.

5. If all guests order the same entree, the last person served could find the look of the food picked over and unappealing.

Russian and French Place Settings

Because the two types of service are so similar, the place settings are identical. In both services, the place settings are shown in Figure 3–9.

The difference between this setting and the basic setting is that the dessert fork and spoon are already on the table. One other difference is that the knife is on the bread and butter plate. Notice the placement of the glasses. There should never be more than three glasses at a place setting.

RUSSIAN/FRENCH PLACE SETTING

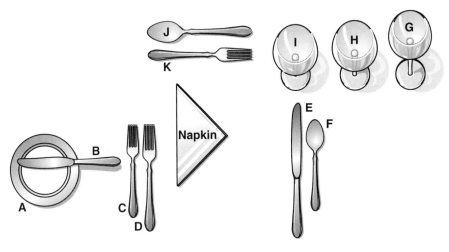

FIGURE 3–9

Russian and French place settings are identical. The setting is basically the same as American style, except for a dessert spoon and dessert fork placed above the center of the place setting.

A bread-and-butter plate
B bread-and-butter knife
C salad fork
D main course fork
E dinner knife
F coffee spoon

GLASSES
G white wine glass
H red wine glass
I water glass
J dessert spoon
K dessert fork

History of Spoons

The spoon is the oldest and simplest of all eating utensils. The earliest ones were made out of wood. The Egyptian spoons were carved from ivory and wood or various metals. Elaborately shaped handles were designed and were often decorated with lotus blossoms.

The spoon was a mark of class in medieval society. Each person brought his or her own set of utensils to dinner. Children were given their own set when they were old enough to eat with company. The expression "to be born with a silver spoon in your mouth" came about because wealthy families started the practice of giving a set of spoons to their children at birth. This phrase meant that the children came from a well-to-do family.

Cesar Ritz

French cooking was becoming more popular and common in the 1800s. More restaurants were opening. Russian service, as well as French, was being experienced by more guests. More restaurants were finding that Russian service was more economical to use. Waiters did not get as much respect as the talented chefs de rang of French service. Cesar Ritz (1850–1918) is credited with making serving guests a profession.

His great learning took place when he worked as a commis de rang (assistant waiter) at the most famous restaurant in Paris, le Voisin. He took the job at le Voisin so he could learn the best methods in serving techniques. He learned to deal well with people, and was so responsive to their wishes that before long, guests were insisting on being served by him. He was a master at details and soon was in demand to manage restaurants and hotels all over Europe.

The following incident was typical of his quick-thinking mind and obsession with details. He was working at a mountain-top hotel in Switzerland called the Rigi-Kulm. A group of 40 Americans were arriving for lunch. The temperature was eight degrees below zero, and the heating system broke down. He had no way to cancel the party.

Ritz changed the setting of the party and the menu to give the guests the impression of warmth. The 40-seat table was moved into a small room and covered with a red tablecloth. Four large copper bowls were filled with methylated spirits; when the guests arrived, each of the bowls was lit. For each guest a hot brick was wrapped in a flannel cloth and placed under his or her feet. The guests began the meal with a hot consommé and ended with crêpes flambées. Because of Ritz's obsession with details, the guests had no complaints about the temperature, and the luncheon was a success.

Ritz's name and fame soon spread. His treatment of guests and his staff's service was legendary. He and Escoffier, the great French chef, began working together. Ritz would be in charge of the service, Escoffier of the kitchen. Escoffier created new dishes and named them for a favored few of their customers. Ritz chose the customers. Peach Melba, Melba toast, and Sauce Melba were created and named for the great Australian opera singer Dame Nellie Melba. His waiters were taught to give dignified service. They served in silence but were always at hand when needed. The dining room was always planned to be elegant and attractive enough to invite the most elegant of ladies.

In 1887, at age 37, he married a London hotelkeeper's daughter. While in London, he was asked to take over the management of the Savoy Hotel, where he made the biggest impact on the restaurant industry. He revolutionized dining out and even changed the habits of society. Restaurants were required by law to close at 11:00 P.M. He got Parliament to change the hour, and soon the Savoy's restaurant was open until 12:30 A.M.

Sunday dining become a feature of the week. The Savoy became known as the place to go and to be seen. Ritz hired orchestras to play dinner music; the first one was led by Johann Strauss. He made evening dress compulsory and banned unaccompanied ladies from the dining room. He was accused of breaking up home life by making dining out fashionable. Because of him, men's clubs suffered a loss of business. Men now took their wives out to dine at the Savoy instead of going to dinner at their men-only clubs. The common people could now go to a fashionable restaurant and dine with the aristocrats. In short, the common people could now "put on the Ritz."

Setting the Cover

As Ritz made it a policy to have elegant surroundings for his restaurants, modern restaurant managers should also have standards for their establishment. Every restaurant and banquet house must have a place setting on the table before the guests eat their meal. Our place settings are different from those of ancient Rome and of medieval times. Some establishments have opulent linens, silver, and crystal, whereas others have only the bare essentials. The area or space for all utensils—including salt, pepper, and ashtrays—for each guest is called the **cover**. Many people refer to this as the place setting. However, note that the place setting includes *only* the utensils for the guest to eat the meal, whereas the cover includes all the space for each guest. A restaurant manager should make sure that each cover is set consistently. This is another factor that distinguishes an award-winning restaurant from others. A guest, dining at one of the Ivy or *Nation's Restaurant News* or DiRoNa award-winning

FIGURE 3–10

Space requirements for American banquet service. Each guest needs 24 linear inches. This table is 8 feet long by 3 feet wide. It can seat four guests on each side of the table.

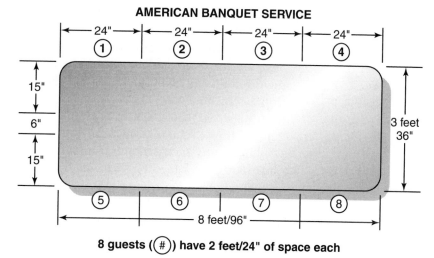

AMERICAN BANQUET SERVICE

8 guests ((#)) have 2 feet/24" of space each

restaurants will notice the placement of the salt and pepper shakers or flowers. Great restaurant managers are sticklers for details. The placement of each item on each table is in the same spot.

TIP$

TO INSURE PROPER SERVICE

An outstanding restaurant—TRU in Chicago, Illinois. There is a comprehensive focus on service, food, and attention to detail. When a guest asks for the location of the restroom, the staff member will escort the guest to the entrance of the rest room.

With any style of service, enough space must be allowed so that guests are not crowded and service staff can serve them safely. French and American services require 24 linear (straight line) inches of space for guest comfort; Russian service requires 30 inches. All should have an area 15 inches deep. Therefore, in American banquet service, a table that is 8 feet long by 3 feet wide can seat four guests on each side of the table, for a total of eight guests (as is illustrated in Figure 3–10). Regardless of the size of the table, the manager must make sure that both the guests and service staff have enough room so that the guests can be comfortable and staff can serve properly.

Placemats and Tablecloths

The choice of what to put under the cover is up to the individual establishment. Some restaurants will use a placemat to cover the area for the place setting; others will use a tablecloth; still others use a tablecloth covered by a glass top.

Originally, restaurants that used placemats were usually low-priced coffee shops. Today, more and more restaurants—regardless of the type or the price of the meal—are choosing placemats rather than cloth because they are less expensive. The placemats range in quality from paper to plastic or cloth. The placemat should be set about 2 inches from the edge of the table. The utensils go on the placemat.

Tablecloths are used for most banquets and, generally, in restaurants that have a high check average. Tablecloths should be placed on tables in banquet rooms by two people. The service people stand on either side of the table while unfolding the tablecloth and laying it on the table. Tablecloths should be hung even with the seat of the chair. In an à la carte restaurant, one person can place the cloth on the table, because the tables are smaller. In an à la carte restaurant, it may become necessary to change the cloth without exposing the bare tabletop to the guests. Changing a cloth should be done discreetly, without any flourish that would distract the guests.

How to Change a Tablecloth

1. Remove all dirty plates and napkins from the table and place them on a tray, which is set on the tray stand, not on the table.
2. Move to one side of the dirty tablecloth all salt shakers, pepper shakers, flower vases, sugar bowls, and any other items that are part of the cover and must remain on the table.
3. Fold back one edge of the dirty cloth and place the clean cloth on the bare part of the table.
4. Unfold the clean cloth to the center of the table so that it is almost touching the cloth to be changed.
5. Return all the items that are part of the cover to the clean tablecloth.
6. Complete unfolding the tablecloth.
7. Set the cover in the proper way, as required by management.

When service persons change cloths, they should never expose the bare table nor should they place anything—clean or dirty items—on the chair. All personnel should know how to change a tablecloth and reset the cover. No guests should ever be allowed to sit at a dirty table.

T I P $ **TO INSURE PROPER SERVICE**
Catch a staff member changing the tablecloth correctly. Reward him or her with a small token of appreciation, like a bottle of wine or a lottery ticket, where legal.

Glass Tops

Some restaurants have discovered a new way to cut costs while still using tablecloths to make the restaurant look nice. The table is covered with a tablecloth, then a glass top—which has been specially made for each table—is placed over the cloth. The cover may be set directly on top of the glass. One disadvantage is that the glass has to be cleaned with a glass cleaner after every meal. The smell of the cleaner might be offensive to some guests. Another disadvantage is that the use of glass tops adds to the noise level in a restaurant.

Completing the Cover

To complete the cover, the table is finally set with a napkin, either cloth or paper. The napkin should be the last item placed on the table. Before the service person places the napkin on the table, the cover must be correct. The napkin can go in the center of the place setting, in a water glass, or in the center of the starter plate for establishments that use a starter plate. The napkins should not go under the forks. Depending on the policies of the restaurant, management may have the napkins folded in an artistic manner. The appendix of this book has a section on how to fold napkins.

Napkins

The use of table linen began when the very rich started to cover their dining room tables with expensive decorated linen or silken drapes. The dining tables of that time were long and narrow. The cloths were generally square. To make the dining room look as attractive as possible, the cloths were set diagonally along the table. A corner of the cloth would hang over the edge of the table in front of each guest.

The eating habits and table manners of the guests were not good. It was common practice for the guests to wipe their greasy hands on their clothes and spill food and drink on the cloths. It was not long before guests realized that there was no need to wipe their hands on their clothing and get their fine clothes dirty. They quickly figured out that this linen would be a great convenience for wiping their hands. Because of the way the cloth was situated on the table, they began to tuck the corner of the cloth under their chins to prevent the food from falling into their laps. And, of course, they wiped their face with the linen at the end of the meal. As early as the fifteenth century, hostesses had their servants make square pieces of cloth to match their tablecloths which is how napkins were discovered.

Attention to detail, especially in regard to table settings, is critical for a guest's first impression of your establishment. Tablecloths should be draped evenly at all tables. The proper length is 14 inches. When the drape of the tablecloth is longer or shorter than 14 inches, the dining or banquet room looks unappealing.

Whatever type of tablecloths, placemats, and napkins are used in a restaurant, they should be attractive, clean, and appropriate to the restaurant's style.

The History of American Service

Dining in America was affected by the Puritan influence. There was only one purpose for eating: to refuel the body. To dine strictly for pleasure or enjoy the meal was thought to be bad.

The restaurant business in America got its start in the 1800s at taverns and roadhouses. Service at the beginning of this century was terrible. American service was and is still characterized by "food on the plate, no wait." This was the American custom. All food was put on one plate and served to the guest, as opposed to French service, where separate plates for vegetables were used. All guests sat in a common room and ordered from a very limited menu. Large quantities of food were served to the guest. The eating hours were set for the convenience of management.

During the 1830s, a great influx of French immigrants entered America, bringing their ways of serving food. At about the same time, many German and Italian waiters and cooks came to the United States, because they had heard that the streets were paved with gold. They also brought with them a better style of service than was available in America. As they found employment in America, they introduced their methods of service in the places where they worked. Eventually, service got better, and a style of service began to develop.

Another reason that service got better was that employers went to Europe and got entire kitchen and dining room staffs to come to America. The owners paid for the workers' trip over. This was a way to get to those gold-paved streets. The owners would offer to pay wages to the cooks but told the service staff they could work only for tips. Restaurant owners did this to cut down on their labor costs. It worked; many people were looking to go to the New World, and they were pleased to have the opportunity.

America had always been tipless. When the restaurant owners returned from Europe with their new staffs, they introduced tipping into American culture, claiming that it was an established European practice.

At the same time the great influx of immigrants was arriving in the United States, Delmonico's opened in New York City (in 1832). This restaurant gets the credit for teaching the American public how to enjoy fine dining. It also set the standard for elegance that all other restaurants in the United States tried to match. Delmonico's offered the first à la carte menu, courteous service, private dining rooms, flowers, music, and fine wines to its guests.

Oscar Tschirky, employed as the maître d'hôtel at the Waldorf-Astoria, worked exclusively in the dining room. He elevated service to the highest standards in America. No waiter was allowed to have chin whiskers or a mustache, as he considered facial hair to be unsanitary. He also got American restaurants to cut down on the abundance of food.

Thanks to Delmonico's, Oscar Tschirky, and European immigrants, America evolved its own unique type of service, which took the best parts of French and Russian service and combined them with American ingenuity.

American Service

American service is characterized by portioning all the food on the dinner plate in the kitchen. It is also referred to as plate service or German service. It is the fastest of all types and requires the least amount of skill to wait on guests. One service person generally works a station—a group of tables in an area of the room—containing between 14 to 18 seats. The main difference in serving food in American service, as opposed to French and Russian service, is that all food is served from the guest's left side with the service person's left hand, and all beverages are served from the guest's right side with the service person's right hand. Raymond J. Goodman theorizes in his book *The Management of Service* that the practice of serving food from the guest's left side occurred because Americans consume more beverages and more varieties of beverages than Europeans.[3] Because the glasses are positioned on the right of the place setting, it was easier to serve the food from the left side, so as not to disturb the guest when he was drinking or reaching for his glass.

See Figure 3–11 for a condensed list of advantages and disadvantages of American service.

ADVANTAGES AND DISADVANTAGE OF AMERICAN SERVICE

Advantages
1. A simple service to teach and learn.
2. A skilled service staff is not necessary.
3. Cost of equipment is low.
4. Service is fastest of all three methods.
5. Less dining room space is required for guests.
6. More guests can be served.
7. Menu prices can be lower than in other services.
8. Quality control can be excellent.

Disadvantage
1. Service is not as elaborate as in French or Russian service.

FIGURE 3–11

Advantages and disadvantage of American service.

The advantages of American service far outweigh the one disadvantage:

1. It is a simple service to teach and learn. The staff only has to put a plate in front of the guest. They do not have to know how to cook, carve, or flambé.
2. A skilled staff is not necessary. Almost anyone can be trained to serve American style.
3. The cost of equipment is low, as there are no guéridons or silver trays to purchase.
4. Service is extremely fast.
5. Less dining room space is required for each guest.
6. Because service is fast and less space is required per guest, more guests can be served during the meal period.
7. Menu prices can be lower for the same meals compared to other services.
8. Portion and quality control are excellent, as all foods are plated in the kitchen.

There is just one disadvantage in using American service: The service is not as elaborate as the other two.

American service is widely used in restaurants around the world today because the advantages are so numerous. Most restaurant managers will borrow parts of French and Russian service and incorporate it into their particular service style. For example, many restaurants in the United States offer salads made tableside (French); or they may serve a dish like lobster Newburg, portioning it out in front of the guests (Russian). American service is the best type of service to use for most restaurants.

Banquet Service

A **banquet** is a meal where all the food has been preselected by the host before the guests enter the room. Banquets are served using **American, Russian,** or **buffet** style. All have advantages and disadvantages. The key factor in serving banquets is for the service person have as much needed equipment on the guests' table before they enter the room. The purpose of banquets is to serve guests faster than in à la carte dining. This is because most banquets are arranged for a special purpose—a dance, testimonial, or awards presentation—not just to eat. A brief description of all types of banquets follows.

Origin of the Word Banquet

At large dinners in medieval times, the seating arrangements were precise. The feudal lord and lady sat on a raised dais at one end of the room. The children and relatives sat on removable benches along the walls. The term *banquet* comes from the French work for bench, which is *banc*. Servants stood behind the chairs of the wealthy couples to make certain that the food was not poisoned. At medieval and Roman banquets, there were not many spoons, so the diners used their fingers or short, pointed daggers to bring the food to their mouths. There were no forks or napkins or place settings.

American Banquet Service

Like American service, this is an easy service to provide. One waiter can usually serve from 16 to 24 guests. The service is the same as American, except for the place setting.

American Banquet Service Place Setting

The place setting for **American banquet service** is similar to American à la carte service. However, the place setting changes with every banquet. A separate utensil is needed for each course. Because the purpose of the banquet is to serve guests as quickly as possible, the utensils should be preset.

Therefore, the meal illustrated in Figure 3–12 needs two forks, three spoons, and two knives. The place setting appears in Figure 3–13. Note that the coffee cup and saucer are preset with the cup up and the handle in the correct position.

FIGURE 3–12

The menu for a typical banquet, with the utensils needed to serve one guest. Two forks, three spoons, and two knives are needed. A bread and butter plate, cup and saucer, napkin, and water glass are needed as well.

TYPICAL BANQUET MENU	
Item	**Utensil Needed**
Fresh Fruit Cup	Teaspoon
Salad, House Dressing	Fork
Prime Ribs	Knife to cut, fork to eat
Baked Potato, Green Broccoli	
Rolls and Butter	Butter spreader
Chocolate Mousse	Teaspoon
Coffee	Teaspoon

Figure 3–13 is the correct place setting for the menu as it appears in Figure 3–12. However, a banquet house may not have enough spoons to place three at each setting. Therefore, a banquet manager might be forced to use only two spoons.

AMERICAN BANQUET PLACE SETTING

A coffee cup
B fruit spoon
C coffee spoon
D dessert spoon
E dinner knife

F main course fork
G salad fork
H bread-and-butter plate
I   water glass

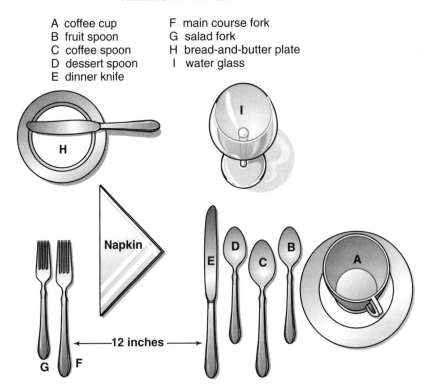

FIGURE 3–13

An American banquet place setting.

TIP$ **TO INSURE PROPER SERVICE**
Develop positive relationships with your competition to borrow equipment and with a business that rents equipment for banquets.

If a restaurant is going to be in the banquet business, it is strongly recommended that the establishment purchase enough equipment to do the job properly.

History of Forks

The first types of forks had two prongs. They were used to hold sacrificial meat, but not for eating. People ate by picking the food up with their fingers or the pointed end of a knife. Two people are credited with introducing the fork to modern society. A Byzantine princess introduced the fork in the eleventh century to the people of Venice, Italy. Queen Catherine de Medici was the second person. She introduced it to the aristocrats of France after returning from Italy in the mid-1500s. At first, it was used more as an amusement than as a serious eating utensil. By the 1600s, forks became fashionable and were more acceptable than eating with one's fingers.

Like spoons, forks became very elaborate. These forks sometimes were as elaborate as a piece of jewelry. When people were invited to dinner, they carried their precious forks with them in special cases. Forks were introduced to England by Tomas Coryate, who brought back samples of them from Italy, where he first used them.

Governor John Winthrop of Massachusetts brought the fork to America. When he came to the colonies in 1630, he brought one along with his personal knife in his personal case.

By the 1800s, forks had become acceptable throughout the Western world. Some restaurants started to provide all utensils for guests.

Russian Banquet Service

Russian banquet service is the most elegant of banquet services. Two service people are generally assigned to work in pairs, serving a total of 20 guests. Food is served from platter to plate. One server serves the main course, while the other follows with the potatoes and vegetables. A skilled staff is needed for this type of service.

Russian Place Setting

Like the American setting, all utensils are put on the table. However, each guest has his own set of salt and pepper shakers. The dessert fork and spoon are set above the place setting. As in American banquet service, the amount of silverware needed changes with each banquet, depending on the menu.

Buffet Service

Buffet service is characterized by the guests obtaining either their whole meal or parts of the meal from food that is displayed in the dining room. One service person can be assigned as many as 35 guests. The place settings for banquets have only enough utensils set to do the job.

There are three types of buffets. The first is simply called **buffet**. In this service, guests obtain all their own food and drinks. The service person has only one job: to clean up dirty dishes.

The second is called **modified deluxe buffet**. Tables are set with utensils and guests are served coffee, and perhaps dessert, by the service person.

The third is the most elegant, called **deluxe buffet**. The guests are served the first and second course, as well as their beverages and dessert. They obtain their main course from an elegant buffet. The service person must serve and clear many courses. They must have all the dirty plates cleared before the guest returns from the buffet table. One service person is needed for 20 guests in this style of buffet service.

Because it is a banquet, the place setting of the buffet is determined by what food is offered on the buffet. Management should train their staff not to allow guests to bring back used plates and utensils to the buffet line. Instead, the guests should be given a new plate each time they come to the buffet line. In addition, there must be enough utensils on the buffet line so that the guests do not use their fingers to pick up food or dip bread or raw vegetables into the food. By taking these precautions, the establishment will prevent cross-contamination. However, the manager must use common sense in determining how many utensils to set.

Another type of food service is the **food station** or **grazing service**. Strategically placed around the banquet room, different types of foods are set up. One table or station may have cheese, crackers, fruit, and vegetables. Another station may have cooks preparing stir fry items. Beef, pork, or turkey may be carved and put on rolls at other stations. The type of food that is served at these stations or grazing service is only limited by the imagination and the cost considerations of management and the person paying for the event. At every station, there should be utensils, plates, and napkins available for the guests. In effect, this service resembles buffet service, because the service staff circulates throughout the room assisting the guests with their dirty plates and dishes. In this type of service, the key to success is to have the staff constantly circulating throughout the room.

Manager's Message

(Courtesy of Jackie Appeldorn, General Manager, Mohonk Mountain House, A National Historic Landmark, New Paltz, New York)

"Service that exceeds guest expectations is the vehicle for distinguishing your property from others. Facilities, physical features like pools and mattresses are important to guests, but other properties can provide the same pool, the same mattress. Outstanding service is the link between your physical property and your guests. It creates a connection that becomes an integral part of the guest experience. This is especially important at a resort, where guests are spending their leisure time."

—*Jackie Appeldorn*

Mohonk Mountain House stands at the heart of a magnificent 26,000-acre natural area. It overlooks Lake Mohonk, a half-mile-long, sixty-foot-deep, mountain lake. This sprawling Victorian castle is one of the last of the great nineteenth-century mountain resorts. This all-season resort has 251 guest rooms, six guest cottages, three spacious dining rooms, 150 working fireplaces, 200 balconies, a half-dozen parlors, and three inviting porches lined with rockers. Mohonk accommodates vacationers and conferences year-round.

SUMMARY

1. Service evolved from traditions—like the knife being set on the right side of the guest so that the right-handed guest could quickly grab it and defend himself if attacked. Each country added its own uniqueness to service. Restaurant owners have taken the best parts of a particular style of service and adapted it to their own restaurants. Service was learned through the "pass-it-down system." Many of the service skills were passed down correctly, but others were passed down incorrectly. The job of waiting on people evolved from slaves serving their masters.

2. French service is characterized by grand flourish and show and having food prepared in front of the guest. Food is brought to the table on a guéridon and cooked or reheated on a réchaud. The chef de rang cooks the food and serves it to the guest; the commis de rang places orders in the kitchen and then brings food to the chef de rang and clears the dirty dishes. Russian service is characterized by having all food cooked and preportioned in the kitchen and placed on silver

trays. The waitperson serves the food from the trays onto the guests plates. American service is "on the plate, no wait." The complete meal is placed on a plate, and the waiter transports the plate from the kitchen and serves it to the guests.

3. The main advantages of French, Russian, and American services are as follows: French provides the guest with a high degree of personal attention; the food looks impressive while being served in Russian service; American service is simple to teach and learn. The main disadvantages of French, Russian, and American services are as follows: French requires highly skilled waitstaff; Russian service requires service people to be skilled in serving from platter to plate; American is the least elegant of the three types of service.

4. Diagrams of how to lay the cover for French, Russian, and American à la carte service are shown in this chapter.

5. American banquet service is the quickest service. Food is placed on plates and served in assembly-line style. Russian service is an elegant service. Food must be served from platters to guest's plates. Buffet service is characterized by having all the food displayed in the dining room. The guests choose their selections from the buffet and may bring their plates to their seat. In some establishments, the waitperson will assist the guests with bringing their plates to the table.

6. The main advantages of American, Russian, and buffet banquet services are as follows: American service is fast; Russian service is elegant; and buffet service provides guests with a great variety of foods. The main disadvantages of American, Russian, and buffet banquet services are as follows: American service is not elegant; Russian service requires waitpeople with skills and is the slowest of all services; buffet banquets generally provide the least amount of service for the guests.

7. Diagrams of how to lay the cover for Russian and American banquet service are shown in this chapter.

8. The cover is the area or space for all utensils (including salt, pepper, and ashtrays) for each guest. Knives were originally carried by individuals for hunting and protection. Spoons are the oldest of all eating utensils, and the earliest ones were made of wood. The original forks had two prongs used to hold sacrificial meat, not for eating.

9. The use of table linen began when the very rich started to cover their dining room tables with expensive decorated linen or silken drapes. Today, the purpose of table coverings is to make a room look more attractive or to cover tables that have a surface that is not pleasing to the eye, and to provide a sanitary surface. This chapter gives the reader step-by-step instructions on how to change tablecloths during the busy times.

REVIEW QUESTIONS

1. How did American service first begin, and how did it evolve?
2. Describe the differences in the three types of à la carte services.
3. Compare the advantages and disadvantages of the three types of à la carte services.
4. Diagram correctly the place settings for French, Russian, and American à la carte service.
5. Describe the different banquet styles: American, Russian, and buffet.
6. What are the advantages and disadvantages of the three buffet services?
7. What must a manager know before he or she can diagram the place setting for American, Russian, or buffet banquet services?
8. What is a cover, and how were eating utensils introduced?
9. Explain how to change tablecloths during a busy period.
10. How many guests is a service person expected to serve in each of the following services: American, French, and Russian à la carte; American and Russian banquet; buffet, modified deluxe buffet, and deluxe buffet?

DISCUSSION QUESTIONS

1. How would you, as the banquet manager for a party, solve this equipment shortage problem: Each person should have three forks at his or her cover: one for salad, one for main course, and one for dessert. You need 600 forks, but you have only 400. In addition, the rental company sent you 200 bread-and-butter plates, but you need 600: 200 for the first course (melon), 200 for the place setting, and 200 for the last course (pie).
2. The customer paying for all of the food and beverages at a cocktail party wants the manager to have a place setting for every guest, along with a seat at a table. Is this a good or bad idea? What do you base your decision on?
3. Your waitstaff tells you that the size of their stations is too small. They would like to double the size of their station. What factors would you take into consideration to make your decision? What would your decision be?
4. When the dining room is set up before the guests enter the room, there is plenty of room for the waitstaff to get between the tables to provide proper service. After the guests are seated, the waitstaff cannot serve properly because there is no room for the waitperson to

move between the tables. What is the cause of this problem and how does a manager prevent this from happening?

REFERENCES

1. Janet McKenzie Hill, *The Up-to-Date Waitress* (Boston: Little, Brown, and Co, 1906): vi.
2. Christine Terhunne Herrick, ed. *Consolidated Library of Modern Cooking and Household Recipes* (New York: Bodmer, 1904): p. 25.
3. Raymond J. Goodman, Jr., *The Management of Service for the Restaurant Manager*, 2nd ed. (Dubuque, Iowa: William C. Brown Co., 1983).

4

Proper Guidelines for Service

OBJECTIVES At the completion of this chapter, the student should be able to:

1. Define competency as it relates to proper service.
2. Understand how to properly pick up, load, carry, and put down a tray.
3. Define a sidetowel and explain its purpose.
4. Recite and properly use the seven guidelines for providing competent service.
5. Understand how to properly serve coffee and tea, and change ashtrays.
6. Explain the different ways in which food is served in American, French, and Russian service.
7. Explain the proper method of serving guests at tables and booths.

KEY WORDS

competency	seven guidelines of	trays
Gretzky service	service	traystands/sidestands
hand service	sidetowel	
in the weeds	trayjacks	

Excellent Service

All restaurants and banquet halls strive to give their guests excellent service. Some of them succeed; but many of them fail miserably. It is a known fact that one of the major causes of restaurant failure is poor service. As was stated in Chapter 1, survey after survey have shown that the American public values good service and despises poor service.

Many people, including restaurant reviewers, restaurant owners, and guests, have stated that excellent service can compensate for average food; but great food cannot compensate for bad service. Excellent service is the result of two factors: *competency* and *friendliness*. Competency is serving food and drinks to the guest in the correct manner. Friendliness is a characteristic that the dining room or banquet manager must encourage in service staff. At times, the manager has to be concerned if the service staff become too friendly with the guests: such friendliness leads to informality and then to sloppiness. But if done correctly, friendliness is an extremely important aspect of excellent service. However, the service staff must also be competent in order to provide excellent service.

Importance of Competency

The manager must teach and reinforce correct serving methods to the service staff so that these methods become second nature. *Random House Dictionary* defines *competent* as "having suitable skill, experience, etc., for some purpose."[1] Competent service in a restaurant has one main purpose: for the guest to leave the establishment pleased with the dining experience. **Competency** in a restaurant can best be described in the following way: Competency occurs when the customers do not have to ask the service person for any item during a meal, the water glasses are refilled, and the meals are served without the service persons asking which guest receives which menu item. In short, the guests know they have had a great dining experience, because the service person brought all items to them before they could think of asking for it.

Sweet or Sour

~~~~~~

Competency—when a waitperson has it, what a difference it makes in the dining experience! Three people went out to eat at their local, neighborhood restaurant. They were seated on the patio overlooking a lake. Their orders were taken, and after the server departed from the table, the husband and wife changed seats. When the waitperson returned with their order, she served them correctly without having to ask who ordered what.

How to Obtain Competency

Great restaurants instill competency in their service staff through great attention to detail, training, and follow-up. The success of a restaurant depends on the manager: if the manager overlooks the little details, the service staff will also overlook the little details; however, if the manager pays attention to details, the service staff will consistently follow the manager's lead.

Competency comes from management. Management must teach their staff the proper way to serve their guests. Training at Walt Disney World concentrates on competent service methods. In addition, management continuously monitors their service. The staff must be reminded about what they are doing correctly and incorrectly. Anything being done incorrectly must be corrected immediately. Managers are taught to be coaches who groom players in the correct way to serve. The key to competent service is *training*. A guest will immediately notice things that are right and wrong about the establishment. Restaurants that have all details in place usually are excellent at service. Establishments that look disorganized usually give merely adequate or even poor service.

TIPS

To Insure Proper Service
As a manager, keep in mind the old Irish saying: "If you don't know where you are going, any road will take you there."

Another factor involving the importance of competency has to do with anticipating the guests' wants and needs. **Gretzky Service** is a term resulting from an answer to a question asked of the great professional hockey player, Wayne Gretzky. He was asked how he became the most prolific goal scorer in that sport. His response was that most great hockey players skated to the puck, while he skated to the open space where the puck was going to be played. A great service person should use "Gretzky service" to anticipate guests' needs—refilling wine and water glasses, obtaining more bread—and satisfy them before they even realize they have a need.

The Key to Competency

Competency does not happen automatically (see Figure 4–1). Restaurants that have competent waitstaff—for example, TRU in Chicago; the White Barn Inn in Kennebunkport, Maine; Le Bernardin in New York City—have them because of their successful training methods. People are not just hired and called a service person: managers and owners set policies for staff and train them thoroughly.

A How-Not-To Story

A wedding reception was held at a country club in one of the richest and most elegant communities in America. The first thing guests saw upon entering the dining room was that all the tables and covers were set in a haphazard manner. Some coffee cups had their handles at the four o'clock position, some at the five o'clock. The cups were placed at the top of the place setting, mixed in with the bread-and-butter plates. It appeared that there was a problem with taking care of details. Sure enough, the concerns were justified. After being served an adequate meal—nothing outstanding, nothing poor—the wedding cake was served; however, the tables had not been totally cleared of the dishes from the main course. Nevertheless, the service staff brought the cake to the table and pushed the dirty dinner plates to the center. What was an adequate meal turned into a disappointment for the guests as they had to eat their wedding cake while staring into leftover broccoli, stuffed baked potato skins, and fried chicken.

In some restaurants, all new service staff and bartenders are required to study a service manual and to pass a written test. Included in the manual are all the minute details through which service is accomplished. For example, the placement of tomatoes on the salad dish is explained, as well as how to remove dishes. Even the proper way to stand in the dining room—upright and with hands behind the back—is covered.

The key to excellent service, however, is the constant supervision and implementation of policies. Manuals and training are worthless if the manager does not enforce the guidelines set forth in those books. The authors interviewed a waitperson who has worked in four different types of restaurants and compared the type of training and follow-up she received. She noted that all of the restaurants varied in their training. At the family restaurant, she was told she was a waitress. That was the extent of her training. Her next job was at a chain restaurant. She had to study and memorize menus and policies and was then assigned

THE KEY TO COMPETENCY

Training by management
plus
consistent observation of the service staff
plus
coaching and complimenting
and
repetition of proper serving methods
by
the manager

FIGURE 4–1
The key to competency.

Chef's Choice

*(Courtesy of
GALE GAND,
CHEF/PARTNER,
TRU,
676 N. ST. CLAIR ST.,
CHICAGO, ILLINOIS)*

Gale Gand, chef–partner of the 100 seat TRU in Chicago says TRU's servers are almost as knowledgeable about the dishes' preparation as the cooks are, and that is by design. Each week she and her partner, Chef Rick Tramonto, change the menu. Their servers taste the new dishes at least two times before the menu changes. In addition, the dining room team is treated to monthly seminars on wine and food pairing. They also have in-depth tastings on such foods and beverages as cheese and tea. The culinary staff provide detailed menu description for the service people and the other dining room personnel to study at home. "Since we are a chef-owned restaurant it makes sense that the service people are as educated about the preparation and ingredients of a food item as the person who prepares the meal."

Restaurant service is the next bastion to become legitimized. Chefs used to be considered blue-collar workers. Now being a chef is actually a fairly noble profession and part of our developing food culture. Gale states that "you don't feel embarrassed to admit that you are a chef" at a family party. "And now that we chefs are coming into our own, service is being appreciated and understood as integral to wonderful dining. Servers are getting the respect they have always deserved; and they are being appreciated."

Dining at TRU was one of the most memorable events the authors have ever experienced. At this 100-seat *prix fixe degustation* restaurant, the food and service are exceptional! The quality service begins when a patron first contacts the restaurant about making a reservation and continues throughout the dining experience until the guest walks out the door. Dress and other policies are explained to the guest by knowledgeable personnel. Arrival at TRU brings smiles and a warm welcome by the hostess. The food choices on the menu are interesting and unique. Questions about food and wine are answered knowledgeably and immediately by the service people.

Both the service and the food are outstanding. No detail is left to chance. Upon being seated, a purse hassock is brought to the table so that the guest does not have to place her purse on the floor, lap, or back of the chair. The presentation of food, from the staircase of caviar appetizer to Chef Gand's decadent desserts on mirror plates, is spectacular. And the service exemplifies our definition of great service—competency and friendliness! We observed that each course was served to all the guests in a party at the same time. For the two of us, we had our plates brought to us by two service people; the party of ten next to us, by ten service people. When the guests finished their course, the plates were removed in the same manner. It was like watching a ballet to behold the timing and precision of the service people.

tables to serve. When she worked at a franchise chain restaurant, she had to pass three written tests before being assigned as a waitress. However, at all these places there was no follow-up to her training. She considers her most successful training to have been at Walt Disney World, because of the follow-up training she received.[2]

Restaurants that have competent waitstaff engage in follow-up training. Managers note the errors made by staffers and correct them, thus maintaining excellent service. The key to a competent serving staff is good initial training plus excellent and consistent follow-up training. As in all learning, repetition is the key to success. The dining room and banquet manager must stress and reinforce the competent way to serve the guest.

In The Weeds

In our business, the phrase **in the weeds** is often stated or even shouted by a staff member in the kitchen or dining room. Restaurant personnel use this phrase to mean that the volume of business they must service overwhelms them. For instance, a waitperson may have too many guests to wait on; a broiler cook has too many steaks to cook. It puts the staff member in a stressful position which is neither great nor enjoyable. *Restaurant Startup and Growth* reported that "based on our best sources, its origin in the United States dates back to the Prohibition era, when restaurant and bar owners would hide liquor 'in the weeds' when the police showed up."[3]

The Sidetowel

All professional service people must have with them a napkin to use as a **sidetowel**. As the veteran waitperson Sam Bubonia at the DeWitt Clinton Hotel in Albany, New York, used to say, "You are not a professional waiter unless you have a sidetowel with you."[4] Unfortunately, use of a sidetowel is a rarity at most establishments.

The sidetowel has two purposes. First, it can be used as an insulator; the service person can pick up and serve dinners with the sidetowel rather than risking getting burned from handling hot plates. Second, if there is any type of spill, the service person has a cloth to clean it up. There is no need to waste valuable time running back to the kitchen to obtain cloths to clean up the mess. Therefore, the sidetowel becomes a time-saver.

When the sidetowel is not used for any of these purposes, it should be placed over the service person's left arm, not stuck in the back pocket like a handkerchief. It must always be clean. If the service

FIGURE 4–2

A service staff ready to greet guests. The first server has the sidetowel properly positioned over the arm. The second has the sidetowel improperly positioned on the shoulder. (Photograph by Randall Perry)

person is not using the sidetowel as an insulator to serve food, then the sidetowel should be placed over the right arm. Figure 4–2 shows three service staff ready to greet guests.

Trays

A wonderful invention was made for waitpeople: the tray. Two basic types of **trays** are used in the restaurant industry: large trays, called *hotel ovals*, are used to carry food and plates to and from the guest; the other type are small round, rectangular, or oval trays called *tea trays*, which are generally used to serve drinks.

Large trays enable the service person to carry many items at once, as opposed to delivering food as they do in diners and coffee shops, item by item. It may be impressive to see a service person carrying eight dinners stacked up on both arms; however, using a tray is much more professional looking, efficient, safe, and sanitary than using the style called *arm service*.

Many of the best establishments insist that waitpeople use a tray to carry all items. The server must use a tray even to carry a water pitcher or one coffee cup. Waitpeople should not be allowed to serve guests directly from the tray without putting the tray on a traystand, as it creates a safety hazard.

As the family approached the restaurant for their Easter dinner, they saw an ambulance at the entrance. Entering the restaurant, they heard a child screaming.

Once the child was taken to the hospital, they were told what had happened. After the child's family (grandparents, parents, and children) had finished their meal, the mother asked for coffee. The service person carried the hot, steaming cup of coffee to the table without a tray. The mother swung around in her chair, hit the server's hand, and the hot coffee spilled on the child, causing second-degree burns. All because the server did not use a tray. Not a pleasant way to celebrate a holiday!

Dining room and banquet managers who insist that the service staff use trays will have a much more competent service staff than managers who do not. Once the service staff form the habit of using trays, it becomes second nature. Soon their service improves, because they are carrying more items on each trip between the dining room and the kitchen. As a result, they make fewer trips and save themselves a most valuable commodity: time.

Besides enabling servers to carry more food and beverages to tables, using a tray is safer and more sanitary than using arm service. The tray is bigger than a plate. Therefore, anyone walking past will most likely see the tray and avoid a possible accident. Using a tray is more sanitary, because the plates do not slide down the server's arm into one another. When this happens, one guest's gravy ends up on the other guest's plate. Using a tray is more appealing and pleasing to the guest because the plates do not slide down the server's arm into one another. However, the greatest reason for using a tray is that all the food can be delivered to the guests' table at the same time. This makes the guests' meal more enjoyable, and the restaurant more efficient.

Small trays are used to bring drinks from the bar or one or two items from the kitchen. Some establishments will allow their servers to serve the guest directly from the tray, but that may create a safety hazard. Other establishments, like Walt Disney World, insist that the servers place the tray on a **sidestand** and serve from the sidestand to the guest.

For the most part, using a tray to serve food is much more efficient than using arm service.

Hand Service

For most restaurants the authors advocate the use of trays to bring food from the kitchen to the dining room. There are some restaurants that provide better service by eliminating tray service; these restaurants use **hand service** in their dining rooms. An individual plate is carried from the kitchen to the dining room by a service person. In order to have all guests served simultaneously, a restaurant must train their service people to work as a team, using as many service people as needed to bring, serve, and remove the plates to all the guests at the same time. To accomplish this type of service, the restaurant must invest time and money in training. Individuals who become service people must train for weeks learning the intricacies and timing of the service system before being allowed to work as a service person. The cost of the constant training and staffing of the restaurant will be reflected in the expensive menu prices.

TIP$

TO INSURE PROPER SERVICE

"The service at a restaurant is the number-one reason the customers will or won't come back," says Linda Lipsky of Linda Lipsky Restaurant Consultants Inc. "Food is the number-one reason why customers go to the restaurant in the first place, but service determines whether or not they'll come back."[5]

Traystands and Sidestands

There must be a place for the waitpeople to place their trays. Trays can be set down on a permanent table in the dining room, called a *sideboard* or *service station*; or they can be placed on lightweight devices called **traystands** or **trayjacks**.

Traystands are excellent for use in a restaurant or at banquets because they are light enough to be carried by the server in one hand, while carrying a tray of food in the other hand. Therefore, the service person can carry the stand right to the guests' table. This saves the service person time and extra steps, because the tray is right next to the table instead of being located a distance from the table. Traystands open easily and are secure, so they are easy to use and safe. Using trays and having traystands located near the guests' table is the most efficient way to deliver food to the guests. After the food is served from the tray to the guest, the service person should place the tray on his/her shoulder, fold up the traystand, and remove it from the dining room. In other words, do not leave an empty traystand in the middle of the dining room.

The Correct Way to Lift and Put Down a Tray

There is a correct way to lift and put down a tray on the traystand. First, when training the staff, they should be taught the parts of the traystand. Make certain that they know all the parts and how they operate.

There are two legs that open up and have cloth supports that hold the traystand together. The service person's body must be lined up parallel with the cloth supports. If the waitpeople line up correctly, their hands will not get tangled with the metal supports when they put down or pick up the tray. Figure 4–3 shows the proper way to line up to pick up a tray from the traystand.

Proper Way to Lift a Tray

Waitstaff should be taught to line their body up even with the traystand. The opening of the traystand should be at a right angle with the server's body. They should bend down at the knee, as if they are about to kneel, as illustrated in Figure 4–3. Figure 4–4 and Figure 4–5 illustrate proper and improper ways to pick up a tray. In order to protect their clean shirts from the dirty tray, service persons should place a clean napkin or cloth on their shoulder. The tray should be in balance before reaching the shoulder. The tray is then slid onto the service person's shoulder. Most waitpeople pick up the tray with their left hand under the tray and slide it onto their left shoulder, because they

FIGURE 4–3

The proper body position to pick up a tray from the sidestand. The server's body is parallel with the cloth supports. This position makes it easy to slide the tray onto the shoulder without getting the hands tangled up in the wooden supports. The server is squatting, not bending over to pick up the tray. (Photograph by Randall Perry)

FIGURE 4–4

The proper manner to pick up a tray. The tray is balanced correctly with dirty dishes neatly stacked. On the server's shoulder is the sidetowel, which protects the shirt from getting soiled. The tray rests on the right shoulder, and the server is lifting the tray with her legs. A sidetowel is placed over the tray to prevent spillage. (Photograph by Randall Perry)

FIGURE 4–5

The improper way to carry a tray, positioned in front of the server and poorly balanced with dirty dishes. In addition, the server has no sidetowel. (Photograph by Randall Perry)

control the tray with their right hand. However, it does not matter which shoulder the tray is carried on as long as it is carried properly.

The service person's hand should be placed under the tray. If the tray is going on the left shoulder, it should be the left hand, as shown in Figure 4–4. The larger tray or hotel oval is usually carried while it is resting and balanced on the palm of the server's hand. More experienced waitpeople will balance the tray on their fingertips. The inexperienced server should grasp the front of the tray with the free hand (as shown in Figure 4–4) for stability. The service person lifts the tray by using leg muscles, not back muscles. A tray should never be carried as illustrated in Figure 4–5; this is too dangerous and may result in injury to the server.

The authors have observed a much higher traystand than the traditional ones. With this traystand, the service person has less bending to do.

T I P $ **TO INSURE PROPER SERVICE**

How to Carry a Large Tray

1. Line up your body parallel with the cloth supports on the traystand.
2. Bend down at the knee, as if you are about to kneel.
3. Slide the tray onto your shoulder and use the palm of your hand to balance the tray. If you are right-handed, put the tray on your left shoulder in order to have your right hand free to control the tray (you may put a clean napkin on your shoulder to protect your shirt from getting dirty).
4. The arm from elbow to wrist should be at a right angle to the tray.
5. Stand up, using your legs to give you the strength to lift the tray. Your right hand is controlling the tray.

T I P $ **TO INSURE PROPER SERVICE**

How to Carry and Serve from a Small or Tea Tray

1. Carry the tray waist high.
2. If transporting a beverage, carry with your left hand; if food, carry with your right hand.

   If your manager allows you to serve guests from the tray:

3. Serve beverages with your right hand from the guest's right side, holding the tray in your left hand.
4. Serve food with your left hand from the guest's left side, holding the tray in your right hand.

How to Put Down a Tray

The procedure is the reverse of that for lifting a tray. The server must align his or her body so that the tray can easily be slid onto the cloth supports. The server should then bend down at the knee and slip the tray onto the traystand. Employees should be taught never to bend over at the waist. If they do, they may injure themselves because they are using their back instead of leg muscles. Once the tray is on the stand, the server takes the sidetowel off the shoulder and places it in the proper position, either over the arm or as needed as an insulator for the hot plates.

The smaller tray or tea tray is carried waist high. Because this tray is so light, the service person can place it on a sideboard without bending down. If the dining room manager allows drinks and food to be served directly from the tray, it must be held in the correct hand. With drinks, hold it in the left hand; with food, the right hand.

Loading a Tray

The first thing a server must do is check that the tray is clean on both the top and bottom surfaces.

Trays are designed with either a nonslip surface such as an abrasive material, or without one. If the tray does not have a nonslip material, the staff should be taught to take a damp, clean cloth, and put it on the tray. Even if the tray is made with a nonslip material, a clean cloth placed on the tray will make the service look more professional.

When loading a tray, the heaviest items should be placed on the side of the tray that will be closest to the server's body. This will allow the server's shoulder to bear the brunt of the weight and allow the server to have more control over the tray. When more experienced servers carry the tray by balancing it on their fingertips, they place the heaviest items in the center of the tray.

The lighter items and glasses are placed to the outside of the tray or away from the service person's shoulder. Items with spouts and handles should have their spouts and handles facing the center of the tray.

When serving food, waitstaff should be instructed to keep all hot items together. If it is necessary to carry both hot and cold food on the same tray, instruct servers to separate the cold food from the hot food. Plates should never be stacked on top of each other unless plate covers are used. When serving soup, the cups should be placed around a stack of saucers. The soup should not be placed on the saucers until the server places the tray on the traystand.

When removing dirty dishes, the establishment should have an organized system for loading trays so that all plates are stacked neatly. This means all bread-and-butter plates are stacked on each other, instead of having a dinner plate on top of a bread-and-butter plate with forks, knives, and spoons stuck in between them. Figure 4–6 and Figure 4–7 illustrate proper and improper methods of loading dirty

FIGURE 4–6

The proper way to load a tray of dirty dishes. The silverware is separated from the plates. The top plate has all of the left-over food on it. When the server brings the food into the kitchen, it will be easy to unload the tray. (Photograph by Randall Perry)

FIGURE 4–7

The improper way to stack dirty dishes. The dishes are placed on the tray in no specific arrangement. This makes for a dangerous and hard-to-carry tray of dirty dishes. (Photograph by Randall Perry)

dishes onto a tray. After the tray has been loaded correctly, the service person should place a sidetowel over the dirty dishes, before the tray is picked up and carried through the dining room to the dishwashing area.

It must be emphasized that the only way the staff will load their trays properly is if they are taught correctly by the manager. Once the training is complete, there must be consistent reinforcement by the manager; that is, correction and reinstruction if done incorrectly, and praise if done correctly.

Guidelines for American À la Carte and Banquet Service

For a restaurant to have competent service, certain standards must be met by all servers. The following **seven guidelines of service** have evolved over many years of serving. Originally, they were thought of as rules, but they should be renamed *guidelines* because rules are too rigid for the dining room business. Perhaps that is why they were not and are not enforced consistently. Due to circumstances beyond the server's control, common sense must often prevail when serving guests. The server will often have to serve from the "wrong" side because of the physical constraints of the room or for the guest's comfort (for example, when the guest is talking to the person on the side from which you normally serve). However, these guidelines should be enforced whenever possible.

The Seven Guidelines Explained

1. Women Are Served Before Men

When there is a party of two couples (two men and two women), the service person serves one woman and then the next woman. The service person serves in this order: woman #1, woman #2, man #1, man #2. If the server can easily determine who is the older woman at the table, she should be served first (see Figure 4–8 and Figure 4–9).

There are instances when the server would ignore this guideline. Children should be served before adults, then women are served then the men. People always wonder if this can be done. Does it make any sense?

When guests dine at The Publik House in Sturbridge, Massachusetts, they indeed see that it is possible to serve children first. The server first took the order for drinks. She returned and served the

FIGURE 4–8

The seven guidelines of service.

THE SEVEN GUIDELINES OF SERVICE

1. Women are served before men (if children are present, they should be served first, then women, then men).
2. Food is served from the guest's left side, with the service person's left hand.
3. Beverages are served from the guest's right side, with the service person's right hand.
4. All guests' food must be brought to the table at the same time.
5. Do not remove guest plates from the table until all guests are finished eating their meal.
6. Never stack or scrape dirty plates on the guest's table.
7. Dirty dishes are cleared from the guest's right side with the service person's right hand.

FIGURE 4–9

The proper sequence to serve a table. The server should serve the table in order 1, 3, 2, 4. The women are served first, and then the men are served.

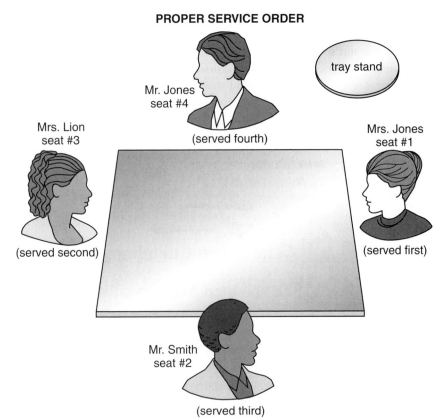

PROPER SERVICE ORDER

tray stand

Mr. Jones
seat #4
(served fourth)

Mrs. Lion
seat #3
(served second)

Mrs. Jones
seat #1
(served first)

Mr. Smith
seat #2
(served third)

youngest child his cola, then walked past the mother to serve the older son his soda. She returned to their mother to serve her drink. Finally, the father was served his drink. It did not take long to serve all four guests. She served all drinks from the guests' right side with her right hand. Throughout the meal, service was performed quickly and competently. The dining room—which seated over 100—was filled and the service was superb. It added to the great food and pleasant atmosphere of the restaurant. Having explained this first guideline, the authors recognize that the times are changing. There are some individuals who object to serving women first. While they feel that it is acceptable to serve either gender first, serving women first is still the norm.

Another exception to this guideline is when serving a banquet, where the room is set up with long banquet tables seating more than 10 people. With long banquet tables it makes little sense to skip over the men, because there are so many guests at the table. If a server is working at a banquet where the banquet table has 10 or more people on each side of the table, it is more logical to serve the guests in sequential order.

2. Food is Served from the Guest's Left Side with the Service Person's Left Hand

There is a logical and practical reason for this guideline: if the service person served with the right hand from the left side of the guests, it would create a potentially dangerous and awkward situation. The service person is putting his or her arm right in the faces of the guests. This could be most unappetizing if the waiter has body odor. Also, the guests would have to back away in order to prevent the service person from brushing or hitting them with his arm. It is also dangerous for the service person. Figure 4–10 and Figure 4–11 illustrate proper and improper ways to serve food in American service. There are times when a guest does not pay attention to the service person and moves unexpectedly. When the service person sees the guest moving quickly, the server's arm can be swung out and away from the guest if the serving is done correctly. The chance of an accident is reduced by proper service.

Because the service person is serving with the left hand, service should proceed in a clockwise direction. Many people have trouble with the concept of clockwise and counterclockwise; a simple way to remember the correct direction is "to follow your nose." Proceed in the direction that your nose is pointing. Serve food from guest's left side with your left hand and follow your nose. Figure 4–12 illustrates the proper direction to serve a party of four.

There are a couple of exceptions to this guideline. Serving food to guests seated at a booth or table positioned against a wall requires a different set of procedures. The service person must serve and pick up with the same hand (see Figure 4–13). The server should serve the guest in seat A, using the left hand. The guest in seat C is served using

FIGURE 4–10

The waitperson is serving food properly to the guest. He is serving from the guest's left side with his left hand. His side-towel is used as an insulator between his left hand and the hot plate. His right hand is behind him. (Photo-graph by Randall Perry)

FIGURE 4–11

The waitperson is serving food incorrectly to the guest. She is serving with her right hand from the guest's left side. Her sidetowel is on her shoulder and her hair is flowing onto the guest's plate. (Photograph by Randall Perry)

FIGURE 4–12

The proper direction for serving a meal. The service person would serve guest 1, then 3 going in a clockwise direction. Returning to the tray, guest 2 would be served followed by guest 4.

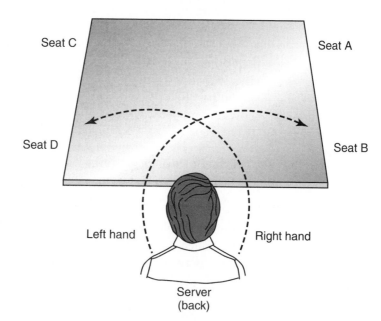

FIGURE 4–13

Service at a booth. The server serves and picks up with the same hand. Guests in seats A and B will be served and dirty dishes picked up with the left hand. Guests in seats C and D will be served and dirty dishes picked up with the right hand. The same rules for serving women before men apply.

the right hand. Removing dirty dishes, the service person would use the same hand that was used to serve the meal. This allows the server to keep his or her arm out of the face of the guest. The same rules for serving women before men apply.

When two guests are talking to each other, the service person does not interrupt their conversation by serving the food properly. Instead, he or she serves one guest from the left side, the other from the right side. When serving from the right side, the right hand should be used. If there is a physical item in the way (like a pole) or the table is positioned in such a way that makes it impossible to serve the guests from their left, they should be served from their right side.

3. Beverages Are Served from the Guest's Right Side with the Service Person's Right Hand

Because a large majority of people are right-handed, the glasses and cups for beverages are put on the right side of the guest. It is logical that the service person would pour beverages from the right side of the guest. Therefore to be consistent, all beverages are served from the right side.

When serving an alcoholic beverage, a cocktail napkin should be placed in front of the guest. The beverage should then be placed on the cocktail napkin. If there is a meal in front of the guest, the service person will place the beverage above the spoons and knives on the right side of the guest.

When service people pour water, wine, or coffee into a glass or cup already on the table, they must not pick up the glass or cup, unless leaving the glass or cup on the table would create a safety hazard.

The proper way to pour water is to pour with the right hand, keeping the left hand folded behind the back. Some establishments prefer that the service person hold the sidetowel under the lip of the glass with the left hand to catch any drips or spills. Water glasses should be filled three quarters to the top of the glass. Figure 4–14 shows the proper way to pour water.

T I P $ **TO INSURE PROPER SERVICE**

Leave glasses and cups on the table when pouring beverages into them.

Coffee should be poured with the right hand while the left hand holds a coffee shield. This shield—bread-and-butter plate—is placed at an angle between the coffee pot and the guest to protect the guest from coffee spills and steam from the hot pot. Figure 4–15 illustrates the correct way to pour coffee.

FIGURE 4–14

The waitperson is pouring water the correct way, from the guest's right side with her right hand. The glass is not removed from the table. (Photograph by Randall Perry)

FIGURE 4–15

The waitperson is pouring coffee the correct way. Served with a coffee shield, from the guest's right side with the service person's right hand. The sidetowel is on the right arm. (Photograph by Randall Perry)

Tea should be brought to the guest in a small pot and be placed above the coffee cup. The teabag should be in the pot steeping.

A competent service person is always aware of a guest's needs. If a guest is left-handed, the service person will switch the water glass or coffee cup to the left side. When this occurs, the server should serve from the guest's left side with the left hand. One important rule is never to reach in front of the guest. For example, when the service person is pouring coffee and the guest has moved the cup to the left side, the service person would never reach across the guest. The proper way to serve is to move to the left side of the guest and pour coffee into the cup on the left side of the guest. However, generally, all beverages are served from the right side with the right hand.

T I P $

TO INSURE PROPER SERVICE

Right-handed people usually wear their watch on their left arm; left-handed people on their right arm. When a service person observes a watch on the right arm, try the following tip. Say to the guest, "It is proper service to serve beverages from the right side, but I will be moving your water and wine glass to your left side and serving you from the left since you are left handed." The guest will be amazed, and the server will see an increase in tips.

4. All Guests' Food Must Be Brought to the Table at the Same Time

One of the most annoying situations for a guest is to be served first and then have to wait for others at the table to be served their food. This creates two problems for guests: those with proper manners will wait for the whole table to be served before they begin to eat their meal. Most likely their food will get cold, as the service person has to return to the kitchen to obtain the rest of the food, which is annoying for the guests. Colleen Sherman says that "the supervisors at Walt Disney World never let a service person go to a table without the complete order."[4]

The manager should insist that all food reach the table at the same time. This is especially true at banquets, when the guests have their choice of two main entrees. All guests must be served the meal at the same time even if half of them are eating chicken and the other half beef. The manager must devise a system (which is explained in Chapter 12) by which all guests are served at the same time.

5. Do Not Remove Any Guest's Plate from the Table Until All Guests Have Finished Eating Their Meal

This guideline means exactly what it says. It is a mystery why wait-people remove plates from guests before all the guests at the table have finished eating their meal. This implies to the guests who have not finished their meal that they are taking too long to eat and must hurry and finish. Of course, if a guest is done and pushes the plate to indicate he or she wants it to be cleared away, then take the plate away even if the others have not finished.

Another part of this guideline is that a new course must never be served until the dishes from the previous course have been removed from the table. This is another of the strict competency rules that are enforced at quality restaurants. A server must remove the soup course before being allowed to serve the salad course.

Sweet or Sour?

This guideline is called "The Aunt Daisy Rule." Our Aunt Daisy always takes longer to eat her meal than her friends. Far too many times we have observed that she stops eating her food after a waitperson removes the plate of her friend or friends. We have asked her why she stops eating her food, and she tells us that she is too embarrassed to continue eating once the other plates are removed.

The maximum amount of five lemons goes to the waitperson who takes plates away from guests without asking if it is okay to remove the plates.

In Peggy Post's "Etiquette for Today," column in *Good Housekeeping* magazine (July 1998), she discusses what she calls "The Restaurant Rush." She states that "one complaint I've been hearing a lot lately is that waiters in restaurants often remove diners' plates as soon as they're finished, even though other people are still eating. It's frustrating and annoying!" She explains that in the early 1900s, quality service meant that empty plates were always removed promptly and clean ones substituted the instant a diner was done. By the time the last person had finished, the entire table was reset for the next course. But slower eaters protested so loudly that the practice was scrapped, and it became the custom instead to wait for the entire group to finish.[6]

The only exception to this guideline may occur during a banquet. Because most banquets are on a strict time schedule, if the banquet manager waited for all guests to complete every course, it could put the banquet behind schedule. If a guest has not finished eating his or her salad course, and the main course is ready to be served, the banquet manager could instruct the service staff to remove all the finished salad plates. If a guest is finished eating his or her salad when the service person brings out the entree, the service person should remove the dirty dish before serving any of the main entrees. If the guest is still not finished with the previous course, the service person should ask permission to move the plate. The server should then move the dish above and to the left of where the entree will be placed.

6. Never Stack or Scrape Dirty Plates on the Guest's Table

This is the most irritating and unappetizing habit a service person can have. Some waitpeople take the dirty dishes and stack them—one on top of another—right in front of the guests, as is illustrated in Figure 4–16. It is even worse if the service person scrapes all the leftovers onto one plate in the center of the table. Some of them will even dump the cigarette and cigar ashes from the dirty ashtray into the leftover mashed potatoes.

FIGURE 4–16

The improper way to clear a table. The server has the guest's dishes stacked in front of her. In addition, the server is picking up from the guest's left side and has the sidetowel over the shoulder. (Photograph by Randall Perry)

If the restaurant or banquet establishment allows smoking, there is a proper way to change the ashtrays. The service person should bring a clean ashtray to the table. The clean ashtray should be turned upside down and placed over the dirty one (capped ashtray). This acts as a cover, so as the service person removes the ashtrays, no ashes will spill onto the guests' table or into their food. The server places the capped ashtray behind his back, and with his free hand places the clean ashtray—the cap—back on the table.

7. Dirty Dishes Are Cleared from the Guest's Right Side with the Service Person's Right Hand

The guest's dirty dishes must be cleared with the service person's right hand, except when it makes more sense to clear from the left side, using the left hand. Figure 4–17 illustrates how the waitperson uses common sense by removing the bread-and-butter plate with her left hand from the guest's left side. She does so because if she removed the bread-and-butter plate from the guest's right side, she would have to reach in front of her. A service person should never reach in front of the guest, as in Figure 4–18.

FIGURE 4–17

The waitperson is using common sense to remove the dirty bread-and-butter plate from the guest. She is removing it with her left hand, from the guest's left side. (Photograph by Randall Perry)

FIGURE 4–18

The waitperson is clearing the dirty dishes incorrectly with her right hand, from the guest's left side. The sidetowel is improperly positioned on the shoulder. (Photograph by Randall Perry)

T I P $

TO INSURE PROPER SERVICE
First remove the utensils, then pick up the dirty plate.

The correct and efficient way to remove dishes from the table is as follows: From each guest, the service person will first remove the silverware with the right hand and transfer it to the left hand. Next, the dirty plate will be removed, and it will be transferred to the left hand. "Following your nose" (going counterclockwise), the service person will remove the next guest's silverware and dirty plate. The server will then step back, out of view of the guests. The leftover food will be scraped from the plate just removed onto the first one removed. The new plate will be shuffled to the bottom of the stack held with the left hand. The silverware should be held in the fingers of the left hand and laid across the top plate with the food scraps. The dirty plates should be placed on a tray in a neat organized manner as explained in the tray loading section. This procedure takes practice to master, but it is the most efficient way to clear a table.

FIGURE 4–19

The correct way to crumb a table. From the guest's left side, the waitperson uses her left hand and sidetowel to brush crumbs off the table into a bread-and-butter plate held in her right hand. (Photograph by Randall Perry)

Before serving the dessert course, the server must "crumb the table." The server would take either the sidetowel or a crumbing device and brush the crumbs from the table into a bread-and-butter plate, as illustrated in Figure 4–19. There are many different crumbers a service person can use. There are some that act like mini vacuum cleaners; others have a tapered edge that the service person can use to crumb the table and then tilt the crumber and remove the crumbs from the table.

Other Helpful Hints for Serving

Whichever hand you are using to serve or pick up, place that foot forward for balance. For example, if serving food with your left hand, place your left foot forward.

If a guest places a dirty dish on his or her left side, to the left of the fork, the service person should use her left hand to remove the dish from the guest's left side.

Diners sometimes are provided with extra hospitality in the form of an extra course. Consequently, the entrée, even though it is prepared exquisitely, is too much food for them to consume. One of the most impressive service traits the authors experienced was from a service person at The Sardine Factory in Monterey, California, who observed that we had finished eating our half-filled main entrees. He asked "may I remove your plates?" instead of removing them without saying a word. He also added "and may I wrap up your entrees to take home?" The waitperson demonstrated competency, friendliness, and "Gretzky" service!

Keep in mind that all these are guidelines, not rules. The most important criteria are the comfort and safety of the guest. If you have to serve from the "wrong" side for the guest's comfort, do so.

Guidelines for French and Russian Style Service

The guidelines are basically the same as for American service, with the exception of guideline 2.

1. Women are served before men.
2. In French service, food is served from the guest's right side using the right hand; in Russian service, food is served from the guest's left side with the *platter* in the service person's left hand, while serving with the right hand.
3. Beverages are served from the guest's right side using the right hand.
4. All guests' food must be brought to the table at the same time.
5. Guest plates should not be removed from the table until all guests are finished eating their meals.
6. Dirty plates should never be stacked or scraped on the guest's table.
7. Dirty dishes are cleared from the guest's right side with the service person's right hand.

The Second Guideline Explained

In French service, food is served from the guest's right side with the service person's right hand. In French à la carte service, the service person has to transfer food from a pan at the guéridon to plate. The plate is then served to the guest from the guest's right side with the waiter using his right hand.

In Russian service, food is served from the guest's left side with the platter in the service person's left hand, while serving with the right hand.

This is the most confusing and contradictory of all the guidelines. In Russian service, clean plates are put down from the guest's right side with the service person's right hand. The food is then brought out on a silver platter. After the food has been presented to the guest, the service person transfers the food from the tray to the plate. This is accomplished by holding the tray in the left hand. The service person should serve the guest from the left side with the right hand. Even though this method will make the service person put an arm in front of the guest, making the guest back away, this is the method that has been taught since the beginning of Russian service.

The method probably originated because it is easier for the service person to transfer food from the platter to the plate. At times it can be difficult to manipulate the serving fork and spoon. There is a chance that the food may slip out of the fork and spoon. In order to be consistent with proper serving techniques, Russian service should be changed to have the service staff hold the tray in their right hands and serve the food with their left hands from the guest's right side. This would be safer and less awkward than the current system.

SUMMARY

1. Competent service in a restaurant occurs when the guest leaves the establishment pleased with the dining experience, because that guest did not have to ask the service person for any item during the meal.
2. Figures 4–3 through 4–7 illustrate the proper and improper methods of how to pick up, load, carry, and put down a tray.
3. The sidetowel is a napkin that all professional service people have with them to use as an insulator and to clean up spills.
4. The seven guidelines of service are as follows:
    1. Women are served before men; if children are present, they should be served first, then women, then men.
    2. Food is served from the guest's left side, with the left hand.
    3. Beverages are served from the guest's right side, with the service person's right hand.
    4. All guests' food must be brought to the table at the same time.
    5. Do not remove guest plates from the table until all guests have finished eating their meal.

6. Never stack or scrape dirty plates on the guest's table.
7. Dirty dishes are cleared from the guest's right side with the service person's right hand.

5. Coffee is served from the guest's right side, with the service person's right hand. The service person uses a bread-and-butter plate as a coffee shield; this shield is placed at an angle between the coffee pot and guest to protect the guest from coffee spills and steam from the hot pot. Figure 4–15 illustrates the correct way to pour coffee. Tea should be brought to the guest in a small pot and should be placed above the coffee cup. The teabag should be in the pot, steeping. Changing an ashtray, if smoking is allowed in the restaurant, is accomplished in the following manner: The waitperson should bring a clean ashtray to the table. The clean ashtray should be turned upside down and placed over the dirty one (capped ashtray). The server removes the capped ashtray from the table, places it behind his back, and with his free hand places the clean ashtray (the cap) back on the table.

6. In American service, food is served from the guest's left side with the waitperson's left hand. In French and Russian Service, food is served from the guest's right side with the waitperson's right hand.

7. Serving guests at a table should be done by following the proper guidelines of service, going in a clockwise direction. Serving guests at a booth is accomplished as illustrated in Figure 4–13, which shows the waitperson serving and picking up with the same hand.

REVIEW QUESTIONS

1. Define *competency* as it relates to the service staff.
2. Can excellent service compensate for average food? Explain your answer by giving examples to justify your position.
3. What is a *sidetowel*, and what is its purpose for a service person? How should it be carried when it is not in use?
4. Describe the proper manner in which a tray should be loaded with dirty dishes. What is a traystand, and how should a tray be picked up from the traystand?
5. Why should trays be used to carry food or beverages?
6. List and explain the seven guidelines of service.
7. Are there any differences between American and other types of à la carte service with regard to the guidelines of service?
8. Why are the guidelines of service called guidelines and not rules? Is there any part of the guidelines that is a rule?

DISCUSSION QUESTIONS

1. What problems must the manager foresee regarding the friendliness of the staff with the guests?
2. How does the dining room manager obtain competency from his staff with regard to proper service?
3. You, the manager, have an excellent waitperson. Guests like him; they always tell you he is an asset to your establishment. He constantly outsells all the other staff in desserts and wines. However, he breaks all the guidelines of service: He serves from the wrong side, picks the glasses off the table to pour water, and so on. In short, he ignores proper guidelines of service. How would you get him to adhere to the guidelines? Or, do you think it is not necessary for him to adhere to the guidelines since he is such a great waiter?
4. Should a waitperson take away a guest's empty dish when it is pushed to the side while the other guests are still eating their main course? What factors should be considered before removing the dish?

REFERENCES

1. *Random House Dictionary*, s.v. "competent."
2. Colleen Sherman, interview with the author in Schenectady, New York (April 2, 1987).
3 Bill Marvin, "Is the Guest Always Right?" *Restaurant Startup and Growth* (October 2006), p. 49.
4. Sam Bubonia, interview with the author in Albany, New York (February 15, 1969).
5. James Peters, "Casual Dining Raising Service Bar to Boost Appeal," *Nation's Restaurant News* 34, No. 35 (August 28, 2000): 4, 43–48.
6. Peggy Post, "Etiquette for Today," *Good Housekeeping* (July 1998): 26.

5

The Styles of Service

OBJECTIVES   At the completion of this chapter, the student should be able to:

1. Give the names and responsibilities of the four typical service positions in a dining room for a restaurant that provides American service.
2. Describe and explain the three service options in a restaurant that provides American service.
3. Define the term *station*, and demonstrate the proper method of setting up stations.
4. Explain the importance of sidework and how to assign it to maintain a smooth-running operation.
5. Describe and organize a dining room using the team method of service for the service staff.
6. Explain the advantages and disadvantages of the three types of service. (team, individual stations, and captain) in the American restaurant.
7. Teach the service staff the proper sequence of serving a meal.
8. Describe how to open wine and serve it to guests.

KEY WORDS

Aid	four-top	six-top
busperson	lead	sommelier
captain	seating	team system
deuces	service person	wine steward
follow-up	sidework	

American Dining Room Service Styles

The American dining room is unique in the world of service. In other countries, such as France, there are clear rules that each restaurant follows to provide its guests standard service. A standard has been set, and all restaurants follow the same standards.

Because the United States is a melting pot of cultures and different types of service, there is no one style used by restaurants. One restaurant may have a captain to take orders and service people to serve the meal; whereas another, just a block away, eliminates the position of captain and has the service person do all the service. A third, a few doors further on, has three people waiting on one table of two guests. All three restaurants are successful, yet all use different styles of service.

Dining Room Service Personnel

In American restaurants there are four traditional job titles for individuals who serve the guests. They are: the **service person**, the **busperson**, the **captain**, and the **wine steward** (or **sommelier**).

Because there are no firm standards followed by American restaurants, establishments may call their employees by one title and combine them in other job descriptions. Therefore, job titles and responsibilities change with each restaurant. In some restaurants, a captain will be assigned to take food and wine orders. Another restaurant will have a wine steward to take wine orders and serve the wine selections.

All restaurants must have people, called the *service staff*, who serve the meal. Many restaurants have a person, called a *busperson*, to assist the service staff. In some types of services, the jobs of captain, wine steward, busperson, and service person are combined into the service person's job. In other restaurants, a team of two or three works together to provide service.

The following sections describe the responsibilities of each job and the qualities needed by dining room personnel.

Qualities of Successful Dining Room Personnel

Certain qualities are needed that will make the dining room personnel successful in dealing with the guests. The manager must be aware of these qualifications when hiring service personnel.

The personal appearance of applicants must be excellent, as stated in Chapter 2. They must have excellent communication skills, both oral and written. Dining room personnel must be sensitive to their guests' and fellow employees' feelings and needs.

Sweet or Sour?

While dining at the Otesago Hotel in Cooperstown, New York, we asked our waitperson, Thomas, what he enjoyed about his job. His reply, "You might not understand this, but to me to serve is joyous." Thomas' technique was not flawless, but his attitude was exemplary.

Personnel must be able to work well under pressure. Being a service person is an extremely stressful job. They will have to be able to gather a variety of information, understand it, and make correct decisions, often in a split second. In addition, they must be organized and efficient.

T I P $

TO INSURE PROPER SERVICE

Danny Meyer, owner of Union Square Cafe, states in his newsletter, "We're acutely aware that in the long run, awards mean nothing: it's your last meal that counts the most!"

Captain

In general, the job of captain is found in restaurants with higher priced menus. The surroundings are more elegant than in an average restaurant and the clientele are usually willing to spend a great deal of money for a meal. One establishment that uses the captain system is the New York Racing Association at its Aqueduct, Belmont, and Saratoga racetracks. The captain is usually responsible for an area of the dining room with as many as 60 seats and four service people. Because the tables are only used for one meal period—called a **seating**—and time is not a factor, the stations at racetracks are larger than normal. A more typical station has between 35 and 40 seats, a captain, and two service people.

Captains have the following responsibilities:

- supervising the service staff and buspersons in their station
- greeting guests who have been seated at the tables in the station
- merchandising (selling) and taking all drink and food orders
- tableside preparation, if called for

- sometimes serving the meal, but more often the service person does the serving
- insuring that the service staff and buspersons clear the dirty dishes and reset the tables

Usually the captain has been a service person and has been promoted to this position after demonstrating proficiency in selling and serving; this is a sales position. As the captain is the first person the guest talks to about the meal, the captain must be personable; and able to manage employees, because this position is also a supervisory one.

Wine Steward (Sommelier)

As the name implies, this person is responsible for suggesting and serving wines to all guests in a restaurant. This job requires a personable individual with a knowledge of wines. The wine steward must know which wine will complement which food on the menu. It is the responsibility of the steward to suggest, sell, and serve wines to the guests. Usually, one wine steward is sufficient for a restaurant. If there is no wine steward, this job becomes the responsibility of the captain or the service staff.

The sommelier has to be knowledgeable about which wine complements which menu item, how the wine tastes, and be able to explain and answer questions about the wine. For example, one of the most confusing wines in America is a wine called "Chablis." A wine that comes from France that is labeled Chablis may only be made from chardonnay grapes grown in the geographical region of Chablis, France. This wine always tastes dry and will complement a fish dish such as salmon or tuna. Contrast that knowledge with a wine made from an American producer that is labeled Chablis. The American Chablis can be made from any grape grown anywhere in America. The sommelier will explain that this type of labeling is called generic and means only that the wine will be white in color. It may taste sweet, semisweet, or dry.

Busperson or Dining Room Attendant

The busperson or dining room attendant is basically an assistant to the service staff. For many years, this job was filled by individuals who were unskilled or illiterate. Many managers placed individuals in this position who had no idea how critical the job was in the successful operation of the dining room.

The specific jobs of the busperson are:

- setting the place settings on the table
- clearing the dirty dishes from the dining room and bringing them into the kitchen

- assisting the service person whenever necessary in clearing away dirty plates from a table and restocking the service area with condiments, plates, glasses, and other items needed for the smooth running of the dining room

Because these jobs seem so straightforward and easy, managers usually assigned one busperson to work with two or as many as four service staff. The busperson was usually poorly trained, if trained at all. That is when the so-called easy job turned into a problem for the manager, service staff, and guests. The busperson could not keep up with the pace of a busy dining room. In the middle of the rush hour, the service staff would find themselves with dirty tables and not enough clean linens or plates or condiments.

The busperson should not be an unskilled worker, but a person who is training to become a service person. The busperson must be as organized and efficient as a service person. If the busperson is not organized, then the whole dining room may suffer and the guests may receive poor service.

The Service Person

Service people are the eyes and ears of the dining room manager. They interact directly with the customers. The guests are more likely to tell *them* what is good or bad about the restaurant than they are to tell the manager. In the eyes of the guests, the person who waits on them *is* the restaurant. The chef of the restaurant could have been awarded three stars by the Michelin guide; the restaurant could have won an award for interior design; the manager can have excellent financial and managerial skills; but if the service staff do not perform up to the guests' expectations, the restaurant is unsatisfactory. Guests are the ultimate critics. If they leave dissatisfied, they will tell many of their friends. Therefore, the manager's number one priority must be hiring, training, and supervising the service staff for the purpose of providing service that excels. It has been proven over and over again that proper service can make a restaurant successful. Even more reliably, poor service can ruin a restaurant.

Service people have very specific duties. They are responsible for the total service of the meal. In most American restaurants, service people work alone. They have no one else to assist them in serving the meal. If the host seats too many people at their table at once, or if there is a complaint about the food, they find themselves unable to serve or to attend to all their guests' needs, or they are—as it is known in restaurant slang—*in the weeds*. They have no one else

Sweet or Sour?

A couple had an 8:00 reservation for dinner. They were seated right at 8:00 P.M. As they looked around the beautifully designed room, they noticed the fresh flowers on the white-clothed tables. Classical music was played in the restaurant by talented musicians. The food served to the tables around them was attractive and plentiful. It was obvious by the looks on the faces of the other guests that the food was excellent and many people were enjoying themselves. However, it was 10 minutes before anyone approached their table to take their drink order. Finally, an order was taken and delivered. The service person put it down and disappeared for 15 more minutes. At 8:32 the service person came back and took the order. The wait between the courses seemed like an eternity for the couple. Finally, the main course was served at 10:03. It was served to them in a very formal, noncaring manner by the service person. The food was excellent and plentiful. What do you think the couple told their friends about the dining experience? Will they ever return to this restaurant for another meal?

to rely on. They must greet the guests and serve them flawlessly through the end of the meal; their only assistance comes from the busperson. They may have a station with three to seven tables seating between 12 and 24 guests.

Specific responsibilities of the service person are:

- obtaining any specific instructions about reservations and policies for the meal period
- preparing the station, checking chairs and place settings for cleanliness, and making certain all tables are set correctly
- greeting customers
- suggesting menu items and taking orders
- serving food and drinks
- inquiring about the guests' satisfaction with the meal
- clearing dirty dishes
- refilling drinks and bread by anticipating customers' needs
- suggesting desserts
- serving dessert
- preparing and collecting bill
- offering a closing remark to guests
- doing preparation work for the next shift

Each restaurant has its own specific tasks for the service person. The tasks should be outlined in an employees' manual. One restaurant chain requires its employees to know all the facts covered in its 228-page training manual. The chain tests the employees for proficiency in an extensive training program that may last up to one year. There is a constant reinforcement of the policies by veteran service staff employees.

The manager must know all the job tasks of the service person. Once the manager knows and understands the tasks of the service person, another task is at hand: understanding how implementing and assigning stations makes a dining room run smoothly.

Stations

All restaurants should divide their dining room up into small sections called *stations*. Each station has between 12 and 24 seats, depending on the size of the tables and other factors. By using this method, the service people are responsible for one part of the restaurant, rather than for the whole dining room.

Many restaurants assign one service person to one station. Other restaurants assign a captain and two or four service people to a station that may have up to 60 seats. Still other restaurants use a system that has a three-person team responsible for up to 60 seats.

A manager should organize the stations to maximize excellent guest service. For example, suppose a dining room has four tables of four seats and two tables of two seats with a view of the ocean. Even though this is only a total of 20 seats, it should *not* be one station. These tables will be requested by the guests first, so it is best for the manager to split up these tables into two or three stations; but the tables in the station must be together. See Figure 5–1 and Figure 5–2. If you were a manager, which plan would give your guests the best service?

Several factors must be taken into consideration when the manager divides the room into stations:

1. distance of guest tables from the kitchen
2. number of guests seated at each table
3. physical attractiveness of the station
4. amount of food preparation required at the table
5. union contract requirements
6. competency of staff
7. tables most frequently requested by guests
8. location of waitstaff workstations, if not in or by the kitchen

FIGURE 5–1

Stations set up for a 96-seat dining room. Five servers all have their tables close to one another. Juan has the most tables because his station is closest to the kitchen door. Jim is an inexperienced service person. Tom is the best service person, so his station has more tables, but his area also has the rest rooms, which are not a desirable location. Lisa has 20 seats, and Elsa has 22 seats to serve. This is the correct manner for setting up stations.

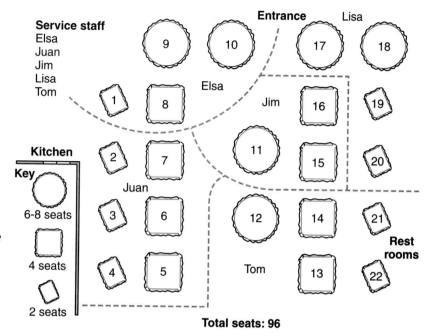

FIGURE 5–2

This dining room also has 96 seats. Each service person should have 24 seats to serve, because there are only four of them. All four have their tables scattered all over the dining room. The service in this restaurant will be poor, mainly because of poor station assignment by the manager. This type of station assignment is incorrect.

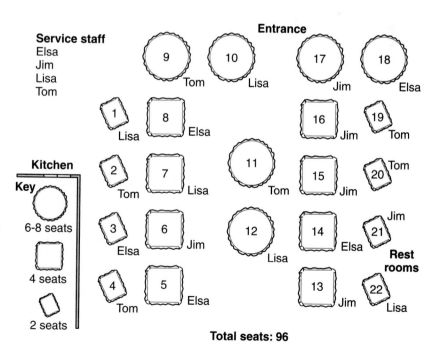

Distance of Guest Tables from the Kitchen

The station that has the fewest number of tables should be the one farthest from the kitchen. Because of its location, it will take the service person longer to obtain the food. Therefore, fewer guests can be accommodated in this station than in the other stations.

Number of Guests Seated at Each Table

A mixture of small tables that seat two—called **deuces**—and larger tables, called tops—four people, **four-top**; six people, **six-top**—is ideal for organizing a station. There should be a maximum of 24 seats in a station for one service person to serve. The 24 seats should not be made up of 12 deuces, however. That would be almost impossible for a service person to serve, because there are too many parties to wait on at once. Ideally, the station should consist of a six-top, three four-tops, and three deuces. Of course, this station must be close to the kitchen area. All stations should be designed with a variety of tables that seat different numbers of guests.

Physical Attractiveness of the Station

In every restaurant, there are tables that are more desirable to the guests than others. Traditionally, tables by the kitchen or rest rooms have been designated as the poorest tables. Tables by the windows, with a view of nice scenery, are considered the best. When there is entertainment in the restaurant, tables closest to the entertainment will be the most popular. The popular station should be smaller than the one by the kitchen door, because many guests will request the popular tables (see Figure 5–3).

Managers should rotate the assignment of the desirable tables to all servers.

Amount of Food Preparation Done at the Table

If the menu of the restaurant has a lot of items that will be prepared or finished off at guest tables, the number of seats at the station should be fewer than 24. Because the service staff has to do a lot of tableside cooking and tossing of salads, they will spend more time at the guest tables. Tableside cooking (usually with French service) will require more space between the tables because of the cart and food preparation equipment. The stations should be smaller than in American service (see Figure 5–4).

FIGURE 5-3

Popular stations, such as ones by a fireplace, should be smaller because many guests will request these. (Photograph by Randall Perry)

Union Contract Requirements

A union contract may state the number of guests a service person can serve at a station. If that number is exceeded, a per-person bonus must be paid to the service person who has served the extra guests. One of the purposes of a union is to provide jobs for their members. It is in the best interests of the union and management to keep the size of the

FIGURE 5-4

Tableside cooking requires extra space between tables. (Photograph by Randall Perry)

stations reasonable. Therefore, this bonus fee discourages management from making the stations too large, as the fee will generally be more expensive to the restaurant than employing another service person.

Competency of the Staff

Every manager will realize that some service people are more competent than others. Highly competent service people can serve more guests than others, so a manager must take this into consideration when assigning stations to staff.

A caution to future managers—Many a well-intentioned new manager has made erroneous changes in stations without asking for input from the staff. A manager should always obtain input from staff and customers before making changes. Because tips make up most of service staff's wages, as opposed to a set hourly wage, planning and consultation with the staff are vital before changes are made.

Assigning Stations

There are two methods of assigning stations, after all the relevant factors have been considered: the first is the *seniority* method, the second is the *rotation* method.

Seniority Method

In the seniority method, service people with the most seniority are assigned permanent stations. The station truly becomes their little restaurant. On their day off they are replaced with a relief service person, usually one with little seniority. Normally, in this system, the best stations are assigned to the service staff who have been employed at the restaurant for the longest time. This system is used in restaurants where guests dine daily at the same restaurant. The guest has a standard reservation for the same table and wants the same service person to serve him or her every day. Once this method is put into place, it is almost impossible to change.

Rotation Method

This method is favored by many restaurant managers and employees. The service staff is rotated among all the stations on a daily basis. One service person is responsible for station one on Monday, station two on Tuesday, and so on throughout the week. This system allows the manager to close off the poorer stations when business is forecasted to be light. It requires more planning and organization than the seniority method, but it allows all service staff to have the better as well as the poorer stations.

Whichever method is chosen for a restaurant, guest satisfaction must be the determining factor. Because much of guest satisfaction depends on the attitude of the service staff, the method selected must satisfy the needs of the restaurant, guests, and service staff. Once the decision concerning stations has been made, the next issue that managers have to deal with is that of sidework.

Sidework

Sidework is one of the necessary jobs that must be done by the service staff. It is a job that is not well liked, because it does not produce tips directly. However, the manager should explain to the staff that sidework is a positive factor in making the restaurant a success. For instance, if the salt and pepper shakers are filled before the guests enter the restaurant, the service person will not have to interrupt service to fill up the shakers during the restaurant's busy time. Therefore, service people can serve more guests, and the income of both the restaurant and the service people will increase. The restaurant is displaying competency, and service people are less pressured and more able to spend more time talking or doing suggestive selling with their guests. Sidework can be defined as all the extra jobs that service people must do to get the restaurant ready to serve the guests. Sidework can be assigned before the shift or after the shift. Examples of sidework are filling salt and pepper shakers, restocking condiments, cleaning the coffee stations, and folding napkins.

Manager's Message and Chef's Choice

(Courtesy of TED BALESTRERI, COFOUNDER, AND BERT P. CUTINO, COFOUNDER AND CHEF, SARDINE FACTORY RESTAURANT, MONTEREY, CALIFORNIA)

"If we made you feel at home, we have made a million-dollar mistake, because you may as well stay at home. Our job is to make you feel better than at home."

—*Ted Balestreri*

"All great service in a restaurant begins and ends in the same consistent manner . . . pleasing the customer and meeting the standard of excellence that they expect as well as what we pride ourselves on providing."

—*Bert P. Cutino*

Ted Balestreri and Bert Cutino are leaders in our industry. They were recognized as two of the 50 Power Players in foodservice in the United States by *Nation's Restaurant News* in January 2000. In 1968, they cofounded the 72-seat Sardine Factory Restaurant in a nearly abandoned area known as Cannery Row. The restaurant was located in a building that once fed sardine workers. Cannery Row, with its approximately 30 restaurants, over 100 specialty shops, hotels, and visitor attractions now draws 51 percent of the tourists that visit Monterey's Peninsula. Balestreri and Cutino were innovators in serving California wines and implementing the premier-wine program in the United States. From the 72-seat beginning, the Sardine Factory Restaurant has grown to five rooms and has more than tripled its seating capacity, to 250. The restaurant is one of the most successful, widely recognized, and highest-grossing dining establishments in the country. Since 1993, the Sardine Factory has been the recipient of virtually every major restaurant and wine award in the industry, including

(continues)

Sidework can create many problems for a restaurant if the manager does not establish a policy. If a restaurant manager has to staff for more than one meal period, like lunch and dinner, there are often disagreements between the two shifts over which one is doing more sidework. The restaurant's policy must define the exact duties and responsibilities of the service staff concerning sidework. Employees must be taught about the importance of sidework and the reasons why it contributes to the success of the restaurant. They must understand that the tasks must be completed, but that the guest is still their most important responsibility. The restaurant manager should not allow any staff member to finish a shift and leave until that server's sidework is completed.

Manager's Message and Chef's Choice

(continued)

the prestigious DiRoNA Award; with their 30,000-wine-bottle inventory and 1,375 labels, they have earned the Wine Spectator's Grand Award every year 1982; the *Nation's Restaurant News* Hall of Fame Award (1981); *Restaurant and Institutions* Ivy Award (1980); and the list continues. Chef Cutino and Mr. Balestreri have held national offices in our industry. Chef Cutino has been head of the American Academy of Chefs, and Mr. Balestreri was president of the National Restaurant Association. Mr. Balestreri said about starting the business, "Here we had no money, and we built a restaurant on the wrong side of the tracks. We broke every rule. We were underfinanced, it was an ugly building, stairs had to be climbed, there was no marketing program or theme. We had nothing, and we created it all when we built the Sardine Factory." Mr. Cutino adds that "success has been achieved through an unwavering commitment to quality. Every person on the staff, from waitpersons to kitchen staff, must be able to present him or her self as a professional and strive for excellence!"

The Sardine Factory delivers quality to its guests. This is what Cindy Railing said when asked about her favorite restaurant in Scoop, "Hands down, the Sardine Factory in Monterey. I love the way I'm greeted at the door—I'm remembered. Care is taken with each and every dish. Everything is ultra- premium; everything shows great attention to detail. I go in and I'm treated like a famous celebrity who's walking into Spago. It's a restaurant with great soul. In this world, there's less and less people interaction. What I like about going out to dine is the people connection and the warmth."[1]

Sweet or Sour?

One evening a couple went out for dinner at a local diner. The food was served quickly and correctly by an efficient waitperson. Because it was near closing time, as soon as the food was served, the waitperson went to an area where there was a lot of stainless steel equipment. She proceeded to wipe it down and make sure it was clean for the next day. She was a master at doing this sidework. The stainless steel was shining, and the condiments were replaced. However, she did not return to the guests' table to see how the meal was or to offer dessert, and it took a long time for her to bring the check; but her sidework was completed.

Scheduling Sidework

The manager must plan out the specific tasks needed in the restaurant and decide how many people are required to do those tasks. Sidework should be scheduled on a daily basis. All assignments concerning sidework, just like stations, have to be posted for all the employees to see. The sidework can be rotated, just like the stations are rotated. In some establishments, the sidework becomes a part of a certain station (see Figure 5–5). For example, the service people assigned stations one and two have to fan-fold 100 napkins each day. Therefore, if Elsa is scheduled for station one today, she knows that she must fold 50 napkins. This method creates accountability for both the manager and employees.

Each restaurant has its own specific jobs for sidework. The key is that the manager must be organized and follow-up to make certain that sidework is completed. When the manager does this, sidework becomes an integral part of the success of the dining room.

FIGURE 5-5

A sidework chart designed for a restaurant with stations. By organizing the sidework duties in this manner, all employees know their responsibilities.

SIDEWORK DUTIES	
Station	**Daily Duties**
1 & 2	Fan-fold 50 napkins
3	Refill salts, peppers, and sugar bowls
4	Wipe down all stainless steel
5	Clean and straighten flowers
6	Dust woodwork and window sills

Note: On days when there are fewer employees, sidework duties will be combined.

Restaurant Success

One of the main reasons for a restaurant's success or lack thereof is the service that the guest receives. The dining room manager is the key person to insure that the guests receive a high level of service. The manager is responsible for hiring and training the service staff, and the training should not be a one-time session but continuous. The manager must follow-up on training through observation and evaluation. Service standards must be explained and maintained. As repetition is the best teacher, here again are the seven guidelines of service:

1. Women are served before men; if children are present, they should be served first, then women, then men.
2. Food is served from the guest's left side with the service person's left hand.
3. Beverages are served from the guest's right side with the service person's right hand.
4. All guests' food must be brought to the table at the same time.
5. Guest plates should not be removed from the table until all guests are finished eating their meal.
6. Dirty plates should never be stacked or scraped on the guest's table.
7. Dirty dishes are cleared from the guest's right side with the service person's right hand.

Serving the Meal

The sequence of serving a meal is relatively the same from restaurant to restaurant. Meals generally are served in the following sequence:

- drinks
- appetizers
- rolls and butter
- salads
- entrees
- coffee/tea
- desserts
- wine when requested—either with dinner or immediately

In some restaurants, the salad course is served in the European tradition, after the entree.

Special instructions should be given by the manager to the staff concerning substitutions; furthermore, menu items should be clearly explained, and the service staff should be knowledgable about ingredients and preparation.

More and more restaurants give tests as part of their training program, and passing a test is one of the criteria for obtaining a job with the restaurant. This makes the applicant and the employees realize that the restaurant is serious about providing proper service.

T I P $

TO INSURE PROPER SERVICE

Bruce Griffin Henderson states in his book, *Waiting*: "There are three main components to the job of waiting tables. 1. Selling food and beverages; 2. Delivering food and beverages to the table; and 3. Representing the business to the public. Any restaurant consultant will tell you that a waitstaff can make or break a restaurant; the chef or owner will tell you that their unique genius is responsible for any success the restaurant has, but the waitstaff is responsible for any and all failure. Most restaurant customers never have any contact with the chef or the owner, so their impression of how they were treated is created by their interaction with the waitstaff."[2]

Methods of Service

Staffing in an American dining room depends on the management of the restaurant. There are three ways in which the dining room can be organized for service: The most common method has one person waiting on a specified number of tables, aided by a busperson; the second is borrowed from the French system, which has a captain responsible for an area of the restaurant. The captain is assisted by service persons and buspersons. The third method is the **team system**. As the name implies, teamwork is needed to make this system succeed.

The manager needs to know how each of these systems works, in addition to their advantages and disadvantages. It is then up to the restaurant manager to decide what type of system will work best in his establishment. The critical part of making any system work is training and follow-up. All of the systems explained here will work if the manager trains and reinforces the policy constantly.

Regardless of the method of service a restaurant uses, all follow the general sequence stated earlier. Lists of the advantages and disadvantages of each system follow.

FIGURE 5-6

The individual service person. He is responsible for presenting the menu, taking the order, and serving the meal and beverage. (Photograph by Randall Perry)

Individual Service Person Method

The service person is assigned a small area of the restaurant called a *station*. It is the sole responsibility of that service person to provide expert service to all the guests at that station. The service person must be extremely well organized. If any mistakes are made, or if the service person cannot handle the problems in the station, the guests will receive poor service. The station generally has between 12 and 24 seats. Many restaurants provide buspersons—one for every two to three service staff—to assist in clearing the dirty plates. Figure 5–6 shows a service person completing his responsibilities.

The advantages of the individual service person method are as follows:

1. It is an easy method to teach and learn.
2. The guests know their service person.
3. The manager knows who is responsible for service.
4. The service person gets to keep all the tips.
5. The service person knows that she is responsible for the serving and guest satisfaction of the total meal.

However, this method has disadvantages as well:

1. If there is a problem, the service person can become overwhelmed and the result will be poor service.
2. Service people may have no one to rely on if there is a problem. However, many times servers will back each other up if there is a problem.
3. Because training is simple, employees can easily move from job to job. This system does not encourage loyalty to the restaurant.
4. The service person is responsible for serving the entire meal. If the service person is performing poorly, the guest will have a poor dining experience.

Captain Method

This system is characterized by having a captain responsible for a double or triple station. The captain may have been promoted from service person. The service staff assist the captain in serving the station. There may even be a busperson to assist the service staff and captain. The captain is usually in a supervisory position and acts as a sort of public relations person. Captains generally stay in the dining room, while the service staff obtain and serve food from the kitchen.

The advantages of the captain method:

1. The restaurant has other supervisors besides the host or manager in the dining room.
2. The guests will have more than one person to serve them.
3. If a problem develops, the captain can assist the other service staff in the station.
4. The guests will have the benefit of having an experienced and personable individual to take their order.

The disadvantages:

1. A restaurant must have an individual experienced in both supervision and waiting to fill this position.
2. The job descriptions and roles are clearly defined; thus, not much flexibility is built into this system.
3. The guest is expected to leave a larger tip because it must cover both the captain and service staff.

Team System

A system that was characterized as an idea whose time had come was highlighted in *Nation's Restaurant News*: the team system.

Ross Sponder owns the 48-seat diner restaurant called the Palace Café in Santa Barbara, California. In his system, a service person takes the initial order and informs the customers that any of the 12 waiters or waitresses can help them with whatever they want. Each table has a pamphlet that states: "Our staff works as a team in order to better serve you. You need not look for the person who initially took your order for additional service. Just ask anyone! This system of service is designed to help you enjoy your time here by making everyone on our staff available to take care of your table."[3]

Sponder has virtually no employee turnover. His biggest challenge has been breaking the service staff of the habit of sticking to their individual territories or stations. But the problem was overcome by requiring dining room servers to pass an intense, practical examination.

The teamwork concept has turned out to be a highly efficient style that makes jobs easier, provides better service, and results in higher gratuities (see Figure 5–7). As Figure 5–7 illustrates, a restaurant that uses the individual service person to wait on the guest may have one service person at a station with as many as 24 guests. The illustration using the captain in Figure 5–7 shows that the captain may be responsible for up to 72 guests. In both of these instances, that is a lot of guests to serve and still be attentive to their needs. It is extremely difficult to practice Gretzky service, mainly because it becomes hard to observe all of the guests in the station. On the other hand, using team service, there are three individuals constantly checking on the guests in their station of up to 50 guests (see Figure 5–7). By using this illustration, it should be logical that the team system—if done correctly—will provide the best service for the guests in the dining room.

La Paloma in North Miami, Florida, uses a similar system. A service person takes the orders and gives them to the kitchen staff. Speed runners bring food to the tables, while the service staff answer customer questions. The result is speedier and more efficient service. The late Michael Hurst of 15th St. Fisheries believed that restaurants should keep servers at their stations. He used runners to bring food from the kitchen at his restaurant.

FIGURE 5–7

The typical number of guests a service staff should be responsible for at a station.

SIZE OF STATIONS	
Type of Service	**Number of Seats at Station**
Individual Service Person	up to 24
Captain	up to 72
Team	up to 50

How the Team System Operates

The team is divided up into three positions: an **Aid**, a **Lead**, and a **Follow-up**. The two critical jobs are the Lead and the Follow-up. Normally, a team is responsible for a station with 12 to 14 tables and 40 to 50 seats. A restaurant of 150 seats usually has three teams serving the guests. It generally takes five months to master the concept of team service; because of the long training period, this reduces the normally high turnover of service people.

The Aid

The first job that is learned is that of the Aid. Of the three positions, the Aid training takes the longest to master: about three to four weeks. This is because the new employee must learn the policies, menu, and organization of the restaurant. The Aid has the following responsibilities:

1. The normal duties of the busperson
2. Picking dinners up from the kitchen and delivering them to the guests—this is the only part of the meal in which the Aid participates, in some restaurants this job is also referred to as a *food runner*. The food runner or Aid must know where all tables are located, and a system must be in place so that the food runner or Aid is not asking the guest who gets what food item.
3. Taking dirty entree dishes from the guest table, if the Lead requests

The Lead

The Lead is the first member of the team that the guest comes in contact with in this system (see Figure 5–8). The Lead should be personable and should be a *suggestive salesperson*. The two main duties of the Lead are *suggestive selling* and the *timing of placing dinner orders* with the kitchen. The duties of the Lead are as follows:

1. suggestive selling for drinks and appetizers
2. serving drink orders
3. taking the guest's drink and dinner orders
4. obtaining additional drinks for the guest
5. selling and serving wine
6. setting the place of service for the other two team members
7. turning the dinner order into the kitchen and timing the dinners

The Follow-up

The Follow-up is the quarterback of the section, making sure the station runs smoothly. This is the most mentally demanding of the three jobs. This person must run the section, making sure the guests are

FIGURE 5–8

The team system. The Lead presents the menu and takes the order. The Follow-up is holding the tray, and the Aid is holding the water pitcher. (Photograph by Randall Perry)

satisfied and solving problems. The Follow-up is the one member of the team who should never leave the station. If it is necessary to leave the station, the Follow-up should have the Aid and Lead assume the duties. The Follow-up has the following responsibilities:

1. checking guest satisfaction with meals
2. conversing with the guests about their meals
3. assisting the other two members of the team in taking orders (Lead) or serving meals (Aid) if necessary
4. solving any problems concerning the meals
5. clearing dirty dishes from the guest's table
6. suggesting and selling dessert
7. totaling up and presenting the check to the guests
8. collecting the money for the guest check

Advantages and Disadvantages of the Team System

The team system, when executed properly, provides the guest with the best service, because there is always a service person available if the guest has a problem. One member of the team is on the floor of the restaurant at all times. The team members are always available, but they are not hovering over the guest, as is the case with an individual service person.

The biggest problem for the guests is that they frequently become confused because they are being waited on by three people. Guests do not understand how the team system works and are confused over who is getting the tip.

The advantages of this system:

1. There are three people to take care of the guests' needs.
2. A professional service staff is obtained through a thorough training program.
3. It provides an organized system for anticipating guests' needs.
4. There is a constant peer evaluation of service.
5. Jobs are clearly defined, but flexibility is built into the system.

Its disadvantages:

1. An extensive training period is needed.
2. The system may be difficult for experienced service people to accept.
3. Guests become confused about who is serving them.

The team system has nontraditional job titles and names, but the job descriptions resemble the traditional jobs found in restaurants that provide their guests with American dining room service. Once the team system is mastered, restaurants are reluctant to go back to the old method of service.

Wine Service

Regardless of the type of service a restaurant uses, staff should be instructed in the proper method of opening and serving wine. Knowledge of wine and wine service by the service staff is essential for guests' enjoyment of their meal.

The service staff should encourage restaurant patrons to enjoy wine with their meal. To do this, the service staff must be knowledgeable about wine. For instance, the staff must know what wine best complements food, and how to present, open, and serve wine properly. This section is not a comprehensive guide on matching food and wine. Service people should take courses on wine and sample wine with foods to become confident and knowledgeable on the subject.

As a general guideline, red wines complement foods that are hearty, like prime ribs and steak. White wines are generally served with lighter dishes, and sparkling wines are used mostly for celebrations. If a guest asks for the "wrong" type of wine with a meal, the service person should not challenge the guest's choice of wine. There are some white wines that complement a hearty dish, or the guest may have a favorite wine that is consumed with every meal. The service person may suggest a selection that complements the food, but after determining that the guest indeed wants the particular wine requested, it should be served without further hesitation.

Sweet or Sour?

After selecting a wonderful sounding Italian entree, we decided to order a bottle of Melani Chianti to complement the meal. When our waiter took our wine order, he proceeded to tell us that we had mispronounced the name of the wine!

Presenting Wine

Once the guest has selected a wine, the server should bring it to the table and present it to the guest for inspection, as illustrated in Figure 5–9. The bottle should be presented with the label facing the guest so that the guest can ascertain that the bottle is exactly what was ordered. The server should present the bottle resting on the sidetowel for two reasons:

FIGURE 5–9

The correct way to present a bottle of wine. The bottle is held with the sidetowel, with the label facing the guest. (Photograph by Randall Perry)

one, if the bottle is wet, the sidetowel will keep the bottle from slipping from the server's hands, two, the sidetowel acts as an insulator and will not transmit as much of the server's body heat to the wine. Serving wine at the correct temperature adds to the enjoyment of the wine.

As soon as the guest approves the bottle, the server should open it—at the service stand, not at the guest's table.

How to Open Wine

The waitperson uses a corkscrew to open any still wine that has a cork. The corkscrew is *not* used to open sparkling wine. Follow these steps to open wine using a corkscrew.

1. If the wine has a foil or capsule, use the knife and cut it at the lower lip of the bottle neck (see Figure 5–10).
2. Remove the cap or wax seal with the edge of the corkscrew knife (see Figure 5–11).
3. Insert the worm into the cork a little off center (see Figure 5–12).
4. Twist the corkscrew clockwise until one spiral of the worm is showing (see Figure 5–13).
5. Push the handle of the corkscrew back so that the lever can be placed on the lip of the bottle.
6. Place one hand over the lever, holding it in place, while lifting the handle straight up with your other hand.
7. Once most of the cork is visible, grip the cork and gently remove it from the bottle.

Opening Sparkling Wine

1. Remove the foil hood from the bottle.
2. Turn the wire cage eight turns to loosen the cage.
3. Grasp the cork with a napkin with one hand.
4. Gently turn the *bottle* with your other hand, *not* the cork.
5. The pressure in the bottle will push the cork into the napkin.

The cork should be presented to the person who has ordered the wine, and a small tasting should be poured into the glass. The guest will sample the wine and either approve of it or will tell the service person it is not acceptable. More and more wines are being bottled with a screw top instead of a cork. Obviously, this eliminates the need to open the bottle using a corkscrew. It does present a problem for the service person of what to do with the screw top. There are two points of view on the service of wines with a screw top. In both instances, the service person presents the wine to the guest for approval as shown in Figure 5–9. Once the guest approves of the wine, the service person

FIGURE 5-10

Using the knife on the wine corkscrew, the foil should be cleanly cut below the lip of the bottle and removed to allow access to the cork.

FIGURE 5-11

More producers are now using wax blends to seal their bottles. This bottle has a pull-tab to allow removal of the wax top.

FIGURE 5-12

Insert the worm into the cork a little bit off center. It is important to insert the worm straight to allow for a clean and easy removal of the cork.

FIGURE 5-13

Twist the corkscrew to the right until one spiral of the worm is showing. This will ensure that the waitperson has enough leverage to fully remove the cork from the bottle.

simply twists the cap off of the bottle. The service person, if the guest requests the cap, either places it on the table—as is the tradition with the cork—or simply removes it and puts it in their apron.

The purpose of having the guest who appears to be the host taste the wine first is steeped in history. In ancient times, the way to eliminate your enemy was to invite him or her to your dwelling to share a bottle of wine. It was easy to hide poison in wine. The guest was offered the wine first, drank it, and died. Before long, guests demanded that their host sample the wine first, reasoning that if the host drank first, the wine would be safe to drink. The tradition carries on today.

T I P $

To Insure Proper Service

Always ask your guests this question: "Who would like to sample the wine?" Do not assume that the person who orders the wine will automatically do the sampling.

Unacceptable Wine

If the wine is not acceptable, the service person should ask if the guest would care for another bottle of wine. The service should not challenge the integrity of the guest, but should inquire what is wrong with the wine. Depending on the policy of the restaurant, the guest may or may not be charged for the wine.

Restaurants that have expensive bottles of wine often employ a different method of handling wine service. When a guest orders an expensive bottle of wine, the manager is called to the guest's table. The guest is told the conditions of the purchase. For instance, the manager may say, "You have made an excellent choice with the 1898 Chateau Lafite Rothschild. However, because the wine is so old, the restaurant cannot guarantee the quality of the wine. If we open the wine for you, you must pay for it." The guest then has the option of accepting or refusing the wine.

Serving Wine

When the guest approves the wine, the server should pour the wine into the guests' glasses using the guidelines for serving beverages. Red wine glasses should be half-filled. White and sparkling wines should be poured three-quarters to the top of the glass. Sparkling wines should be served in two steps. The service person should pour an amount into the glass so that the bubbles and foam will not overflow the glass. Then the other glasses are poured in the same manner. The service person should then go back to the first glass that was poured and continue to fill up that glass so that the guest receives a glass that is three-quarters filled. As the service person finishes pouring any type of wine, the bottle should be rotated to the right to prevent the wine from dripping.

Red wines should be placed on the guest's table. The sparkling and white wines are placed in a container to keep them at their proper temperature. This container is either an ice bucket placed near the guest's table or a container that retains the cold temperature and sits on the table. Throughout the meal, the service person should return to the table and refill the guests' wine glasses when needed.

TIPS

TO INSURE PROPER SERVICE
Servers should check guests' wine glasses frequently and replenish as necessary.

Proper Serving Temperature of Wine

Serving wines at the proper temperature is essential for guest satisfaction. When wines are served correctly, they offer incredible perfumes and bouquets. Proper temperature balances the sweetness and acidity in wine (see Figure 5–14).

White, rosé, and sparkling wines should be served chilled. Sparkling and sweet dessert wines should be served at 35 to 45 degrees Fahrenheit. Rosés and dry white wines should be served at 45 to 55 degrees Fahrenheit. These wines should be stored in a cooler for at least two hours. If they are not, and the guest orders a wine that should be served chilled, the service person can put it in a bucket with ice and water; it

FIGURE 5–14

The proper serving temperatures of wines.

PROPER SERVING TEMPERATURES OF WINE	
Name of Wine	**Serving Temperature (°Fahrenheit)**
Wine coolers, Rosés, Beaujolais, White	45 to 55
Red	55 to 65
Sparkling, Sweet White Desserts	35 to 45

will be the proper temperature in about 15 or 30 minutes. However, any restaurant that sells wine should have proper refrigeration.

Red wines should be served at the old European temperature of 55 to 65 degrees Fahrenheit. A red wine served too warm goes out of balance and becomes overwhelming. Particularly robust reds that contain more than 13 percent alcohol begin to smell like ether. Serving reds too warm also causes a slight warm sensation in the wine drinker's throat. If red wines are served too cold, they lose their aroma and bouquet. Coldness brings out the astringency in the tannin and makes the wine taste harsh. If possible, a red wine should be opened half an hour before serving to let the wine breathe; this breathing makes the wine taste smoother.

Serving wine with a meal adds to the pleasure of the dining experience. Restaurants with service staff that are knowledgeable concerning wines and wine service offer their guests an additional benefit.

T I P $

TO INSURE PROPER SERVICE

Every time you try a wine, keep a note about what you liked or disliked about the wine. The note should include the name of the wine, along with the vintage and what food you ate with it. This is a great method to build up your knowledge of wine and food.

SUMMARY

1. There are four typical service positions in American service: captain, wine steward or sommelier, service person, and the busperson. The captain is responsible for taking food orders and overseeing the service in a section of the dining room. The wine steward or sommelier is responsible for suggesting and serving wine. Serving food and beverages is the responsibility of the service people. The busperson assists the service people by laying the cover and removing plates from tables. In some establishments, the busperson serves coffee or tea to the guests.

2. In American service, there are three options to serve guests: Restaurants may assign an individual service person to serve guests in a section of a dining room. Other restaurants may employ captains who have the responsibility to greet guests, take food orders, and supervise a section of the dining room. The third option for American service is to use a team system. In this system, a Lead greets the guests and takes their orders, the Follow-up serves the food, and the Aid clears dishes and serves coffee or tea.

3. Stations are small areas of the dining room that are comprised of 12 to 24 seats. Stations should be set up by management using criteria such as distance of the guest tables from the kitchen, number of guests seated at each table, physical attractiveness of the station, amount of food preparation required at the table, union contract requirements, competency of staff, tables most frequently requested by guests, and location of waitstaff workstations.

4. Sidework should be assigned in an organized fashion for a smooth-running restaurant. Specific tasks to be done on a daily basis must be scheduled by management. These tasks should be posted for all employees to see.

5. Using the team method of service, the manager would divide the dining room into stations of 40 to 45 guests. The three members of the team—the Lead, Follow-up, and Aid—would work the station together. The Lead would take orders, the Follow-up would serve the food, and the Aid would remove dirty dishes and serve coffee or tea.

6. The individual station method, which uses one service person, has these advantages: it is an easy method to teach and learn, the guests know their service person, the manager knows who is responsible for service, the service person is responsible for all service to the guest and keeps all tips. The disadvantages are that the waitperson can become overwhelmed and end up in the weeds, which results in poor service for all guests in the station. Because training is simple, service people can easily quit a position at one restaurant and find a job at another restaurant, creating a turnover problem for the original restaurant. Since the service person is responsible for serving the guests their entire meal, if the service is poor, the guests will have a negative impression of the restaurant.

   Restaurants that employ the captain method have these advantages: there is more supervision in the dining room than with the individual station method; guests have more than one person to serve them; the captain can assist service staff with problems; and guests will have the benefit of having an experienced, personable individual to take their order. Disadvantages of this system are: restaurants need individuals experienced in both supervision and service to fill these jobs; there is not much flexibility built into this system; and guests are expected to leave a larger tip because of the extra service.

   The team system has the following advantages: three people will serve guests; it provides an organized system for anticipating guests' needs; there is constant peer evaluation of service; jobs are clearly defined; flexibility is built into the system. Disadvantages of the team system are: an extensive training period is needed for the staff, the system may be difficult for experienced service staff to learn, and guests become confused about who is serving them.

7. The proper sequence in serving a meal is as follows: drinks (alcoholic or nonalcoholic), appetizers, rolls, salads, entrees, coffee/tea, and desserts. Wine is served when requested, either with dinner or immediately.

8. Wine that a guest has ordered is presented for inspection. The service person removes the protective covering over the cork, inserts the corkscrew into the cork, and removes the cork from the bottle. The cork is presented to the guest for inspection, and a small amount of the wine is poured into the guest's glass for sampling. Once the guest approves of the wine, the wine is poured by the service person following the seven guidelines of service. Throughout the meal, the service person should refill the guests' glasses as necessary.

REVIEW QUESTIONS

1. What are the four traditional job titles for dining room service personnel? Explain the duties of these employees.
2. List and explain five qualities that applicants must have to be successful as dining room service personnel.
3. What is the main difference between the captain system and the team system in dining room operations?
4. Explain the jobs of the wine steward and dining room attendant.
5. What are the stations? What factors contribute to assigning stations?
6. What are the two methods for assigning stations? In your opinion, which is the better method? Explain your answer.
7. What is sidework? Why is it necessary in a restaurant? What are its benefits for the service staff?
8. Explain and list the seven guidelines of service.
9. What is the sequence of courses in a typical, American à la carte restaurant? Is there ever any change in the sequence of courses? If so, explain when and why.
10. What are the three positions in team service, and what are the individual responsibilities?
11. What should a service person know about wine service? What are the proper temperatures at which wine should be served?

DISCUSSION QUESTIONS

1. What is the best system for your restaurant? Now that you have read and know about the three systems, which one would you choose for your restaurant? Give specific reasons why you would choose one system over the others.

2. What percent should a guest leave for a tip on a bottle of wine? Should the amount of the percent change if the wine costs $45.00 a bottle compared to $1,000 a bottle?

3. Your restaurant is open for three meals. The day shift employees claim that the night shift is not doing sidework. What would you do to solve this problem?

4. What percent of the check should a captain be tipped in the caption system? Explain your reasoning for the percentage tip you will give to the captain.

5. The guests at table 42 have ordered the most expensive bottle of wine on your wine list. They are regular customers who have been coming to your restaurant each Thursday night for the past 22 years. When the wine is poured in the host's glass, he says it is spoiled and unacceptable. You taste the wine and it seems fine to you. What do you do?

REFERENCES

1. Katie Ayoub, "People Connections, An Interview with Average Diner," *Chef* (September 2000): 20.

2. Bruce Griffin Henderson, *Waiting: Waiters' True Tales of Crazed Customers, Murderous Chefs, and Table Side Disasters* (New York: Plume/Penguin Press: 1995).

3. Charles Bernstein, "Teamwork Service: An Idea Whose Time Has Come," *Nation's Restaurant News* (August 10, 1987): 13.

Dining
Room
Management

Training the Service Staff to Serve the Meal

OBJECTIVES   At the completion of this chapter, the student should be able to:

1. State the importance of thorough knowledge of the menu.
2. State why service persons should know the ingredients of all menu items.
3. Write down and organize food and beverage orders so that there will be no question about who gets what item.
4. Explain the importance of cooking times.
5. Understand the importance of suggestive selling and merchandising.
6. Define the term 86ed, and tell how to avoid problems with 86ed items.
7. Order food from the kitchen.
8. Give the serving sequence of a meal.
9. Explain the importance of training, testing, and evaluating employees.
10. Explain the purpose of a substitution or no substitution policy.
11. Understand the value of a computerized register system.
12. Understand the sequence of placing orders using a point of sale system.

KEY WORDS

anaphylactic shock	fire the table	standard abbreviations
chef's creation	MICROS	suggestive selling
dupe	point-of-sale (POS)	underliner
86ed	systems	

The Manager's Role

The dining room manager is the key to a successful restaurant, since the manager sets the tone and pace of the establishment. The success or failure of the restaurant is determined by the manager, who should not be at the restaurant 24-hours a day, or even 18; but the restaurant should run as if the manager were there.

How do successful restaurant managers make their businesses run effectively, even when they are not present? By proper selection, teaching, training, and continuous evaluation of all employees. A dining room manager is like an orchestra leader: The orchestra leader does not play an instrument, and the dining room manager does not serve food; but both of them are responsible for their guests' enjoyment. They both have to select, teach, train, and evaluate their talented employees so that the guests will have an enjoyable experience. In addition, the restaurant manager's attitude is passed to the patrons by the employees.

The importance of competency and friendliness have been emphasized in previous chapters. There are many types of service available for the restaurant manager to choose from, but all this does not make good service. The final important element in providing excellent service occurs because the staff *knows* and *communicates* information that adds to the guests' enjoyable dining experience.

Parts of the Meal

All dining experiences can be broken into four parts, as related to service: the first part is getting prepared to serve the guests, the next part is merchandising and taking the meal order, the third part is the actual service of the meal, the last part is presentation of the guest check.

It does not matter if a restaurant offers French, American, or Russian service to the guests; nor does it matter what the style of service—team, individual service person, or captain—the manager chooses. The following information will apply in all settings.

Learning the Menu

The dining room manager should insist that all employees know all the information about items on the menu. Employees should know which foods or beverages are offered, their pronunciation, their ingredients, and their styles of preparation. It is the responsibility of the manager to prepare this information for the employees. The information must be clearly written in a manual and given to all employees. Many restaurants, such as specialty restaurants and Casa Lupita Mexican restaurants, are using this type of training method.

In order to make certain that the employees become knowledgeable, they are tested on the material. Casa Lupita stresses to its employees that customers have no idea what it is like to open a restaurant. Guests do not think about the problems of a restaurant; they simply want good food and service. Applicants should be told when hired that knowledge of the material in the training manual is a requirement to start and keep the job. The Barnsider Restaurant chain manual clearly states the purpose of knowing the information. They inform their applicants that they must know the material before they are allowed to work on the floor of the dining room, because they do not use their guests as guinea pigs for training the service staff. So before any person becomes a service person, he or she must know the material required by the chain. The appendix of the manual contains a series of tests that may given to applicants. The applicants are required to know 90 percent of the answers to the questions before they are allowed to work on the dining room floor. All managers should set up a policy of testing employees on material. There should be a test covering all the items that the manager feels are important to make the guests' meal an enjoyable experience.

Reimund Pitz, one of fewer than 60 certified master chefs in the United States and a past president of the American Culinary Federation, stated that "Up until now, I don't believe the service staff has received as much education as it needs. We concentrate so much on training the kitchen staff. The servers aren't taught about the food, and yet they are the people who have contact with the customers. I think it's time that changed. I think the time has come to educate servers and turn them into true food experts."[1]

Sweet or Sour?

A couple went out for dinner in a popular summer vacation resort. The waiter approached the table to inquire if the guests wanted a before-dinner drink. The woman ordered a whiskey sour and the man asked, "What kind of ale do you have?" The waiter thought for a moment and then blurted out "Ginger, sir." The man had to explain to the waiter that he was inquiring about an alcoholic beverage, not a soft drink. Obviously, the service person had very little or no training. He certainly did not know all the items on the menu.

The training manual must cover such things as general policies, food prices and descriptions, beverage prices and descriptions, and specific information about the restaurant. Is it hard to set up a training manual? Is it hard to evaluate employees? Does it take a lot of the manager's time? Of course, it does. But it pays off in guest satisfaction, return business, and—in the long run—profits!

What Should the Service Person Know?

Before a manager allows employees to wait on guests, there are many facts they should know. The first group of facts deals with specific policies about the restaurant. Acceptable standards of appearance, dress, and attendance should be explained before the service person is hired. Additional items, such as what time to report to work, food and drink policies concerning consumption both on and off the job, and serving hours, should also be explained to the employees. These facts must be reinforced in a training booklet.

The next set of facts should deal with the establishment. The purpose of having these facts known is so the service people can answer any and all questions that guests ask. The guest will feel assured of the competency of the service person if he is able to answer questions intelligently and confidently.

A third group of facts should be concerned with the physical layout of the restaurant. It should explain how to order and pick up food and beverages. There should be an area that explains how to write and read guest dinner checks. The list is long but important for a successfully run restaurant.

Knowledge about the Restaurant

Guests evaluate service people in two ways: are they friendly, and can they answer questions? Guests will ask many questions. Most of them are legitimate, but others may seem silly. However, they are not silly to the guest.

All of the employees must know the history of the business. For example, questions will be asked concerning the ownership of the restaurant; how long it has existed; and the names and locations of other restaurants in the chain.

Other facts employees should know are the days and hours of operation for their restaurant. If there are any other restaurants on the premises or in the hotel, the employees should know *their* hours of operation, types of food served, the general price range, and the dress code. One section of the manual should outline trivia and historical information about the community and the restaurant. There should be a daily listing stating what events are occurring in the restaurant, hotel, and community.

All of this information is vital for the service persons who must answer questions intelligently and converse with guests. This knowledge demonstrated by the service person will make the guest feel comfortable and confident in the server's ability. Occasionally there will be a question the service person cannot answer, so management should provide a method for service people to obtain the answer. Many establishments compile a fact book that is kept at the host stand or, in a hotel, at the front desk.

Physical Layout of the Restaurant

For the service staff to take orders and deliver food correctly to the guest tables, all employees should receive a floor plan of the dining room. The floor plan should have the size and number of each table in the dining room. The diagram should be planned so that the employees will be able to understand it. Confusion should be kept to a minimum. For example, instead of numbering the tables in a haphazard manner, all tables should be numbered sequentially, as illustrated in Figure 6–1. In the diagram, the first table in row one is assigned the number 10. In each row, the first table is numbered by starting by the number of the row. Therefore, table 40 would be the first table in the fourth row. The remaining tables in each row are numbered sequentially, so table 32 would be the third table in the third row. All tables are Statler tables, which have leaves that can be pulled up to turn them into a table that can seat six guests; or, if the leaves remain down, they can accommodate two to four guests. If a party is larger than six guests, two or three tables can be put together to accommodate everyone. Using this numbering system, communication between the manager, host, and staff is logical. When a large party is scheduled, the host can say to the service person, "Put tables 42, 43, and 44 together for 12 guests." As most dining room tables remain in the same location day after day, the staff will know the location of each table. It is much simpler for a manager to say, "Check table 40 for a problem," than to say, "The guy over at the table by the window has a problem." All employees will know exactly where table 40 is located by memorizing the floor plan.

Some restaurants have tables that are different sizes and shapes to seat their guests. The floor plans for these restaurants should also label

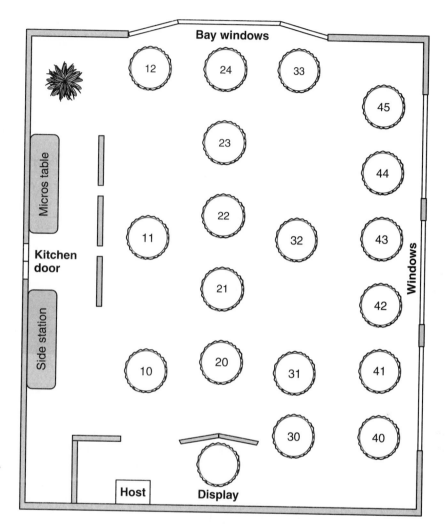

FIGURE 6–1

A numbered, floor-plan diagram. The tables are numbered in a logical pattern to make it easier for the service staff to do their jobs efficiently.

the actual size of the tables. However, most service people are not concerned with the actual size of the table (e.g., 60 inches in diameter); instead they are concerned with how many guests each table seats and must state the number of guests each table seats and must state the number of seats at each table. An easy method for diagramming the sizes and numbers of tables is illustrated in Figure 6–2. Notice that all tables are numbered in the manner described earlier. Some of the table numbers have a circle around them, others have a rectangle, whereas others are drawn at an angle. In addition, some tables are drawn larger in size than the other tables—another helpful visual reminder. By designing the floor plan carefully and making the employees memorize it, service will run more smoothly.

FIGURE 6–2

A numbered, floor-plan diagram. The tables are numbered in a logical pattern to make it easier for the service staff to do their job efficiently. Tables illustrated with a circle, such as table 20, seat from six to eight guests; those with a rectangle, like table 22, seat four guests; and those drawn at an angle, like table 10, seat two guests.

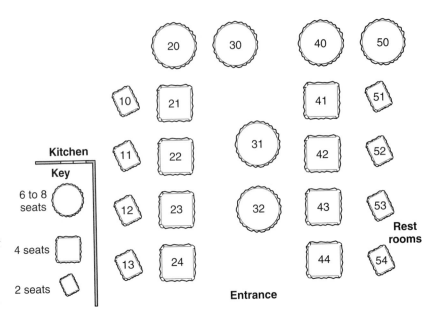

Writing and Reading the Order

The manager should stress to employees the correct way to write and read a guest check. The manager must translate all the menu items into **standard abbreviations**. Each item must have its own abbreviation.

All employees—including kitchen staff—are required to know and use the abbreviations when ordering food from the kitchen or serving food. This is to prevent any confusion. For example, what does *SS* on the check mean? Would the guest receive shrimp scampi, sirloin steak, or swiss steak? Abbreviations are used for all menu items, including accompaniments. For example, *BAK* would mean a baked potato, whereas *BAKy* means that the guest has requested sour cream with the baked potato.

Many times restaurants offer a children's menu. The children's portion would be abbreviated with the letter *C* in front of it. For example, if *SS* means sirloin steak, a *CSS* is a child's portion of sirloin steak.

With the advent of computerized systems, which transmit orders directly to the kitchen, does a service person still need to know the importance of using abbreviations? Yes. It will help the service staff know which guest gets which meal for one thing. Also, in the case of an electronic or computer failure, the service staff should know how to use this method.

Knowledge of the Menu

Many times guests are not familiar with your menu, so they ask the
service person about the entrees. For example, a guest will ask, "What
is the shrimp scampi?" The service person should know the names of
all items, how to pronounce them, and how to describe them. The
training manual should have a description of all menu items. Shrimp
scampi is as follows:

Shrimp Scampi

Pronounced *Shrimp Skamp-ee*
Abbreviation SKP
  Five sized 15/18 shrimp sautéed in garlic butter and served over a
bed of wild and white rice.

All items on the menu should be described in this manner, and the
staff must know all of them before they are allowed to wait on guests.

We often dine at a local, family-run restaurant. One evening we
received a pleasant shock, because the restaurant was short of service
personnel. Our server was the chef–owner. That evening he gave up
his cooking duties and was working as a service person. The pleasant
shock occurred because he knew the ingredients of each menu item
in detail and how they were prepared. His special for the evening—
we believe it should have been called *chef's creation*—was described in
such appealing detail that all three guests ordered the item, which
was the highest priced entrée on the menu; and it lived up to his
description!

Ingredients

Many people are allergic to certain spices and foods. In the description
about the shrimp scampi, the ingredient garlic is mentioned. The
manager should list any spices or ingredients that are predominant in
the recipe. For example, when a guest asks if there are any sulfates in
a food item, they are asking for a specific reason. In addition, the manager should also instruct the service persons to ask the chef about the

ingredients in the food if they do not know them. The service person should not guess about ingredients in food. Guests have gotten ill because a service person guessed rather than knew the ingredients of a dish.

Some people have severe allergic reactions to some foods, spices, additives, or other ingredients. Allergic reactions have killed individuals who unknowingly or accidentally ate a particular food item or ingredient. About 11 million Americans—or about one in 25 people—suffer from a food allergy, with 6.5 million allergic to seafood and 3 million allergic to peanuts or tree nuts, according to the American Academy of Allergy, Asthma and Immunology.[3] Eight foods account for 90 percent of the allergic reactions. They include peanuts, tree nuts (walnuts, pecans, etc.), fish, shellfish, eggs, milk, soy, and wheat. Peanuts are the leading cause of severe allergic reaction, followed by shellfish, fish, tree nuts, and eggs. Most individuals who have had a reaction ate a food that they thought was safe.[4] It was reported in *Nation's Restaurant News* that 30 percent of emergency room visits—and between 150 and 200 deaths per year—are the result of anaphylactic shock.[5]

At Levy Restaurants Bistro 110 in Chicago, executive chef–partner Dominique Tougne created a multipoint food-allergy response system that offers personalized service to his guests. The restaurant, which serves about 700 people daily, typically has at least one customer per day with a food allergy. When a guest informs the service person that they have a food allergy, the staff member alerts the floor manager. The floor manager inquires about the severity of the allergy and asks if the guest carries emergency medication, like an Epi-pen. The manager communicates all this information to the chef. One cook at Bistro 110 is designated to make all food for allergic customers on surfaces that are free from cross-contamination. The cook then personally delivers the dish to the table to insure that it has not been contaminated or switched inadvertently coming from the kitchen.[3]

TIP$

TO INSURE PROPER SERVICE
Make certain your service staff know all the ingredients in menu items (see Figure 6–3).

If your staff do not know the ingredients, the consequences could be serious. The family of Janet Walker of Plaistow, New Hampshire, sued Bertucci's, a Massachusetts restaurant chain, for $10.4 million in Massachusetts state court, claiming the woman was killed by an allergic reaction to Bertucci's pesto sauce. The woman went into a coma

FIGURE 6–3

Having the chef explain particular items is a good way for the service person to learn the menu. (Photograph by Randall Perry)

after she ate part of a chicken pesto sandwich at a Bertucci's in New Hampshire. She died a week later.

Mrs. Walker's lawyer, J. Albert Johnson, said Mrs. Walker specifically asked her waitress if the pesto sauce contained nuts. The waitress allegedly told Mrs. Walker that the sauce contained only basil and other herbs, failing to mention that it also contained walnuts and pine nuts, both of which Mrs. Walker was allergic to.

The lawsuit claimed Bertucci's withheld from the waitstaff a list of the ingredients for the "secret sauce."[6]

Figure 6–4 shows a variety of food presented on a buffet. The service staff should know the names and ingredients of all the foods.

FIGURE 6–4

For a buffet, the service staff must know the names of the items and the ingredients used to make them.

(Photograph by Randall Perry)

Garnishes and Substitutions

In the manual, there should be an area that explains how each food item should be garnished. A diagram or picture of where the garnish is placed and how it looks is helpful. For instance, the manual would state that all hamburger plates are garnished with a leaf of romaine lettuce and an orange slice at the three o'clock position on the plate, as shown in Figure 6–5.

Also in the food item section, should be an explanation of what each guest receives as accompaniments. For example, all beef items will be served with *BAK*.

It is a good idea to use the abbreviations in the manual so that the employees will realize the importance of learning and using them. Of course, management should include in the manual a definition page for all abbreviations.

Finally, this section should state what—if any—the substitutions are for each item. For example, *RIC* (rice) can be substituted for any

Manager's Message and Chef's Choice

(Courtesy of JOYCE SLATER, DINING ROOM MANAGER, AND BARRY CORREIA, EXECUTIVE CHEF/ EXECUTIVE DIRECTOR, CANYON RANCH IN THE BERKSHIRES HEALTH RESORT, LENOX, MASSACHUSETTS)

"At Canyon Ranch, the ingredients are the key component to our signature dishes. The ingredients are the finest quality and some organics. Our servers are well educated to meet the needs of many guests with allergies and special food requests to insure their safety."

—Joyce Slater

"At Canyon Ranch we make knowledge of ingredients a top priority for the waitstaff. Knowing the profile of each dish can make the difference and possibly save someone's life."

—Barry Correia

Since 1979, Canyon Ranch has set the standard for health spas as the quintessential health and fitness choice. At Canyon Ranch a guest can choose from a rich array of programs and services that have made Canyon Ranch the overwhelming best spa choice among readers of *Condé Nast Traveler* magazine throughout the 1990s. Chef Barry and his staff at Canyon Ranch know that taste matters as much as nutrition. He does not serve celery sticks, sprouts, or stuff that tastes like cardboard. Gourmet cooking and the highest nutritional standards are the foundation of every menu item. Menu items range from lobster to lamb chops, chowders, pizza, vegetarian specialties—even hot fudge sundaes and cheesecake. For an autumn season presentation, Chef Barry prepared Butternut Squash and Apple Cider Soup with Cranberry Drops, an Asian Duck Salad, and a Pumpkin Crème Brûlée.

BAK. It is important to have a clearly stated policy for substitutions. Some guests will have a legitimate reason for asking for the substitution; others only do it to get more food for their money. As an example, one customer would always order a hot roast beef sandwich with a special request. The special request was "hot roast beef sandwich with no bread." He felt that when the cook placed the correct amount of beef on the plate without the bread, the entree would look as if there was not enough food on the plate. It was the guest's hope that the cook would replace the bread with additional beef. If service people have questions about what items may be substituted, they should be instructed to ask the person in charge of the restaurant.

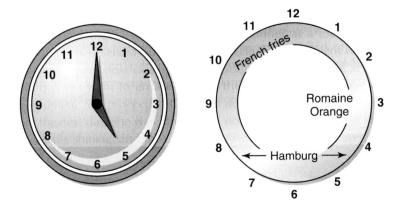

FIGURE 6–5

Diagram of the positions of items on a plate using a clock as a guide.
The hamburger is placed from 4 to 8 o'clock, the French fries from 9 to
1 o'clock, and the romaine and orange at 2 and 3 o'clock, respectively.
When served to the guest, the orange is placed at the 3 o'clock position.

No matter how large or small the restaurant is, if the manager writes out the policies, the guest will receive the same meal and the same answers to the questions regardless of the service person. Most likely, the restaurant will be profitable, because guests will feel comfortable knowing that there is consistency every time they dine at the restaurant. They will not be frustrated because one time they are allowed to substitute *RIC* for *BAK* and the next time they are not.

Cooking Methods

Guests often inquire about terms on the menu that are unfamiliar to them. For instance, a guest may ask the meaning of *sauté*. Each employee should know the more common preparation methods for cooking foods—there are at least 12. This information is also needed in the manual. An example of two cooking methods:

baked—cooked by dry, continuous heat in an oven
sautéed—browned or cooked in a small amount of hot fat

Preparation Time and Cooking Doneness

This is a critical part of the service person's training. Knowing how long it takes to cook an item and knowing what *medium* or *pittsburgh* means is important for ordering and picking up food from the kitchen.

A chart of the cooking times of all menu items should be listed. The chart should range from pittsburgh to well done, with the normal cooking time for each item.

TO INSURE PROPER SERVICE
Knowing the approximate cooking time of an item may make the service person a star to the guest who is in a hurry.

In addition, there should be a description of what the terms for cooking doneness mean. A diagram of all the types of cooking doneness that the chef can prepare is most helpful. For example, a steak ordered medium would be described as having a pink, hot center. One way to cook meat is referred to as *pittsburgh*. A steak done in this manner is raw on the inside and black on the outside. It is cooked by having the cook drop fat onto the fire. This causes a big flame to rise through the grill. The cook chars the outside until it is black; the inside is raw and cold to touch.

Tableside Cooking and Flambé

The authors recognize that some establishments finish cooking off foods at the table or flambé food or drinks for a spectacular effect in the dining room, but this is occurring in fewer restaurants mainly because of liability issues. This book does not include recipes for tableside preparation of Caesar salad, bananas foster, or chateaubriand for two. Our goal is to teach individuals how to be a proper server, not how to prepare these foods. We encourage readers who have an interest in learning how to prepare foods tableside to consult the many cookbooks that address the topic of flambé. However, if the restaurant prepares food tableside, the service follows the seven guidelines of service detailed in Chapter 5.

Alcoholic Beverages

As with the food, there should be a description of every beverage the restaurant has available. In addition, there should be a description of how the drinks are made, the glass the drink is served in, and the proper garnish. The brand names of all wines and beverages must also be included in the section on alcoholic beverages. Here is an example of a drink description:

Margarita
Pronounced *Marg a rita*
Abbreviation MARG

Made with tequila, triple sec, lemon, and lime. Served in a fiesta grande, straight up ( ) or on the rocks (v). Garnished with salt around the rim of the glass and served with a lime wheel.

Glasses

There should be a diagram or a picture of all the glasses used for drinks. Beneath the picture should be the name of the drink served in the glass. There should also be a description of the glass. For example, a *fiesta grande* glass would be described as a "16¾-ounce glass used for all frozen margaritas."

Pricing

Because menus are constantly being changed, a separate price sheet should be distributed with current prices. Owing to the fluctuation of prices, putting prices into the manual would be a waste of time and money. The prices will most likely change more often than any other information in the manual. When done on a separate sheet, the manager only has to print the new prices instead of the entire manual.

Tasting the Food and Beverage

This is another part of the training for the service staff that must be continuous. However, many restaurant managers refuse to let their staff taste the food. Instead, they serve them an employee meal each evening. The feeling is that it is too expensive to serve it to the staff. In reality, it is too expensive *not* to serve it to the staff. The guests are going to ask the service person how the food tastes. If they have never been allowed to sample the food, how will your service staff know what to tell the guests? The service staff should taste all food and beverage items as soon as it is practical. This does not mean that each night, the service staff should have a gourmet meal; but they must taste the food that they will be recommending and serving to their guests. One way of accomplishing this is by having meetings where service staff sample the menu items. Another way is for management to encourage service staff to dine with their families at the restaurant by offering employees and their families a discount.

Once employees have mastered the knowledge of the restaurant and menu by the testing criteria set up, it is time for them to move on to the second part: serving the meal.

Sweet or Sour?

At a restaurant, you are asked by the service person if you want a salad. You reply, "Yes." The service person says, "And what would you like on your salad?" That's it: That's all they say. They figure you must be a mind reader. The next time someone says that to you, reply "Poppy seed vinaigrette" or some other made-up salad dressing, and watch the expression on the person's face!

Merchandising Food and Beverage

Merchandising food and beverage is another term for *selling*. Selling occurs because the guest feels confident in the service person's ability.

Training should be done by placing the service staff in common situations that occur daily in the restaurant. This is called *role playing*. For instance, have service staff ask the "guests" what type of salad dressing they want, using the example of the problem stated earlier.

The service person should assess the mood of the guests as they approach the table. Are they celebrating and in a festive mood, or do they appear somber, as if they have just returned from a funeral? Once the service person has assessed the situation, the server's behavior should be appropriate.

Each guest deserves and expects a warm, sincere greeting. If the staff person knows the guest, the guest should be addressed by name. Furthermore, staff should acknowledge the presence of the guest immediately, and take care of any requests as soon as possible. This will make the guest feel as though the restaurant appreciates the patronage and will help make the dining experience a positive one.

Assisting the Guest with the Order

Many times guests will know exactly what food they wish to order; other times they cannot make up their minds. There is a trick that experienced service people use to sell items and help guests make up their minds. If guests are asked for their order and they hesitate, count backwards from seven. If the guests have not made up their minds by the time the server reaches zero, then they need help, which opens it up for the service staff to do some suggestive selling.

Suggestive Selling

The first step in **suggestive selling** is having the guests feel confident in the service person's knowledge. Once this happens, the guests will respond to the service person's suggestions. The guests now trust the service person's knowledge and judgment. He or she has answered all the guests' questions about the restaurant, told them what is happening in the area, and is perceived to be knowledgeable.

The next question the guests usually ask is, "What's good on the menu?" "Everything" is a poor response. Instead, train your staff to turn the question around and ask the guests what type of food they like: fish, chicken, or beef? The service person may then describe a meal that tastes and looks great based upon their preference. This is the main reason why employees should be required to taste all items on the menu: they are then able to describe how the food tastes and can base their recommendations on what the guest desires.

Sweet or Sour?

⌣⌣

After the server stated the soup special, a guest asked how it was. The reply: "It's OK." No orders of soup were sold at that table!

The key to suggestive selling is for the service person to keep a positive attitude. Staff must put themselves in their guests' place, then use mouth-watering descriptions of the menu item for the purpose of selling the item. The service person should never say, "Would anyone care for dessert?" Instead, servers should describe the desserts available in tantalizing detail.

Sweet or Sour?

♫♫ ♫♫

A typical suggestive selling job occurred when a veteran waiter was removing the dinner plates at the end of the meal. While he was crumbing the table, he said, "May I get you coffee?" As soon as the guests said "Yes," he added, "By the way, if you like chocolate, I tasted our great, new, decadent dessert, the triple chocolate cake. I'll be back with your coffee and a dessert menu." The service person had obtained the guests' trust, and he put the idea of a specific dessert in their minds. They all ordered dessert.

If a service person does not suggest desserts, or merely asks the guests if they care to see a dessert menu, too often the answer is "No." By suggesting a specific dessert and using mouth-watering descriptions, the rate of success at selling desserts will be greatly enhanced.

Another technique used by experienced salespeople is to suggest *last* the item they wish to sell. This is because people usually remember the last thing said to them.

Suggestive selling can build the profits for the restaurant by encouraging guests to order extra items that they normally would not have ordered. It also builds up the check total; and as most guests tip on the total bill, the tip for the service person increases.

Sweet or Sour?

We dined at the California Grill in the Contemporary Hotel at Walt Disney World in Florida. Our waiter was a true professional. His service, as well as his suggestive selling, set a standard—both in competency and friendliness. When he first approached the table, he greeted us, inquired if we had been at the restaurant before, and told us his name. After we answered that we had never dined at the California Grill, he proceeded to explain the type of food served there with pride. He explained that the restaurant prides itself in offering superb California wines by the glass and by the bottle. He then explained the items on the menu to us using descriptive words and telling us which items were his favorite and why. Of course, his two favorite meals and his two favorite appetizers just happened to be the most expensive items on the menu. But because he was so sincere—or at least appeared to be—and due to the fact that all the selections he suggested appealed to both of us, we ordered them.

He then suggested that we have wine with the meal. "But," he said, "instead of having a bottle, because one of you is having duck and the other filet of beef, why don't you have wines by the glass?" He said, "Let me bring you over some to try." Over he came with six wine glasses. He poured a sample for us to try in the first glass. We tried it, and he informed us of the name. He also did this for selections two and three. In doing this, he gave us three choices, all different prices and styles. We chose four different glasses of wines, which were much more expensive in total than if we had bought one bottle. We were pleased with our selections of food and wine. The waiter had made it a pleasurable experience by suggesting—and even letting us sample—different wines.

After dessert, he brought the check over. Instead of just placing it on the table and walking away, he first shook both our hands and thanked us for coming in and dining at the California Grill. He used the knowledge that a Cornell University study discovered: When a wait person touches the guest, their tip increases by 29 percent.[7] Even though we paid the most money we have ever paid for one glass of wine, we felt that our experience was phenomenal, thanks to our waiter.

The Special of the Day

What is the special of the day? Whether you are shopping in a supermarket or department store, a special means reduced prices. Does a special in the restaurant mean reduced prices? Not necessary. It usually means a special item prepared by the chef with a special price. In some cases it is priced lower, or "best buy," and in other areas it is higher than a normal menu item.

A manager might do well to change the name of the special of the day to the **chef's creation**. Then the service staff can approach the table and explain the chef's creation to the guests. Should the service staff be instructed to inform the guests of the price of the chef's creation?

In an Ann Landers column, a reader wrote in for advice about etiquette in a restaurant. The reader stated that service people rattle off the specials of the day, and although they all sound wonderful, they don't tell you the price. When the bill comes, it is a lot higher than if you had ordered from the menu. Would you buy a shirt or blouse without knowing the price?

No one has ever satisfactorily explained why prices are not given when a special item is offered. In keeping with the premise of this book—that the restaurant's job is to please the guests—the service staff must recite the prices to the guests. This is another positive factor that builds trust between server and guest. Another annoying custom is for restaurants to instruct their service staff to offer an item—such as blue cheese dressing—and state it is *à la carte*. Most guests have no idea what *à la carte* means. The service staff should inform the guests the price of all items.

Sweet or Sour?

St. Patrick's Day: A time for a traditional Irish meal. The waitperson approached the table and informed us of the specials of the day. "Our chef has prepared Irish lamb stew for $6.95; corned beef and cabbage for $7.95. We also have a sirloin steak available tonight." I thought to myself, the sirloin sounds really good, but something is strange here. I then asked her the price of the sirloin. Her answer: $22.00. *That* price certainly was special!

Wine, Dessert Tables, Gimmicks

Other techniques may assist the service staff in selling additional items. These are usually associated with wine and dessert sales.

More and more restaurants include wine glasses at the place setting. Others sell a sample, two-ounce portion of wine to the guests. Still others put a bottle of unopened wine on each table to encourage guests to order wine with their meal.

Desserts provide the opportunity to increase sales enormously. Even though the American public is becoming more nutrition conscious and eating lighter meals, survey after survey have found that guests will order desserts. Many restaurants display their desserts so that guests can view them before they begin their meal. This technique has been used successfully by many restaurants for merchandising desserts. If the desserts are kept attractive and eye-appealing, the guest will be more apt to order dessert. However, if the cart or table becomes messy and unappetizing, it does the restaurant more harm than good.

Another excellent way to merchandise desserts is to bring out a sample tray of all the desserts. The service person brings the trays to the guests' table and describes the desserts to them. This method eliminates the problem of the desserts looking unattractive, because the desserts on the tray are not served to the guests. Instead, the service person obtains the desserts from the kitchen. As soon as a dessert on the tray looks unappealing, it is replaced.

One of the best selling gimmicks—one that has been used for ages—is initiated by the manager. If done properly, it can increase sales and repeat business dramatically. It involves the manager giving away an item that will call attention to that item. For example, a restaurant sells flaming coffee. The manager should approach a table in the center of the dining room, where other guests can see the coffee being prepared. The manager should introduce herself to the guests, inquire about their meal, thank them for their business, and offer to buy them an after dinner coffee. Once the coffee is being prepared, all the eyes in the dining room are attracted to the coffee presentation. This display will encourage other guests to order the coffee after their meals. This can be done with a fancy dessert, a large glass of beer, or any type of fancy entree. The cost of this to the restaurant is the cost of the item. In addition, the guest will feel special, because the manager gave away an item (back to Maslow's hierarchy).

The manager must encourage the service staff to sell extra items, since the guests have already made the decision to patronize the restaurant. With suggestive selling, the service staff can increase profits for the restaurant. However, one word of caution: The manager must make certain that the service staff do not push so hard that the guests become upset with their selling aggressiveness and have a bad dining experience.

Taking the Order

Training your staff to take a guest's food and beverage order correctly is critical. There are many correct ways to take the order. All of them should have one goal: to serve the meal to the guest without having to ask who gets what.

The manager should teach the service staff how to talk to the guests and how to take meal orders. The staff should not be allowed to say to the guest, "Whadda ya want?" instead of "May I take your order?" Avoid addressing guests as "hon," "doll," "fella," "you guys," and other words that could be interpreted as derogatory. The staff should be encouraged to address people by their names: always by the last name, unless the guests tell the service people to call them by their first names. A study by Garrity and Dagelman discovered that when waitpersons introduce themselves by name to their guests, their tips increase by 53 percent.[8]

The manager must impress upon the service staff that they should treat the guests as if they had never dined at the restaurant before. They do not know how the specials are prepared or what salad dressings are available. It must be impressed upon the service staff that this will be the first time the guest hears the specials. Even though the service staff may have repeated them 100 times that evening, employees should be taught to explain every item to each guest.

The manager must train staff to explain in detail the chef's creation of the evening. When it is time to offer the guest the choice of salad dressings or vegetables, explain what they are. Rather than let the staff say, "And what would you like on your salad?" encourage them to say something like: "A salad is included in the meal. Our choice of dressings are: blue cheese; Russian; Italian; and our house dressing, which is a sweet and sour dressing made with mustard and honey." The same should be true for vegetables, potatoes, and chef creations, especially if the item is new or is not normally served in the area where your restaurant is located. Included in the explanation can be the ingredients, how it is prepared, and the price.

Finally, the order should be repeated back to the guest. By doing this, your service staff will avoid any misunderstandings of guest orders. However, the method used should not be annoying to the guests. For instance, a service person who echoes every single item that the guest orders will be annoying. It is much better to wait until the complete order is taken, then repeat the main course back to the guest. Should one guest change his order, the service person, in order to avoid a misunderstanding, could say, "Your final choice was _____" or "Am I clear that you wanted _____?"

The job of the service staff should not be just to serve the food but to be the human link between the kitchen and the guest. This is why the importance of verbal communication between the service staff and the guest must be stressed. It gives the restaurant personality.

Where to Stand

There are two opinions on where the service persons should be standing when they take the guests' order. Both agree that order taking should follow the proper guidelines of service: children first, then women, then men. There is an exception: when one person is the host of the party and he or she is ordering for the entire table.

The first method states that the service person should stand to the left of the guest and take the order, then move to the next person, following the proper guidelines of service. The problem with this method is that if the service person takes the order by following proper guidelines, it may be necessary to skip over one male guest to take the next female's order. The service person will then have to return to the man, and move back and forth, creating much unnecessary confusion.

The second method is to have the service person stand in one spot and take all the guests' orders from that spot, following the proper guidelines of service. This works well at a table with two to four guests. However, for more than four guests, especially with rectangular-shaped tables, the service person may have to move to different spots to hear the order. More restaurants are having their waitperson move next to the guest when taking the order and squat, which allows the waitperson to make eye contact with the guest. Also, the tip will increase by $1.00 according to a Cornell University study.[9]

Whichever method is used, the management should set guidelines for their own restaurant, keeping in mind that guests should be served smoothly and efficiently.

86ed Items

The term **86ed** in the restaurant business means to be out of an item. When a restaurant sells all of its orders of prime ribs, the chef will tell the service staff, "Ribs are 86ed." Before a service person takes a dinner order from guests, they should know what items are 86ed. Managers must set up a system that provides a list of 86ed items to the service staff, through oral communication or a blackboard. The manager should train his chef and kitchen staff to inform the service staff when there are ten servings of a particular entree left. The service staff will then be able to inform the guest that they think that the dinner item is available, but will have to check with the kitchen. This will avoid embarrassing the service person and annoying the guest. It is a bad situation to have the guest decide on shrimp scampi, have the service person take the order, and then come back to say, "I'm sorry we are out of the shrimp, what would you care for now?" It gets even more annoying to have the guest then decide on another item, only to find that the kitchen is out of that too. Who will make the third trip to the table to tell the guest?

86ed

This phrase, according to the show *Secret Passages* on the History Channel, comes from the prohibition of selling alcohol in the United States. During Prohibition there was a speakeasy (a restaurant that served alcohol illegally) named Chumley's in New York City. Its location was identified by its address, number 86. When police raids occurred at Chumley's, the patrons would throw their illegal alcoholic beverages away. To warn the guests of the raid, 86 was yelled out. That is how this term has been incorporated into the hospitality industry.

Home Base

Many of you have experienced the auction game. The service person comes to the table with two dinners and asks "Who's the beef and who's the shrimp?" It sounds funny, but it can be embarrassing and insulting. This should never happen, but it happens frequently in those restaurants that use food runners. The most common way of taking orders to avoid this is referred to as the *home base* system.

The system works in the following manner: The manager decides on one focal point in the restaurant as the home base. It may be a clock, the kitchen door, or some other easily observable item in the restaurant. Management has all the tables numbered. At each table, chair one is the one closest to home base; the other chairs are numbered clockwise so that there is no confusion. Confusion could occur because of a table placed at an angle to home base. Once every staff person knows the location of chair one, this allows any staff member to serve food or drinks to the guests without having to ask who gets what item. Figure 6–6 and Figure 6–7 illustrate how this system works and shows home base at a four-top with only two guests at the table. In Figure 6–7, using the clock as home base, chair *A* would be the first chair.

Order Forms

Once staff know where the home base is, the next procedure the manager must teach them is how to write the guest orders. The system must be explained simply enough so that any employee who picks up

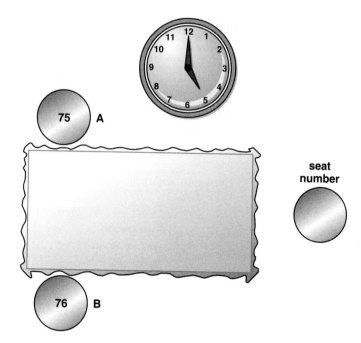

FIGURE 6–6

Using the clock as home base, the seat closest to the clock is chair one. Seat A is chair one.

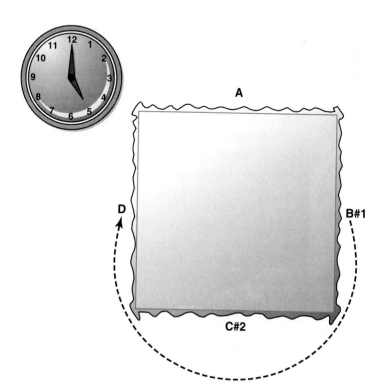

FIGURE 6–7

Using the clock as home base, seat A still remains chair one, even though no guest is seated in seat A.

the food order can deliver it to the guests without having to ask who gets what.

Each person should be provided with a standard form with which to take orders. The service person must be organized; but it is up to the manager to devise this policy in such a way that all employees will know who gets what item. Some managers, in addition to using the home base system, will have their staff put an X next to the seat number of the women. This is a variation on the system called *code order*.

Here is an example of a guest's order form:

Order Form

Table Number 49   **Time 7:02**

Seat	D	App	MC	Sal	Pot	Veg
1	ws	sc	ss	bc	b	gb
2x	ws	os	NYS	it	m	c

In the above example, the woman is seated at seat 2. By putting an X next to her number, all employees will know that an X means a woman is seated there. Because all employees know the standard abbreviations, this form can be used by all staff. The time and table number are also on the form to tell the service person what time the order was taken. This form can be expanded to include desserts and after-dinner drinks; however, it would be preferable to use a new form for these items. Across the top of the form is *D*, which stands for before-dinner drink; *App* is for appetizer; *MC* is for main course; *Sal* is for salad; *Pot* is for potato; and *Veg* is for vegetable. Because more restaurants are using computerized systems, the manager would be wise to institute this system. The computer system provides for the food order to be transmitted directly to the kitchen, without the service person's entering the kitchen. The printer is programmed to print orders based upon cooking time with the longest item to cook shown first. Even though the computer system relays the order to the kitchen, when it is ready, the restaurant has to have a system in place for the employees to know what guest gets what food item.

Ordering on the Guest Check

Some restaurants use a system that has the guest check remain at the table, in a slot provided in each table. The duplicate check or **dupe** is brought into the kitchen to order the food. The guest check can have the system for who gets what directly written on the check. The service staff will write the check in the following manner: The seat immediately to the left of the slot is the number one seat. Going in a clockwise direction, the seats are numbered consecutively. The management arranges the tables so that the slots are always in the same position relative to home base.

On the bottom of the check, the server writes in the table number and the last three digits of the check. This information appears on the dupe that is turned or transmitted to the kitchen. An example of a check follows:

Sect 5					245667
Chair				Food	Bar
1	NY	mr	Xs	24.95	
2	Rib	end m	BQ	25.95	
3	Smp +S	r	p	20.95	
4	FsOs	m	1p	26.95	
	Amarone 1–4 (3)				45.00
2	Bq2,4			8.50	
1	mk 3			4.95	
2	c cho 1,3			7.00	
2	wit 2,4				4.50
1	vo w 1				4.25
1	jb v 3				4.25
26/667					

An Explanation of the Check

This check combines many different techniques for taking orders. The service staff must know what all items and abbreviations on the check mean. Working from the bottom of the check up, the 26 represents the table number. Since the staff know the layout of the restaurant, they will all know where table 26 is located.

The last three digits of check number 245667 are represented by the 667. Any person who picks up the food in the kitchen will know that the food will be delivered to table 26. Once the food is placed at table 26, the staff member can verify that it is the same check by comparing the last three numbers on the dupe with the guest check in the slot at the table. If there is a problem at table 26, such as food not being served quickly enough, the manager can go into the kitchen and check on the status of the dupe.

The *1 jb v 3* for $4.25 means that there is one order of J & B scotch served with Vichy to the guest in seat number 3 for $4.25. The server can see that it is a drink because the price is listed under the bar column.

Reading up the check, the first food item is the *2 c cho 1,3* for $7.00. This means that there are two orders of clam chowder served to the guests at seats 1 and 3. The total price of $7.00 ($3.50 each) is placed under the food column.

Continuing up the check to the *Amarone 1-4(3)*, the service staff knows that the table ordered one bottle of this red wine, with four glasses. The *(3)* means that the guest seated in seat 3 ordered the wine.

Above the line, the ordering is different. The chair numbers are written, and then the entrees are ordered. For instance, the guest seated in chair 1 is to receive a *NY mr Xs* for $24.95. Translated, this means a New York sirloin, cooked medium rare and a baked potato (*x*) with sour cream (*s*).

These are two methods for writing guest orders and determining who gets what order. There are other methods, but they all have one thing in common: they are set up in an organized manner that can be easily learned. The key is to have the manager decide on one system and have all of the staff use only that system.

Code Order

Another system for determining who gets what is the *code order*. This system is not recommended, because too much confusion and embarrassment can result. The code order system was used in the past when a single service person was responsible for the station. The service person would write next to the order a code to identify the guest. The code would represent some distinguishing feature that made one guest stand out from another, such as a blue tie or red hair. This system can create problems because not all the service staff would understand the system. It also could be embarrassing if the service person used a code that was derogatory toward the guest, such as fat, bald, or grey.

Placing Orders in the Kitchen

Correct ordering in the kitchen is a must for guests to receive their dinner cooked and served properly. Since the service staff know the time it takes to cook every item, they should submit their orders based on the mood of the guests and how long it will take to cook the meal. In most restaurants, the time to submit the order is when the service person picks up the guests' salad from the kitchen. In restaurants with a salad bar, the service person is instructed to turn the order in to the kitchen when the guests go to obtain their salads from the salad bar. However, each manager can determine what works best.

One of the critical parts of placing orders in the kitchen is controlled by the phrase **fire the table**. When the service person tells the kitchen staff to "fire table three" that phrase informs the kitchen that it is time to start cooking the main course for table three. Before leaving the kitchen, the service person must receive an acknowledgement that the command was heard.

Depending on the system used, the service people may be required to order all entrees at top of the check. They may put all the cold items at the bottom. Others may have a computerized system that prints all the orders in a priority based on cooking times. It does not matter how it is done, as long as all members of the staff use common abbreviations and the same system.

Serving the Meal: Timing Is Everything

Timing is a critical part of the meal. If the meal is served incorrectly, the dining experience can be ruined. Suppose the server has ordered the meal correctly, it has been cooked properly, and the kitchen is waiting for the service person to serve it to the guest in the dining room. But instead of being picked up and delivered to the guest, it sits in the kitchen, becoming colder and less appetizing. Timing is of the essence, and staff must get the meal to the table as soon as it is ready. If dinners sit too long, the quality suffers, and the guests become impatient.

More and more restaurants are using electronic means to notify the service person that the meal is ready. These electronic devices may include a light system, a vibrating beeper, or other methods. Some restaurants use the food-runner system. As soon as the food is ready, it should be brought to the table. But before doing so, the person responsible for delivering the food should take a few seconds to check that all the food items on the dupe match those that have been prepared by the kitchen. He or she must also check to see that all special instructions on the dupe have been followed. The tray will be loaded by placing the cold items first then the hot items. Hot items should be placed on the tray last so that they will not cool off fast. The food on the tray should be arranged to serve the guests in the most efficient manner. Any condiments and garnishes should be brought to the guests' table along with the entrees.

Sequence of a Typical Meal: Team System

The sequence for serving a typical meal using the team system is as follows:

1. All the sidework has been completed, and the service staff are prepared to receive their guests. Staff know the chef features of the day and what items are 86ed. They have their guest checks and duplicate order forms to take orders.
2. Guests are seated by the host and presented with food and wine menus. Chef features are recited or given out using a chef-feature menu printed daily.
3. The Lead approaches the table, greets the guests in a friendly manner, answers questions about the menu, and offers to take drink or wine orders.
4. Drinks are written on the check and the order form using the system that has been taught to all service staff. In the team system, the check never leaves the table; it is placed back into the slot in the table.
5. Drinks are served on a cocktail napkin in the center of the setting. If the setting has a show or starter plate, the drink is placed on center with the starter plate. All drinks are served from the right side of the guest with the service person's right hand.
6. The food order is taken by the Lead, who merchandises additional items. After the order is taken, the menus are collected by the Lead.
7. The order is placed on a duplicate check which the Lead holds until it is time to turn it in to the kitchen to order the food.
8. The Aid picks up the appetizer (first course) from the kitchen and serves it to the guests. When an appetizer is served and there has not been a piece of flatware included in the cover for an appetizer, flatware is brought with the food. For example, if a bowl of soup is served, the soup is served from the left side with the left hand, and the soup spoon is placed on the right side of the guest. Staff should not reach across the front of the guests, but walk behind them to put the spoon in its proper location.
9. Rolls and butter are served by the Aid, who places them in the center of the table.
10. The first course is removed from the guest's right side with the Aid's right hand.
11. In the absence of a salad bar salad is served. If a guest requests salad dressing on the side, it is placed in a separate container and served on a bread-and-butter plate, called an **underliner**. The

salad is placed in the center of the place setting or on the starter plate.

12. When salads are served, the Lead turns the check in to the kitchen for the food to be cooked.

13. Wine is served at this point, unless it was served as soon as it was requested. The Lead shows the label to the person who ordered the wine. Once the guest verifies that this is the desired wine, the Lead opens the bottle and presents the cork to the guest. The guest should feel the cork—it should be wet—to determine if the wine was stored properly. The Lead then pours about an ounce into the glass of the guest. Once the guest approves the wine, the Lead pours the wine into the glasses of the other guests, using proper serving techniques. Glasses of red wine should be filled half full; white, three-quarters full. The bottle of red wine is placed on the table, whereas the white wine should be placed in an ice bucket.

14. Salad plates are removed, as well as the starter plate. If guests tell the service staff that they would like to finish their salad with the meal, the staff person should move it to the left of the place setting.

15. When the food order is ready, the kitchen informs the Aid to pick up food by following whatever system is used for informing service staff when the food is ready to be served.

16. The entree is picked up in the kitchen. The plates are placed in the order written on the duplicate check. The Aid compares the food to the duplicate check. If any mistakes are found, they are corrected immediately. It is the responsibility of the person picking up the food to make certain that the plate is appealing, complete, and the proper temperature.

17. Before food is served to guests, the service person makes certain that plates are the proper temperature, attractive (no gravy or juices slopped on the rim of the plate), and garnished correctly.

18. All entrees are brought to the table simultaneously. If the service person has more entrees than can fit on the tray, another service person carries out the remaining food. All guests receive their food at approximately the same time; no one has to wait while the service person returns to the kitchen to pick up the additional meals.

19. The entree is served without asking who gets what. If vegetables or potatoes are served in a side dish—called monkey dishes—they are placed above and near the main entree dish. Staff never put one course in front of the guest before the previous course has been removed. If a guest had not finished eating her salad when the service person remove the other salad dishes, her salad dish is removed before her entree is placed in front of her.

20. Condiments that accompany the main courses—such as sour cream, catsup, and so on—are placed on the guests' table.

21. All meat items are placed in front of the guest with the meatiest part facing the guest, so when the guest cuts the meat, she cuts into the most tender part. If starch and vegetables are served on the same plate, they are placed farthest from the guest.

22. As soon as all entrees are served, the service person checks the table to determine if more rolls and butter are needed or if more wine is to be poured, and the server then inquires if there is anything else that the guests would like.

23. Throughout the meal, the Lead checks the tables to determine if guests need more drinks. In order to save time, the Lead learns to take more than one table's order at a time. Then the Lead can order 10 or 12 drinks at once instead of having to make four separate trips back and forth.

24. The service staff check back at the table as soon as the guests have sampled their food to inquire if the food is done to their satisfaction. The question is not, "Is everything okay here?" because that assumes that it is not. Instead, it is "Is the steak cooked the way you ordered it?" Any problems are taken care of immediately. Food is returned to the kitchen and recooked if is is not done well enough. If food is done too well, the service person informs the guest that it will take extra time to cook the meal over and offers an alternative item that is already prepared and can be served immediately, such as prime ribs.

25. Once the guests inform the Follow-up that the food is done to their satisfaction, the guest check is flipped over so that the other members of the team can see that the table has been checked.

26. The service staff returns to the table to pour extra wine and water throughout the meal. Water glasses are filled as soon as they are half empty.

27. Plates are removed as soon as all guests have finished eating their meals. The staff can determine this as guests put their utensils across their dinner plates or push their dinner plates away from them when finished.

28. If any guests have not finished their main course, an inquiry is made to determine if the guests would like to have the remainder of the meal wrapped so that they may take it home. If the answer is "Yes," the server takes one plate at a time to the sidestand to wrap the leftover food and bring it back to the guest. This eliminates having the guest question whether the food they have received is their own. The service people bring wrapping

material with them when they are preparing to clear the dirty dishes.

29. The staff remove all the dirty dishes, including bread baskets, bread-and-butter plates, butter plates, dirty glasses, and wine glasses.

30. The service staff crumb the table with either the sidetowel or a crumbing device. The crumbs are swept onto a bread-and-butter plate.

31. The staff inquire if the guests would like coffee or tea. They merchandise dessert by using descriptive words, such as "our delicious triple chocolate dessert."

32. Coffee is served by the service person using a coffee shield. Tea is served by placing the teapot above the coffee cup. Cream, sugar, and lemon are served with tea and coffee.

T I P $

To Insure Proper Service

Always tell the guest which coffee cup is the decaf. Don't make a mistake, because if you serve regular coffee to a person who wanted decaf, he will be awake all night! Also, there are people who have been advised by their doctors not to drink regular coffee.

33. Dessert is served to the guests. If one dessert is ordered for two people, bring two forks. If the dessert is gigantic, inform the guest and bring extra plates and flatware for other guests to share the dessert.

34. The staff serve second and third cups of coffee and tea before the guests have to ask for additional beverages. Once the dirty entree dishes have been cleared and the coffee and dessert have been served, the meal is not over! The guests deserve as much attention at the end of the meal as they received at the beginning of the meal.

35. The check is presented to the guests. If the staff cannot determine who is the host of the party, they place the check face down in the center of the table.

36. When the guests pay the bill, they are thanked for their patronage and encouraged to return.

37. After the guests leave, the staff reset the table for the next party.

38. Throughout the meal, the service staff are always thinking of ways to save time. They never go into the kitchen empty-handed or come out empty-handed, and they are attuned to when and how to change the ashtrays.

The preceding illustrates a typical sequence of serving a meal using the team system; however, this typical meal will work with any system. Depending upon the restaurant's menu, steps may be changed to fit the individual needs of the operation.

Sequence of a Typical Meal: Individual Waitperson System

The sequence for serving a typical meal using an individual waitperson system follows many of the same steps as the team system. The system is as follows:

1. All the sidework has been completed and service staff are prepared to receive their guests. The service staff know the chef features of the day and what items are 86ed. They have their guest checks and duplicate order forms to take orders. In restaurants that have a computerized system, they have signed in using their identification number.

2. Guests are seated by the host and presented with food and wine menus. Chef features are recited or given out using a chef-feature menu printed daily.

3. The waitperson approaches the guests, greets them in a friendly manner, answers questions about the menu, and offers to take drink or wine orders.

4. Drinks are served from the guest's right side with the service person's right hand.

5. If the guest requests coffee or tea, cups and saucers are brought to the table, along with cream and sugar. Coffee is served from the guest's right side with the service person's right hand. The service person uses a coffee shield—a bread-and-butter plate—held in the left hand. This shield is placed between the guest and the coffee cup to protect the guest. A teapot is brought to the table with hot water, a lemon wedge, and a selection of teas.

6. If wine is ordered, the waitperson brings the bottle to the table and presents the bottle to the person who has ordered the wine, called the *host*. The host inspects the label of the wine to make certain that the bottle is what was ordered. The waitperson opens the bottle, asks who would like to sample the wine, and pours a small amount into the glass of that guest. Once approval is granted, the remaining guests' glasses are filled. Glasses for red wines are filled half full and those for white wines are filled three-quarters full. White wine is placed in an ice bucket; red wine is placed on the table. In some restaurants the wine is moved away from the table

to a sidestand. Throughout the meal, the waitperson continues to pour wine with the right hand from the guest's right side.

7. The order is taken from each guest using the system that has been taught to all service staff. The order is either brought into the kitchen—for those restaurants that do not have computers—or it is entered into the computerized point-of-sale system.

8. The appetizers are picked up from the kitchen when ready. All soups and pasta bowls are served with underliners. The waitperson has condiments and other items, like peppermills and cheese grinders, on the tray.

9. Appetizers are served from the guest's left side with the service person's left hand. Before serving any dishes, the service person wipes any spills with the side towel. If plates are hot, the service person uses the side towel. The guest should always be told when a plate is hot.

10. When guests are three-quarters of the way done with their appetizers, notify the kitchen. This is referred to as *firing the table*. For example, the waitperson will come into the kitchen and say, "fire up table 10." Before leaving the kitchen, be certain that the kitchen acknowledges that the command was heard.

11. Clear appetizers from the table when all the guests are finished eating. Plates are cleared from the guest's right side with the service person's right hand.

12. All used and unused utensils for that course are removed. Crumb the table with a crumber or folded side towel and a bread-and-butter plate. Replace any used utensil with clean ones before returning to the kitchen to pick up the food.

13. The entree is picked up from the kitchen. The food is served from the guest's left side using the left hand. The meat on the plate should be placed at the 6 o'clock position in front of the guest.

14. Give the guests a few minutes to try their food. Return to the table and inquire if you may get the guest anything else. Correct any situations that are not acceptable.

15. Refill all beverages, bread, and butter as needed.

16. Clear the entrees when all guests are finished. Plates are cleared from the guest's right side with the service person's right hand. All used and unused utensils for that course are removed. Remove bread and butter, salt and pepper, and any remaining condiments.

17. Crumb the table with a crumber or folded side towel and a plate.

18. Dessert choices are presented, either with a menu or by showing the desserts to the guests.

19. Dessert orders are taken.

20. Dessert orders are placed in the kitchen or entered into the POS system.
21. Desserts are served from the guest's left side with the service person's left hand.
22. Refill coffee and tea.
23. Total the guest check, bring it to the table, and place it in the center of the table. Inform guests that you will take the check when they are ready to pay.
24. Bring check and payment to the cashier.
25. Unless the guest gives the waitperson the exact amount of the check, return to the table with the change. If the guest has paid with a credit card, return the guest's credit card and have the guest sign the credit card voucher.
26. When the waitperson is finished serving the guests, thank the guests for patronizing the restaurant and invite them to return for another dining experience.[10]

TIP$

TO INSURE PROPER SERVICE
When removing dirty plates, always pick the utensils up off the plate before the plate is removed. Observe which utensils have been removed and replace them with clean ones.

Computerized Systems

There are many computer systems designed to make a restaurant more efficient. Some of these **point-of-sale (POS) systems** allow the server to transmit the order directly to the kitchen with a hand-held electronic order pad. Other systems have computer terminals throughout the dining room to allow waitstaff to enter information for the kitchen. Such systems are a benefit for the guests, servers, and management.

Traditional face-to-face service is being transformed by technology. The *Wall Street Journal* reports that at the Stinking Rose in San Francisco, waiters record orders on a hand-held computer. With the push of a button, the order is sent to the kitchen, where it is printed out for the chef. This wireless ordering shaves as much as 10 minutes off a meal. "We can handle more diners at night, because everything comes out faster," says Edward Saravia, the restaurant's general manager. And each waiter now handles a dozen tables a shift—twice the load handled before adopting the hand-held devices.[11]

Other restaurants are using electronics to better address customer tastes. With technology becoming more affordable, independent restaurants can compete with chain operations. For instance, the Chili's chain, owned by Brinker International, has instituted a frequent-diner program. When a guest makes a purchase at a Chili's, credits are placed toward free meals or prizes. The same type of program has been put in place in independent restaurants.

New computer technology is changing the restaurant industry. We recommend that readers keep their eyes and ears open to the changes that will be a direct result of this new technology. For example, some restaurants are having guests settle their checks right at the table. Guests swipe their debit cards, put in their personal identification number, and take their receipt—all without the card leaving the table.[12] This will stop the practice of dishonest service people who change or increase the amount of the tip on the credit card receipt after the guest leaves the restaurant. This actually happened to us. After receiving an excellent meal but only mediocre service, we left a 15 percent tip, which amounted to $10.00. On our American Express bill, the tip had been changed to $20.00. We had no way of knowing that the tip was changed because we never saw the final dollar amount entered into the computer.

Another bit of new technology reported in *Nation's Restaurant News* is a wireless device being used at the Fatz Café in Rock Hill, South Carolina. When a guest needs to summon a service person for anything, they simply page the service person through the device. The service person wears a wrist device that flashes and vibrates to tell the service person where they are needed.[13]

Step-by-Step Method of Using a MICROS System

All computer systems work by using a logical system. Each POS computer system has its own unique characteristics. The following illustrates the steps a waitperson uses to enter orders and close out checks using a **MICROS** system.

A. At the beginning of the shift the waitperson clocks in.
    1. Press [CLOCK IN/OUT].
    2. Enter the identification number assigned to you by your manager or swipe your MICROS card.
    3. Press [ENTER].
    4. Confirm your job code (for example, one may be wait staff, three may be host, etc.).
    5. Press [ENTER].

B. To start transactions:
    1. Enter your identification number or swipe your MICROS card.
    2. Press [SIGN IN].
C. To begin a new check:
    1. Press [BEGIN TABLE NUMBER].
    2. Enter the table number.
    3. Press [ENTER].
    4. Enter the number of guests at the table using [ENTER # GUEST].
D. To order food:
    1. Enter the number of meals served by pressing [LUNCHES OR DINNER SERVED].
    2. Press [APPETIZERS] if guests have ordered appetizers.
    3. Press choice of appetizers [APP], [SALAD], or [SOUP].
    4. Press the [———] line key. This will separate appetizers from entrees.
    5. Press [ENTREE].
    6. Press the choice of entree as identified on the keyboard: [MEAT], [CHICKEN], [FISH].
    7. When meat is ordered, use the appropriate key to specify rare, medium, or well done or press [PASS].
E. To send the order to the remote printers, press [SERV].
F. To print a guest check, press [PRINT].
G. To add on to an order:
    1. Enter your identification number or swipe your MICROS card.
    2. Press [SIGN IN].
    3. Press [ENTER].
    4. Press [SHOW OPEN TABLE].
    5. Press the table number that you want to add items to.
    6. Press [ADD ON].
    7. Press [DESSERT], [BEVERAGE], or [WINE] as appropriate.
H. To send the order to the remote printers, press [SERV].
I. To print a guest check, press [PRINT].
J. To cancel a transaction:
    1. Press [TRANS CANCEL].
    2. Press [ENTER].
K. To void the last item, press [VOID] *twice*.
L. To void a previous item within a transaction:
    1. Press [VOID].
    2. Press [LINE UP] to the item highlighted.
    3. Press [ENTER].
    4. Enter the reason code number.

      5. Press [ENTER].

      6. Continue with the transaction.

M. To void an item from a previous transaction:

      1. Follow the directions to void a previous item within a transaction above.

      2. A manager must approve the change.

N. To close out a table when the guest is paying using cash:

      1. Input the table number that will be closed.

      2. Press [PAY].

      3. Enter the cash amount received.

      4. Press [CASH].

O. To close out a table when the guest is paying using a credit card:

      1. Input the table number that will be closed.

      2. Press [PAY].

      3. Enter the amount of the credit card payment, including all tips.

      4. Press the appropriate credit card key, such as [AMERICAN EXPRESS], [VISA], and so on.

      5. If the tip is correct, press [ENTER].

      6. If the tip is incorrect, press [CLEAR] and re-enter the correct amount.[14]

As with any computer system, management must train the staff properly; and the more a server uses the technology, the easier it is to understand. The computer has changed the way restaurants, managers, and servers do business.

Presenting the Guest Check and Accepting Payment

It has been the authors' experience that too often service falls off at this part of the meal. In Europe and in some Canadian restaurants, the waitstaff will not give guests their check until it is requested. In the United States, that is not the case. The guest check should be brought and placed in the center of the table as soon as the waitperson determines that the guests will not be ordering any additional items. If it is a breakfast or lunch meal, many restaurants have a policy that the guest check is placed on the table as soon as the main course is served. Whatever the policy of the restaurant, this part of the dining experience is critical: both for the guest who would like to leave the restaurant and for the restaurant that needs the table for another party. If the check is presented on a tray or in a book, this means that the server will be back to pick up the payment and bring it to the cashier. Otherwise, the guest should bring the check and payment to the cashier. Once the waitperson has delivered the check and has accepted payment, the guests should be thanked and invited back.

Sweet or Sour?

My barbers, Joe and Tom, tell me they always pay cash for their meals. They wanted to know who trains the waitstaff in the following technique: The bill is placed on the table. It is for $35.00. A $50.00 bill is placed down for payment. The waitperson asks, "Do you need any change?" Joe and Tom complain about this practice every time I get a haircut, and the complaint ends with the comment, "This really ticks me off." So for Joe and Tom, always bring the change to the guests, and let the guests determine the amount of the tip.

SUMMARY

1. Employees of a restaurant should know all the information about items on the menu. They should know which foods or beverages are offered, their pronunciation, their ingredients, and their styles of preparation. This will allow any employee to answer a guest's question about a menu item.
2. Service people must know the ingredients of all menu items because many people are allergic to certain spices and foods. Knowing what foods and spices are used to prepare a menu item and communicating that information to the guest will prevent an allergic reaction to the prepared item.
3. Each restaurant should develop a delivery system so that when menu items are brought out, any server will be able to serve the guests the item that they ordered without having to ask who gets what.
4. Some items that have been cooked in advance take relatively no time to prepare and plate in the kitchen. Other items may take 30 minutes or longer to cook and plate. Service people must know how long it takes to cook an item, because they must be able to time the sequence of service to the guest. The salad course should be finished and cleared before the main course is brought to the table. If the service person waits too long to serve the salad, the entrees may be ready to be picked up and served before the guests have finished their salads.

5. Suggestive selling and merchandising food and beverages are important for the establishment, service person, and guest. A service person who can suggest additional menu items to guests increases sales and profits for the establishment. When the check total is increased, the amount of tip or gratuity that the service person receives also increases because most guests tip on the total bill. An item suggested by the service person, such as bacon with Belgium waffles, will result in a more pleasurable meal for the guest.

6. The term 86ed means that the restaurant no longer has the item available for sale. Kitchens should have a means of communicating with the service staff–like posting 86ed items on a board in the kitchen–so that they do not take orders for a menu item that the restaurant no longer has available.

7. Service people should know the proper method of ordering food in the kitchen. Restaurants have different methods for the service staff to order food depending upon their level of computerization. Regardless of the system used (computer, written, or verbal), there should be a set procedure for all staff to order food in the same manner.

8. The proper sequence in serving a meal is as follows: drinks (alcoholic or nonalcoholic), appetizers, rolls, salad, entree, coffee/tea, and dessert. Wine is served when requested, either with dinner or immediately when ordered.

9. Restaurant managers should train, test, and evaluate employees so that the employees are competent to perform their duties in the restaurant. By training, testing, and evaluating employees, the service people become more proficient in their duties, thereby resulting in a more pleasing dining experience.

10. Restaurants may offer to substitute some food items in place of another. For example, a restaurant may allow guests to substitute coleslaw in place of french fries because some guests cannot eat fried foods. Management must determine when and if substitutions will be allowed because some patrons will try to substitute food to get more food for their money.

11. A computerized register system is of tremendous value to management, service people, the culinary staff, and guests of the restaurant. For management, a computerized system provides numerous reports that can be used to operate the establishment more efficiently. For the service people, a computerized register system saves time because the food order is transmitted to the kitchen quicker than other methods. Food orders are printed in readable language for the

culinary staff. The guests like this system because they can check their bill for accuracy.

12. As with all computers, placing orders on a point-of-sale (POS) system can only be accomplished by following logical steps. Management has to train employees in the proper use of the POS system in their individual restaurants. The sequence of placing orders is accomplished by a precise, step-by-step method.

REVIEW QUESTIONS

1. Why should the service person have a thorough knowledge of the menu?
2. Why is it important that a service person know all the ingredients of all menu items?
3. The cooking times of all menu items are important for a service person to know. Explain why you believe this is true or false.
4. What is suggestive selling, and what are its benefits for the restaurant?
5. What does the term 86ed mean? How can servers avoid problems when an item is 86ed?
6. What is the home base system? Describe how it operates.

DISCUSSION QUESTIONS

1. A check for $15.97 was presented to a guest, who paid it with a $20.00 bill. The service person brought three cents change back to the table, having kept the balance without the guest's offering the tip. Is there any problem here? And if there is, how would you handle the complaint from the guest and make certain that it never happens again?
2. What would you do as a manager if a guest refused to pay a bill because it is the policy of the restaurant not to tell the guests the "special prices"?
3. Should guests be allowed to substitute items on the menu?
4. If asked by a guest, "What should I not miss seeing in your town?" how would you respond?
5. Describe the method or methods that you would use to train your service staff to master the art of serving courses to the guests without having to ask who ordered what. Include in your answer the use of role playing.
6. Study and respond to the following scenario:

Dining Out: What Went Wrong?

A party of six had dinner at a restaurant. The restaurant seated about 150 on several levels. There was a large rectangular bar with tables surrounding it. About four tables were occupied, with a total of 15 guests in the restaurant. One bartender, a hostess, and six service people appeared to be staffing the restaurant.

The guests were seated at an eight-top. Next to the table were two round tables, both six–tops. One of the guests asked the hostess if the group could move to one of the six–tops, and the hostess instructed the waitress to move the party.

The waitress moved the menus and place settings to the new table, and began taking orders. A guest ordered salad and asked her what the salad dressing choices were. The waitress said she didn't know because that was her first night on the job, though she had worked at the restaurant during the summer, before she went away to college. She asked the server next to her for the choice of salad dressings and then repeated them back to the guests. One of the guests was reading her menu and did not hear the choices. When she ordered her salad, the whole process had to be repeated, with the waitress again asking the other server for the choice of salad dressings.

It came time to order the main course. The first guest ordered a burger without a bun and a Diet Coke; she had asked for her dressing to be served in a separate dish for her salad. The other guests ordered their main courses also.

Five of the six meals were delivered to the table. The order for the first guest—the hamburger—was served on a bun. There were three other meals, besides the hamburger, which were to receive french fries as an accompaniment. Each meal had on the plate the sandwich, an orange garnish, a sprig of parsley, plus a large area of white space left on the plate. Five minutes later, the waitress brought a community basket of french fries to the table, explaining that they had not been ready when she had brought out the other food. The sixth meal—Cajun-style shrimp—was finally brought to the table along with the french fries.

Coffee was asked for and brought. The coffee was served with a napkin between the cup and saucer. The coffee spilled all over the napkin. The waitress asked the customer if she wanted a new napkin. The customer felt like saying, "No, I'd rather slop it over my dress."

What is wrong with this restaurant, and who is responsible for this mess?

REFERENCES

1. *Restaurant & Institutions* (August 12, 1992).
2. *Nation's Restaurant News* (May 4, 1987): F4.
3. Erica, Duecy, "Food Allergies Nothing to Sneeze at, Chains Say" *Nation's Restaurant News* 38, No. 38 (September 20, 2004): 1, 143.
4. Food Allergy Basics. Food Allergy Questions and Answers. http://www.foodallergy.org.
5. Elissa, Elan, "Students' Activism, Allergies Top Agenda at NACUFS Confab" *Nation's Restaurant News* 40, No. 32 (August 7, 2006): 8.
6. "Restaurant Chain Is Sued in Death Blamed on Pesto," *Wall Street Journal* sec. A (August 8, 1995): 2.

7. John Clark, and Don Nichols, "Facts of Life, Service with a . . . Name," *Southwest Airlines Spirit* 9, No. 8 (August 2000): 146.

8. Ibid.

9. Ibid.

10. Robert Payne and Kimberly Williams, *Casola Dining Room Training Manual,* Schenectady County Community College, Schenectady, New York.

11. G. Pascal Zachary, "Restaurant Computers Speed Up Soup to Nuts," Wall Street Journal sec. B (October 25, 1995): 1, 7.

12. Stacy, Hirsh, "Pay at the Table Systems Coming Soon to Restaurants," *The Baltimore Sun* (September 3, 2006): C6.

13. Dina, Berta, "Operators Use Wireless Technology to Connect Customers, Employees", *Nation's Restaurant News* 40, No. 50 (December 11, 2006): 4, 66.

14. Payne and Williams, *Casola Dining Room Training Manual.*

Organizing the Dining Room to Accept Guests

OBJECTIVES   At the completion of this chapter, the student should be able to:

1. Give a historical background of the host's job.
2. List the qualities that make a good host.
3. Explain the importance of stations and sidework as they relate to the host's job.
4. Recite the five Ps of management and know what they mean.
5. Discuss the factors that affect scheduling.
6. Organize a dining room to accept guests.

KEY WORDS

deuxieme maitre d'hotel	forecasting	maître d'hôtel de carre'
directeur du restaurant	host	occupancy rate
five P's of management	logbook	tact
	maître d'hôtel	

FIGURE 7–1

A host at a restaurant, which in some cases may be the owner, is often the first person that the guest comes into contact with. (Photograph by Randall Perry)

The Host

The key person in the dining room is the individual who greets the guests. This person may be called the *maître d'hôtel*, the *director of service*, or the host or hostess (referred to as **host** in this chapter). The host must be staffed by a competent individual. In many instances he is the first human contact the guest will have with the restaurant. Therefore, the host represents the restaurant to the patrons. (See Figure 7–1.)

Guests often decide to patronize a restaurant based upon the greeting and attention they receive from the host. The mood for the evening is set by his actions. As stated in Chapter 1, Ben Franklin said, "The taste of the roast is determined by the handshake of the host." In addition to greeting the guests, the host is responsible for the operation of the dining room; he is the one who must insure that the guests have an enjoyable dining experience; and must solve any problems that may arise.

TIP$

TO INSURE PROPER SERVICE

Give customers "the free gifts they cherish most: recognition, recommendation, and reassurance," said the late Michael Hurst of the 15th Street Fisheries.

A Historical Overview

The job of the host has evolved from the classical restaurant. In this type of restaurant, the job titles were as follows: *directeur du restaurant; maître d'hôtel; deuxième maître d'hôtel;* and a *maître d'hôtel de carré*. This type of staffing had a host for each area of the restaurant.

The **directeur du restaurant** had complete charge of the restaurant, including the kitchen and dining room staff. He was also responsible for long-term planning, food and beverage cost controls, and service.

The **maître d'hôtel** was the host of all the dining rooms in the hotel. He was responsible for what occurred in all the different restaurants in the hotel, and he was in charge of the dishwashers, cleanup crew, and linen service. If the hotel was large, there may have been a second or **deuxième maître d'hôtel**, who was responsible for one dining room.

The **maître d'hôtel de carré** had the responsibility of a section of the dining room similar to the captain of today.

Because of the high labor cost involved in employing a large number of individuals in a restaurant, many operations have consolidated these jobs into the position of host. However, there are larger restaurants that still have a director of food and beverage and also a host. Figure 7–2 compares the early job titles to the responsibilities of restaurant personnel today.

Authority of the Host

The authority and respect of the host has deteriorated over the years. As service became more and more lax in America, the job of the host was considered an entry-level position. Restaurant owners paid the host minimum wage because the owners felt that a host did not directly produce money like a service person. Consequently, the person

FIGURE 7–2

Early job titles compared with the responsibilities of restaurant personnel of today.

THE HOST'S POSITION		
Early Days	**Responsibility**	**Today**
Directeur du Restaurant	Total Restaurant Operation	Food and Beverage Manager or Host
Maître d'Hôtel	All Dining Rooms	Food and Beverage Manager or Host
Deuxième Maître d'Hôtel	One Dining Room	Host
Maître d'Hôtel de Carré	One Section of the Dining Room	Host or Head Service Person; Captain

who was given the host position was poorly trained if trained at all. This position changed from one of prestige, power, and respect, to a job that restaurant owners felt anyone could do. Instead of having experienced waitpeople striving to become the host, they avoided it, because it did not pay as much money as their tipped position. Guest service and the industry suffered tremendously.

Today, the pendulum has begun to swing back to the experienced and respected host. Restaurant owners are realizing the importance of having a well-trained host. A well-informed and personable individual holding the job of host will make the restaurant a success. Restaurant owners are now compensating their hosts at a higher pay rate than minimum wage. As the laws regarding tip reporting and taxes become more stringent on restaurant owners, more and more are instituting a fixed service charge. From this fixed service charge, the host is being paid a much higher wage than minimum. Restaurants that still have a voluntary tipping policy may make the service staff contribute part of their tips to the host.

Restaurant owners are, once again, realizing the importance of having a competent, personable host to greet their guests.

Host Selection

Selecting a person for the host's job is important and challenging for the manager or owner of the restaurant. This is because a major portion of the job is dependent upon the host to observe a situation or problem, weigh the positive versus the negative aspects, and make a decision—all in a few seconds. Because the ability to think quickly and react to situations positively is a necessary qualification, the manager must try to select an individual who is personable and can work well under stress. The selection process should be structured in such a manner as to determine the personality of the applicants and how they handle stressful situations. Figure 7–3 lists the criteria for selecting a host. In addition, the manager should look for some specific

CRITERIA FOR HOST SELECTION

Individual selected to be a host must:
1. be personable
2. work well under stress
3. be able to think quickly
4. be able to make decisions

FIGURE 7–3

Criteria for host selection.

qualifications that have been identified with excellent hosts. These qualifications are discussed in the next section.

T I P $

TO INSURE PROPER SERVICE

To determine the personality of his applicants, the late Michael Hurst would ask, "What is the funniest thing that ever happened to you?"

Qualifications of the Host

The qualifications for a host fall into two general categories: physical and behavioral (see Figure 7–4). The first relates to the appearance of the individual. The second refers to the manner in which the person interacts with people.

In most instances, the host is the first person guests see when they walk into a restaurant, therefore the physical appearance of the host must be exemplary. Figure 7–1 shows a host at his restaurant. This host makes a positive physical appearance. As with the service staff, cleanliness is essential. Any uniform must be neat and clean, as these are a symbol of professionalism. The host should be proud of wearing the uniform.

The behavioral qualification is the ability to deal with people. The host must be able to meet the needs of the restaurant's guests and employees. Sometimes this is not easy. Many guests are not pleasant, because they may be having a bad day or are not used to waiting for a table, or for a myriad of reasons that the host has little, if any, control over. Employees provide another challenge. They will complain about the amount of tips that the guests have left and about their stations, for example. The host must have the ability to satisfy all the employee and guest complaints, whether legitimate or not.

Who's in Control Here?

George Goldoff, the author of the foreword to this book, tells about an incident that occurred when he was the manager at the Rainbow Room in New York City and the extreme measures he took to solve the problem. In this case, he was able to take control of the situation. Four guests came into the Rainbow Room. When they were brought to their table, they told him that they did not like the table assigned to them. He explained to them that all of the other unoccupied tables were reserved for that night. When he left the table, the four of them moved to the table they wanted. He went to the group, told them that they would have to move back to the original table. They refused. He had his staff go to the table and physically remove it from the dining room. He then went to the table and informed the guests that he did not have a table for them. This is a technique that would only be used as a last resort.

FIGURE 7–4

Qualifications of a host.

QUALIFICATIONS TO BE A HOST	
Physical	**Behavioral**
Positive appearance	Personable
Able to stand for long periods of time	Outgoing
	Ability to work well with others in all situations

Useful Behavioral Tips

For the host to do the job effectively, other behavioral traits are needed. The book *The Professional Host* lists some of them: attentiveness, courteousness, dependability, economy, efficiency, honesty, loyalty, knowledge, preparedness, quietness, sensitivity, skill, tact, productivity, and persuasiveness.[1] Even though it would appear that every person has the common sense to know and use these traits, many do not. The following information will give examples of the importance of the specific traits.

Attentiveness

The host must be ubiquitous. He must know what is occurring in the dining room at all times and must appear to have eyes in the back of his head. The host must know the status of all tables at all times; whether table three has been served the main course; if table five needs more wine. An absentminded person or daydreamer does not belong in the position of host. This job requires a person who will be consistently alert to the guests' needs.

T I P $

To Insure Proper Service
Sirio Maccioni, founder and owner of Le Cirque in New York City and Las Vegas, tells everyone on his staff that if a guest calls them over, the thing to say is, "What can I do for you?" Do not ask, "Is everything all right?" That is very pretentious. When you ask, "What can I do for you?" people open up.[2]

Courteousness

The host must treat the guests as though they were guests in his home. Words such as "please" and "thank you" are thought by many to be magic. Guests appreciate hearing these magic words, and the host is encouraged to use them whenever appropriate. Greeting and addressing the guests by name throughout the dining experience, the host should return to the table to show his genuine concern for their satisfaction. By using the magic words "please," "thank you," "excuse me," and especially the guest's name, the host will not only impress the guest by his courtesy but will provide a positive model for the service staff to follow.

Courteousness also includes assisting guests with little things that show concern. These little things are not something that will make a person jump up and down and say, "Wow, did you see what the host did!" Instead, they are displays of courteousness that will make the guests feel that the restaurant really cares about them and is happy to receive their business. Examples of courteousness are: assisting guests removing or putting on coats; pulling out chairs for guests as they are shown to their table; and checking back with guests to determine if the table and temperature of the room are pleasing. Pulling the shades down so the sun will not shine in guests' eyes is another example. The difference between a great restaurant and a good restaurant is taking care of the details—and courteousness is a detail.

Sweet or Sour?

On a hot August night, we climbed up the stairs and entered The Sardine Factory restaurant in Monterey, California. The host—we later discovered his name was Marty—welcomed us and asked if we had a reservation. When we replied no, he said it was no problem and asked for my name. I responded with "Toby." He seated us at a great table that afforded us the opportunity to observe his skills as a host. Each guest who entered The Sardine Factory and approached the host's podium was met with a smile, enthusiasm, and a welcoming tone. The host let all of the guests know that he was happy to have them dine at The Sardine Factory. As we watched him deal with the many requests—late reservations, guests requesting table changes—he handled them with confidence, tact, and diplomacy. His most impressive trait was that he thanked every guest who left the restaurant and called them by name! We were impressed that he knew all of the names of the guests and thought that they all must be regular customers. Once we paid our check and were ready to exit the restaurant, Marty said "Goodbye, Toby, and thanks for dining with us." This treatment confirms the truth of the statement in the last paragraph of the Manager's Message and Chef's Choice by the owners of The Sardine Factory in Chapter 5. Marty had never met us before we walked in; but he made us feel as though he and The Sardine Factory appreciated us and welcomed our business, which is exactly what a host should do.

Dependability

Dependability is a trait that is valued highly by restaurant owners. It is a sign of maturity. Basically, it means that the employees will be responsible for their own actions. It also includes the fact that the employees will accomplish the goals that have been set, either by management or by the employees themselves on their own. This trait is important in all positions, but is extremely critical for any person who will hold the job of host.

T I P $ **TO INSURE PROPER SERVICE**
Offer to take pictures of guests together when you see them taking pictures.

Economy

Economy means keeping costs at a minimum. This will be the host's responsibility. The dining room is an area where costs can rapidly get out of control because of improper scheduling, improper use of linen, and food waste. If the host schedules too many service people, the labor cost will be a drain on the restaurant. If staff are allowed to use extra equipment—like extra side towels—when they are not needed, money is lost. Common sense is important in keeping waste to a minimum. An example of economy is to save and reuse individual packaged jellies if they have not been opened.

Efficiency

Efficiency means finding the quickest and easiest way to do a task without jeopardizing guest satisfaction. The ability to organize reservations in a systematic manner is an example of efficiency. By having an efficient reservation system, the host can take reservations correctly. This will allow him to spend more time in the dining room or working the floor instead of trying to straighten out a mess caused by an inefficient reservation system. An organized host has more time to spend with the guests.

Honesty

A person who deals with the public, especially in the host's job, will have to make many decisions that will test his honesty. For example, a guest approaches the host and asks for a table. The host has all the tables reserved and informs the guest of this. The guest produces a $50 bill and asks, "Are you sure?" The host and the guest both know that the patron is buying the table. What should the host do?

Other opportunities will arise to deceive the customer as well as the employees. In all instances, if the host is dishonest and allows the staff to be dishonest, word will spread that the establishment is dishonest. This will result in negative word of mouth from both guests and employees, and the business will suffer.

T I P S

TO INSURE PROPER SERVICE

Danny Meyer of the Union Square Cafe says, "It's less appropriate to 'grease the palm' of a maître d' to get a better table on your way in. Maître d's who 'sell' good tables for tips are not providing good service for other guests."[3]

Loyalty

Loyalty is another highly rated trait for a host. It can be defined as being, or giving the impression to the public of being, totally supportive of the ideas and philosophies of the restaurant. An example of not being loyal is downgrading the establishment to the guests with such comments as, "Management has no idea how to run this place."

Knowledge

As with the service staff, the host has to know all facets of the operation of the restaurant. In fact, he must know more about the operation than the service staff, because the guests perceive the host as the key figure in the restaurant. The host should know *everything*, including the preparation and service of food and beverage. In addition, the host has to be aware of the physical layout of the restaurant, how to deal with credit card charges, and the accounting procedures of the restaurant. With today's ever-changing technology, knowledge of computers and computer systems is critical.

Knowledge of community events and area attractions is an important aspect of the host's concern. If a guest asks a question and the host does not know the answer, he will have to find out the answer and return to the guest with it.

Sweet or Sour?

A couple invited two friends to dinner and a play on Saturday evening. A reservation was made at one of the couple's favorite restaurants; in addition, that restaurant was to provide the catering for the theater where the party of four were to attend the play. While driving to the restaurant, the host turned to the invited couple and said, "Well, we won't be late for the play, but we will be a little early, because our tickets are for next Saturday. I called and tried to exchange the tickets and get us seats for tonight; but as the theater only seats 200 people, they are sold out." When they arrived at the restaurant, the host–owner greeted them warmly and inquired whether they were going to the play or were there for a leisurely dinner. The guest explained the problem. The owner asked for the tickets and said "Let me see what I can do." By the time the salad arrived, the owner was back at the table to inform the group that he had secured tickets for that evening's performance.

Preparedness

Nothing is more frustrating for guests than to have to wait for a reservation, food, or drinks. The host has to be ready to accept guests into the dining room at its stated opening time. If a guest is promised a 3:00 P.M. reservation, then the table should be ready for them at 3:00 P.M. Preparedness is the act of planning and organizing all equipment and supplies so that the guest will not have to wait for service.

Procrastinators do not belong in the hospitality industry. The host should have a plan for each situation and consider alternative plans in case of a problem.

Quietness

A good host is always available when needed. However, the host has to be aware of the proper time to talk to guests and when to leave them alone. When talking to the guests, it is done in a courteous manner, not in a loud or boisterous one. The host must act with dignity, and do the job quietly.

Sensitivity

Restaurants are where many special occasions are celebrated, such as engagements, wedding anniversaries, births, and job promotions. Unfortunately, it is also the place where many marriages and relationships are ended. People often choose a restaurant in which to tell their spouse or lover that the relationship is finished, because they think that the hurt party will not make a scene in so public a place. The host has to be sensitive to the needs of the guests and observe their actions to determine how much attention they want. Sensitivity is a two-part trait: first, to observe what is occurring between the guests or to the guests, then act appropriately; if the guests have just become engaged, congratulations should be offered. A dessert or drink may be offered, compliments of the restaurant. If the couple obviously is having a fight, then staying away from the table is best. Going to the table to ask how the food is would not be appropriate, but would show a lack of sensitivity.

T I P $ **TO INSURE PROPER SERVICE**
Provide immediate service recovery by immediately resolving a guest service failure before it becomes a problem.

Skill

A skillful host knows how to "work the floor." He knows how to obtain the most efficient or effective use of the tables in the shortest period of time. The skillful host knows how to keep the guests happy and how to motivate them to return. Skill also involves making salads tableside, carving meats and poultry, and pouring wine.

Tact

The ability to say the right phrase at the right time without offending the guest would be a definition of **tact**. Saying to a guest, "Where have you been, I haven't seen you in a long time: can be interpreted by many guests as tactless. A more tactful way of saying this would be, "It's nice to have you visit us, we're glad to see you here again." This says the same thing, but it will not offend the guest.

Tact is also involved when inquiring about the guests or their families. The host has to be aware of what is happening in the community. Reading the local newspapers will give the host information needed to avoid embarrassment and appearing tactless. For example, in last week's newspaper, the host read that John Smith had been cut from the professional baseball team. When Mr. and Mrs. Smith come to the restaurant, the host would not ask them, "How is your son's baseball career going?"

Productivity

Productivity is defined as the ability to get the maximum amount of tasks accomplished in the shortest period of time. There are times when the host must take reservations, greet guests, take their orders, and return to their table to see if the meal is to their satisfaction. In addition, the host must monitor the service staff's performance, seeing that the sidework is being done and that the dining room is operating to its maximum potential.

Persuasiveness

This is another important behavioral trait, especially when dealing with guests who have problems. Persuasiveness could be used to convince the guest to take a different table, or to take a different time, because the restaurant is booked solid. Convincing the guest to change his or her mind about something requires persuasiveness.

Manager's Message

(COURTESY OF DENISE VOLPICELLO, GENERAL MANAGER, EAST HAMPTON POINT RESTAURANT)

It would be a wonderfully simplistic business if restaurants were only about food. The reality is that it is about people, the ones that keep you in business, and the ones that work for you. It is no longer just a meal out; people are paying for an experience.

Everyone has heard the expression "you never get a second chance to make a first impression." This cannot be more stressed about the host or, now more popularly titled, "reservationists" in your restaurant. The initial telephone greeting, including the tone of voice, inflection and verbiage tells the guest what kind of experience is ahead of them. Finding the right person to "read" a guest through the phone is invaluable. You want every guest to hang up and think that was the nicest person they ever spoke to. They should "feel" a smile through the phone.

As for the host that actually greets your guests upon arrival, there are many skills required that need constant maintenance. Smiles, now more than ever, are paramount. It tells the guest we are happy to see them, whether they have a reservation, or not. Conveying to the guest that you have anticipated their arrival, and are anxious to accommodate them sets the pace for their entire experience in your restaurant. Displaying the appropriate sense of urgency, reading body language, comfortably using their name tells them they can relax; they are in the hands of hospitality professionals.

(continues)

There are many more behavioral traits that the reader will be able to identify; however, an individual has to exhibit some, if not all, of the traits reviewed here in order to be an excellent host.

The Host's Responsibilities: The Five Ps of Management

For any restaurant to run efficiently, the host must be prepared. The key to having a successful restaurant or banquet are the **five Ps of management**: *Prior Planning Prevents Poor Performance* (see Figure 7–5).

This phrase and the meaning of it are important for all restaurant employees. However, this philosophy is especially critical in the host's

---

Manager's Message

(continued)

Upon departure, the ideal host has anticipated the guest's departure, asked them by name how their experience was, and invites them back soon. The host then genuinely thanks them and says goodnight.

In the end, they felt cared for. The entire experience started and ended with the host. The food was someplace in the middle.

Denise Volpicello
General Manager
East Hampton Point (Restaurant)
East Hampton, New York (EastHamptonPoint.com)

The East Hampton Point restaurant is on the eastern end of Long Island located on the water. This is a 450 seat restaurant with 2 kitchens. It is a seasonal restaurant, open from April to Labor Day. After Labor Day, the restaurant does special events, mostly high end weddings for not less than 100 people.

The food is progressive American, with an emphasis on local seafood and produce. They also own 3 other restaurants in East Hampton, NY which are open year round: Citta Nuova; Wei Fun; and the 1770 House.

General Manager Volpicello has had experience working for restaurants such as the Striped Bass in Philadelphia and Morton's Steak House in New York City.

FIGURE 7–5

*The five Ps of manage-
ment.*

THE FIVE Ps OF MANAGEMENT
PRIOR PLANNING PREVENTS POOR PERFORMANCE

job. The five Ps of management mean that if all tasks are planned in advance, problems will be kept to a minimum.

Therefore, a plan is needed before each meal period. This plan may be in the form of a checklist, as illustrated in Figure 7–6. Each restaurant may design one that fits the needs for that particular unit. By completing it, the host ensures that the restaurant is prepared to accept guests. The following are some examples of what items may be on the checklist and why they are important.

The list should include checking both the men's and women's rooms for all paper products and for cleanliness. If the host does not do this, it will have to be attended to during a busy time, taking valuable time away from the guests.

Another important area to check is the physical cleanliness of the dining room. Are the floors free of crumbs or lint? If the floor is dirty, it will have to be cleaned or vacuumed before the guests arrive. All light fixtures are inspected for burned out bulbs or cobwebs. The host may think, "It's not my job," but the host is responsible for the operation of the dining room. The guests want to feel that they are eating in a clean and safe restaurant. Burned out light bulbs, dirty floors, and cobwebs send a message to the guest that the restaurant does not care about cleanliness.

FIGURE 7–6

*A sample checklist for
the host, to be done
daily.*

HOST'S DAILY CHECKLIST FOR OPENING THE DINING ROOM
1. Inspection of the service staff for proper grooming guidelines
2. Men's restroom and women's restroom:
• Clean
• Paper products
3. Physical cleanliness of the dining room:
• Floor free of crumbs and lint
• Light fixtures clean and no burned-out bulbs
4. Printers have enough paper to complete meal period
5. Menus are clean and chef's creations have been added
6. Reservations have been blocked
7. Computer system has been programmed with the chef's creations
8. Host is neat and clean, ready to accept guests

For restaurants with a computer system, printers have to be checked to see whether there is enough paper to last though the meal period. With some computer systems, if the paper runs out, the computer will not work. All prices and new items should be put into the memory of the computer before staff take their first orders.

The host may assign an employee to complete any task not completed. The first responsibility of the host is to prepare the dining room to accept guests. The host must have the dining room ready to accept guests when it is scheduled to open its doors. As has been said before, the difference between a good and a great restaurant is attention to detail. A good host will anticipate and avoid problems. A great host will use the five Ps of management to have an excellent restaurant.

Organization of the Dining Room

Knowledge of the menu, pricing, ingredients, and all facts essential to the smooth and profitable operation of a restaurant is as essential to the host as it is to the service staff. In addition, the host has to supervise the service staff.

The host is responsible for making the service excellent. Successful restaurants constantly evaluate service throughout an employee's career. The host is responsible for the training and performance of the service staff. In addition, the host has to schedule employees and assign stations and sidework to make the dining room operate at maximum efficiency.

Factors that Affect Scheduling

Have you ever been to a restaurant where you are served slowly because there are too many guests and not enough staff? Sometimes there is an obvious shortage of service staff to serve the guests. For example, a restaurant has 120 seats filled and only two service people to tend to the guests. The person responsible for scheduling has not scheduled enough service staff to meet the demand. The host must schedule the correct amount of staff to meet the demands of business, while not overstaffing the restaurant. Overstaffing causes a loss of money and, at times, even results in poor service. In order to schedule effectively, the host must take certain factors into consideration and then schedule the employees correctly. The first step begins with forecasting.

Forecasting
Planning for anticipated business based upon previous history of the restaurant is called **forecasting**. Reservations and events that are

planned for the community that will affect the business must be taken into account. A formal written forecast on a weekly basis is the most important aspect in scheduling.

Scheduling

There are many factors that affect correct scheduling. The first has to do with the qualifications of the individual waitpeople. The next has to do with the type of menu and style of service that the restaurant offers. The third involves events occurring in the community in which the restaurant is located. If the restaurant is located in a hotel, expected occupancy rates of the hotel will play a major part in scheduling. Another factor is based upon the history from previous years' business. The final factor would be the number of reservations for the meal period. Scheduling is one area where the five Ps of management are extremely important.

The first consideration is qualifications of the individual waitpeople. For example, one service person may be able to work best waiting on a lot of small parties; another may work better with large parties. Knowing this information allows the host to compensate for the strengths and inadequacies of the staff.

Next, the host has to consider the type of menu and the style of service offered by the restaurant. If the restaurant uses American service, the number of guests that can be served efficiently by one service person is anywhere from 12 to 24. Individual restaurants determine how many guests a service person is required to serve. This depends on the menu, the meal period, and the atmosphere of the restaurant. The host can use this standard in forecasting and scheduling.

The third factor that affects scheduling are events occurring in the community that will positively or negatively affect the restaurant's business. For example, if there is a parents' weekend at the local college, and the restaurant serves breakfast, then it should be staffed to accommodate extra guests. If there is a youth sporting event scheduled in the community, and the restaurant appeals to that market, it will be busier than usual. The host, the service staff, and the cooks want to avoid surprises. No one likes to be swamped with business when they are not prepared to handle it.

T I P $ **TO INSURE PROPER SERVICE**

Manage your restaurant from the front door, not from the kitchen. In other words, be visible so that you can observe what is occurring in your restaurant and the guests can see that you are in control of the operation.

The next factor is particularly for restaurants located in a lodging establishment. Almost all hotels send out a forecast of the prospective **occupancy rate**; this is the anticipated number of guests staying in the establishment on a certain night. If the rate is expected to be 100 percent, then the restaurant will be very busy for breakfast. It is amazing that when a hotel has 100 percent occupancy, the restaurant is not staffed properly for breakfast: the meal that will be eaten most often by the hotel's guests. Effective staffing in this category also means scheduling employees to work at the correct time. Having employees come in from 8:00 A.M. to 4:00 P.M. would be a mistake if the hotel's clientele are business people. They want to be out of the restaurant by 8:00 A.M. It is easy to obtain advance occupancy figures, thereby reducing the probability of an insufficiently staffed restaurant. A word of caution: The restaurant manager has to determine if the high occupancy rate is the result of a large convention. If so, the manager must determine what banquet meals have been planned for the convention. For example, at the American Culinary Federation National Convention, breakfast, morning break, luncheon, afternoon break, and dinner are included in the convention. At this convention, the vast majority of attendees would be eating all their meals at banquets, not in the à la carte restaurant.

The next factor is determined by the history of the restaurant. Every restaurant needs a book at the host stand—some call it a **logbook**—for the purpose of recording the history of that day's business. Included should be the number of meals that were served for each meal period, the weather, and special events that were occurring in the community, such as conventions. The guest history also includes how much money was generated per hour and per meal period. This information may be computerized. This will assist the host in forecasting the staffing for the same day of the week next year. In addition, it is recommended to have an area where the day shift host can leave messages for the night shift host concerning important items, such as, "Jane called in, and she will be 20 minutes late tonight."

Finally, the manager reviews the number of reservations normally taken on a particular day. If the restaurant is booked up far in advance, all the reservations will be factored into the scheduling.

By no means is this a complete listing of the factors that the host must consider when staffing the restaurant; however, these items will help the host in this regard. This planning allows the host to staff the restaurant properly for all types of business, including the least busy nights. For example, the night before Thanksgiving is traditionally not busy in a hotel dining room. However, the dining room must be open.

Using the previous history, plus the expected occupancy rates, the host can schedule a skeleton crew. On the other hand, one of the biggest business days at a restaurant like Churchill Downs in Louisville, Kentucky, is Thanksgiving. At the racetrack, the restaurant must be staffed to accommodate the large group of guests. Taking into account all necessary factors, the host can develop a schedule to satisfy the demands.

Scheduling the Employees

Based upon the factors that were discussed previously, the host can determine how many service people are needed for a certain time period. This time period is usually a week. It is beneficial to the host and employees to have the work schedule completed and posted in advance. This lets all employees know when they are scheduled to work.

The restaurant industry has a reputation for not treating its service staff decently. Many times, restaurant owners engage in day-to-day scheduling. When service persons ask for their schedules, they are told to call at 10:00 A.M. the next day. Then they are told to work or not to work. This type of scheduling negatively affects morale. Posting the schedule on the same day every week for the same period of time will alleviate the problem.

The busiest days in the restaurant business are the times when everyone else is enjoying themselves—weekends and holidays. Employees should be told when hired that they will have to work weekends and holidays. The host should strive to give his employees two days off in succession.

The authors have designed a system to improve scheduling that resulted in improved morale. First, the schedule was made every Wednesday and posted every Thursday. As an example, the schedule went from Friday, April 1, to Sunday, April 10. The employees would know a week in advance who had to work the following weekend. The next week's schedule went from Friday, April 8, to Sunday, April 17. Using this method, the host plans for seven days but always schedules for ten. An example of the two-week schedule is in Figure 7–7 and Figure 7–8. Notice that the last weekend (April 8, 9, 10) of Figure 7–7, and the first weekend (April 8, 9, 10) of Figure 7–8 are the same.

This method improves morale, and it will allow the employees to plan in advance if there is a special event they wish to attend. For instance, Justina knows on Wednesday, April 6, that she has the weekend of the 16th and 17th off.

FIGURE 7–7

A 10-day schedule for restaurant employees.

WEEKLY SCHEDULE, APRIL 1–10									
Name	**1**	**2**	**3**	**4**	**5**	**6**	**7**	**8**	**9**	**10**
	Fri	*Sat*	*Sun*	*Mon*	*Tue*	*Wed*	*Thu*	*Fri*	*Sat*	*Sun*
Justina	7-3	7-3	7-3	OFF	OFF	7-3	7-3	7-3	7-3	7-3
John	7-3	7-3	7-3	7-3	7-3	OFF	OFF	7-3	7-3	7-3
Bill	7-3	7-3	7-3	7-3	7-3	7-3	7-3	OFF	OFF	7-3

FIGURE 7–8

A 10-day schedule for restaurant employees.

WEEKLY SCHEDULE, APRIL 8–17									
Name	**8**	**9**	**10**	**11**	**12**	**13**	**14**	**15**	**16**	**17**
	Fri	*Sat*	*Sun*	*Mon*	*Tue*	*Wed*	*Thu*	*Fri*	*Sat*	*Sun*
Justina	7-3	7-3	7-3	7-3	7-3	7-3	7-3	7-3	OFF	OFF
John	7-3	7-3	7-3	7-3	7-3	OFF	OFF	7-3	7-3	7-3
Bill	OFF	OFF	7-3	7-3	7-3	7-3	7-3	7-3	7-3	7-3

In addition, if the employees wanted a special day or weekend off, they were allowed to switch with other employees as long as the host was told. However, it was made clear to the employees who were scheduled to work that they were responsible for covering the shift. If their replacement did not show up, then the originally scheduled employee would pay the consequences. This system made the host's job easy. The staff was motivated because they knew exactly when they had to work and knew that they could take a day off if some special event occurred. Of course, if employees knew far enough in advance before the schedule was to be made up that they needed a day off, they would inform the host and they would be accommodated.

Stations and Sidework

Regardless of how the stations are arranged in the restaurant (team or individual), stations and sidework responsibilities have to be posted. Sidework should be with the station. Figure 7–9 is an example of how stations and sidework can be planned. Notice that the sidework corresponds to the station assignment.

The host must be flexible and on occasion must combine stations or service staff from different stations when it would benefit the

STATIONS AND SIDEWORK, APRIL 1–10										
Name	**1**	**2**	**3**	**4**	**5**	**6**	**7**	**8**	**9**	**10**
	Fri	*Sat*	*Sun*	*Mon*	*Tue*	*Wed*	*Thu*	*Fri*	*Sat*	*Sun*
Justina	1	3	2	OFF	OFF	1	2	1	2	1
John	2	1	3	1	2	OFF	OFF	2	1	2
Bill	3	2	1	2	1	2	1	OFF	OFF	3

1. Fold fifty napkins
2. Salt and pepper shakers; perform sidework of station 3, when only two people are scheduled
3. Housekeeping of all coffee and beverage machines

FIGURE 7–9

A 10-day schedule of corresponding sidework for restaurant employees.

guests. For example, a party of 12 went to a restaurant on New Year's Day. The host assigned two service people to take care of the table even though it was on one station. The group was served more quickly than if one person had served them.

Menus and Checks

The host is usually responsible for making sure the proper meal period menus are clean and ready to distribute to the guests. In some establishments, the host has to write or print out the daily specials to insert into the menu and/or write them on the blackboard. When putting the specials into the menus, the host also checks the condition of the menus. Dirty, torn, or smudged menus should be discarded. If the restaurant serves three meals a day, the host checks that the menu is correct for that meal period. Have you ever received a menu that was for lunch when the other guests in your party had a dinner menu?

Guest checks are sometimes given out to the service staff by the host or cashier; at other times, computer systems print them automatically. All service staff are responsible for the checks they receive. At the end of the meal period, the host verifies that all guests' checks have been returned.

Staff Inspection and Daily Meeting

Before each meal period, the host has to conduct a staff inspection and hold a daily meeting.

It is at this time that the host inspects the employees regarding the grooming and cleanliness policies set by the restaurant. If a member of the staff does not meet the grooming standards that have been set, the host cannot allow that individual to work. Allowing a service person to work who has not met the restaurant's standards will make it diffi-cult to enforce the rules to the other staff members. Once the service staff realize that the grooming and cleanliness policies will be enforced, they will comply.

The daily meeting usually consists of a short information session that the host conducts before each meal period. Information is shared with the staff, such as the description and price of the day's chef cre-ations. Any new wines or beverages that the restaurant is featuring will be explained. The soup or vegetable of the day and items that the restaurant is temporarily out of are also communicated by the host. Any special requests from the reservations, such as a birthday cake for the Smith reservation at 8:00 P.M., and any new promotions are also explained.

This informational session should not last long. There will be reg-ularly scheduled meetings for the purpose of tasting food and wine, reviewing policies in depth, and soliciting new ideas from the staff. This meeting is only informational in nature so that the dining room runs smoothly for that particular meal period.

SUMMARY

1. The host's job historically evolved in the classical restaurant. In clas-sical restaurants, each area of the restaurant had a host. Today the host may also serve as an owner, food and beverage director, or manager of the restaurant—all depending upon the size of the restaurant.

2. The host must be attentive, courteous, dependable, honest, loyal to the establishment, tactful, knowledgeable, sensitive to guests' needs and moods, and persuasive.

3. The host should have a knowledge of where stations are located in the restaurant and the sidework that has to be completed by staff. On occasion, the host must combine stations or service staff from differ-ent stations when it would benefit the guests. Stations and sidework should be posted by the host so that service people know their duties and responsibilities. This will create a accountability for the duties to be performed by staff.

4. The five Ps of management are *Prior Planning Prevents Poor Performance.* To have the dining room run smoothly, the host should have a plan. With a plan, when change occurs, the host will be able to make adjustments as necessary to insure a favorable dining experi-ence for the guests.

5. Many factors must be taken into account by a host to schedule correctly. Among major factors that affect scheduling are: forecasting of business; qualifications of the individual service people; type of menu; style of service; and events occurring in the community.

6. The host should have knowledge of the menu, pricing, ingredients, and all facts essential to the smooth and profitable operation of the restaurant. In addition, the host has to supervise the service staff. Scheduling employees and assigning stations and sidework must be planned. Training, evaluation, and supervision of service must also be done for guests to have a favorable dining experience. To organize the dining room to accept guests, the host must take all necessary factors into consideration, along with making certain that the restaurant is physically clean.

REVIEW QUESTIONS

1. Compare the jobs of the host today with the four job titles of earlier times.
2. What qualities should a manager look for when hiring a host?
3. What behavioral traits should a person have to make a good host?
4. What are the five Ps of management, and why is this phrase important in the restaurant industry?
5. What is forecasting, and how does it affect scheduling?
6. What is the purpose of having a 10-day schedule? Do you think it is a good idea? Explain your answer.
7. What factors have to be taken into consideration when scheduling?
8. What is a logbook, and what is its purpose?

DISCUSSION QUESTIONS

1. You are the manager of the dining room. Your morning host is a bright, articulate, and personable individual. All the staff love him. You have received many letters from guests complimenting him on the way he treats them at breakfast. However, he has an alcohol problem. About once a month he goes on a binge and does not show up for work, though his wife does call in for him. What do you do?
2. The host has all the tables reserved and informs the guest of this. The guest produces a $100 bill and asks, "Are you sure?" The host and the guest both know that the patron is buying the table. What should the host do?
3. What does the phrase "The taste of the roast is determined by the handshake of the host" mean?

4. The restaurant where you are employed is located in a geographical area that has many colleges. What factors must be taken into consideration in forecasting for graduation weekend so your restaurant achieves the highest profitability?
5. Referring to Discussion Question two, how does a manager determine if guests are truly tipping the host for great service or if they are giving the host extra money to get a good table? If the host is actually "selling tables," what action should the manager take?

REFERENCES

1. The Food Service Editors of CBI, *The Professional Host* (Boston: CBI, 1981): pp. 11–13.
2. Mervyn Rothstein, "Sirio's Circus of the Chic," *The Wine Spectator* (May 15, 1995): pp. 71–80.
3. Danny Meyer, *Union Square Cafe Newsletter* (Autumn/Winter 1994).

8

Planning Reservations and Blocking Tables

OBJECTIVES At the completion of this chapter, the student should be able to:

1. Take reservations.
2. State the advantages and disadvantages of a reservation policy.
3. State the advantages and disadvantages of a no-reservation policy.
4. Demonstrate how to block tables when reservations are accepted.
5. Plan and organize a system to seat guests who come into the restaurant with a reservation.
6. Explain the problems that occur when taking guest reservations and propose solutions.
7. Recognize the problems with no-shows and know how to reduce their number.
8. Understand how call-ahead seating works.
9. Understand the concept of first-priority seating.

KEY WORDS

blocking
call-ahead seating
check–off method
first available seating

no-shows
open seating
overbooking
priority seating

reservation
reservation manager
residence time
walk-ins

The Decision on Whether to Accept Reservations

Each restaurant must decide whether it will accept reservations or rely on walk-ins to fill up its tables. A **reservation** is a promise for a table in a restaurant. **Walk-ins** are guests who patronize the restaurant without making a reservation; in effect, they walk in the door expecting to obtain a table (see Figure 8–1).

Many restaurants will not take reservations. Instead, guests are seated on a first-come basis. However, before the decision is made not to take reservations, some factors must be considered.

One of the most important considerations in not accepting reservations is the location of the restaurant. A restaurant located in an

FIGURE 8–1

A restaurant, such as the one pictured, can take both walk-ins and reservations. (Photograph by Randall Perry)

area where there is a large population, or in a busy tourist area, may prefer not to take reservations. A large population guarantees the restaurant the number of potential guests needed to fill up its tables. The same is true in a busy resort area that caters to tourists. If the establishment is located in an area where guests have to travel a long distance to reach it, this will be a negative factor.

A second negative factor would be the absence of other restaurants of the same quality in the general area. The guest will take both of these factors into consideration and most likely will not attempt to patronize the restaurant. Why should a guest drive for a long period of time and not be assured of getting a table?

The next factor is the size of the party. Because most restaurants have the majority of their tables as deuces and four-tops, they are not equipped to accommodate groups of more than six people. It would be difficult if not impossible to accommodate a group of ten people at one table. Imagine a busy night at a restaurant where all the tables are occupied. A large group appears at the door and wants to sit together. The host would have to wait until three tables next to each other become vacant all at once. Then the host would have to move the tables so that they could accommodate the party. To avoid this problem, reservations should be accepted for large parties. The definition of *large* would depend upon the size of the tables in the individual restaurant. Usually, a party of five or more guests is considered large.

All restaurants are not alike, which requires them to have different policies for seating. In gambling casinos it is common to have two separate lines to seat guests. One line is for guests who have earned special privileges by spending a set amount of money gambling. The other line is for the rest of the guests at the casino. It is common practice in many restaurants for management not to reserve all of their tables; instead they hold a couple of tables back for regular or special customers. The key to being profitable is to build loyalty among your repeat guests. What will happen to future business when, a regular guest—a person who entertains weekly at the restaurant—has unexpected business clients arrive in town and calls for a reservation at the last minute only to be told that you have no tables? Or how about the guest who has just lost a huge sum of money playing blackjack and states that he wants to eat at the best restaurant in the casino? This scene is played out in restaurant after restaurant throughout the world.

Reservations should always be accepted on holidays. Easter, Thanksgiving, and Mother's Day in particular are special days for families; they want to be assured that they can arrive at a restaurant, enjoy themselves, pay the bill, and leave in a definite period of time. For many people, holidays are the only time of the year that family members can have a meal together. Because of the great age differences in most family groups—between young children, parents, and grandparents—having to wait for a table would not be tolerated or even considered.

Accepting Reservations

Once the decision has been made to accept reservations, management needs to create a policy to deal with reserving tables for the guests. As was stated previously, some establishments only reserve a certain percentage of tables; but many restaurants prefer to be reserved completely. A gourmet restaurant, like Victoria and Albert's Restaurant in Walt Disney World's Grand Floridian Beach Resort only takes reservations. Some restaurants are so popular that there must be a policy on how far in advance reservations are taken. This practice is common for restaurants that are in demand and have a limited amount of seating.

T I P $

To Insure Proper Service

Guests will be reasonable if policies are explained to them. The Schenectady County Community College restaurant takes reservations for its meals only two weeks in advance of the desired date starting exactly at 10:00 A.M. When guests are told that the policy was designed to be fair to all, they express their appreciation.

A reservation is a promise for a table in a restaurant. The promise works in two ways: The restaurant promises to have a table available for the guest for a certain time period, and the guest promises to show up for the reservation.

Reservations provide a mutual benefit to the guest and the restaurant. Guests know that a table will be available for them without having to wait for the table, or even worse driving to the restaurant to find out they cannot be accommodated.

Reservations have advantages and disadvantages for both the restaurant and guests. The benefits for the guests are:

1. The table is available when requested.
2. The restaurant can be informed of special requests and have them available when guests arrive.
3. The host learns the guests' names.

The benefits for the restaurant are:

1. Management knows how many guests to expect; forecasting and scheduling are easier.
2. The menus and service staff can be planned exactly.
3. The host knows guests' names and can use them to create ego gratification.
4. A mailing list can be developed for future promotions.
5. If reservations are taken correctly, the restaurant will run smoothly, because the restaurant controls when the guests dine. The restaurant can prevent too many guests from showing up at the same time, thereby avoiding a strain on the kitchen and dining room.

However, reservations can also be a disadvantage. Among the disadvantages for the guests are:

1. If restaurants do not know how to take reservations and plan correctly, reservations may not be honored at the stated time.
2. Some restaurants reserve more parties than they have tables available for. This practice is called **overbooking**. Restaurants do this to avoid losing revenue in the event that guests who have reservations do not show up. Others overbook because they do not know how to plan reservations.

The possible disadvantages for the restaurant are:

1. When guests do not show up—called **no-shows**—revenue from that reserved table is lost.
2. When guests arrive late, the reservation plan may be put in disarray.
3. Restaurants that do not know how to block tables correctly lose money because they are not getting maximum use from tables.

Taking reservations is a benefit to the guest and the restaurant only if both know their responsibilities concerning reservations. Training the person who takes reservations is important. When guests make a reservation, it is an essential part of the reservationist's job to explain to the caller their responsibilities (e.g., arrive 15 minutes prior to the reservation time).

TIPS

TO INSURE PROPER SERVICE
Another of Michael Hursts' tips: Greet customers by name; make a game of remembering names.

Factors that Affect Taking Reservations

As stated in the list of disadvantages for the guests, one of the main problems is overbooking by the restaurant. First, management must establish a system that allows people taking reservations to know exactly how many tables can be reserved for the day. Also, if the restaurant takes more than one seating for the meal period, the **residence time** must be established. Residence time is defined as the time it takes a party to eat the meal and pay the bill. For example, 90 minutes are required for a complete meal with appetizers, drinks, main course, and dessert for a party of up to four people. Thus, leaving enough time to reset the table, reservations should allow two hours residence time. Guests who have larger parties will take longer to eat, so the residence time must be adjusted. Other factors also influence the residence time; music, lighting, decor, mood, ambience, and special events make the difference in how quickly or slowly the guests will eat. A menu that is easier to prepare will speed up the residence time.

Once the residence time is known and the system for taking reservations has been developed, reservations can be taken.

Taking the Reservation

Reservations are taken via telephone, the Internet, or in person. The people who take the reservations have to be trained properly so they know what information to obtain from the guests and can explain to them the policies of the restaurant.

The person answering the phone must be competent in taking reservations but also must have excellent telephone manners. This is the guest's first contact with the restaurant. To insure a good first impression, management may check their reservation procedures by conducting mystery calls to determine the competency of the reservationist. It is common telephone courtesy for people answering the phone to identify the restaurant as well as themselves. A sentence such as this is appropriate: "Good day, thank you for calling the Specialty Restaurant. This is José speaking; how may I help you?"

Reservations should be taken and placed on a preprinted form like the one shown in Figure 8–2, or entered directly into the reservation book. Which system to use depends on the size of the restaurant: A small restaurant would be able to put reservations directly into a book. A large restaurant would have to use forms and then transfer them to the book afterwards. Some restaurants use personal computers with software developed to manage the reservation process.

FIGURE 8–2

A typical reservation form. The host will fill in the information in the appropriate space.

RESERVATION FORM	
Day & Date of Reservation _____	Time_____
Guest's Name _____	Number of Guests ____
Phone Number, Home_____	Business _____
Special Instructions_____	
Taken By _____	Date Taken_____

Operations that have multiple restaurants at one location have a centralized call center to take reservations for all restaurants located in the hotel, like Atlantic City, or in a small geographical area, such as Walt Disney World. By implementing this system, a guest may call for a reservation at a time that the restaurant is normally closed. If the restaurant they request is filled, the guest will be given a choice of other restaurants.

Regardless of what type of form the restaurant uses, the information required from the guest is generally the same.

Information to Obtain from the Guest

The Name of the Guest
Included in this step is getting the correct spelling of the guests' names.

The Date the Reservation Is Desired
Ask for the date that they request with the day of the week and date. For example, when the guest says "April second," reconfirm by saying "Saturday, April second." If the date is open, proceed with other questions. If the date is booked, suggest a different day. If the guest is adamant and insist on that date, take their name and phone number and tell them they will be placed on the waiting list. Depending upon the restaurant, there should be a maximum number of parties that can be on the waiting list. Inform waiting guests that they will be called when a date opens up.

The Time of the Reservation
If the time is booked, suggest other times. At this point, the host should explain the policy concerning holding reservations. For example, a restaurant may have the policy that when guests make a reservation,

they are told they must be at the restaurant 15 minutes early. It is further explained to guests that if their reservation is for 6 P.M., they must show up at 5:45, and if they are not *there* at 5:45, the table is given to a walk-in.

The Number of Guests in the Party and Any Special Requests

If guests need a birthday cake or special seating, this should be noted. One of the reviewers for our book offered the following advice: A

Manager's Message

*T*he following article, written by Kate Harrigan, managing editor of Chef magazine, is reprinted with permission.[1]

There's been a lot of editorializing over the past couple of years about a wave of incivility, punctuated by the occasional road-rage-related shooting, that is leaving the country awash in hurt feelings. Poor service in the hospitality industry is hardly news, but people in the business ought to be aware that, as bad manners rage epidemic, customers are not becoming inured to the discourteous behavior of those who profess to serve them. In fact, many now are quite sensitized to the whole issue, and are less likely than ever to smile in the face of contempt.

Each month, *Chef* magazine interviews "Average Diner" in "Scope," reporting his or her hopes and expectations, desires, and disappointments. Reading a few of these interviews makes clear how similar we all are, no matter how different the places we come from or the lives we lead. People, whether walking into a white-tablecloth restaurant in San Francisco or a simple neighborhood bistro in New York, want to be greeted with a warm smile and waited on by a polite and efficient server.

As editors, not once have we heard, "I like those restaurants where some person who looks like she hasn't eaten in four months greets me at the door with a disdainful yet haughty expression and makes me chase after her while she stalks across the restaurant to my table." Okay, fine, so a handful of readers already are penning their responses in defense of contemptuous hosts or superior servers. But the truth is that most people are just looking for a little tenderness.

The alarming demise of basic manners at some restaurants came up at a recent editorial meeting, the topic rung in by indignant editors who had fallen victim to various ill-mannered restaurant

(continues)

significant part of my luncheon clientele consists of groups from nursing homes and many of my guests are in wheelchairs. When we take reservations we make a point of asking if any guests will be in wheelchairs and if so, how many. The information is entered in the reservation book. We allow one-and-half times the space for a wheelchair place setting when we set up the tables and allow additional space around the table for ease of access. I have noted with interest that when I ask the question the first time—as I make a point of

Manager's Message

(continued)

managers and hosts. One editor had spent five minutes on hold the previous day, standing at a pay phone in a strange city trying to make a restaurant reservation. "I lost my quarter. I certainly didn't feel special," he said. "No wonder there are so many of those online reservation services. You don't have to talk to anybody."

My own impressions of an establishment I was writing about changed considerably after I called to confirm the spelling of the chef's last name. The woman who answered the phone asked me who I was, and then put me on hold before I could answer. At any rate, I certainly hope she thought I couldn't hear her say, "Bite me."

Another editor told of calling a Boston restaurant and asking to speak with the manager. She simply wanted to find out if they served a tapenade, she said. She was a bit taken aback when the manager picked up the phone and said, "Yeah, what's your problem?"

Do these restaurants receive a lot of calls from process servers?

On the stress and aggravation scale, I'd say working in a restaurant falls somewhere between answering the phone at a computer help desk and working triage in an emergency room on a Saturday night. People calling for reservations radiate an air of entitlement that ought to be reserved for the owner's mother. Diners vent the day's frustrations on waitstaff and other innocent bystanders. And there are times when the customer, quite frankly, is wrong.

But despite the tide of boorishness and discourtesy lapping at the steps of our dining establishments, the best defense against such behavior remains scrupulous manners. Those unwilling or unable to respond in kind will find it more difficult to escalate the confrontation. And the more emotionally flexible may find themselves enjoying their meal.

knowing my clients, I seldom have to ask a second time—I am usually asked in a defensive manner, "Why do you want to know that?" Having explained my reason, the person booking the group almost always says, "That's really nice. I have never been asked that before." Before the client has even walked in the door, our actions have created a positive feeling towards us.

The Guest's Phone Numbers

Take both the home and business numbers, if possible. If there is a problem, the host can contact the guests. The host may want to contact them after the meal to find out how they liked their dining experience.

To illustrate this point, here is a true story that happened in New York State. A popular restaurant received a phone call asking for a reservation for 22 people on a Saturday evening. The arrangements were made from the guest's place of employment, therefore the manager had the guest's work phone number. Because the party was large, management asked the person making the reservation to preorder the meals.

The guest also asked the manager to suggest a hotel where these guests could stay. The manager suggested a local hotel and made a note of it. The manager also insisted on obtaining the guest's home phone number.

The Friday before the event, all details (food and wine ordered) of the dinner were confirmed. On Saturday morning, two guests stopped at the restaurant to make certain they knew how to get there from the hotel. On Saturday evening the party of 22 guests never showed up for the meal. The manager went to his reservation book and called the hotel that he had recommended. When he inquired if the guests were staying at the hotel, the desk clerk not only volunteered the information that they were, but he also mentioned overhearing them say that they were going to a local restaurant in town. The manager called the restaurant and asked to speak to the individual who arranged the party. She got on the phone and said that they had never firmed up the final details and also said that they never paid a deposit. She then hung up on the manager. The manager recalled the restaurant and the person refused to talk to him. The manager was faced with a loss of revenue for this party for 22 guests.

In a fit of either anger or brilliance, he called the woman's home phone number. Her husband answered, and the manager identified himself and asked if he knew where this group of 22 were, since they did not show up for the reservations. The husband said, "You must have the wrong number, my wife is in Boston on a business trip."

At this point the manager said, "No, your wife is in our community, at this restaurant, at this phone number, and staying at this hotel."

About an hour later, the manager of the restaurant received a call from the wife of the firm's owner—who had been to the restaurant many times. She was called by the guest's husband after the phone call from the manager. She apologized to the manager and asked that all the cooked food be donated to charity. The manager complied and sent the bill to her. It was paid in full.

As a postscript, the owner's wife still comes to the restaurant regularly; however, the husband has not been seen since the divorce.

Other Items on the Reservation Request

There are other items that the person taking the reservations should place on the reservation form. By placing these items on the form, they can be used if any problems arise, as well as for planning future reservations.

The Name of the Person Who Took the Reservation

The people who booked the party must sign their names. This makes them responsible, and if a problem arises, the host will know whom to ask. If the guest calls and changes the reservation in any way, the person who took the changes must also sign and date the reservation request form.

The Date the Reservation Was Taken

Noting the date that reservation was taken allows the host to determine how far in advance reservations are demanded.

Explaining Policies of the Restaurant to the Guest

Before the person taking the reservation thanks the guest and hangs up the phone, the guest will appreciate being informed of any special policies of the restaurant. For example, if the restaurant requires jackets for men in the dining room, this should be told to the guest at this time. The guest can be told that a gratuity is automatically added to the check. Each restaurant should develop its own reservation checklist to make certain that the guests are informed of all pertinent policies.

T I P \$

To Insure Proper Service
Restaurants should give out confirmation numbers for reservations, as hotels and airlines do.

In order to avoid mistakes, the reservation information taken down by the person who answered the phone is repeated back to the guest. Finally, the guest is thanked for calling, and told, "We look forward to seeing you on Saturday, April second, Mr. Smith."

Not Accepting Reservations

Advantages for the Restaurant

When factors warrant not taking reservations, the advantages for the restaurant are much greater than for the guest. Many no-reservation restaurants will take reservations for larger groups—usually five or more. There are four main advantages for the restaurant:

1. Maximum use of tables is obtained.
2. No overbooking occurs.
3. Little preplanning of reservations is needed.
4. No-shows are not a problem.

Maximum Use of Tables Is Obtained

Many restaurants that accept reservations will lose the use of tables for a period of time, if the host reserves the tables incorrectly. For example, if a party of 10 has a reservation for 8:30 P.M., the host puts three tables together and sets the table up at 5:00 P.M. Those tables are lost for the first three-and-a-half hours. Even when the host reserves tables correctly, some time will be lost. When tables are not occupied because the table is reserved and other guests are waiting for a table, a reservation policy loses money for the restaurant and service staff. With a no-reservation policy, the guests are seated on a first-come basis, and the restaurant is not losing money from unoccupied tables.

No Overbooking Occurs

With a no-reservation policy, there is no danger of reserving more tables than the restaurant has to accommodate the guests.

Little Preplanning of Reservations Is Needed

The host only reserves tables for large parties. At all other times, the host will seat the guests at any table that is available.

No-Shows Are Not a Problem

Because reservations are not accepted except for large parties, there is no danger of holding a table and not having the guest show up to use it. Even if the large party fails to show up, the host can reset the tables and accommodate the guests waiting for a table.

Disadvantages for the Restaurant

There are a couple of disadvantages for the restaurant that has a no-reservation policy:

1. Business may be lost because reservations will not be accepted.
2. Guests may refuse to patronize the restaurant because they believe they will have to wait for a table for a long period of time.

Both of these disadvantages have to do with the attitude, convenience, and beliefs of the guests. Many guests do not want to wait for a table. They want to be assured that they will have a table when they arrive at a restaurant. If reservations are not taken, the guest may decide to go to another restaurant, where accommodations can be secured without waiting.

The second disadvantage occurs after the restaurant has been in business for some time. When a restaurant is a success and attracts a large volume of business, the wait for a table becomes longer than an hour. The word-of-mouth network that the public uses so well informs other potential guests of this fact. This works negatively for the restaurant. Many people will not want to wait that long, so they do not try to get into the restaurant. Eventually, because so many people decide to go to other restaurants, the amount of business decreases. However, the belief that the restaurant still has a long wait time persists, even though it might not be true.

Advantages and Disadvantages for the Guest

In a no-reservation system, there are no outstanding advantages for the guest. It might be argued that everyone has the same opportunity to obtain a table; however, it is a common practice in many no-reservation establishments to push regular customers to the top of the waiting list.

The disadvantages for the guest are:

1. The guests have to wait for a table; a large party may experience an extended wait if the restaurant does not take *any* reservations.
2. If the guests are planning some other event besides dinner such as the theater, there is no guarantee that they will be seated in time to attend.

Regardless of whether the restaurant has a no-reservation policy, knowing how to reserve tables is an integral part of the host's job.

All restaurants should take reservations on holidays and for large parties of five or more guests.

Reserving Tables and Blocking Reservations

The term **blocking** means to reserve a certain table at a certain time for a guest. Its purpose is to enable the host to avoid overbooking. As was previously stated, each restaurant must determine the residence time for each meal period. Once this is known, the dining room can be blocked correctly. The process of blocking begins with taking the reservation correctly. All reservations should be taken on some kind of standard form, like the one shown in Figure 8–2.

Successful blocking depends upon an organized system. There are a few common procedures involved in all systems. Regardless of the method that is used, all blocking is to be entered in one place, such as in a three-ring binder, which is preferable to individual sheets of paper, which may get lost. The physical layout of the dining room—complete with tables and numbers—is designed and duplicated. Restaurants that have entered the computer age may block tables using a computer program. However, all methods use the same basic principle: A table can only have one party reserved to use it at a time.

Blocking in a Small Restaurant

The simplest way of blocking tables occurs when a restaurant has set meal periods and a limited number of tables. In addition to the preprinted reservation pad, all that is needed is a chart. The chart should be designed as in Figure 8–3.

Across the top of the chart is the day of the week and date. Obviously, the restaurant would have a different chart for each day

FIGURE 8–3

A blocking form for a small restaurant.

SUNDAY, APRIL 14, 20__			
Table Number	**# Seats**	**5:30**	**8:00**
1	4	Smith (2)	Yi (4)
2	6	Cohn (6)	Larkin (5)
3	2	Bhutta (2)	Woodcock (2)
4	4	Gepfert (4)	
5	2		Geleso (2)
6	4		Malary (4)

of the week and for each meal period. The next line of headings shows the table number, the number of seats at each table, and the times of the reservations. The restaurant in Figure 8–3 is only accepting reservations at 5:30 P.M. and 8:00 P.M.

The chart in Figure 8–3 is an easy one for the host to use to avoid overbooking. Notice that table 3 seats two people. It is booked for the evening. If a guest requested table 3 for Sunday, April 14 , the host would see that the table is booked. In this restaurant of six tables with 22 seats, there are only three unreserved tables. By using this form, the restaurant can avoid the problem of overbooking. All employees know at all times how many tables can be reserved. When a guest desires a reservation, the host can turn to the date in the book to see if the party can be accommodated. Then all the information needed for a reservation can be obtained from the guest.

Restaurants without Set Meal Times for Reservations

Some small restaurants will take reservations on a first-come, first-seated basis. They will take reservations at any time during their meal period. Basically, the blocking is accomplished in the same manner as in Figure 8–3, but with three differences: First, the restaurant must know the residence time of the guests. This residence time is then incorporated into the planning for reserving tables. Second, the times that the restaurant will take reservations are stated in time segments at the top of the chart. Third, the guests' names must be written on the chart and their residence time blocked out. Figure 8–4 illustrates how to block in this type of restaurant.

FIGURE 8–4

A blocking form for a restaurant that takes reservations with open seating.

Table Number	# of Guests	Time 5 5:30	Time 6 6:30	Time 7 7:30	Time 8 8:30
		SUNDAY, APRIL 14, 20__			
1	4	Lee- - - - - - - - - - - - - - -			
2	2		Jones- - - - - - - - - - -		
3	2	Malary- - - - - - - - - - - - - - - - - -			Khan- - - - -
4	6				Glock (5) - -
5	4		Zorn (3)- - - - - - - - - - -		
6	2				
7	2				

Notice that in Figure 8–4, the Zorn party at table 5 is booked from 6:00 to 8:00 P.M. The residence time for their party of three is two hours. The restaurant can take another reservation at 8:00 P.M. What problems do you envision using this type of system? Will the restaurant obtain maximum use of their tables? This is another example of a system that works well for a small restaurant; but how does a large restaurant avoid overbooking?

Blocking in a Large Restaurant

A decision must be made whether to accept reservations at any time the guest desires or only at specified times set by the restaurant. The principle of blocking tables in a large restaurant is the same as for a small restaurant, but it is impossible to block out reservations using the same method because of the large number of tables involved: There would be too much paperwork at the host's desk. The system in a large restaurant relies on having a person responsible for the planning and blocking of all reservations. This person is also responsible for informing those who take reservations about the number of tables left for each meal period. A large restaurant may have a person whose sole job is to be the **reservation manager**.

Blocking with Set Meal Times

This method of blocking tables requires four steps and is referred to as the **check-off method**. The first thing that the manager determines is the number of tables available to be reserved. For example, a restaurant has 4 tables that seat six to eight people; 12 tables that seat two; and 16 tables that seat up to four. A chart like the one shown in Figure 8–5 is made for the 2:00 P.M. seating and placed into the three-ring binder or entered into the software program where reservations are recorded. Each seating has its own individual chart.

The person taking the reservations checks off the size of the table that has been reserved. When Mrs. Smith reserves a table for six at 2:00 P.M., the reserving and blocking would occur in the following manner: The person taking the reservation would look at the check-off sheet for Mother's Day at the 2:00 P.M. seating. Seeing a table available, all information would be obtained on the preprinted reservation form. The first table under the "6–8" column would be crossed out, and the name Smith would be placed next to it. The first line of the chart would appear as it does in Figure 8–6.

The chart would continue to be crossed off and filled out until all the tables are used. If a guest desired a reservation for more than eight

SUNDAY, MAY 12, 20__ (MOTHER'S DAY)		
2 P.M. Seating		
2	**4**	**6–8**
12	16	4
11	15	3
10	14	2
9	13	1
8	12	
7	11	
6	10	
5	9	
4	8	
3	7	
2	6	
1	5	
	4	
	3	
	2	
	1	

FIGURE 8–5

A check-off sheet. The check-off sheet is used to assist the reservation manager in blocking.

SUNDAY, MAY 12, 20__ (MOTHER'S DAY)		
2 P.M. Seating		
2	**4**	**6–8**
12	16	4̶ (Smith) (6)

FIGURE 8–6

The check-off sheet after a reservation for Smith has been taken.

people, the reservation manager would have to establish a policy for accepting or rejecting the request. As large parties require combining existing tables, the reservation manager must carefully plan for them or overbooking will occur.

Each restaurant should decide the maximum number of large parties that can be accepted. A set formula has to be determined for checking off tables so the restaurant will not overbook. For example, a reservation for 12 may include putting together four 4-tops and a deuce. When a reservation is made for a party of 12, four 4-tops and a table for two must be crossed off.

The reservation manager, to assist in the planning of reservations, will have a printed diagram of the dining room and will block the guests' names and times next to the table that they have been assigned, as shown in Figure 8–7. The Jones, Casola, and Mardigian

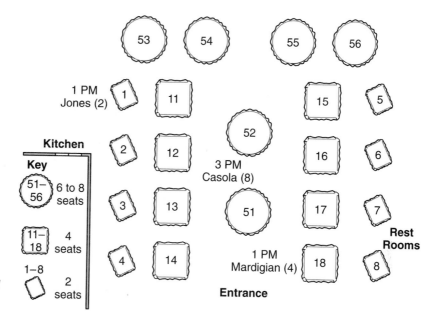

FIGURE 8–7

The dining room blocked with three reservations.

reservations have been blocked off. As more reservations arrive, the remainder of the dining room can be blocked off.

The key factor in making this system work is to have constant communication between the reservation manager and the people taking the reservations. Some restaurants use a software program that has been programmed and designed to do the blocking, and it generates alphabetical lists of the reservations for that meal period.

Accepting Reservations at Any Time

If the restaurant allows guests to reserve tables for any time—called **open seating**—then even more planning and organizing is required to avoid overbooking. The check-off sheet would be used, except that the sheet would have the guest's name and the time of the reservation. Figure 8–8 shows how the sheet would look after the restaurant accepted the first reservation for the Jones party of two.

FIGURE 8–8

The blocking sheet for open seating after the Jones reservation has been accepted.

SUNDAY, MAY 12, 20__ (MOTHER'S DAY)		
Open Seating		
2	**4**	**6–8**
~~12~~ Jones (1 P.M.)	16	4

The reservation time is placed next to the Jones name to inform all people taking reservations that a table has been booked. Since the people taking reservations know that the usual residence time for a guest table is two hours, they may accept another reservation at 3:00 P.M. for the table. However, this system could become very confusing when multiple reservations are made or when guests come late or early or overstay the residence time. Therefore the reservation manager would be well advised to block out tables daily on the master chart of the dining room, as shown in Figure 8–7. Each day, an updated sheet should be put in the three-ring binder, showing the number of tables left to reserve. It is easy to understand why a computer software program that reserves seats would be ideal for a large restaurant.

Blocking Effectively

The previous examples show how blocking can be done in one step. For the small restaurant, this is a simple process. Large restaurants, however, create more of a challenge. Blocking involves much planning and organization so that the guests will have their tables available when they arrive. To block effectively, the reservation manager needs three items: a *diagram* of the dining room, the *reservations*, and the *check-off sheet*.

The diagram of the dining room must show the table number and the number of people that can be seated at each table. The reservations are on preprinted forms that the person taking the reservations has completed and the check-off sheet is the control sheet located where the reservations are taken.

Blocking is accomplished by the way of an organized process. First, the reservation manager assigns the reservation to an appropriately sized table. Then, the guest's name and time is placed on the diagram at the table, as shown in Figure 8–7. Figure 8–8 shows the blocking sheet for open reservations.

Finally, an alphabetized listing of the guests arriving is completed alongside their expected arrival time and their assigned table. An example of the list is shown in Figure 8–9. From the list and a copy of the blocking diagram, it is easy for the host to know what tables are blocked and what guests are to be seated at which table. Because the reservations are set up first by time and then alphabetized, the host's job is made easier, as much planning has taken place before the guest has arrived. This system works well if planned and executed properly.

However, there are some problems that can be associated with this system. First, if the guests do not like the table they have been

FIGURE 8–9

The alphabetized reservation list. After the reservation manager has blocked the tables, the guests' names are organized on a reservation form.

RESERVATIONS FOR SUNDAY, APRIL 28, 20__		
Name	**Number in Party**	**Table Assigned**
1 P.M.		
Feldman	4	12
Jones	6	51
Khan	2	4
1:30 P.M.		
Collins	4	16
Malary	6	55
Zorn	2	8

Sweet or Sour?

The reservations system works only if the host does not deviate from the system. A restaurant that only takes holiday reservations is a good example.

On Easter Sunday, the restaurant accepted reservations and served over 800 guests. A month later on Mother's Day, it served over 1,200. For both holidays, it used the open-seating policy on taking reservations. In addition to the regular dining room, it also used three banquet rooms for parties of six or more.

The dining rooms at Easter were running smoothly until 4:00 P.M. At that time, the staff began to get tired—both dining room and kitchen—and the residence time increased. Some guests had to wait for their assigned tables. As a solution, the hosts deviated from the plan, putting guests at tables that they were not assigned. From 4:00 P.M. to 6:00 P.M. the staff had a mess on their hands. Guests were being brought to tables that should have been vacant and were not. The hosts could not keep up with the changes that were being made and for those two hours confusion reigned. Fortunately, they learned from their mistakes.

A few weeks later, Mother's Day was almost perfect. The restaurant's planning took into account the fatigue factor of the staff. It increased the residence time of the guests for later in the day and did not deviate from the plan. The result of the planning was that just one party of guests was not seated at its assigned time. When the guests arrived, an explanation was offered to them, admitting that it was the restaurant's problem, not theirs'. To show its concern, the restaurant invited them to go to the bar and have complimentary drinks or complimentary Champagne with their meal. In addition, the host kept checking back with the guests to advise them how long it would be before their table was available.

The result was phenomenal: over 1,200 guests served with only one problem!

assigned, the host may have a problem with the guests. The host has a few options: For example, the guests' table could be switched to another comparable table (a four-top for a four-top); or an apology could be offered and an explanation given as to why the guests cannot have the table they desire (e.g., all the tables are reserved). If the host ever does switch a table for the guest, the master sheet also has to be updated.

Second, if guests stay beyond the residence time, the next party will have to wait for their table. Another problem that can occur is to have a party appear for their reservation and state that they have a few more people to add to the party. This can create a real headache for the restaurant. The host must calmly talk to the person in charge of the reservation and assure him or her that the restaurant will accommodate the party as soon as it is possible. Next, the host should make whatever arrangements are necessary to seat the guests (add an extra seat to a table, put two tables together, etc.). This is one of the situations in which the host has to use good judgment, tact, and diplomacy to keep everyone happy.

Taking reservations and blocking require a lot of organization and preplanning, but these allow the restaurant to have a table ready for guests and to avoid overbooking. Some would say it is too much work to do all that preplanning. Some might take some shortcuts and not put the names next to the table. This can work only if the host is experienced and knows the room. A person using this system initially should follow the steps described here, and the problem of overbooking will be eliminated. Once again, the reader can see the importance of the five Ps of management: *Prior Planning Prevents Poor Performance.*

Call-Ahead or Priority Seating

Many guests will not patronize a restaurant that does not take reservations. Long waits for a table prompt many complaints from guests. Restaurants have a technique called **call-ahead seating** or **priority seating** to manage this.

Guests call the restaurant and have their name added to the seating list. It holds a waiting spot for the guest for dinner that day. The guest's name is logged immediately onto the seating list so that when he or she arrives, the wait will not be as long. It does not guarantee the guest a table for a certain time, but a place in line. The guest does the waiting somewhere other than in the restaurant; therefore, this system keeps the wait time in the restaurant to a minimum. For example, a man calls the restaurant and states that he would like a table for four people at 6:00 P.M. His name is added to the list under the four-tops, and when he arrives at 6:00 P.M., his party gets the next available table.

Other restaurants have instituted a system called **first available seating**. A guest asks for a reservation for 6:00 P.M. and the reservationist informs the guest that a reservation has been made at 6:00 P.M. for first available seating. It is explained to the guest that the first table that becomes available around 6:00 P.M. will be for their party. It may be at 6:02 or 6:04 or 6:15 P.M. Using this type of system helps the restaurant manage its flow of guests. It also is a benefit because some guests may stay at their table longer than the residence time. When the party arrives for their 6:00 P.M. first available seating, they will be seated immediately if a table is available. If one is not, many restaurants now have pagers that are given to guests waiting for a table. One type vibrates when paged. The other sends out a visual message; both may have a verbal message stating "Your table is now ready."

How to Alleviate No-Shows

A major problem that restaurants face in taking reservations is with guests who do not show up for their reservations. Restaurants have been trying to solve the problem of **no-shows** for many years. Some proven methods have been found that work for reducing the number of no-shows.

The first step in preventing no-shows is to properly train the people who take reservations. Proper training means informing guests of restaurant policies pertaining to the reservation. Also, when the guest makes a reservation, information has to be obtained and recorded clearly and correctly.

Some restaurants request that the guest call them back on the day of the reservation to confirm. However, many people object to this, because the restaurant is making the guest do the work.

A better method is to inform the guests that on the day of the reservation, the staff will contact them within a certain time frame—for example, between 12:00 P.M. and 3:00 P.M.—to confirm the reservation. The guests are told that if they are unable to be reached, their reservation will not be honored unless the guest confirms the reservation.

Other restaurants have begun to employ the same methods as hotels do for lodging rooms: They take a deposit for the reservations. In towns where there is a large demand for tables, restaurants have asked for a guest's credit card number or for cash to hold the table.

Some owners use a personal computer to keep track of guests who are no-shows. Once the guest becomes a no-show, the name is put on an alphabetized list for the reservation taker. When a guest calls and asks for a reservation, the name is checked against the list. If the name is on the list, the employee informs the guest that there was a reservation scheduled for a certain date for which the guest did not show up. The policy is further explained to the guest that if he or she does not show up for the reservation and does not cancel, then the restaurant will no longer take any reservations under that name.

By using one or a combination of these methods, the number of no-shows in the restaurant will be greatly decreased. One person took drastic action concerning a no-show. David Pelzman, owner of David's on Main in Columbus, Ohio, a 46-seat American bistro, sued customer Jeff Burrey, who was a no-show on New Year's Eve.

Pelzman decided to sue Burrey after his party of four did not show up on New Year's Eve. The table was held and Pelzman calculated that he lost $240 in revenue, or $60 per person. The $240 suit was dropped by Pelzman after Burrey's attorney presented the judge with a thank-you letter sent to Burrey for his donation to the Mid-Ohio Food Bank. (Earlier, Pelzman had requested that Burrey make a donation for any amount to a food-service charity in exchange for Pelzman's dropping the suit.)

David's on Main now requires advance credit card payments for reservations on New Year's Eve.[2]

SUMMARY

1. A reservation is a promise for a table in a restaurant. Walk-ins are guests who patronize the restaurant without making a reservation.

2. There are advantages for a restaurant that takes reservations from guests: Tables are available when requested, the host learns the guests' names, and any requests are ready when guests arrive. Forecasting and scheduling are made easier for the restaurant because the number of guests coming to the restaurant is known. The host knows guests' names and can use them to create ego gratification. A list of patrons' addresses can be developed by the restaurant for future promotions. Restaurants will be able to control when guests dine, which avoids a strain on the kitchen and dining room. There are disadvantages for guests. Reservations may not be honored at the stated time and reservations may overbook.

   Restaurants have disadvantages too. A loss of revenue occurs when guests do not honor their reservations, or reservationists do not know how to block tables. When guests are late in arriving, the reservation plan is put in disarray.

3. Benefits exist for restaurants that do not take reservations. The maximum use of tables is obtained, no-shows or overbooking do not occur, and little preplanning of reservations is needed. The major disadvantage for a restaurant is that guests may not patronize the restaurant because they cannot make reservations. The benefit for the guest is that presumably all guests are treated the same. The disadvantage for the guests involves the fact that the guests cannot have a table when they desire it; they have to wait for the restaurant to have one available for them.

4. Blocking of tables for reservations is accomplished by having an organized system. The restaurant must have a floor plan of the restaurant and know the residence time for parties.

5. The restaurant, in order to seat guests with a reservation, will use a blocked reservation system.

6. Problems for restaurants that take reservations occur when guests arrive late for their scheduled time or stay longer than their residence time at the table. Restaurants have to inform guests about their policies. When guests stay longer than the residence time, management may use subtle and not-so-subtle methods to encourage guests to finish their dining experience.

7. Controlling no-shows is solved by informing guests about the restaurant's policies and may take a nonrefundable deposit to hold the reservation. Some restaurants have the guests call back the morning of the reservation to reconfirm, whereas others call the guests back to reconfirm the reservation.

8. Call-ahead seating is like a reservation. The difference is that call-ahead seating is used when the restaurant is open for business and holds a waiting spot for the guests for the meal period.

9. The concept of first priority seating is also like a reservation. The guest requests a reservation for a certain time. When the guest arrives at the restaurant, she will be seated as soon as a table is available.

REVIEW QUESTIONS

1. What are walk-ins? How are they different from guests who have a reservation?

2. What are the benefits and disadvantages for the guest at a restaurant that takes reservations?

3. What are the benefits and disadvantages for a restaurant that takes reservations?

4. What are the benefits and disadvantages for the guest at a restaurant that does not take reservations?

5. What are the benefits and disadvantages for the restaurant that does not take reservations?
6. What information should be obtained from a guest when taking a reservation? Why is this information important?
7. Explain how reservations can be structured to avoid overbooking. Include in your answer reservation taking, blocking, and drawing up seating charts.

DISCUSSION QUESTIONS

1. Your superior wants to have a no-reservation policy. The restaurant is located in a large metropolitan city. What reasons would you give your superior to have a no-reservation policy? What reasons could you give for accepting reservations?
2. Based on Figure 8–3, what type of cuisine would the restaurant that uses this type of blocking system have to make the system work? What will be the cost of the typical meal: high, average, or low? In other words, what factors must exist for a restaurant to use this system?
3. Guests arrive at the restaurant where you are the host. They have a reservation for 7:00 P.M. It is 6:45, but they are not dressed according to the restaurant's dress code. What do you do?
4. Should restaurants overbook when they take reservations? Explain your answer.
5. All of the tables have been blocked for reservations in the restaurant. A table of four overstayed their residence time by 25 minutes because they ordered extra wine, appetizers, desserts, and after-dinner drinks. The second seating of guests for the table has arrived. What steps would you take to make both groups of guests happy?
6. Should a restaurant ever limit the amount of reservations they will take?

REFERENCES

1. Kate Harrigan, "Wrong Number," *Chef* 10, No. 7 (July 2000): 8.
2. "David's Settles No-Show Suit," *Nation's Restaurant News* (November 21, 1994): 11.

Managing the Dining Experience

OBJECTIVES   At the completion of this chapter, the student should be able to:

1. Recite, recognize, and know how to correct or avoid the seven deadly sins of service as stated in this chapter.
2. Explain the method of handling the complaints of guests who have a problem with reservations, the food, or any part of the dining experience.
3. Use a turnsheet and know its purpose.
4. Work the floor.
5. Seat guests—those with reservations, as well as walk-ins—using the tools available to the host.

KEY WORDS   turnsheet   time in   working the floor
                 waitlist   time seated   turning tables
                 est. wait time

The Operation of the Dining Room

A pleasurable dining experience will result in guests' returning to the restaurant for another meal. Return business is the key to making a restaurant profitable.

The restaurant business world would do well to adopt the model of service created by Swedish businessman Jan Carlzon. In the early 1980s, he sought to make the financially troubled Scandinavian Air System the best airline in Europe. He was able to change it from a losing prospect to a profitable one by using service as its main strategy. Carlzon keyed his system to "the moment of truth." A moment of truth occurs each time a guest comes in direct contact with the restaurant's people or systems. The model states that the service image of a business is the sum of all its moments of truth.

The host is a key player in a restaurant's moment of truth. Many times, the first employee of the restaurant who comes in contact with the guests is the host. The host may also be responsible for training and managing the service employees in the dining room. Service staff have many moments of truth with the guests. Karl Albrecht, author of the book *Service America*, stated at a conference of chain restaurant executives in Orlando, Florida: "Your service image is not in the hands of your managers. Rather, it's won or lost by your service personnel."[1] It becomes the responsibility of the host to insure that the staff excels in giving the guests positive moments of truth.

The Seven Deadly Sins of Service

Karl Albrecht also states that there are seven deadly sins of service. They are listed in Figure 9–1. Being aware of them and of how to prevent them is the obligation of both the host and the service staff. The seven deadly sins of service are *apathy, the brush-off, coldness, condescension,*

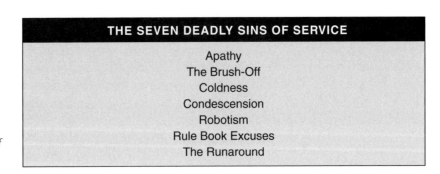

FIGURE 9–1

The seven deadly sins of service.

THE SEVEN DEADLY SINS OF SERVICE

Apathy
The Brush-Off
Coldness
Condescension
Robotism
Rule Book Excuses
The Runaround

robotism, rule book excuses, and *the runaround.* Let's examine how each one of these sins relates to the job of the host.

Apathy

Apathy can be described as a lack of emotion or interest. An example of an apathetic host is found in the following example: The guest enters the restaurant and sees the host standing at the host's podium. The host does not acknowledge the guest's presence. Instead, the host appears to be interested in reading something that is much more important than greeting guests.

To avoid the sin of apathy, greet guests immediately. Studies have shown that the impression made in the *first 30 seconds* determines the feeling of the guest about the total dining experience. This is the first moment of truth for the restaurant. The host can create a positive impression by greeting the guest warmly within 30 seconds of arrival.

Sweet or Sour?

It was a bitterly cold night in a major metropolitan city. Our reservation was for 6:00 P.M. at one of the most highly praised restaurants in the city. We asked our concierge at the hotel how long it would take to reach the restaurant by cab. "About 10 minutes, but because it is the rush hour, I would allow myself more time." So at 5:30 we took a cab to the restaurant. As luck would have it, the trip only took 10 minutes. We were dropped off right at the door of the restaurant. As we walked into the restaurant, the hostess said to us, "We won't open until 6:00 P.M." She did not give us a welcome, instead she turned us away. She offered us no seat at the bar, did not ask if we had a reservation, and basically told us to go outside and wait until 6:00 P.M. As we walked the unfamiliar neighborhood in the subfreezing temperature, we could feel the heat rising—the heat from anger! Finally, after walking the street for 15 minutes, we went back into the restaurant. The same hostess seated us without any acknowledgment that we had been in the restaurant 15 minutes before. How was the food and service? If it was exceptional, we could not remember. What we know is that we will never recommend this restaurant to anyone!

The Brush-Off

Brush-off is a slang term that means *rebuff,* according to the *Random House Dictionary.*[2] Relating it to the host's job, an example of brushing off the guest occurs in the following cases: The guest approaches the host and asks, usually in a timid manner, "When will my table be ready? You told me it would be ready now and it isn't." The host replies, "In a few minutes," and walks away from the guest without any explanation or comment. The second moment of truth has been negative for the restaurant. To prevent committing the second sin, the host should strive to give the guest undivided attention. To avoid brushing off the guest, the host should apologize to the guest and assure that the party will be seated as soon as possible. The host will then seat that party when the next table is available. If the problem persists and a table is not ready, it becomes the responsibility of the host to tell the guest about the status of the seating. Eye contact should be made with the guests, so they do not get the impression that the host is trying to brush them off.

Coldness

Have you ever been to a restaurant where the food was excellent and the prices reasonable, but you still felt something was missing? That something was a problem that you could not identify but it may have been that the restaurant left you with a cold feeling toward it. The host who responds to the guest's question with one-phrase or one-word answers is guilty of committing the sin of coldness. For example, a guest might ask the host, "How long has the restaurant been in business?" The host answers, "Two years." The next question is also answered with a brisk reply. This is the one opportunity for the host to make the guest the restaurant's ally; instead, the host has turned off the guest. Answers are best if they are complete and friendly. This will benefit the restaurant in two ways. First, the guest will have questions answered; second, it will create a warm feeling toward the restaurant.

T I P $

TO INSURE PROPER SERVICE

"Basic service is giving the customer what they want, when they want it, and at a price they are willing to pay," states Peter O'Connor, senior vice president of the 418-room Hard Rock Hotel and Resort in Bali in Indonesia, which includes five restaurants and the Hard Rock Cafe.[3]

Condescension

Condescension can be described as an air of superiority that an individual shows toward another person. A host who is guilty of the sin of condescension would give the guest the impression that the guest does not belong in the restaurant. Unfortunately, condescension is frequently directed at high school students. This most often occurs when they have a prom and go out to dinner before the dance. The host's attitude conveys the impression to the staff that the high school students are not very good customers. Notice the word *customers* is used, not *guests*. That is an example of a condescending attitude. To correct this problem, the host should lead by setting an example and should treat all the individuals who enter the restaurant as guests when all guests receive positive treatment by all employees, repeat business for the establishment will increase. Neither the host nor the staff should convey the feelng that they are better than any of the guests. By treating the high school students as guests, and by realizing that this is an important night for them, the host can make them feel important. Therefore, the host should greet them warmly and treat them like the valued, respectable guests they are.

Robotism

Robots do not belong in the dining room of a restaurant. A robot can do many repetitive, boring tasks well. However, the job of the host is not repetitive or boring. An example of robotism is when the host seats guests. The host picks up the menus and says, "Follow me," and then sprints to the table. The host then places the menus at the place settings and says, "Have a good meal." The next group of people are treated to the same robotic antics. This method of dealing with guests is eventually transferred to the actions of the service staff. It becomes especially obvious when the service person is going through the "Hi, my name is ____" canned speech. To alleviate the sin of robotism, the host should act natural and should encourage the staff to act natural also. The host's movements should be energetic, and his speech should be cordial toward the guests. A robot would be great to do the dishes, but not to manage the dining room.

Rule Book Excuses

Rules are a necessary part of any business. However, when a host manages only by rules, and does not use common sense, the restaurant will suffer.

The host must not commit the sin of rule book excuses, and may bend the rules when it benefits the guests.

Sweet or Sour?

A couple decided to try a new restaurant that had windows overlooking a beautiful view. The tables directly in front of the windows were all booths for four people. When the hostess seated them at a deuce away from the windows, they asked for a window seat. The hostess said "I'm sorry, but I have to save those seats for parties of four." They tried to buy the table by giving her a tip. She still said that she could not give them the table. The time was 5:00 P.M., just when the restaurant opened, and there were no other guests demanding to be seated. The couple could not understand why they could not have the table they desired. During their meal, they watched the table to see how many people she sat at the booths. When they left an hour and a half later, there still were no guests seated at the table they wanted. Of course, they never returned to the restaurant. Apparently, not too many others did either, because the restaurant went out of business. This hostess failed her moment of truth.

The Runaround

The final sin of service has been experienced by everyone at one time or another in life: we call it the runaround. An example of this is when the guest is waiting for a table at a no-reservation restaurant. The guest approaches the host and asks how long it will be before the party is seated, and the host replies, "Just a short time." The guest waits, and after 20 minutes returns to the host and asks the same question. Again the host says that it will be just a short while. When the guest demands a specific time, the host pretends to check the dining room and gets sidetracked.

The definition of the runaround is to give vague answers or to refuse to answer the question by ignoring or changing the meaning of the question. The way to avoid the runaround is for the host to give definite answers. A definite time will satisfy the question "How long will it be before a table is ready?" An appropriate answer would be "15 to 20 minutes," not "in a short while."

Knowing and training the staff to recognize and avoid the seven deadly sins of service is important, because the restaurant business is filled with many moments of truth. A restaurant cannot afford to have sins committed at any time.

The first moment of truth comes when a reservation is made or when the host greets guests; the last occurs when the guests leave the establishment. Throughout their meal, they will experience a series of moments. All of these moments of truth add up to the total service in the restaurant. If staff fail in one of these moments of truth, service will suffer.

The Greeting

The host is exactly that: a host. The greeting should be warm and cordial, just as it would be in the host's home. The first 30 seconds are critical for the guest. In that time, the guest forms an opinion about whether the restaurant wants or does not want the guest's business. This is all determined from the greeting offered by the host.

The size and volume of the restaurant determine the number of hosts on duty and their responsibilities. Smaller restaurants usually have one host, who must perform all the jobs. At larger establishments, there may be as many as four hosts: one remains at the podium to greet guests, take names, and assign tables; another finds the guests in the waiting area or at the bar; the other two show the guests to their tables, each being responsible for one half of the dining room.

Other establishments use three hosts. One remains at the podium to greet guests, take names, and assign tables. Another gets the guests when their table is ready. The third seats people and does table checks.

Regardless of the size of the establishment or the number of hosts employed, one host is always responsible for greeting guests. This individual is always in a position to see when a guest enters the restaurant.

Once a guest enters the restaurant, it becomes the host's responsibility to greet them immediately. If the host recognizes the guests he will greet them by addressing them by name. If the guests are new to the restaurant, the greeting is cordial. When at the podium receiving guests, the host should not be leaning over the desk, chewing gum, smoking, or drinking. Instead, the guests receive the undivided attention of the host. If the restaurant takes reservations, the first question after the greeting will be, "Do you have a reservation?" If the guests do have a reservation, the host takes them to their table.

If the restaurant does not take reservations, or the guests do not have a reservation, an inquiry will be made about the size of the party. The host should be aware of obvious facts; avoid saying to a single person, "Table for one." Instead say, "I have a nice table for you, sir; would you please follow me?"

TIPS

TO INSURE PROPER SERVICE
"Always greet every guest with a smile, using the guest's name whenever possible," says Peter O'Connor, senior VP of the Hard Rock Hotel and Resort in Bali.[4]

Assigning Tables

As with everything else in the restaurant business, there is a correct way to assign tables. There are also those hosts who take shortcuts and create problems for the guests, service staff, and the restaurant. Assigning tables correctly is another step toward insuring that the restaurant obtains maximum income and the guests receive excellent service.

A good tactic used by many restaurants is to seat the guests who arrive when the restaurant opens at a table by the window. Studies have shown that people would rather dine in a busy restaurant than one that is not busy. If the host seats guests near a window, people walking or driving by will see the guests enjoying a meal, and it will create an impression in their minds that the restaurant is a good place to dine.

Rotation of the seating of the guests among the different stations is also advised. The wrong way to seat guests is for the host to seat the first 20 guests at one station and then fill up the next section. Instead, the first party is seated at station one, the second at station two, and so on. Rotating the seating in this manner allows the service person to give the guests excellent service. If the service person's station were filled up all at once, it would be difficult to give the guests good service, because the server would be overwhelmed, or *in the weeds*, with too many guests to serve at once. The rotation of assigning tables is also considered when stations are made and reservations are being blocked.

Occasionally a guest will request a special table or a different table from the one the host assigns. If the host can honor the request, it is good policy to do so. If there is a legitimate reason not to honor the request, it should be explained to the guest. For example, many times guests will request a four-top for their party of two. If there is not too much business forecasted for the day, the host can give them the table they desire. If the host expects a high volume of guests or has a reservation for the table they desire, the guests should be told the reason why they cannot have the table. Of course, if they are regular guests, the host should try to accommodate them and provide them with the table they request. Always seat parties of two at four-tops if those tables are not in demand.

When a large group of people request a table together, the host should inquire whether they are on a time schedule; guests may have some event to attend and only a limited time to eat. If they are on a schedule, it would be wise for the host to explain that it would be faster if the party broke up into groups of four. The host could then seat the guests at different stations in the dining room, where they will have more service staff to wait on them, instead of just one service person.

Forms Needed to Seat Guests

In addition to the ability to think quickly, the host needs a few forms that will facilitate doing the job correctly and efficiently. The forms needed are 1) a diagram of the tables in the restaurant; 2) the reservation list; 3) the turnsheet; 4) a table check form; and 5) a waitlist. These forms can be generated by the old fashioned method—on a piece of paper using a pen or pencil, or by a computer printout. Regardless of the method, the same principles are applied to effectively and efficiently seat guests.

A Diagram of the Tables in the Restaurant

At the host's desk, there should be a diagram of the floor plan of the restaurant. Many restaurants place this diagram under a glass top. The hosts are given a grease pencil so that they can write on the glass to indicate the vacant or occupied status of the table. Using the grease pencil and glass top makes it easier for the host to keep track, since it is easier to erase and neater than trying to keep track on individual paper diagrams.

Some restaurants have their seating charts on software programs. These are generally chain restaurants that have similar floor plans, so they can spread out the cost of developing their software over their many units. The host uses a computer that is located at the host station.

For independent restaurants, a software seating program is challenging because of the different configurations of dining rooms. These restaurants do not have the time, expertise, or money to develop a software program for seating. In addition, the time and learning curve involved in training hosts to use the software make it prohibitive for smaller restaurants. They will likely prefer to use the grease pencil method, because it is simple and fast.

The Reservation List

Along with the diagram of the restaurant, the host should also have list of the names of the guests who have reserved a table. Included on the list beside the name should be the number of guests and the table number assigned. The list should be set up in chronological order and alphabetized. This will allow the host to check off the names as the guests come in to the restaurant and will make for a smoother operation. Figure 9–2 shows the reader how the reservation list should be set up.

The listing would continue throughout the entire day. By setting it up in an organized fashion, the host can spend time attending to the guests' needs. If the host did not write this seating out in advance, he would have to spend an enormous amount of time and effort correctly seating the guests with reservations.

The Turnsheet

The next form needed to seat guests effectively is called a **turnsheet**. Figure 9–3 illustrates how this form allows the host to keep track of how many guests have been seated at each station and what station should receive the next party.

Our turnsheet shows that we have five service staff. After each person's name there is a series of numbers. Find the 6/6 fraction after Tom's name. The top number of the fraction represents the number of guests in the party. The bottom number is the cumulative total of all guests seated at Tom's station during this meal period.

FIGURE 9–2

A reservation list set up for the host.

RESERVATIONS FOR SUNDAY, APRIL 28, 20__		
Name	**Number in Party**	**Table Assigned**
	1 P.M.	
Feldman	4	12
Jones	6	51
Jaypel	2	4
	1:30 P.M.	
Collins	4	16
Malary	6	55
Zorn	2	8

FIGURE 9–3

A turnsheet keeps track of how many guests have been seated at each station and what station should receive the next party.

TURNSHEET			
Name			
Jan	3/3	3/6	4/10
Chenusa	2/2	4/6	7/13
Jim	1/1	2/3	8/11
Sheryar	4/4	4/8	2/10
Tom	6/6	2/8	

From this example, Tom has only had 8 guests, while Sheryar and Jan have had 10 each, Jim 11, and Chenusa 13. The host will seat the next party at Tom's station. Most hosts use a turnsheet to seat guests equitably among service staff. However, when the restaurant becomes busy, often the host has no choice but to seat the guests at the next available table. To avoid any controversy with the service staff, it is advisable for the host to keep track of the guests served by using a turnsheet.

Sweet or Sour?

Restaurants that do not take reservations or those that only reserve a small percentage of tables, need a method to seat guests. When there are tables available, there are no problems; guests are seated at an available table. Problems arise when all tables are occupied.

No guest wants to be treated in the following manner. In a no-reservations policy restaurant, when guests approached the host and asked for a table, the host would seat them. However, if the dining room was full, the host would tell the guest to go to the bar and check back in a few moments. The guest would say, "Aren't you going to put my name down?" The host would reply, "No." The guest wanted to know how he would know when his table would be ready. "Just come back, and if there is a table you get it," said the host. The guest suggested that a better method would be to take his name down. The host replied, "What do you think I am, a secretary?" The host is no longer employed at this establishment.

Table Check

The **table check** (see Figure 9–4) is a tool that allows the host to know the point of the meal that each table has reached. This form is continuously updated throughout the meal. For instance, some restaurants will have it done every 20 minutes. The table check is

FIGURE 9–4

A table check form allows the host to easily see the status of every table.

TABLE CHECK					
No. in Party	JS	SS	Entree	Coff	Up
2	11	14	75	71	74
4	24	34	64	62	61
Big Table	17	18	19	20	
8:20 P.M.					

completed by one of the hosts whose job it is to walk around the dining room and observe each table's progress. The host writes down the course each table is on under the appropriate column. For instance, if table 71 is having coffee, a 71 goes under the coffee column, as shown in Figure 9–4.

From Figure 9–4, the reader can see that table 74 is available for a party of two, and table 61 is available for a party of four. *Up* means the table is available; *JS* refers to just seated; *SS* means soup or salad; *Entree* means the guests are eating their main course; and *Coff* means the guests are having coffee. Using the table check, which was completed at 8:20 P.M., the host greeting guests at the podium knows the status of all tables at all times. When a party of two approaches the podium and requests a table for two, the host can seat them immediately at table 74. The next party of two will have to wait until table 71 finishes their coffee. The host will know that it generally takes 15 to 20 minutes before that table will be vacant. When all the tables are filled, the table check gives the host a guideline of how long it will be before the guests can be seated. The approximate waiting times would be as follows:

If the guests are on:	Table available in:
Soup and salad	45–60 minutes
Entree	30–45 minutes
Coffee	15–20 minutes

Some restaurants do table checks every 20 minutes, whereas others do table checks informally. The Perry Restaurant Group and Hooters use electronic devices to assist with the table check. The host remains at the desk greeting guests, while another employee roams throughout the dining room communicating the availability of the tables directly to the host via a headset microphone. Once the host knows how long the wait will be, the proper method of informing the guests can be used.

Informing the Guests about the Wait

When a guest arrives at a restaurant that does not take reservations and there is a long waiting time, the host has an obligation to tell the guests approximately how long they will have to wait for a table. Most guests do not mind waiting; however, some guests will object. The host should never state to a guest that it will just be a few minutes for a table. Instead, the host should give the guest an approximate time. This time has to be one that the host can honor; so, if the host knows that a table will be vacant in 15 minutes, the guest should be told that there is a wait of *15 to 20* minutes. If the guest is seated before the 15 minutes, that will be great for the guest. If the wait is more than 20 minutes, the restaurant has failed in this moment of truth.

When the host informs the guest of the length of the wait, the responsibility of staying or leaving rests upon the guest. Many restaurants have a friendly working relationship with their competitors. Sometimes a host will even phone the competitors and find out how long the wait is there. The host can use this information in a variety of ways to assist the guests. First, if there is a long wait at the competitor's restaurant, this knowledge relayed to the guests may keep them at the host's restaurant. This is especially true after the guests have to factor in driving time to the other restaurant. However, if the competitor has space available or a much shorter waiting list, this can be relayed to the guests.

The host should keep guests informed whenever possible regarding any problems that arise that may keep the table from being available when promised. If guests cannot be seated when promised, management policy may allow the host to give the guests some complimentary item to let them know that their business is appreciated. One restaurant takes this a step further: Any guests who are told the waiting time and decide that it is too long for them to stay receive a card that can be redeemed for a complimentary drink on their next visit.

The Waitlist

All restaurants that take walk-ins must have a **waitlist**. This form allows the host to seat guests in an organized manner. The waitlist is used when all the tables are occupied and guests are waiting for a table. The waitlist is shown in Figure 9–5.

The waitlist is set up with the names of the guests who are waiting for a table. The next column is for guests who want a table for four or

FIGURE 9–5

*The waitlist form allows
the host to seat walk-in
guests in an organized
manner.*

THE WAITLIST						
Name	4 or 6 Guests	Est. Wait Time	Time In	Time Seated	2	Table Number
Smith	(51)	30/45	8:02	8:32	2	51
Jones	4(62)	30/45	8:15			
Brown	6(22)	30/45	8:17			

more guests. The number in parentheses, 51, represents the table that the host plans to use for that party. **Est. wait time** refers to the amount of time the host has estimated that the guest will have to wait for a table. **Time in** refers to when the guest entered the restaurant. **Time seated** is when the guest has been seated at the table. The next column is for parties of two. Finally, the table number where the guest was actually seated is recorded. In our example in Figure 9–5, Mr. Smith entered the restaurant at 8:02 P.M. and wanted a table for two guests. From the table check chart, the host decides to seat Mr. Smith at table 51 because the guests at the table are on their entree. He informs the waiting guests that there will be a 30- to 45-minute wait, whereupon Mr. Smith decides to stay and have dinner. The host gives Mr. Smith a card with Mr. Smith's name on it, instructs him to give it to the host when his name is called, and keeps a duplicate copy for himself. This stops guests from trying to claim a table when it is not their name being called.

Informing Guests that Their Table Is Available

Different establishments have different methods for informing their guests when their tables are ready. Many have loudspeakers that announce the names. A more professional method is to have a system that instructs the bartenders and cocktail servers to ask the guests if they are having dinner. If the guests say they are, they ask them for their card. When their table is ready, the host calls the bar and informs the bartender that there is a table available for the Smith party of two. Another method is for the host to walk through the waiting area and announce the names of the guests whose tables are ready.

Electronic Devices

Restaurants have discovered the value of using electronic devices to manage the dining room. Instead of using the common industry standard for communicating, which is searching on foot for the person and having a face-to-face conversation, many restaurants have turned to these electronic devices. From informing guests that their table is available to instant communication between the podium host and seating host, electronic devices are proving invaluable to the restaurant manager.

For example, at the Perry Restaurant Group's Dakota Restaurant in Latham, New York, when there is a wait for tables, the podium host gives the guest a pager. This pager vibrates to inform the guests when their table is available. The podium host punches in the corresponding number of the pager into a master unit. If a guest has pager number 33, when that table becomes available, the hostess enters in the number 33. A word of caution is given to the guests when they receive their pagers: the host must inform guests that if they leave a certain geographical location, the pagers will not work.

Managers at Dakota also use the same pagers that the guests use. These are used for instant communication. Each manager is assigned the same numerical pager daily. The pager can be set up to give one, two, or three vibrations, depending on how important it is that the manager come to the host stand. Management must develop a system so the manager knows the meaning of each vibration. Using this type of electronic device, the host need never leave the podium to communicate with guests that their table is available or to inform the manager that he is needed at the host's stand.

Another electronic device is a two-way radio. This can increase seating and sales for the restaurant. Lightweight headsets are available that have a range of up to 200,000 square feet indoors. The podium host and the two or three seating hosts (depending upon projected business) each have a wireless radio. While the seating hosts are working the floor, they can instantly communicate to the podium host the status of each table. As soon as a table is cleared, this information is communicated to the podium host, who can then page the guest using the pager system.[5]

Keeping the Waitlist Accurate

The host must keep an accurate waitlist to avoid problems in seating guests and to aid in planning future business. All restaurants have their own codes to assist them with the waitlist. At one restaurant, when a guest requests a table for six, the host places a big, black mark around the guest's name. This is to signify that they have a large party waiting. Since the number of tables that will accommodate six people

Chef's Choice

(*Courtesy of*
Aram Mardigian,
Executive
Chef,
Spago
Restaurant,
Palo Alto,
California)

"Good service entails many things. It's not only being on the spot with drinks and clean napkins. I believe knowledge of the menu and wine list is essential. This applies to all levels of the restaurant business. If I'm in a five-star restaurant and I ask the server about a sauce or a selection on the wine list, I expect them to know the answer. If I'm in a small sandwich shop and I ask the server what condiments they offer, again, I expect them to know the answer. I'm a chef and I'm driven by food, but when I'm dining out, it's the service that really makes the difference. If the service is excellent and the food is just good, I'm happy. If the food is exceptional and the service is horrible, I probably won't be back. Remember, we are in the hospitality business."

—*Aram Mardigian*

Chef Mardigian has worked around the country with Wolfgang Puck. Before becoming executive chef at the Palo Alto Spago, he was executive sous chef at Postrio Restaurant in the promenade of the Venetian Hotel in Las Vegas, Nevada. He has also assisted in the opening of two other Las Vegas restaurants for Chef Puck. Previously, he worked at Spago in Hollywood Hills, California, and helped to open Spago in Chicago, Illinois. Chef Mardigian often assists Chef Puck in the preparation of food for special events throughout the United States and on his television show. At Spago, Chef Mardigian presents the culinary style that Wolfgang Puck has made famous for over two decades. Spago's elegant menu and seasonal specialties are always made from the finest producers in the region. Baby beet salad with Harley Farms goat cheese, Pan roasted Sonoma Quail with Brioche Stuffing, Atlantic Salmon with Citrus Vinaigrette and Fennel, and Wolfgang's Austrian favorite Spicy Beef Goulash make this the best dining experience in Silicon Valley.

is limited, the host does not want to make the guest's party wait longer than they are told. In addition, once the host sends for a party, he or she underlines the name with the black pen. When the person has been located, the host puts a double mark under the name. If a person is not found, the host writes down the time the guest was called and gives them 15 minutes to appear. If they are not there in that time, the host writes in large letters *NS* for *No-Show* through their name.

The information gained from the waitlist can be valuable for the host, who can see how many guests had to wait for a table, the time the first guest had to wait, the average waiting time, the longest waiting time, and other factors that will help him staff and plan for the business. Above all, the waitlist will provide a fair and organized tool for seating the guests.

T I P $

TO INSURE PROPER SERVICE
Never tell your guests that their table is not ready because you have a problem. They do not care: They just want their table.

Leading and Seating Guests

The guests now need to be shown to their assigned table. The host has to take into account the age and physical condition of the guests. Once the host determines the condition of the guests, he gauges the walk to the table at a comfortable pace. It is not a good idea to sprint to the table if the guest is elderly because the guest may not be able to keep up with the pace.

Once the host reaches the table, it is proper to pull out chairs for the guests—women first—and assist them with seating. If the table is against the wall, it has become traditional to offer the seat that faces into the dining room to the female, while the male is seated facing the wall. The napkins are removed from the table by the host, opened, and handed to the guests.

Menus should be distributed next, both food and wine, if appropriate. Women are given their menu first. It is advisable to open up the menu to the entree page. This accomplishes two things: First, the host can make sure the menu is correct; second, it is another small detail that the guest will not have to attend to.

T I P $

TO INSURE PROPER SERVICE
Check to make sure that you give each guest the right menu for that meal period: dinner menus are for dinner, not lunch menus.

Communicating Information

Next, the host must communicate important information to the guests. This is an area where most hosts fall short. Many hosts bring the guest to the table, drop off the menus, and are never seen again. After the guests have been seated and handed menus, the host should inform them of any chef's creations—and their prices—that are not listed on the written menu. The restaurant should not have more than three chef's specials because guests may become confused. Many restaurants use an alternative method. The host gives a list of daily specials to the guests along with the regular menus. The host points out the list, which includes prices, to the guests as they are seated. It is strongly suggested that the host use the guests' names as much as possible.

Once the guests have been told the additions to the menu, the host may also ask them if they would like to order a beverage. This is a key moment of truth in the restaurant business. According to Professor Gary Brenenstuhl of Schenectady County Community College, this is transition time. It is the time when the host turns the guests over from his care to the care of the service person. When the guest must wait for the service person to approach the table and take the drink order, the wait can be an uncomfortable one. Professor Brenenstuhl says that "the guest should have the drink order taken immediately." By having the host take the drink order, the guest will have been served immediately. The restaurant is saying to the guest, "We value your business and do not want you to wait for anything." In addition, there is the possibility of selling more drinks, whether they are alcoholic or nonalcoholic.

This serving or taking of a drink order should be done with every meal period. At breakfast, the host would offer coffee to the guest immediately. The last thing the host should do as he leaves the table is to tell the guests the name of the service person. To be most effective, it should be done in an informal manner, such as, "Jan will be your server and she will be right over with your drink order." As the host leaves the table, the drink order is given to the service person so that it can be delivered as soon as possible. The host can now concentrate on working the floor.

Working the Floor

Working the floor is a phrase used in the restaurant business to mean that the host is circulating around the dining room, talking to guests, and assisting service staff. When the guest has been seated by the host, the host should not go back and stand at the podium waiting for the next guest to come into the restaurant. Instead, the host should walk around the dining room and make certain that the guests are being served properly. One of the key factors in working the floor is to communicate with the guests. If the host notices that the guests are sitting at the table with their menus for a long period of time, he should approach the table and ask, "Has Jan been here to take your order yet?" Is she has not, the host should take the order or find Jan so that she can take the order. The host should not just walk around the dining room, but should stop at tables and talk to guests—by name, if possible.

Working the floor also involves getting your hands dirty. This means that the host—and dining room manager, if they are not the same person—may bus tables, serve food, serve drinks, and reset tables if a service person needs assistance. The host should be a vital, working member of the staff.

The final responsibility of the host is to make sure that the guests are completely satisfied with their dining experience. As the guests complete their meals, the host inquires about their dining experience and shows appreciation to the guests for patronizing the restaurant. This appreciation can be shown in the form of a "Thank you," buying the guest a free dessert or after-dinner drink, or some other gesture that makes the guest feel special. Other establishments empower the host and waitstaff to give a card to their guests that offers them a free appetizer or dessert upon their next visit.

Sweet or Sour?

A couple were at a restaurant. They watched and listened as the host approached and spoke to a party of two after they had finished their meal. One guest had ordered swordfish that was served on a bed of pasta. The host inquired about the food, asking how they liked it. The guest said that the swordfish was great, but the pasta was not cooked enough. The host replied that all the pasta is cooked, *al dente*. He further added: "If you want, you can take the pasta home with you and microwave it. It will taste really good that way. The next time you come in, make sure you ask to have it cooked longer."

Seating Guests with Disabilities

Title III of the Americans with Disabilities Act (ADA), which became effective in 1992, requires that any private place of business be accessible for all guests. There are specific guidelines for both new and existing restaurants that must be followed. The dining room manager should be aware of this law and the guidelines that must be followed. If the restaurant is not accessible, a plan should be put into effect to make it so. As an example, it has been reported that Planet Hollywood in Washington, D.C., installed a ramp leading to the front entrance, placed an accessible restroom on the first floor, lowered counters in the bar and retail areas, built a ramp into the science fiction theme dining area, and installed signage required by the ADA. This occurred because of a complaint brought by wheelchair users Atsuko Kuwana and her husband, Michael Winter, after they had to enter through a locked side service door because the three steps leading to the front entrance allegedly were not ramped.

With restaurants becoming more accessible to guests with disabilities, the host has to be aware of what can be done to make their dining experience enjoyable. The type of disability guests have will dictate their special needs as well as the consideration that the host gives them. For instance, a guest with limited vision should be led to the table and have the location of the utensils explained by imagining the table as the face of a clock (e.g., the coffee cup is at 5:00). If the guest has a seeing-eye dog, the host leads the guest to a table where the dog can lie down without being in the traffic flow.

Title III requires that there be an accessible route of travel to get into the dining room. In addition, guests must be seated in the least restrictive environment. A host cannot give people with disabilities the poorest table in the restaurant. The host should seat guests in wheelchairs at a table that is out of the flow of traffic, but where the guest is comfortable.[6] The host may assist the guest in whatever way possible to make the person feel welcome. It may be necessary to move the table so that the guest can position his or her wheelchair comfortably at the place setting. In some instances, it might be necessary to raise the table to a height that will accommodate a wheelchair.

TIP$

TO INSURE PROPER SERVICE
Talk directly to guests with disabilities. One hospitality student we know who is in a wheelchair gets most annoyed when servers ask his wife questions and treat him as if he were not there.

Regardless of the disability of the guest, the host must remember, and impress upon the staff, that these individuals are as valuable to the restaurant as the other guests. The staff has to be taught to treat all guests with courtesy and to put forth the extra effort so that all guests can enjoy themselves and have a pleasant dining experience.

T I P $ **TO INSURE PROPER SERVICE**
Have Braille menus available for guests with such a need.

The Problem Guest

Unfortunately, there will be times when a guest has a complaint about the wait for the table, the food, the services, or prices. The host must know how to handle complaints and be able to resolve the situation to the guest's satisfaction.

T I P $ **TO INSURE PROPER SERVICE**
Never interrupt a guest who is complaining!

Clarify the complaint by repeating it back to the guest. By now the guest should have calmed down. Make the person realize that you understand the complaint. Next, try to agree on some point about their complaint. Finally, solve the problem or offer the guest some possible solutions to the problem. Throughout the meal, return to the guest's table and check to insure that the problem has been solved. Using this approach, the host can turn a bad situation into a good situation. This skill in handling complaints is another area that the host must excel in to create a positive moment of truth for the restaurant. (See Figure 9–6.)

Unfortunately, the restaurant business is easy prey for those customers who make it a habit to use devious methods to obtain free meals. For instance, it has been well documented about guests who bring into restaurants pieces of hair, glass, or other foreign objects and—after eating almost their entire meal—call a waitperson over and show the waitperson the foreign object that they "discovered" in their food. Some of these people have made a living by cheating restaurants. Each restaurant will have to determine its own policy

STEPS TO HANDLE COMPLAINTS

1. Give undivided attention and listen carefully to the guest's complaint.

2. Clarify the complaint by repeating it back to the guest.

3. Agree with the guest on some point about the complaint.

4. Solve the guest's problem. Ask what he or she would like you to do, or explain why the complaint cannot be solved.

5. Check back throughout the meal to be certain the problem was solved.

FIGURE 9–6

List of steps to handle complaints.

for handling these complaints. With time and experience, a manager will realize when there is a legitimate complaint or when a scam is occurring.

Sweet or Sour?

As the restaurant owner was standing at the podium in his small, family-owned neighborhood establishment, a well-dressed middle-aged woman entered the restaurant. When he asked if he could help her, the woman explained to the owner that she and a friend were at dinner the night before and had a problem with the food. He inquired what the problem had been. She said there were too many flies on her food. He had a hard time understanding her and asked her to repeat what the problem had been. She further said that the two of them could not eat their food. Instead, they just asked for their bill and paid the charges. But after thinking about the incident, she felt that she should come back and tell the owner and ask for a refund. The owner realized that he certainly could have had a pest problem. It could have occurred, and he expressed his apology and started to write out a gift certificate to cover the cost of the two meals, but he wanted to know what they had to eat. She said they both had a sirloin steak and baked potato. He asked how they were cooked; she said medium rare. At that point, he reached down and instead of signing his name to the gift certificate, he handed her his menu and said, "Do you care to look at the menu or should I call the police now?" With that the woman ran out of the restaurant. If she had done her homework she would have realized that the Italian restaurant did not serve sirloin steak with baked potato.

*4 LEMONS FOR THE SCAM ARTIST; 4 SUGARS FOR THE RESTAURANT OWNER

Reservations Not Honored

Unfortunately, one of the major problems that occurs in restaurants is that reservations cannot be honored. This happens for a number of reasons. Occasionally there will be a problem because reservations have been taken incorrectly. Other times, guests will stay longer than their residence time. Regardless of the problem or the reason why the restaurant does not have a table for the guests, it is the fault of the restaurant, not the guests.

To solve the problem, the host must seat the guests as soon as a table becomes available. However, he should first explain the problem to the guests and offer an apology for their inconvenience. It is recommended that the host make some positive gesture to the guests to soothe their feelings for their inconvenience. If it is legal in your state, buy them a bottle of wine with the meal or have them go to the bar and buy them a drink. If they don't drink, offer them a free dessert.

In the meantime, the host also has to deal with guests who are staying past their residence time. The host should tactfully find out the reason for the delay. If it is a problem that can be solved quickly and the service person has not given the guests their check, the host can rectify it immediately. The table can now be set—called **turning tables**—for the next guest. If the guests are sitting with an extra cup of coffee, the host may not be able to do anything, or an offer may be made to move the guests to another area, such as the bar or a sitting room, where they can continue their conversation. However, this is a tricky situation, and the host may do more harm than good by asking the guests to move. This is a decision that the host would make after considering whether asking the guests to move would create negative feelings.

After the problems have been solved, the host must identify the reason why the reservations were not honored. Then, adjustments to the reservation policy must be made so that the problem will not occur again. The host must be able to solve the problem of not honoring reservations so that the guest will want to return to the restaurant for another meal.

Final Jobs of the Host

The host's job is not complete until long after the guests leave the restaurant. After the guests have received their entrees, the host works the floor and talks to everyone, inquiring about their meals.

Sweet or Sour?

A couple ventured out one Friday night to patronize a restaurant. With the temperature of –5 degrees Fahrenheit and a wind chill down around –35 degrees Fahrenheit, the restaurant owner, manager, and staff should have been thrilled to see them and should have done everything possible to make their meal memorable.

They walked into the restaurant right at opening time and were shown a nice table for two. It was a cozy seat by the window, so they could see the people rushing by in the cold. But they were nice and warm because of the baseboard heater right at their feet.

They opened up their menus and the wife said, "What a strange menu; there are no appetizers." After comparing both of their menus, they discovered that she had duplicate pages of the entree menu and no appetizer menu. The waitress came over to their table and asked if they would like a drink. They told her they would be ordering wine; please give them a few minutes. She then proceeded to talk to them about the weather and how slow business was going to be that night. She is off to a good start, the couple thought.

She came back to the table a couple of times to see if they had any questions about the menu. Finally, they ordered their wine and food. They were both served properly. She even refilled their wine glasses! The food was acceptable—not great, but nothing special. When they finished, the server came to the table and asked them if they cared to see a dessert menu and have coffee. They said, "Sure, but let us finish our wine before you bring us the decaf and regular coffee." She then proceeded to clear their plates, stacking the dirty dishes on top of one another. She brought the coffee and decaf, making sure she told them which one was decaf. They had their two desserts and coffee, which were quite good.

Then came another moment of truth. She brought the check to the table and placed it down. She failed to ask if they wanted another cup of coffee! There was no excuse for this. She was not busy, the restaurant was not busy, and they would have had to ask for a second cup of coffee. By her lack of perception, she had ended the service negatively. No manager or host ever came to the table throughout the meal to inquire about the meal. The couple paid the check, and as they were going out, the husband recognized the owner. He was putting on his coat in a leisurely fashion. He never spoke to them or the other patrons leaving. As they left, no one, not he, the server, the manager, or the two hostesses said anything to them. This was an opportunity for the restaurant to show a positive sign of hospitality. Instead, the few guests patronizing the restaurant were penalized.

Before the guests leave the restaurant, the host should inquire about the dining experience and offer the guests something free. This could be an after-dinner drink, dessert, or complimentary coffee. The key is to let the guests know that their business is appreciated. The host should have the ability to recognize the mood of the guests. Some guests invite the host to sit down and join them at their table for conversation, while other guests only want the host to recognize them. Do not make the mistake of monopolizing the guests' time by lingering too long at their tables.

When the guests leave the restaurant, it is imperative that the host thank them for their business and invite them to return to the restaurant.

Some restaurants employ a person to call up guests on the following day to inquire about their dining experience. This gives the guest an opportunity to give someone feedback without having to do it face to face, and it gives the restaurant an opportunity to evaluate its performance and find out if there were any problems. If the person calling is told of a problem, the restaurant can take steps to correct it.

TIP$

TO INSURE PROPER SERVICE
Remember the 80/20 rule: Eighty percent of your business comes from 20 percent of your customers—your repeat customers.

When Mistakes Occur

Mistakes will occur in every restaurant. It is inevitable. When mistakes occur, the manager has to address them. In his book *Setting the Table*, Danny Meyer states that "the five A's" for effectively addressing mistakes are Awareness, Acknowledgement, Apology, Action, and Additional generosity.[7]

Awareness means knowing what is happening in the restaurant at all times. Is John in the weeds? Is the printer not working in the kitchen? The couple at table 23 is not eating their entree. As Danny says, "If you're not aware, you're nowhere."[8]

Acknowledgement lets the guest know that you are aware of the situation and you inform them that you are taking steps to correct the problem. "I am sorry that your table is not ready yet. We are resetting it now and we will seat you in less than five minutes."

Apology is a must and can be combined with acknowledgement. The host should never offer an alibi. When I was a dining room manager an irate guest stated that he had been waiting for his table for over an hour. My response was that our dishwasher did not come in that night and we were backed up. The guest looked me right in the eye, shook his finger in my face, and said "That's your problem, not mine." As Meyer states, "It is not appropriate or useful to make excuses."[9]

Action should be taken immediately to solve the problem. When the author was served a wrong entree at Roy's in Honolulu, the waiter immediately apologized and placed the correct order in the kitchen. In the meantime, he returned to the table with a complimentary course so I would not be sitting watching the three other guests eating their entrees.

Additional generosity may involve sending out complimentary desserts or even paying for the guests' bill.

The Logbook

Each restaurant should have a book that includes a record of the important happenings of the day. Items such as the number of meals served, the waiting time for reservations, the time first seated, and other items that will assist in the forecasting of the business may be included in the logbook. In addition, there is usually an area where messages are left for the next shift. By having this special area in the logbook, no messages are lost and there is proof that information was passed on to the next shift. This logbook will help the restaurant run smoothly and efficiently.

Marketing Your Business

All businesses, regardless of type, need a marketing plan. The plan is a blueprint for the business. Because the only constant in the business world is change, the restaurant or banquet manager must complete this blueprint to guide the business for the upcoming year.

Sweet or Sour?   In a little community 10 minutes from Schenectady, New York, is a restaurant called The Bears. The owners of the restaurant, Bob and Pat Payne—or Papa and Mama Bear—along with their son (Baby Bear), operate an excellent restaurant that has been in business for over 35 years.

(continues)

(continued)

Everything works. The food, the service, the cleanliness, and the price value. When guests arrive at The Bears, they are greeted by name and by the owners. The owners act as if they are greeting long-lost friends. The new guests are introduced to the owners by the regulars. Once that is done, the owners return to the kitchen to prepare the meal.

Next, the server explains the menu thoroughly and knowledgeably. However, for most guests, it is not necessary. This is because The Bears is noted for its beef. When the guests make their reservations, the meals have been ordered in advance. Usually, it will be Chateaubriand or prime rib.

Next comes the food, and it is great. Their specialty, Chateaubriand, is so tender that it can be cut with a fork. All the other items are good, and all are presented attractively. The service is proper, and the service staff make certain that they take care of the needs of all their guests.

When the meal is completed, Papa Bear makes it a point to visit each table and ask all the guests if they liked their meal. He then offers them more food if they are still hungry, which almost everyone refuses because there is enough food left over for another complete meal. That leftover food is quickly placed in a container by the service staff to be taken home by the guest.

Guests leave The Bears completely satisfied, and their word-of-mouth promotion fills the restaurant completely, week after week.

A marketing plan addresses the current business. It outlines problems and opportunities by identifying the operation's strengths and weaknesses, as well as its competitors'; and it informs management. Goals are set and strategies are planned based upon analysis of the strengths and weaknesses. The marketing document will state how the plan will be implemented and executed. Included will be a budget to help the operation reach its desired goals. Finally, the plan will have criteria built into it to allow management to determine if the plan has been successful.

One of the best—and often overlooked—marketing tools to have is a copy of the restaurant's menu posted with prices outside the restaurant for patrons to view. This menu has to be kept current. Another tactic used by successful restaurants is to print small menus that guests can take with them as they leave.

Remember that the number one reason for trying a restaurant is a word-of-mouth recommendation. Incorporate that fact into your plan. Here is how one restaurant owner obtained positive word of mouth publicity. The following article appeared in a circa 1940 newspaper.

"Spa Restaurant Owner Refuses Meal Payment"

Ballston Spa—When a restaurant owner refuses to be paid for a meal, that's news. Nevertheless it happened here Monday night. Art Strianese, operator of the local Spa restaurant proved the village slogan that "Ballston Spa is a Friendly Town" when he gave an out-of-town visitor a free full course dinner, simply because a roast beef meal which the customer requested wasn't on the menu. The customer, when informed that the restaurant was out of roast beef, ordered a ham dinner. When he asked for his check, Strianese told him "There'll be no charge, because we didn't have what you wanted," and refused to accept any payment.[10]

T I P $

TO INSURE PROPER SERVICE

As Papa Bear says, "It costs nothing to say thank you to your guests, but the payback is tremendous." Or as Harvey Mackay says, "Anyone too busy to say thank you will get fewer and fewer chances to say it." He also says, "Bad service saves money and loses customers. Good service costs money and saves customers."[11]

SUMMARY

1. The seven deadly sins of service are *apathy, the brush-off, coldness, condescension, robotism, rule book excuses,* and *the runaround.* A person can correct or avoid these seven deadly sins of service by knowing and recognizing them.

2. When a person has a complaint, there are five steps to be taken to solve the problem. First, the guest should receive undivided attention and be listened to carefully by the employee. The complaint should be clarified by repeating it back to the guest. The employee should agree on some aspect of the complaint. Ask the guest what he would like done to solve the problem, or explain why the complaint cannot be resolved. Check back throughout the meal to be certain the problem was solved and the guest is satisfied.

3. A turnsheet keeps a record of how many guests have been seated at each waitperson's table and the size of each party. The host will use

this information to seat guests fairly so the waitpeople can manage the dining room efficiently.

4. *Working the floor* means to walk around the dining room making sure that everything is running smoothly. The manager does a variety of jobs when working the floor, such as clearing tables, seating guests, solving problems, and thanking guests.

5. To seat guests properly, the host uses a variety of methods, including blocked reservations, a waitlist, turnsheets, and electronic devices such as two-way radios, pagers, and headsets.

REVIEW QUESTIONS

1. Why should a restaurant owner or host send business to the competition?
2. List the seven deadly sins of service. Explain what they are and how they relate to the host's job.
3. What is a turnsheet? What is its purpose and how is it set up?
4. How is a table check form set up? What is its purpose?
5. What should a host do when seating a guest? What are the steps required to seat guests properly?
6. What is a waitlist, and what is its purpose?
7. What does the phrase "working the floor" mean?
8. What considerations should be given to guests with special needs?

DISCUSSION QUESTIONS

1. Explain how you would handle the following problem: A party of four comes into your restaurant. The host tells them it will be a short wait for their table. They are asked if they want to go to the bar, which they do. The service person ignores them in the bar. When they finally are seated after their short wait—30 minutes—the service person serves their appetizers almost immediately. One half hour goes by, and then the service person returns to the table and says, "I made a terrible mistake; I forgot to put your order into the kitchen. I just did it now." The food comes out 20 minutes later. One of the steaks was ordered medium well and comes out rare. The guest is upset. She asks to see the manager. You come to the table, and she shoves her plate at you, complaining about your restaurant. What do you do?
2. A guest complains that the cost of the appetizer is too much money. She states that the waitperson did not recite the price and she was

shocked to find that the special appetizer costs more money than her entrée. How would you handle this situation?

3. A party of four guests arrives at the restaurant. One of the guests is in a wheelchair. What considerations would you take into account in assigning them a table?

4. A guest asks for a table by the window with a spectacular view of the falls. The table is blocked on the reservation sheet. You politely inform the guest that the table is not available. She reaches into her wallet and hands you a $100 bill and asks, "Are you sure?" How do you handle this situation?

5. At the beginning of the meal period, how should the host seat guests so that they are not all clumped together in one area? Or should the host seat guests all in one area?

REFERENCES

1. Jack Hayes, "Albrecht Stresses Need to Service America," *Nation's Restaurant News* (March 14, 1988): p. 4.

2. *Random House Dictionary*, New York: Ballantine Books, 1978: p. 116.

3. Peter O'Connor, in a letter to the author, 1996.

4. Ibid.

5. Motorola, "Business Solutions for Group Talk," Collateral Material from Porter Novelli Convergence Group.

6. Danny Meyer, *Setting the Table*, New York: Harper Collins, 2006: p. 223.

7. Ibid.

8. Ibid.

9. From the archived collection of Edward Strianese, Armonk, New York (January 3, 2006).

10. James R. Abbey, *Hospitality Sales and Advertising*, 2nd ed. East Lansing, Michigan: The Educational Institute of the American Hotel and Motel Association, 1996.

11. Harvey Mackay, "Even the Lone Ranger had Tonto," Albany *Times Union*, (Sunday, August 13, 2000): C7.

Part Three

Banquet Management

The Banquet Business and the Banquet Manager

OBJECTIVES   At the completion of this chapter, the student should be able to:

1. Define the term *banquet*.
2. Explain the importance of banquets as they relate to the profitability of any hospitality establishment.
3. List and explain the advantages that the banquet business has over restaurants that serve à la carte meals.
4. Define the difference between a caterer and a banquet manager.
5. List the advantages and disadvantages of a career as a banquet manager.
6. Name the types and styles of service available for banquets.
7. Explain the qualifications for being a banquet manager.
8. List the job knowledge that a banquet manager must possess in order to do the job effectively.
9. Explain the banquet manager's main responsibility as it relates to the client requesting the banquet.
10. Explain the key to being a successful banquet manager.

KEY WORDS

a la carte restaurant
banquet
banquet captain

banquet facility
banquet manager
diplomacy

head banquet waiter
off-premise catering
perquisites ("perks")

What Is a Banquet?

A **banquet** is a meal that has a menu preselected by the client for all of the guests attending the event. A banquet usually occurs in a separate location, and the client generally requests special items, such as a certain color of tablecloths, special centerpieces, a different menu, and so on. The number of guests at a banquet usually ranges from 10 to 10,000 or higher. The only reason there will be a maximum number is because the **banquet facility** has a limited amount of space to accommodate guests.

Any restaurant that can successfully serve a banquet of 10 people can serve any size banquet. This is because the principle of serving a banquet to a large group is the same as serving it to a small group.

Manager's Message

(Courtesy of GLENN GRAY, DIRECTOR OF FOOD AND BEVERAGE, RENAISSANCE AUSTIN HOTEL, AUSTIN, TEXAS*)*

"Catering is the horse that pulls the carriage in the majority of our companies' hotels. The ability to serve great numbers of people at one time, EFFECTIVELY, is an art. If you do it well you will drive loyalty to your product. Competition these days, especially in the Austin market, is fierce, and to establish loyal customers is essential to remain successful. Food and Beverage profits are driven on the catering side of our business. If you do not have a successful catering business in this type of hotel, you will not be in business for long."

—*Glenn Gray*

Mr. Gray is responsible for all of the food and beverage operations at this elegant hotel, which has 476 rooms including 44 suites on 10 floors. He oversees the Garden Cafe, open for breakfast and lunch; the Pavilion, which is a deli open for breakfast, lunch, and dinner; the Trattoria Grande Italian dinner restaurant; the Club Renaissance; and Tangerines, an upscale nightclub. The hotel has 18 meeting rooms, which provide 60,000 square feet of total meeting space. Glenn has worked for Marriott hotels in Marco Island, Fort Lauderdale, and at the Marriott World Center in Orlando, Florida. His career has also taken him to Chicago, Illinois; Westchester, New York; and San Antonio, Texas.

Clients' Reasons for Having a Banquet

There are many reasons why clients hold banquets (see Figure 10–1). Some hold them for the purpose of personal entertaining; some must conduct them for business; some clients hold banquets for special events. Regardless of the reason, the banquet serves one main purpose: it allows the client to invite a large group of people without having to do the planning, buying, cooking, and serving of food. Nor does the client have to clean up after the party is finished. Having a banquet allows the client to greet guests and make them feel at home, rather than act as a service person.

FIGURE 10–1

Reasons for holding banquets.

REASONS FOR HOLDING BANQUETS		
Personal Entertaining	**Business**	**Other Organizations**
Religious Ceremonies	Meetings	Weekly Meetings
Celebrations	Conferences	Sports Banquets
Social Events	Celebrations	Award Banquets

Personal Entertainment

The first thought most people have about the reasons why banquets are held concerns personal entertaining. These banquets are conducted because the client wants to entertain friends. Personal entertainment banquets are usually for religious ceremonies, celebrations, or social affairs.

One of the largest markets in the personal entertaining banquet business comes from wedding receptions; however, there are many other religious ceremonies that add to the list. For example, baptisms, first communions, confirmations, and even funerals. In communities where there is a large Jewish population, bar mitzvahs and bat mitzvahs may make up a large portion of a banquet establishment's business.

T I P $ **TO INSURE PROPER SERVICE**

Read your local newspapers daily to find out what type of clients are holding banquets, meetings, and social events. This will give you an indication of the type of events held in your area.

Some of these events require the banquet manager to understand and know the religious customs of a certain group. For instance, a banquet celebrating a Catholic confirmation would require a different set of rules than a Jewish bar mitzvah. The banquet manager must know the protocol regarding who is to give the blessing and when and how it will be given. The client will often ask the banquet manager for guidance to perform these tasks correctly.

T I P $

TO INSURE PROPER SERVICE
Learn and understand a new religious custom weekly.

The 25th and 50th wedding anniversaries are the ones most often celebrated with banquets. However, birthday and graduation parties and baby and wedding showers also contribute to the social event business.

Finally, there are parties for social entertaining. Guests are invited to a **banquet facility** or to a party catered at the client's house for the purpose of having a party. Many of these events occur during the winter holiday season, but they are a viable business all year long.

The personal entertaining business is an excellent market for a banquet facility or caterer. There will always be a demand for banquets.

Business Entertaining

Entertaining for the purpose of doing business is another large source of income for the caterer or banquet facility. The individual at the business responsible for planning the function is usually employed by that particular business. This type of entertaining differs from personal entertaining because the business, not the individual, pays for the banquet. One of the main purposes for business entertaining is to conduct conferences or meetings (see Figure 10–2). Other reasons are for celebrating a special business occurrence—like an anniversary or grand opening—and for throwing parties to honor employees.

Conferences and meetings are often held off the premises of the business at a hotel or restaurant. Some large companies employ a meeting planner to select the facility for these conferences. The vast majority of companies assign an employee to head the event who has little or no experience in planning and conducting a conference. This person utilizes the experience and organization of the banquet manager to have a successful conference. His or her success in pulling off the event depends greatly on the banquet manager's skills, especially if the designated

FIGURE 10–2

Catering business functions can be a lucrative source of income for the banquet manager. (Photograph by Randall Perry)

employee has had little experience in organizing these types of events. The employee relies on the banquet manager for the planning, name tags, pens—in short, everything. These conferences can last for one meal or for as long as a week, and they usually involve renting meeting rooms and making provisions for food and liquor service.

A great source of income for the banquet manager or caterer are business anniversary parties. Along with these anniversary parties, businesses often have special parties for their employees. These consist of retirement, holiday, and special recognition banquets. Also, many schools have a "welcome party" for their new employees at the beginning of the school year.

The business market is a valuable addition to the caterer's market, as the vast majority of functions are held Monday through Friday, though a certain percentage also are held on weekends.

Other Organizations

Other types of organizations that have banquets are groups of people who belong to organized clubs. Some examples would be service clubs, like the Rotary and Lions. Youth sport groups such as soccer, hockey, baseball, football, and basketball also have a need for banquet facilities. Bowling leagues are another group that can be a large source of revenue for a banquet house. These organizations can bring an enormous amount of business to a banquet house or a caterer.

TIP$

TO INSURE PROPER SERVICE

Have your banquet facility sponsor a youth sporting event.

The Key to Successful Banquet Management

The reasons explained earlier are only a partial list of why people have banquets. The reader can add to the list many more groups of people who would need the services of a banquet manager. However, regardless of the reasons for holding banquets, there is one key to being a successful banquet manager. It is the statement highlighted in Figure 10–3.

FIGURE 10–3

The key to successful banquet management.

THE KEY TO SUCCESSFUL BANQUET MANAGEMENT

The banquet manager must take the
RESPONSIBILITY
for the total event off the client's shoulders
and put it on her own.

Why Banquets?

More and more restaurants are getting into the banquet business for a very simple reason: A restaurant can make more money, with much less chance of failure. Put simply, the profit potential is much greater for selling banquets than for a restaurant that operates as an à la carte business only.

The reason this is true becomes evident when a comparison is made between the way the à la carte restaurant and the banquet house must conduct business.

At a banquet, the establishment knows in advance many more facts about the food it has to prepare than does an à la carte restaurant. First, the banquet manager knows what all the guests are going to eat. Because the banquet has been prearranged, the banquet manager knows how many guests will attend the event and how much food has been ordered.

At the **à la carte restaurant**, the manager never knows what or when the guests will eat. Therefore, the à la carte restaurant has to carry more inventory to satisfy guests' requests, whereas the banquet house only has to buy the food that has been requested for the banquet.

The banquet manager knows in advance exactly how many guests will attend the banquet; as a matter of fact, the client of the party must guarantee the number of guests that will attend. If fewer people show up, the client must still pay for the guaranteed number. On the other hand, the restaurant has to forecast the number of guests that will patronize its establishment. If there is bad weather or some other event is scheduled that the guests would rather attend, then the guests do not show up at the restaurant. In addition, the banquet manager may obtain an advance payment; most banquet houses obtain a deposit large enough to cover all their expenses. The restaurant has to wait until the guests consume their meals before getting any money.

Banquet establishments also determine how much revenue a banquet room should bring in for a time period. When an event is booked in a room, the banquet or sales manager has a formula to determine the minimum amount of money that must be spent to use the room. For instance, if the room commands $15,000 in revenue for a meal period, the host of the party must spend that much money to be able to use the room. Therefore, a party would be booked for 300 guests at $50.00 a person for that room. If two weeks before the event, only 150 guests have responded that they are coming to the party, the host will still be obligated to spend $15,000 for the use of that room. Banquet establishments will then upgrade the food and beverage to have the guest spend $100.00 per person.

Staffing is another advantage the banquet house has over the à la carte restaurant. Because the banquet manager knows the number of people attending, the menu, and the time the food will be served, she can staff for the event without any wasted labor cost. On the other hand, the restaurant has to be prepared for a large group of guests, when in fact no one may show up. The à la carte restaurant may have many people scheduled to work with little work to do. As the restaurant has to pay these employes, their labor costs rise and their profits decrease.

There is virtually no leftover food at a banquet. Everything is purchased in advance and cooked correctly; therefore, waste is kept to a minimum. At an à la carte restaurant, there may be an enormous amount of waste, because the restaurant manager does not know what the patrons will order. Thus, the restaurant may have too much of one item and not enough of another. In an à la carte restaurant, specific items are often sold out; at a banquet, this rarely happens.

The advertising and selling of banquets is easier than marketing for an à la carte restaurant. For an à la carte restaurant to get 200 guests to have dinner at the establishment, it has to convince a large number of guests to patronize it by using a variety of advertising methods—often at a cost of between 3 and 7 percent of its gross sales. On the other hand, for a banquet facility to get 200 guests it has only to convince one or two people—just the client or clients—to have the banquet at its establishment. In addition, because everything is known about the banquet before the guests arrive, the quality of food and service will most likely be higher than at the à la carte restaurant. The end result is that when the banquet house does a superb job on the party, the banquet manager has 200 potential guests to book a banquet.

T I P $

TO INSURE PROPER SERVICE
It is five times more expensive to acquire a new customer than it is to keep an old one.

There was a restaurant in Columbus, Ohio, called Monaco's Palace. The owner of the restaurant, Baldino Monaco, chose to change the business from à la carte and banquets to strictly banquets. The restaurant had a banquet room that seated 400. The room was booked a year in advance for banquets. Baldino had a very good à la carte weekend business; his restaurant would have an hour-and-a-half wait on Saturday night and a short wait on Friday. But during the week, there was never a wait for a table. In fact, business was very slow. He found he was getting more requests for his banquet room and had to turn business away, so he did the logical thing: He eliminated the à la carte business and changed the name of the restaurant from Monaco's Palace to Monaco's Palace: The Banquet Specialists. As a result of the change, he was able to reduce his full-time staff—from about 28 to 5. He also appreciates the banquet business because it is guaranteed, and it has been a lot less strain on him.

More restaurant owners are turning to on-premise parties to increase their profits. High-end restaurants, like the Smith and Wollensky Restaurant group, are increasing their number of private parties. Many operators feel that these parties not only contribute to a healthier profit, but they are also able to charge more than they traditionally would. "Normally you are looking to turn seats," says Allen Susser, chef–owner of Chef Allen's in Miami. "But if it is a private party, you are selling seats for the night. And customers don't mind paying extra for a private room."[1]

The main reason a restaurant would seek out the banquet business is because it is a profit maker. A restaurant that serves banquets knows a vast amount of information about the party before the guest arrives. The restaurant knows how many people will be attending, how much food to order, the time of the event, the food cost, and the labor cost for the banquet. Everything about the banquet is known before the guests arrive. With proper planning—remember the 5*Ps*—costs can be kept to a minimum while profits are maximized.

Catering versus Banquets

Many people do not understand the difference between a caterer and a banquet manager. In reality, there is very little difference. In some areas of the country, there is no distinction whatsoever; both serve the guests by providing them with food, service staff, and cleanup.

In some geographical areas, however, there is a difference: a caterer performs the service away from his own establishment. In other words, the caterer brings the food and the service to the guests. This can occur at many different locations. This is sometimes called **off-premise catering**. On the other hand, the banquet manager usually works at the establishment that has space to hold a banquet and has the guests come to the establishment to partake of the food and service.

Both the caterer and banquet manager basically conduct their business in the same manner. However, the caterer does a tremendous amount of preplanning and organizing to prepare a successful banquet. This is because all the equipment and food must be brought to the job.

TIP$

To Insure Proper Service
It is a major logistical operation to move food somewhere.

The banquet manager has the luxury of working in a familiar facility. If the banquet manager forgets or runs out of some item like salt, it is much easier for him to replace it than for the caterer. The banquet manager will go to the storeroom and get more salt; the caterer will have to find a store that sells salt, which will involve wasted time and money on the caterer's part. The caterer will have to charge for travel time and transportation costs; obviously, the banquet manager does not have such costs. Because the jobs of caterer and banquet manager are so similar, many people use the terms interchangeably. However, there is a difference between them (see Figure 10–4).

FIGURE 10–4

The difference between catering and banquets. In some geographical areas, the terms are interchangeable, whereas other areas this is the only distinction.

DIFFERENCE BETWEEN CATERING AND BANQUETS	
Catering	**Banquets**
Takes place AWAY FROM the establishment	Takes place AT the establishment

Staffing a Banquet Facility

The person responsible for the success of the banquet is the **banquet manager**. In larger operations, the banquet facility may have a sales manager, a head banquet waiter, and banquet captains as well as the banquet manager. But in a smaller operation, the banquet manager performs all the duties.

The job of the sales manager is to book the banquets. Booking of banquets can be done by conducting outside sales or inside sales. The outside salesperson travels to the client's home or business to convince the client to have the banquet at the salesperson's facility. The inside salesperson works at the banquet facility, and clients come to the restaurant to book the party.

A **head banquet waiter** is generally employed at an establishment where there are many function rooms. In these large banquet establishments, many banquets occur simultaneously. The head banquet waiter is responsible for the success of the party in the room he supervises.

Banquet captains are responsible for the service in a section of the banquet room. They would be used when the banquet is large—perhaps over 200 guests. Both the head banquet waiter and the banquet captains are working supervisors. They work along with the employees, and also supervise them.

The banquet manager is the person who has the final responsibility for the success of the banquet. She must make sure that all the details of the party are attended to. She must make certain that whatever the client requested and was promised is delivered. If there are any problems with the banquet, it is the banquet manager's duty to solve them. The key to being an excellent banquet manager is to concentrate on details.

TIP$

TO INSURE PROPER SERVICE

It is just as important to tell the client what you are *not* doing for the banquet. For example: "The price quoted is for food, china, and staff. I am not furnishing flowers for the church or the entertainment."

The banquet manager has one main purpose in doing his or her job: It is not to cook the food. It is not to serve the food. It is *to take the responsibility for the total event off the client's shoulders and put it onto her own*. The main responsibility of the banquet manager or caterer is to allow the host to socialize with the guests while the banquet manager or caterer takes care of all the details of the party.

Banquet Manager Qualifications

A banquet manager has to be a truly unique individual. The job requires a person who can be referred to as a generalist, rather than a specialist. The banquet manager must have the ability to deal with all types of guests. These guests are on many different socioeconomic and psychological levels.

The qualifications for becoming a banquet manager include having a cheerful personality, being attentive to details, having a neat appearance, using tact and diplomacy, being creative during an emergency, having the ability not to become flustered when problems occur, and having the ability to work with many different groups of individuals at the same time. In addition, the banquet manager has to be able to express herself both verbally and in writing. Above all, the banquet manager must be organized (see Figure 10–5).

Personality

The banquet manager will have to deal with a never-ending group of clients that will test her limits of patience and endurance. Her personality must be cheerful, because the banquet manager is almost always dealing with clients who are in a stressful situation. Clients want their

BANQUET MANAGER QUALIFICATIONS

To become a banquet manager, you MUST:

1. have a cheerful personality.
2. be attentive to details.
3. have a neat appearance.
4. practice tact and diplomacy.
5. be able to react quickly to change.
6. not become flustered.
7. have excellent verbal communication skills.
8. have excellent written communication skills.
9. have the ability to work with many different types of people at once.
10. be creative during an emergency.

FIGURE 10–5

Banquet manager qualifications.

party to be perfect. Even though the banquet manager may have conducted a thousand wedding receptions, the parents of the bride may feel that this is the only one that the banquet manager has ever done. All clients—regardless of how rich or poor, no matter the type of education they possess, no matter their ethnic background—share the same trait when they are the host of a banquet: they are all placed in a stressful situation. Because of this stress, they exhibit behavior that will test the limits of the banquet manager's patience. Almost always, their personality changes; they change from kind, friendly, relaxed individuals to stressed out people who need to be treated in a firm yet friendly manner. In short, they could be considered temporarily insane!

Sweet or Sour?

At a very extravagant wedding, both the wedding and reception took place in the same location. The wedding took place in a garden under a tent. When the ceremony was over, the guests were to proceed into one room for cocktails and hors d'oeuvres. After an hour and a half, they were to go into the dining room for the meal.

The parents of the bride had planned everything in a calm atmosphere. They, their daughter, and their future son-in-law were well educated and articulate. The numerous meetings conducted with them were cordial and relaxed. The caterer had explained all that would happen on the day of the wedding.

After the ceremony, the bride's mother came into the dining room and began to panic because none of the tables had been set. The caterer had to calmly escort her out of the room while explaining that the room would be set up in time for the meal. In the meantime, the father of the bride came into the room, and his wife asked him to put some gifts into their car. They started an argument, not because the room was not set up, nor because he had locked the keys in the car, but because they were both so stressed out over the wedding. It was the caterer's job to calm them both down and decrease their level of stress by assuring them that everything would be all right with the wedding reception.

When the room was set up, the bride was brought in to see it. She immediately broke down in tears because the florist had put the wrong type of flowers at the place setting. Because the florist did not have the type of flowers she requested and had never told her, it was up to the caterer to solve the problem. All that could be done at this point—five minutes before the guests were to enter the room—was to give the anxious bride a reassuring hug and again calmly tell her everything would be all right. She calmed down and enjoyed her wedding reception.

A banquet manager will encounter this type of behavior at every wedding and almost all parties that she conducts; so she must have the personality to deal with stressed-out clientele.

Attention to Detail

Attentiveness to detail is considered the most important trait for the banquet manager to have. Being attentive to detail makes the difference between a good banquet manager and a great banquet manager.

TIP$

TO INSURE PROPER SERVICE

So much attention to detail is needed in off-premise catering that you should always use two checklists by two different people.

Sweet or Sour?

A woman was giving a catered party for her husband's 50th birthday. The staff arrived at her house and set up for the party. Everything was progressing smoothly: the food was being unloaded and cooked; the dining room was being set up; and the hostess was acting normal—crazy and stressed out. Then she asked the terrible question that sent her over the edge: "Where are the raspberries?" The response was that the caterer had not sent any raspberries; instead, she sent other fruits as a substitute—mangoes and papayas.

The hostess broke down and started to cry. She said that the party was ruined because raspberries were her husband's favorite dessert and she was promised them by the caterer. The caterer was immediately called, and the hostess talked to her about the problem. The hostess was not at all pleased about the lack of raspberries. The caterer claimed that she had told the woman only that she *might* be able to get the fruit for the party. The woman heard what she wanted to hear—that the caterer would have raspberries for the party. All the guests at the party loved the birthday celebration. But the hostess was convinced the party was ruined.

It is worth repeating: Attention to details makes the difference between being good and being great.

Neat Appearance

A banquet manager should look neat and clean. Her appearance has to be professional at all times, even after 12 hours and 12 functions.

Tact and Diplomacy

The banquet manager must be able to react with tact and diplomacy at all times and must use these traits often in dealing with different groups of guests. Tact is the ability to say or do the correct thing without offending the guest. **Diplomacy** is the ability to act tactfully with the guest.

Sweet or Sour?

At one party, two of the honored guests were seated at the head table. Another guest wanted to buy them an alcoholic beverage. However, because other guests would have been offended if they had seen the two drinking alcohol, the drinks had to be served without calling attention to the fact. An experienced waiter said, "Leave it to me, I'll solve the problem." He went to the honored guests, obtained their order, and served them their drinks. No one knew that they were drinking alcoholic beverages. This waiter was a master in the art of tact and diplomacy. He had exercised tact by not turning down or insulting the guest who wanted to buy the honored guests a drink, and he did not offend any of the other guests by blatantly serving the alcoholic drinks in glasses: he showed his diplomacy in this situation by serving the drinks in coffee cups.

Ability to React Quickly to Changes

Another qualification needed by a banquet manager is the ability to think and react quickly when a change must be made. For instance, there are many times when more guests show up for a party than had been planned. The banquet manager must be able to accommodate the extra guests without the other guests' realizing there is a problem.

Tendency Not to Become Flustered

In the same vein, when a problem occurs, the banquet manager must remain calm and solve the problem without becoming visibly annoyed with the guests. The banquet manager should give the impression that everything is okay, even if there is a catastrophe in the kitchen.

Ability to Work with Many Different Personalities

The banquet manager is a boss. She must manage her staff, as well as interact with the guests. In the banquet room, there may be a guest who holds an important position in the country or community. In the kitchen there are dishwashers and potwashers. The banquet manager may be responsible for the performance of the dishwashers and service people, as well as for the success of the banquet. This means that at one moment the banquet manager may be talking to the dishwasher, and a second later he or she has to return to the banquet room and discuss an item with the host of the party, who may be the Vice President of the United States. Most likely these two individuals come from different social and intellectual classes, but the banquet manager has to be able to converse and act appropriately with them both. The banquet manager must know and understand psychology and must use it to make the banquet a success.

Verbal Communication Skills

The banquet manager must possess excellent verbal communication skills. In addition to the obvious responsibilities of communicating with the guests, at times the banquet manager may have to act as a master of ceremonies for a party. This may involve speaking before a group of guests. The banquet manager also conducts meetings with staff and presents proposals to committees of clients wishing to hold a banquet at the banquet facility.

T I P $ **TO INSURE PROPER SERVICE**
Master the art of working with committees.

Written Communication Skills

The ability to communicate with staff clearly and concisely through the use of memos and forms is another qualification needed by the banquet manager. In addition, the banquet manager must be able to communicate effectively with guests via letters and contracts.

Organizational Skills

Along with taking care of the details, the banquet manager must possess organizational skills: these are critical for a banquet manager. She must be organized to do the vast amount of planning that goes into preparing for a banquet. Food must be ordered, cooking time and service have to be coordinated. Often, the banquet manager arranges for music, flowers, wedding cakes, audiovisual equipment, photographers, and even entertainment. This person must know where to find all of these services and must have an organized system to obtain them.

At times, a second banquet is scheduled within one hour of the first banquet in the same room. The banquet manager must be organized and have a plan so that the room can be reset and ready for the next party at its scheduled time. Regardless of the time factor, without organization, any banquet becomes a disaster.

The list of qualifications presented here is not all-encompassing; but it is a list of the most crucial skills that the banquet manager must have in order to perform the job successfully.

Banquet Manager Benefits

There are many benefits to a career in banquet management. Prestige, salary, gratuities, and perquisites or *perks* are among the benefits a person can expect as a banquet manager.

Prestige

Prestige comes naturally to the banquet manager. This is because the job puts the banquet manager in direct contact with the most important and influential people in the social and business community. A banquet manager who excels at the job soon receives the accolades of the community. In addition, the manager makes valuable contacts that may be used to further his or her career. Because the banquet manager is the most visible employee and the one who comes in contact most often with the guests, the manager *is* the establishment in the eyes of the guests.

Psychic Income

Another important benefit in the prestige category is the factor called *psychic income.* This is not money that the banquet manager receives;

rather it is the positive feeling that the manager gets from doing the job well or from serving important guests and sometimes becoming the confidante of those guests.

Pay

The banquet manager is generally paid an excellent salary. Because she represents the establishment to the guests, they are loyal to the banquet manager, rather than the to establishment. If the banquet manager leaves the establishment and goes to work for a competitor, the guests generally follow. Therefore, the banquet facility does not want to lose good banquet managers, so they pay them handsomely for their services and contacts. In addition, managers may receive a percentage of the service charge as an extra incentive to remain at the banquet house.

The banquet manager deals closely with the hosts of the parties, and in doing so usually creates an excellent rapport. If the banquet manager is competent in performing the job, it appears to be done effortlessly. The client often asks the banquet manager to do jobs that are not normally associated with the position. At the end of the party, it is not unusual for a satisfied guest to give a monetary gratuity to the banquet manager for a job well done.

T I P $ **To Insure Proper Service**
Consider all your benefits as your pay, not just your salary.

Perquisites

Perquisites or perks are additional benefits given to the banquet manager in addition to the regular salary. There is usually an allowance for clothing and for the expense of cleaning the clothes. The banquet manager generally has an expense account for the purpose of entertaining potential or repeat clients. Sometimes lodging may be included as a benefit. The value of the banquet manager to the business will determine the amount of perquisites she is offered.

Drawbacks to Being a Banquet Manager

As in any good job, there are also detriments to the banquet manager's position. Long hours, stressful parties, and the constant availability of tempting foods and liquor are all negative aspects of the banquet manager's job.

Long Hours

The job of banquet manager requires the banquet manager to work when everyone else is playing. Social events occur on weekends, evenings, and holidays. The banquet manager may have had 12 parties during the week, but to clients, their party is the only one that matters. The banquet manager is responsible for all the parties being conducted at the establishment. Many times, this means supervising all the parties. Larger banquet houses will have assistant banquet managers, but the vast majority of operations cannot afford an assistant. Therefore, the banquet manager has to attend all parties.

Stress

The banquet manager is under a tremendous amount of stress to do an excellent job. Even though guests may not expect the same high quality as they do when they go to an à la carte dining establishment, the hosts of the party want a gourmet meal. They also want everything done one way—perfectly. The hosts have chosen the banquet facility with the expectation that the party will be perfect. They want to enjoy themselves. At times this creates an unbearable amount of stress on the banquet manager.

T I P $

TO INSURE PROPER SERVICE
People do not care how much you know, until they know how much you care.

Availability of Food and Liquor

Sometimes the banquet manager, as a response to the stress in the job, may turn to alcohol to solve problems. As a perk, and because of the banquet manager's stature in the establishment, she can consume alcohol as part of the job. By the same token, many people in this profession have poor diets. They have so many different foods available that they reward themselves with a poor diet that is detrimental to their health.

Illegal Activities

In addition to these problems, there is the temptation for the manager to engage in illegal activities, such as drug use and gambling. Because of the contact with people in all walks of life, the banquet manager is often exposed to these types of activities.

Job Knowledge Needed

The banquet manager must know how to sell, plan, organize, and conduct banquets so that they are a success for the clients. There are many details that make the difference between a successful or unsuccessful banquet. The following chapters will go into more depth on these nuances. However, to begin with, the banquet manager must know the following to conduct business successfully:

1. The style of banquets
2. The size of each room in the operation and how to diagram rooms
3. How to book banquets
4. The difference between tentative and firm reservations, and how to make a tentative one firm
5. The variety of menu items from which the client may choose
6. The importance of communication with guests and staff
7. How to construct a menu that will be appealing, nutritionally sound, and that the kitchen will be able to prepare and serve
8. The timing of the party so that the food arrives when the client desires it and the guests are ready
9. The variety of ways in which banquets can be served to guests

Styles of Banquets

There are three general styles of banquets. The first is a sit-down meal, the second is a buffet. Both refer to the type of service the staff gives to the guests. The sit-down banquet refers to the fact that the guests are served their complete meal by the service staff. At a buffet, the guests either obtain a portion or all their food by serving themselves from buffet tables.

Stations represent the third type of service. Throughout the banquet room, foods are served from different locations in the room. At one side of the room, there may be a turkey carving station; on the opposite side, an appetizer station. This allows the guests to graze throughout the banquet, rather than having to obtain and eat their food as they do in sit-down banquets and buffets (see Figure 10–6).

TYPES OF SERVICE AT BANQUETS		
Sit-Down Meals	**Buffets**	**Stations**
American	Simple Buffet	Grazing
Russian	Modified Deluxe	
	Deluxe	

FIGURE 10–6

Types of service for banquets.

Type of Service for Banquets

There are two types of service for sit-down banquets. Restaurants use either American or Russian banquet service. For buffets, there are three types of buffet services: *buffet, modified buffet,* and *deluxe buffet.*

American banquet is the type of service that most restaurants use because it is simple. It is referred to as *on the plate, no wait.* It is easy to learn and use.

Russian service requires more skill by the service staff. The staff must transfer food from platters to guest plates by using a fork and spoon. This type of service most often occurs at expensive banquets, usually in large metropolitan hotels or at an off-premise event.

The service that does not deserve to be called service is the simple buffet. In this option, the guests go through a line and pick up their own food, utensils, and beverages. The only thing the service staff does is clean up the dirty tables.

A modified buffet service requires the service staff to serve beverages and, perhaps, the dessert courses, whereas guests obtain their appetizers, salad, and main entree items from the buffet table.

The deluxe buffet provides the guests with the most service. All the courses except the main course are served to the guest.

Service at a station-type of party is much like the service at a simple buffet. Because the guests are grazing, the service staff must be circulating throughout the room to remove dirty dishes from guests' tables and sometimes offer beverage service. It is common to have sidestands with trays located throughout the room for guests to place their dirty dishes on if they desire.

SUMMARY

1. A banquet is a meal that has a menu that has been preselected by the client for all of the guests attending the event.

2. A restaurant can make more money with a lot less chance of failure by holding banquets. Put simply, the profit potential is much greater for banquets than for a restaurant with an à la carte business only.

3. An establishment that offers banquets has many advantages over restaurants that serve à la carte meals. This is because the establishment knows in advance how many guests will attend the banquet and what the menu selection will be, which avoids over-preparation of food and controls food costs. The time and size of the event is known, which makes controlling labor costs easier than at an à la carte restaurant. Deposits and a guaranteed number of guests or money is contracted far in advance of the event. Marketing banquets is more cost-effective, because only one or two individuals will decide on having the event at the restaurant; in an à la carte restaurant, many individuals make a decision to patronize the restaurant.

4. The main difference between a caterer and a banquet manager is that the banquet manager hosts the guests in his own establishment, whereas the caterer brings the food and service to the guests.

5. The advantages to the banquet manager's position are good pay, prestige, psychic income, the availability of food and liquor, and perquisites. The disadvantages are long hours, stress, the opportunity to abuse food and liquor, and the opportunity to engage in illegal activities.

6. The styles of service available for banquets are *sit-down meals*, *buffets*, and *stations*.

7. The qualities that a successful banquet manager must possess are numerous. Among the most important are attention to detail, tact, a neat appearance, the ability to react quickly to change, the ability to work with many different types of personalities, the ability to communicate well both verbally and in writing, and a high degree of organizational skill.

8. A banquet manager must know how to sell, plan, organize, and conduct banquets that are a success for the clients.

9. The key to banquet management is for the banquet manager to move the responsibility for the banquet's success off the client's shoulders and onto her own.

10. The key to being a successful banquet manager is to take care of all details concerning the banquet for the guests. To be a success, the banquet manager must listen and really hear what the host of the party is requesting. Then the banquet manager must exceed the expectations of the guests.

REVIEW QUESTIONS

1. Define the term *banquet*.
2. Explain the importance of banquets as they relate to the profitability of a hospitality establishment.
3. List and explain the advantages that the banquet business has over restaurants that serve à la carte meals.
4. Define the difference between a caterer and a banquet manager.
5. What are the advantages and disadvantages of the banquet manager's job?
6. What are the types and styles of service available for banquets?
7. What are the qualifications needed to become a banquet manager?
8. What job knowledge should the banquet manager possess in order to do the job effectively?
9. What is the banquet manager's main responsibility as it relates to the host of the banquet?

DISCUSSION QUESTIONS

1. A party of 150 is served a meal. You, as the banquet manager, observe that the noise level in the room is very high. No one is eating the main beef course! It is obvious that there is a problem with the meal. How do you solve this problem?
2. Remember the story about the "promised" raspberries? What should the caterer have done to avoid this problem? Explain how the caterer did not exhibit the trait of attending to details.
3. What are some of the tasks that a banquet manager or caterer would take over to assist and relax the host? Or that would allow the host to enjoy the party?
4. At a wedding reception, one couple makes a special request for two kosher meals. The kitchen is not equipped to produce kosher meals. How will the caterer solve this problem?
5. What factors would the caterer have to take into account to have a successful house party for 200 guests? Include in your answer considerations such as cooking facilities, washing facilities, equipment needs, bathroom facilities, sanitation, and the challenge of weather conditions. What might occur if the caterer does not plan for these factors?

REFERENCE

1. Paul Frumkin, "Operators See Big Profits in Catering to Private Affairs," *Nation's Restaurant News* 34, No. 44 (October 30, 2000): 1, 56.

How to Book Functions

OBJECTIVES   At the completion of this chapter, the student should be able to:

1. Define the term *function*.
2. Name the sizes of the standard banquet tables and their uses.
3. Describe the different types of room setups available for functions.
4. Draw a diagram of a function room in a simple and concise manner.
5. Define the difference between tentative and firm bookings.
6. Explain the importance of a function book or computer program, and how to book functions at the establishment.
7. Explain the word *qualified* as it relates to booking business.
8. Explain the word *guarantee* and its importance in the banquet business.
9. Describe the difference in policies on room rentals.
10. Explain the importance of setting up policies as they relate to payment of functions.

KEY WORDS

firm booking	function book	tentative booking
function	guarantee	

What Is a Function?

A **function** is any use of banquet facilities. The room may be rented by the client, or the establishment may allow the client to use the room at no charge. Examples of functions are meetings, dinners, conferences, and cocktail parties. Clients deal directly with the banquet office for the purpose of conducting these functions. Depending upon the size of the banquet facility, the banquet manager may be the only management person that comes in contact with the client from the initial booking until the function is complete. In larger establishments, there may be a catering and sales manager, as well as a group sales office that has the responsibility of booking the function. Once the event is booked, the responsibility for the success of the event belongs to the banquet manager. Conducting successful functions begins with proper booking of the event.

What Must Be Known about Function Room Setups

Regardless of the type of function that will be booked, the person booking the function must know specific facts about the individual banquet facility. First, the booking person has to know the number of rooms available and each room's capacity for either meal or meeting functions. Second, the type of physical setups that will accommodate guests comfortably and efficiently in each room should be known. Third, the banquet manager has to know the equipment available to be used in the establishment; whether it has been assigned to another function at the same time, as well as how, where, and at what cost extra equipment can be obtained. Finally, the manager will have to be able to perform the job without having to ask any questions about the room layout.

T I P $ **TO INSURE PROPER SERVICE**
Work a day with banquet set-up people to understand the problems they have in physically setting up rooms.

Room Availability and Capacity

Architects and banquet managers never see a room the same way. It has been well documented that most restaurant facilities—especially kitchens—are designed by people who do not or have never worked in a kitchen. The same is true of function rooms. Many times, the square footage available is calculated using the general formula of 8 to 12 square feet of space for each person at a sit-down meal function. Often, even though the formula is mathematically accepted, the projected number of guests will not fit into the room. This is because each function is an individual party that may require different demands on the space, resulting in a different capacity for the room. The location of exits, the shape of the head table, the traffic flow, the dance floor, the audiovisual equipment, and the type of function must be taken into consideration before the realistic capacity of a room, for each function, can be determined. For instance, more people will be accommodated in a room when it is being used for a stand-up cocktail party rather than for a meeting. Therefore, the banquet manager should get the feel of the room by setting up tables and conducting a few sample functions in it. By doing this, the banquet manager will generally know the capacity of each room for most kinds of functions.

Another moment of truth occurs when guests sit down to have their meal. If there is enough room at the table, they are pleased. If the room is too crowded, the banquet facility has failed in their eyes. Each person booking functions has to be aware of the realistic capacity and use of every room for every type of function; do not rely on the proposed capacity determined by the architect.

Types of Room Setups for Functions

Guests do not want to be too crowded into a room; nor do they want a room where there is so much extra space that it looks as if the party is a failure. It is the banquet manager's responsibility to know the different ways a room can be set up to create a successful social or business event. Banquet managers must know how to use room space effectively in order to maximize revenue. In addition, anyone booking parties has to know the definition of the standard types of functions. We will define here those functions most widely used, but the list is not all-inclusive.

Tables

All guests are seated at tables and are waited on by a service person. For social events, such as weddings or dinners, round tables are ideal because they encourage conversation. For business meetings, a block table, a T-shaped table, or an E-shaped table is better because it eliminates unnecessary conversation. Figures 11–1 through 11–3 illustrate the different shapes.

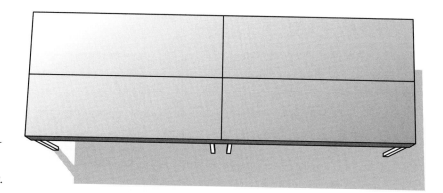

FIGURE 11–1

An illustration of a block table. Four rectangular tables are put together to form a block.

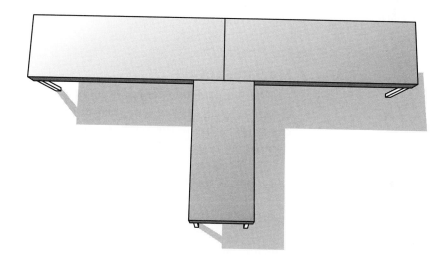

FIGURE 11–2

A T-shaped table made up of three or more rectangular tables.

The block table (Figure 11–1) is made up of four rectangular tables put together to form a block. This is an ideal setup for a maximum of 20 guests at a small business meeting where all guests can communicate freely.

The T-shaped table (Figure 11–2) is ideal to use in a long, narrow room. The illustration shows three rectangular tables; however, in actual practice, four or five tables often make up the "bar" of the T.

The third, the E-shaped table (Figure 11–3) is ideal where a large delegation of guests must be seated at the head table.

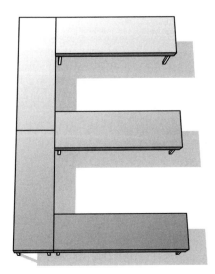

FIGURE 11–3

An E-shaped table made up of five or more rectangular tables.

Meeting Setups

Usually there are two general types of setups for meetings. The easiest one to set up is referred to as *theater style*. The guests are provided only chairs, all facing in the same direction. This type of setup would be used when the guests are attending a presentation.

The second type of meeting setup is a style called *classroom* or *schoolroom*. Figure 11–4 illustrates tables that face the front of the room. Guests are seated on the side of the table facing the front of the room for the purpose of writing notes. This setup would be used for a teaching seminar. Classroom style takes up the most amount of space, which results in fewer guests that may be accommodated in a room.

T I P $

TO INSURE PROPER SERVICE

To impress your clients, use skirting to dress up all tables at meetings.

Head Tables

These tables are placed in front of the room, with the guests seated only on the side of the table from which they are facing the other members of the party. A trend at social events is to have a round head table placed in the middle of the party. This eliminates the formality of the event and allows the guests at the head table to enjoy themselves more.

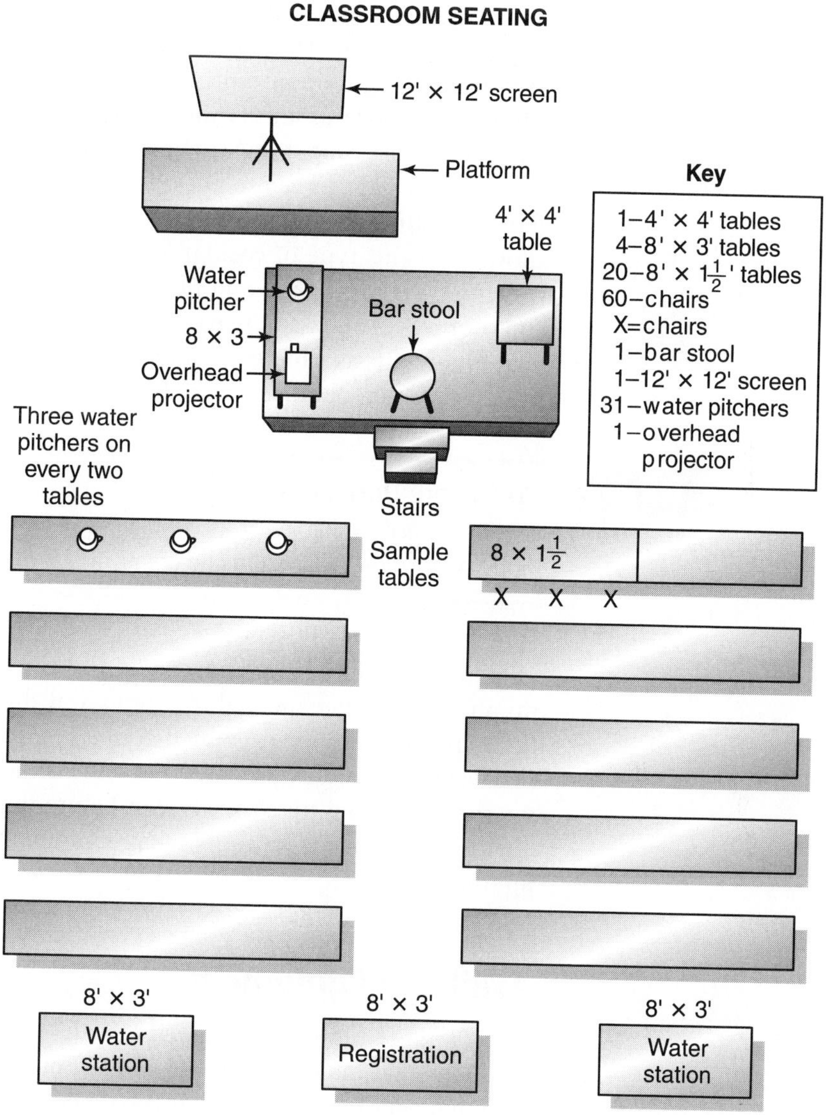

CLASSROOM SEATING

12' × 12' screen

Platform

4' × 4' table

Water pitcher

8 × 3

Overhead projector

Three water pitchers on every two tables

Bar stool

Key

1–4' × 4' tables
4–8' × 3' tables
20–8' × 1½' tables
60–chairs
X=chairs
1–bar stool
1–12' × 12' screen
31–water pitchers
1–overhead projector

Stairs

Sample tables

8 × 1½

X   X   X

8' × 3'
Water station

8' × 3'
Registration

8' × 3'
Water station

FIGURE 11–4

A classroom or schoolroom-style setup for a function. All seats are facing the front of the room.

Cocktail Parties

The flow of guests is important for this type of function. The banquet manager can become creative and use all types of spaces for these parties. These spaces can be the lobbies or pools of hotels, or they can be a function room. The positions of both the bars and the food stations become important for guest comfort and ease of service. Setting up a cocktail party is relatively easy because the banquet manager only has to use a few tables.

At a cocktail party, there should be fewer chairs than the number of guests expected. This forces the guests to socialize. Care must be used in locating food and drink stations away from one another to minimize traffic jams and facilitate mingling. A popular cocktail party concept that has caught on is to have stations where food is cooked and small portions are served to guests. For instance, there may be a pasta station, a stir fry station, and a carving station. More room must be allowed for this type of cocktail party than for the traditional one in which food is precooked and put out for the guests in chafing dishes and on trays. At cocktail parties, during which guests typically stand, many more guests can be accommodated in the same space than at a sit-down dinner, because fewer chairs are needed.

TIP$ **TO INSURE PROPER SERVICE**
Use any space available for a cocktail party: the pool area, a hallway, the lobby of your establishment—be creative!

Once the banquet manager and the client have determined the number of guests expected to attend and the type of setup desired, the manager can decide which room can accommodate the group comfortably and efficiently. A diagram has to be drawn in order for the room to be set up correctly; but before this can be done, the banquet manager needs to know what equipment is available for setting up rooms.

Available Equipment

The manager knows the capacity of all the rooms and the types of functions that may be booked into each one. The next thing the banquet manager needs to know is the types and sizes of tables available, so the function can be planned with comfort for the guests and efficiency for the banquet establishment in mind. Figure 11–5 illustrates the types of tables that are available for the banquet manager to use in setting up functions.

Round Tables

Round tables are used to create a jovial atmosphere. They should always be used when the client wants a function where fun and enjoyment are among the key ingredients for the success of the party.

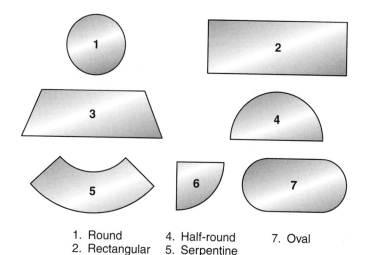

FIGURE 11–5

Shapes of tables available to use in setting up banquet functions.

1. Round   4. Half-round   7. Oval
2. Rectangular   5. Serpentine
3. Trapezoid   6. Quarter-round

Round tables are a must for wedding receptions, since these encourage conversation. Most banquet houses use one of two sizes of round tables: The standard round table is 60 inches in diameter. This will seat 8 people comfortably at a meal. The other common size is 72 inches, which seats 10. The main disadvantage of a banquet facility using round tables is that round tables take up more space than rectangular tables. Therefore, the banquet facility cannot seat as many people at a function using round tables as it could using rectangular tables.

T I P $

To Insure Proper Service
If you are planning to make a name for yourself in social catering, invest in round tables that seat 8 to 10 guests.

Oblong or Rectangular Tables

Figure 11–6 shows the three basic sizes of oblong or rectangular tables. They are 30 inches wide by 96 inches long, called an eight-footer; 18 × 96 inches (8-foot by 1½-foot, or skinny); and 30 × 72 inches, called a six-footer. Each guest needs 24 inches of linear space to be comfortable. Therefore an eight-footer will seat eight people—four on each side of the table. The six-footer will accommodate six people, and the skinny will only accommodate four people. The skinny table is used when guests have to sit on one side of the table, such as at a head table or for a classroom-style setup. A skinny can also be used for a

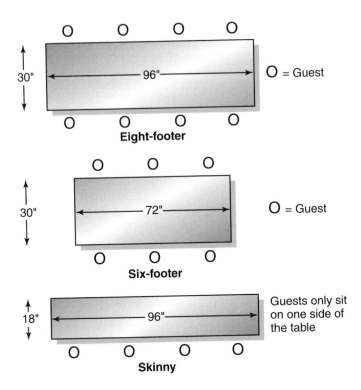

FIGURE 11–6

Three basic sizes of rectangular tables.

block table. A block table is made by putting rectangular tables together to form either a solid or a hollow setup. This style of setup is used when all participants want to be able to see and communicate directly with each other. It is usually used at a meeting, but it can also be used for a small business dinner.

Space Between Tables

When guests are seated back to back, which is the case when rectangular tables are used, it is recommended that 60 inches be allowed between tables. Using round tables, 54 inches of space is needed. Both of these guidelines take into account that chairs are to be placed in the 60 inches and 54 inches of space. However, this is another area in which the banquet manager should experiment by actually setting up the rooms to determine if there is enough space between tables for the guests to be comfortable and for the service personnel to do their job efficiently. When doing this experiment, the banquet manager should instruct the person setting up the chairs not to push them under the tables but to keep them pulled out as if a guest were sitting at the table. The banquet manager will soon discover the capacity of the function rooms in the establishment.

TIPS

TO INSURE PROPER SERVICE

Explain to your service staff the purpose of pulling the chairs out when the room is being set up by the banquet houseperson. The reason: to make sure the service staff has enough room to serve without creating a safety hazard.

Special-Shaped Tables

Trapezoid, serpentine, quarter-round and half-round tables are best used for setting up food or bar stations, rather than for the guests' dining. A banquet manager and chef can create interesting food setups using the different table shapes.

Lecterns

Lecterns are placed in the center of the head table and take up 24 inches—the same amount of space that a guest requires. On the lectern there is a place for the notes of the guest speaker, a light, and a microphone.

Podium

A podium serves the same purpose as a lectern. The difference between the two is that a podium is freestanding, whereas the lectern sits on the table. The podium also takes up 24 inches of space.

Microphones

Every banquet manager has to be aware of the types of microphones available for use in the function room. The banquet manager should know where the power source is for the microphone outlet, how to turn the system on, how to adjust the volume, and how to eliminate annoying feedback. One common mistake most people make when testing a microphone is not setting the volume loud enough. The microphone system should be tested before the guests arrive. Often the person testing the system does not take into account that there will be many more people in the room when the system is in use. A room with 400 guests will produce a higher decibel level of interfering sound than one with no guests; so the microphone must sound loud when it is being tested.

TIP$

TO INSURE PROPER SERVICE
Work with the musicians or disc jockeys to keep the music at a comfortable level so the guests can talk.

Audiovisual Equipment

Most banquet facilities have movie screens, and some may have slide projectors. Other facilities have state of the art rear-projection systems. Regardless of the type of equipment the establishment owns, the banquet manager needs to know how to operate it. If a guest makes a request for equipment that the facility does not own, the banquet manager can rent it. Therefore the manager must know where to obtain rental audiovisual equipment and how much to charge the guest for it.

In larger banquet and conference facilities, the banquet manager's job is simplified because the establishment has its own audiovisual department. The department has a price sheet for all equipment available, listing the prices for LCD projectors, microphones, and other equipment. In addition, the audiovisual department employs professionals who set up and operate the equipment for an hourly fee. On the audiovisual menu, the establishment may also put together equipment packages. The video, VCR/monitor package includes a VHS one-half U-Matic player/recorder that features a roll-around 54-inch projection cart and a 2-inch, full-function, color video monitor/receiver with cable connections. AC extension cords are safely taped. The audiovisual menu also increases sales for the facility by upselling additional items recommended by professional meeting planners. In this package, it is recommended to have an additional 27-inch video monitor and cart that includes cables and connectors for an additional cost.

The audiovisual department can become a revenue producer for the establishment and a convenience for the client.

Sweet or Sour? A few days before a function was to take place, former Governor Nelson Rockefeller's advance man made an appointment with the banquet manager to inspect the facilities for the Governor's speech. They entered the function room, where the windows were checked to make sure the Governor would not be susceptible to a sniper's shot. The advance man told the banquet manager exactly what side the television cameras could be set up on to present the best side of the Governor and then asked to test out the lectern.

(continues)

(continued)

The lectern was positioned on the head table as it would be for the Governor's speech. The advance man took out a tape measure and discovered that the place where "The Man's" (as he referred to him) notes would be placed was 43 inches from the floor. "This will never do," he said. "The notes must sit on a lectern or podium 44 inches from the floor." The question was asked, "Why?" "Because that is the perfect distance that allows the Governor to read his notes without putting on his glasses," he replied. With that information, the problem was solved by getting a carpenter to cut a one-inch piece of wood to fit under the lectern. On the day of the speech, the wood was under the lectern, which elevated it to 44 inches from the floor, and the event was a success. From that day on, the wood was kept in the banquet manager's office and used every time the Governor was the guest speaker at functions at the hotel.

Things to Keep in Mind

Every banquet manager must realize that planning the correct setup of a function room can be an integral part of the success or failure of a business meeting or party. There are a couple of facts about equipment and the use of function rooms that must be stressed.

Especially important is that all equipment must be in the room and thoroughly tested before the guests arrive. For example, if the slide projector is rented, the banquet manager should have extra bulbs available and know how to change them if one burns out during a slide presentation. If the equipment is owned by the establishment, a regular maintenance schedule should be set up for changing bulbs so that there will be no problem during the presentation. All equipment must be in working condition and ready to operate when the guests walk in.

The second fact that the banquet manager must consider has to do with the placement of different types of functions in the rooms. Many facilities have large function rooms that can be made into smaller rooms by the use of movable walls. Many times these walls are not as soundproof as the manufacturer claims. A banquet manager would be wise not to book a business meeting next to a wedding reception, with only the wall separating them.

The banquet manager can play an integral part in the success or failure of a party by the planning and use of equipment. Practice, common sense, and the banquet manager's experience will benefit all the guests. This will result in more repeat business for the establishment.

A Final Point about Room Setups

When scheduling a function, the banquet manager should see to it that there is enough space to accommodate all the guests comfortably in the room. There is one exception to this rule: for a press conference, clients often want to schedule space that is much too small for the number of people that is expected. It is a press conference. This is done to make the event look like an overwhelming success. Think of a room that seats 100. If 100 people show up, the room is filled to capacity. Put the same press conference in a room that seats 500. Even if 200 people attend the event, it still appears that the event was a flop, because there are 300 empty seats.

Physically Setting Up the Function Rooms

Once the banquet manager knows the proper manner of setting up and using the function rooms, the next step is to physically set up the rooms for the function. The banquet manager should not set up the rooms, but should know how to diagram the function so that the set-up crew will be able to accomplish the task without asking any questions.

Most of the time, the people who have the responsibility of setting up the rooms are entry-level workers. If they are trained properly, which is generally the banquet manager's job, they become excellent employees and are a valuable asset for the banquet manager. It is the banquet manager's responsibility to diagram all parties as requested by the client. This prepared diagram is then given to the set-up people so that they can physically set up the room.

Figure 11–7 shows the setup for a wedding reception for 198 guests. There is a key on the bottom of the diagram. All tables are clearly marked with their sizes, and there is a sample table for the set-up crew to follow. The head table has the exact specification of how many guests should be seated and where they should be seated. The key tells exactly how many tables, their sizes, and the number of chairs the set-up crew needs for each table. This diagram makes the setup of this party easy.

Every function should have a diagram such as that in Figure 11–7. Because most setups are done during the night when the banquet manager is not working, the diagrams should be as complete as possible. In the morning, the first thing the banquet manager will do is check the rooms to make sure they are set up correctly. If there is a problem, it can be corrected, and it can be determined whether the mistake was the set-up crew's or the banquet manager's. The banquet manager must know how to diagram function rooms simply and concisely.

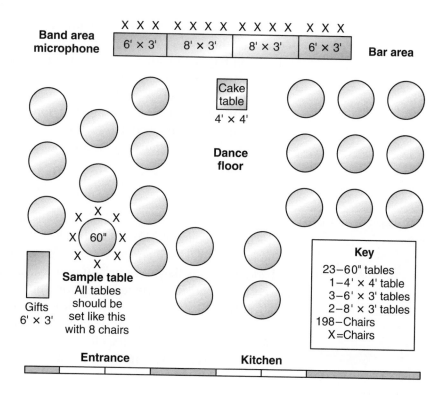

FIGURE 11–7

The correct way to diagram a wedding reception.

Two Final Tips

All illustrations should be done on letter-sized paper so that the set-up crew can carry them around in their pockets easily. The diagrams do not have to be done to scale.

Finally, the banquet manager should try, whenever feasible, to suggest the same physical setup to the next client as was used for the previous function. This will cut down on the banquet facility's labor cost, as well as increase the morale of the set-up crew.

Booking Functions

Once the banquet manager knows the capacity and use of the function rooms, the next task is to book functions. The booking of functions is done by a sales, catering, or banquet manager, or by a secretary. For the purpose of this chapter, the title *banquet manager* will encompass all of these job titles.

The banquet manager has to know exactly what types of meals, accommodations for meetings, and charges for these services the establishment can offer to the client. Usually this information is provided by the owners or the general manager of the establishment after the food has been costed out and the profit margin is added into the meal. Most banquet managers work from a set-price menu; caterers usually do not. Caterers set their prices based upon a variety of factors, such as what the client desires, the location of the party, the day of the week, and how much demand there is for the caterer's services. Knowing all of this information, the booking process can begin.

Sweet or Sour?

One Saturday morning a banquet establishment was setting up for their wedding of 200. As they had just about completed the setup, the waiter looked out and saw the wedding party arrive. He thought this was odd, as they were half an hour early. The banquet manager went out to greet the bride and groom; but to his surprise it was a different bride and groom who showed up. Another manager had booked another wedding on the same day, at the same time, with the same menu. In 30 minutes, the other wedding party of 200 showed up. And no, this is not made up. It really happened!

Function Book

To avoid the embarrassments caused by unprofessional booking practices, every facility must have an organized system to keep its bookings straight. In the past, the tool to use was a function book. Today, the function book is being replaced with computer software. However, whether a banquet establishment uses a function book or a computer, the basic principles are the same.

A **function book** is an organized system for listing rooms that the establishment has to rent on a daily basis. A typical page from a function book is presented in Figure 11–8.

In Figure 11–8, each meal period and each day of the year are in the book. In addition, every room would be listed in the book. The person doing the booking would open the page to the date and see if anything was booked into the room. If there was nothing entered, then the booking person could sell the space to the guest. In Figure 11–8, the booking person can see that the Seville room is booked for Mr. Zorn. Furthermore, AJS booked the party and accepted the deposit on 3/21 and made the notation that the reservation was firm.

If another client wanted the Seville room for lunch on September 12, the client would be told that the room was already booked. The

MONDAY, SEPTEMBER 23, 20__ LUNCH			
Room	**Group**	**Estimated Number**	**Time**
Seville	Society of Wine Educators	250	11–1:30
	Ted Zorn		
	28 Oakbarrel Drive		
	Hammensport, NY		
	617-555-WINE (B)	Firm 3/11/20__	AJS
	315-555-6589 (H)	$1,000.00 Deposit	

FIGURE 11–8

A typical page from a function book. Its purpose is to avoid overbooking.

banquet manager should then attempt to sell the client a different time, room, or a different date. If there are no open dates or if the client cannot change the requested date, the banquet manager may make suggestions or even assist the client in finding another banquet facility that is comparable in service and price. This practice is beneficial to the banquet manager in a couple of ways. First, the client will be impressed that the banquet manager is taking the time to assist in finding an alternative banquet establishment. Second, the competition will reciprocate when it is booked up.

The function book does not provide any information about the menu or the party; only who reserved the room, whether it is a firm or tentative booking, and the approximate time and number of guests that will attend the function. The main purpose of the system is to avoid overbooking, which is having two parties reserved in the same room at the same time.

Care and Storage of the Book

Because the function book is such an integral part of the banquet business, it should be kept in a permanent place. It should not be brought into another office or to a person's home when booking a party. When no one is in the office, it should be kept in a locked area.

T I P $

TO INSURE PROPER SERVICE

Function books are gigantic. They cover all the rooms and all the meal periods. Some establishments have them for a year or more; others only for three or six months. Devise a function book that works for your banquet facility.

The banquet facility must make certain that only authorized people are allowed to make entries into the book. All entries must be made in pencil, and the people who book the parties must identify themselves by putting their initials in the entry.

One advantage computer software has over the traditional function book is that back-up copies of all bookings can be saved or printed. There has always been a fear that if the book was stolen, lost, or damaged by fire, it would be difficult to reconfirm the bookings, and thus, overbooking would occur.

By taking these steps, the establishment should almost eliminate the possibility of overbooking.

T I P $

TO INSURE PROPER SERVICE
Back up your computer software function book at least twice daily.

Qualifying Business

Each banquet establishment has to set up a policy to determine the amount of money that must be made when a room is booked. Once that determination and policy has been set, the banquet manager should attempt to book parties that will bring in the most revenue for the establishment. Some banquet establishments will accept any and all business, whereas others attempt to specialize in certain market areas, such as the social business.

To *qualify* a client means to determine how much money the client will be spending at the establishment. At some establishments there will be more demand for function space during particular months. "September is peak season for us as far as functions go," states the sales and catering manager at The Desmond in Albany, New York. "It is primarily our large conference and convention season. There is minimal space available. If a room is available for 50 guests, we are going to try to find a client who wants an open bar, extensive hors d'oeuvres, a high revenue dinner, and possibly wine sales, in comparison to a cash bar and a chicken dinner."

The second part of *qualifying* means to determine if the client can pay for the party. Some clients have booked parties with no intention of paying for them; unfortunately, this is usually people running for political office. It is best to make political candidates pay for their functions in advance. There are many documented stories about candidates who have both won and lost elections and still owe for their parties. The accepted method of payment should be explained to the client when the party is booked. The establishment has to decide if it will accept personal checks or credit cards only and also how much of a deposit to charge the client.

Once the client is qualified, the date can be entered into the function book as either a tentative or firm booking.

How Far in Advance May Banquets Be Booked?

Each banquet facility has to determine, based upon the demand for space, a policy concerning how far in advance banquets may be booked. The goal of the facility is to obtain the most revenue. For example, a new banquet business would probably book any business, whereas one that is established and more in demand may set a limit on advance bookings. As was explained in the previous chapter, more banquet establishments have determined how much revenue a banquet room should bring in for a specified time period. When an event is booked, the banquet or sales manager has a formula to determine how much money must be spent for the use of that room. The client must guarantee spending the set amount of money regardless of how many people attend the event.

At a particular banquet facility, the guidelines are clearly outlined: They have very specific booking policies. For instance, the group sales office can take bookings far in advance, as long as the client is qualified. On the other hand, the catering office can take social events only nine months in advance of the event. The exception is on holiday weekends. They can book as far in advance as requested on a weekend such as Labor Day. So if they had a request for a wedding, it cannot be booked a year in advance unless it was on a holiday weekend. Small business meetings of between 15 to 25 people may only be booked three months in advance of the date. This is done in order to attract events that will bring in the highest revenues.

Once the guidelines and policies are set, the banquet manager should qualify the client before booking the party.

The Difference between Tentative and Firm

Bookings can be called either tentative or firm. **Firm bookings** are the easiest to understand. A client gives the banquet manager a deposit for a party. Once the establishment receives the client's money—and in some banquet establishments a signed contract for the event—the amount and date of the deposit and the word *firm* are entered into the function book.

A **tentative booking** means that the banquet manager puts the client's name into the function book, and the client has first refusal if another person calls and wants the same room at the same time. Again, a policy is established by the banquet facility regarding tentative bookings. At many banquet establishments, tentative can mean that the space is held tentatively without a deposit for one week. After the week, the person who booked the party will call the client and ask whether he or she is still interested in the date. If the client is still interested, a deposit must be collected. The person who books the function writes in the book the term *firm*, with the date and the amount of the deposit received. If the client does not pay the deposit within one week, he or she is called and informed that the deposit must be brought in before the close of business that day or the booking will be canceled.

Problems with Tentative Bookings

Banquet managers find that some dates are more popular than others. Often, the manager will have a tentative booking and then a client will come in a day later with a deposit for a firm booking. The banquet establishment needs a policy to determine which party to take and which party to refuse.

Deposits

A deposit is required for almost all banquet events. The deposit protects both parties. The banquet house will not sell the date that the client has reserved to another client; the client will not cancel the event without losing the money that has been put down.

Each banquet house should determine the amount of deposit that it will charge. It should be expensive enough to deter the client from canceling the party, while moderate enough not to deter the guest from booking the party with the banquet house. As an example, one banquet facility requires a $200 deposit for social events that occur in any month except December. Deposits on holiday parties vary from $500 to $1,000. Other establishments have a different policy. However, excellent repeat customers are often not charged a deposit.

Different operations have different policies on refunding deposits. Some will never refund a deposit; other places will refund the deposit if the party is cancelled four months prior to the event; still other banquet houses will not give back the deposit unless another group rebooks the date. Of course, there are always circumstances in which the manager will have to determine if giving back or keeping the deposit would be in the best interests of the business.

T I P $ **To Insure Proper Service**
All policies regarding your banquet facility must be in writing and distributed to your clients when the first contact is made.

Guarantees

When booking functions, clients should be informed of the policy on guarantees of the establishment. A **guarantee** is a promise made by the host of the party that a certain number of guests will show up for the party and that the client will pay for that number unless more guests attend.

When a client originally books an event, an estimate is made of how many people will attend the party. Most banquet establishments require that the guarantee must be given three or four days prior to the event. Most establishments will take that number and set up 5 percent above that guaranteed number (100 guaranteed, 105 seats). The client pays for a minimum of 100 people, unless more guests show up. Some banquet establishments will also charge a 10 percent menu premium if the guest attendance is 5 percent or more than the guarantee. The establishment should also state in its procedure sheet that it cannot be responsible for service greater than the guaranteed number of guests. The key to managing successful banquets is to inform the client of all policies when the banquet or function is booked.

T I P $ **To Insure Proper Service**
Use common sense in charging a client when the guaranteed number does not show up because of circumstances beyond the client's control. What long-term benefit does a banquet establishment get from charging a client for 200 guests when a blizzard or hurricane prevented 175 guests from attending the reception?

Room Rentals

Since clients will be using the function rooms differently, some for food and beverage functions and some just for meetings, there are different ways to charge for room rentals.

Manager's Message

(Courtesy of
BRIAN PALAZZOLO,
PRESIDENT, CLASSÉ
CATERING,
ALBANY, NEW YORK)

I cannot stress enough the importance of the service arts professional—we are the front line of our organization. We interact with the guests and can make or break our organization's ability to provide a truly memorable experience to our clients, who may be celebrating the most significant day of their lives.

Keep in mind that in this competitive marketplace event planners and sales staff are forced to sell flawless, world-class service just to get an edge on the competition. So it is our responsibility to fulfill the mission to exceed guest expectations at all times. No matter how high the expectations are or how prominent the guests we are serving, if we do our role exceptionally well, then we are just as important as everyone else.

The Service Arts are my utmost passion. The culture here is that Hospitality is Paramount. And I say this with all sincerity: The mentality has to be, "It is our pleasure to serve you," and we must be passionate about the service of others. If you are not passionate about it and cannot give the perception of passion, then this gig is really not for you. Because in special events, service is a performance and we are always on stage.

We are truly in a performance with scenes, a cast, and props. Our mannerisms impact the guests. I am talking about the chivalry, White-Glove Touches, and the Red Carpet Treatment. It is important to understand *impression management* to help create that magic. The Magic of Service is that the guests will always have what they need without ever knowing how it got there. Great Service is invisible;

(continues)

If a client has a food and beverage function in one room, a meeting in another, and in yet another a food and beverage function, the client may be charged the full price for the meeting room. Naturally, if a client uses just a meeting room, the full price for the meeting room is charged.

At times, meeting room charges can be waived if the client spends additional money at the facility. For instance, if a client has booked 200 rooms at a hotel, the meeting room charge may be waived.

Manager's Message

(continued)

the guests should want for nothing. Our guest service policy is that you are *image empowered*. That is to say that the event personnel can and should do whatever it takes to get the best possible BIG-PICTURE outcome and make the guests' experience truly one of a kind.

—Brian Palazzolo

Classé Catering, established in 1995, is an innovative special events firm specializing in off-premise catering. With Brian's passion-driven leadership, Classé Catering received the Entrepreneurial Excellence Award from the Small Business Council, the Small Business Excellence award from the Small Business Association, and has been chosen as one of the Greatest Places to Work by the *Capital District Business Review*. The company's services include floral and theme design, wedding coordinating, and complete event planning.

Brian Palazzolo is the author of *Masterful Banquet Service*, an internationally distributed service-training DVD, and is the official service consultant for the national catering group *catersource* and for *catersource* magazine, which concentrates on catering, both on and off-premise. He has successfully planned and produced thousands of special events and weddings. Brian has shared his expertise as a featured speaker in Las Vegas at the largest catering convention in the world. He also has been a featured speaker at the New York State Restaurant Association show in New York City. Brian has won awards for his company's designs at a national theme competition and regularly teaches classes in buffet design. He and his staff at Classé Catering are also great community citizens, donating approximately $100,000 worth of goods and services each year to non-profit organizations.

SUMMARY

1. A *function* is any use of banquet facilities. Examples of functions are meetings, dinners, conferences, and cocktail parties.
2. Round tables are 60 or 72 inches in diameter and they seat a maximum of 8 and 10 guests, respectively. These round tables are ideal for banquet meals in which the host would like to encourage conversation. There are three types of rectangular tables that are standard

for functions. An eight-footer is 30 inches wide by 96 inches long. A skinny table is 18 inches wide by 96 inches long. A six-footer is 30 inches wide by 72 inches long. These rectangular tables are used for business meetings, classroom-style meetings, and dinner meetings.

3. Rooms will be set for a social banquet using round tables exclusively. Oblong or rectangular tables are used to create block, U-shaped, buffet, and E-shaped tables. Skinny tables are used for classroom-style events. The banquet manager can create different setups to meet the clients' needs by using a combination of tables to create various setup configurations.

4. A banquet manager must know how to draw a diagram of a function room in a simple and concise manner so that the employees who set up the room will be able to accomplish the task without having to ask questions for clarification.

5. A *tentative booking* means that the banquet facility reserves a banquet room temporarily for the client. The client has a certain amount of time to firm up the booking. If another client requests the room for the same time and date, the individual with the tentative booking is called and he must accept by placing a deposit or release the room. A firm booking means that the client has reserved the banquet room by placing a deposit down for use of the room.

6. A function book system of some kind is critical for reserving function rooms. Before any function is sold, the function book or computer program must be consulted for room availability. All reservations—tentative and firm—must be entered into the function book as soon as requested. This is done to avoid overbooking (having two parties in the same room at the same time).

7. To *qualify* a client means to determine if the client will spend—and can pay—the required amount of money on the function in order to make it profitable for the banquet business.

8. *Guarantee* means that the client must pay a minimum amount of money for the use of the banquet room. This amount must be paid regardless of how many guests attend the event. If more guests attend, the client will pay for the extra guests. A guarantee allows the banquet facility to achieve maximum return on investment for holding a function.

9. Each establishment that has function rooms to rent out will determine the policies needed to maximize revenue for the use of the rooms. Many factors are taken into account by establishments to determine policies. Establishments may take into consideration the

demand for the rooms based upon the day of the week, season of the year, special events, and loyalty of the customers.

10. A banquet establishment must have firm policies concerning payment. These policies should include the schedule of payment required, the types of payment that are accepted, and cancellation penalties. A written policy will maximize profits for the establishment.

REVIEW QUESTIONS

1. What is a guarantee?
2. What is the proper amount of space that should be allowed between each table at a banquet?
3. Explain what the term *qualifying a client* means.
4. What is the purpose of a function book?
5. What does the term *function* mean?
6. What are the sizes of the standard banquet tables, and what type of parties use them?
7. Explain the difference between a tentative and a firm booking.
8. What are the advantages and disadvantages of having a function book on a computer, as opposed to having a hard copy?

DISCUSSION QUESTIONS

1. As the banquet manager for a hotel, one of your jobs is to book events in your one and only banquet room, which holds 200 guests. The geographical area in which you are located has many June weddings. On November 15, Mrs. Bodian and her daughter have an appointment to look at your hotel for a June 21st wedding. Before the appointment was scheduled, you looked at the function book and saw that the room was vacant. At the end of their visit, you have convinced Mrs. Bodian to put a tentative hold on the June 21st date. That evening, you and your food and beverage manager have an appointment with Mr. and Mrs. Coccozzo to book their daughter's wedding for June 28. Your food and beverage manager made the initial contact with the Coccozzo's and tentatively reserved June 28 in the function book. After meeting and presenting your proposal to the Coccozzo's they say "We would love to book our daughter's wedding at your hotel." You say, "Great, we have a tentative reservation for June 28 and we will make it firm with your deposit". They respond, "We tentatively booked June 21 and that is the date that we want." What would you do?

2. Your restaurant has booked a sit-down dinner banquet for the full capacity of the only banquet room you have. A week before the banquet, the host informs you that the number of guests will exceed the capacity of the room by 100 people. How do you solve this problem, so you do not lose this business? Or would it be better to lose this business?

3. Referring to the problem of the two simultaneous wedding receptions that were cited earlier in this chapter, how would you handle the situation?

4. A guest has booked a tentative party. Unfortunately, you did not qualify the business. It is the typical chicken dinner for 50 guests with a cash bar. One of your best customers comes into your office and says that his boss is retiring and he wants the same date as that booked for the tentative party. In addition to being a great customer, he informs you that they want a filet mignon party for 200 guests with an open bar, wine, and a cocktail party. What party should you take, and how will you explain the rejection to the guest to whom you deny the date?

5. Would you give back a deposit if a couple broke up two weeks before their planned wedding? What if the prospective bride got killed in an accident?

REFERENCE

1. Albany Marriott Audio Visual List. Albany Marriott, 189 Wolf Road, Albany, New York (July 14, 2000).

The Banquet Event Order

OBJECTIVES At the completion of this chapter, the student should be able to:

1. Define a banquet event order (BEO) and know its purpose.
2. Understand how to obtain information from the client concerning the event.
3. Suggest options to enhance the success of the event.
4. Complete the information needed on the banquet event order.
5. Explain the different meal options a client can have for a banquet.
6. Define *detail* as it pertains to the banquet business.
7. Explain the importance of details in organizing and planning a banquet.
8. Illustrate how to serve more than one main course item to guests at a banquet.
9. Understand the importance of communication and cooperation with all the staff, especially the chef.
10. Plan, staff, and organize a banquet to result in a perfect event.
11. Explain the different alcoholic beverage choices to a client at a banquet.
12. Set up seating arrangements for a party.

KEY WORDS

Banquet Event Order (BEO)	beverage service cash bar	open bar policy sheet

Organization: The Key to a Successful Banquet

After booking function rooms, the next step in the banquet management process is to obtain all information concerning the event. Once the banquet manager has the information, it has to be transmitted to the staff in a clear, concise manner.

Different banquet managers use different techniques for accomplishing this task. However, they all have one thing in common: every successful banquet manager has an organized system. Some banquet managers use informal lists to keep organized. The banquet manager may be responsible for parties from 10 to 10,000 or more.

Many facilities have a limited kitchen area and equipment to accommodate the large number of guests. The banquet manager must plan and organize the banquets, keeping in mind the limitations of the facilities. He or she also has the responsibility for obtaining all utensils and plates to feed the many guests. In addition, the banquet manager must obtain all the service staff to serve the guests.

Once a party is booked, the banquet manager should make lists of what must be done for the event. By compiling these lists, he or she makes certain that nothing is forgotten. Finally, the banquet manager must have everything the client has ordered and make sure it is served the way the client desires it. Another banquet facility may use a more sophisticated process in the planning and operation of functions. Each day, their sales and banquet staff receive a computerized printout that consists of five parts: deposits due, banquet event order (BEO) due, guarantee due, personal thank you, and signed BEO received.

All tasks are assigned to staff in the sales and catering office. They are to complete these tasks daily. Figure 12–1 illustrates page 2 of the Morning Report for Kimberly A. Spiak. This page is concerned with personal thank you notes and the signed BEO. Once the task has been completed, Kim will check it off.

Organization is one of the keys for a banquet manager to be successful in this business. Without organization, the job of the banquet manager would be impossible to accomplish successfully.

Obtaining Information about the Function

Once the client has reserved a date, the banquet manager must schedule an appointment to discuss all the particulars concerning the event.

DELPHI -- Morning report for Kimberly A. Spiak - KS
2

PERSONAL THANK YOU_____

Group Name	(Account ID)	Arrival Date	Trace Date	Action
Quench Beverage	(Quench Bev)	7/05/08	7/09/08	_ Complete/New Trace: _/_/_
Scarlett County Farmers Assoc.	(Scarlett Farm)	7/06/08	7/10/08	_ Complete/New Trace: _/_/_
APEX Savings and Loan	(APEX S & L)	7/07/08	7/11/08	_ Complete/New Trace: _/_/_
Red Rupert Insurance	(Rupert Ins)	7/07/08	7/11/08	_ Complete/New Trace: _/_/_
Professional Paints	(Prof Paint)	7/07/08	7/11/08	_ Complete/New Trace: _/_/_

SIGNED BED RECEIVED?_____

Group Name	(Account ID)	Arrival Date	Trace Date	Action
Glucose Associates	(Glucose)	7/05/08	7/09/08	_ Complete/New Trace: _/_/_
Wildnut Spring Corp.	(Wild Spring)	7/06/08	7/10/08	_ Complete/New Trace: _/_/_
Ardor, Beetle and Beason, Inc.	(Ardor, Bee)	7/07/08	7/11/08	_ Complete/New Trace: _/_/_
Wearever Tires and Shocks	(Wearev Tires)	7/07/08	7/11/08	_ Complete/New Trace: _/_/_
Peoples Bank	(People Bank)	7/07/08	7/11/08	_ Complete/New Trace: _/_/_

FIGURE 12–1

A morning report form for a banquet manager. This comes from a computer printout that is obtained daily.
It assigns tasks to complete for past and future functions.

At this meeting the banquet manager will listen, suggest, and guide the client toward appropriate choices for the function. Included in the discussion will be the physical setup of the room, planning the program and time schedule, and selecting the food and beverage menu.

The banquet manager usually will offer suggestions to the client to insure the party's success. Often, a client has a general idea of what he or she desires for the function. As banquet manager you must help with details of the event that the client did *not* think about. It is the job and the responsibility of the banquet manager to help plan the event so that it will be precisely what the client desires within the limits of your operation.

In order to do the job effectively, the banquet manager has to rely on the sense of hearing more than any of the other senses. The banquet manager must listen carefully to the client. The banquet manager's mind cannot be thinking of next week's party; all attention must be given to the client. By listening to the client, the banquet manager can offer suggestions to make the party a success.

BANQUET AND MEETING POLICY INFORMATION

Thank you for your interest in our facilities.
The following is an outline of our standard policies:

1. Rooms will be set up one hour before an event is to begin. If the client desires to have the room set up earlier, he or she must pay the standard room rental fee for the time period.

2. One bartender is provided for every 50 guests. Additional bartenders may be requested at the current rate of pay.

FIGURE 12–2

Part of a policy sheet. All banquet facilities need a sheet that lists the policies of the banquet establishment.

The Policy Sheet

Each banquet facility must have a printed sheet that lists specific policies concerning banquets. This **policy sheet** must be given to the client and reviewed at the initial planning meeting. Items on the sheet should include the length of time a room will be reserved; the cost of extra service staff and bartenders; how long in advance a function room will be set up; and the policy on deposits, guarantees, and contracts. The list may be as short as one page, or for conferences it may be several pages. With a printed policy statement, most questions are answered. This alleviates misunderstanding between the client and the banquet management. Figure 12–2 illustrates a portion of a banquet and meeting policy information form.

The Banquet Event Order (BEO)

When the banquet manager and client decide what is needed for the function, this crucial information must be placed on an organized, written document. The purpose of this document is to have the banquet house give the client exactly what has been requested. Everything that the client and the banquet manager have agreed upon appears on this document.

This information sheet has many different names, depending on the banquet establishment. In most cases it is called the **Banquet Event Order (BEO)**, but it could be called the *BEO* or *banquet stencil*. Regardless of the name, the purpose is to list in detail everything that the client desires for the event. Every banquet establishment must have a BEO in order to successfully serve banquets. Figure 12–3 illustrates a standard BEO.

BEOs are generally broken down into three main areas. The top third is information obtained at the time of the booking. Only the

BANQUET EVENT ORDER

Event Date _____ Payment Arrangement _____

_____

Organization _____ Business Phone _____
Address _____ Home Phone _____

Person in Charge _____
Estimated Number _____ Guarantee _____ Set _____
Room _____ Time _____
Food   Program

Liquor
Price _____ Booked By _____
Guest Signature & Date _____

FIGURE 12–3

Banquet Event Order (BEO). All banquet establishments need a standard form to transmit information from the client to the rest of the staff. This is accomplished through the use of BEO.

banquet and sales office employees need this information. Part 1 begins at the top of the sheet and includes the information through the estimated number of guests.

For large establishments that have many banquet rooms, banquet managers, and assistants, Part 1 of the BEO also includes the names of the staff people in the hotel who are responsible for the event. An example of a large facility is Marriott's Orlando World Center in Orlando, Florida. They have 143,000 square feet of public function space, which includes a 40,000-square-foot Crystal Ballroom and a 51,000-square-foot Palms Ballroom. In addition they have three boardrooms for high-level meetings and 14 other meeting rooms. When conventions occur, job assignments are broken down into specific areas. Regardless of how big or small the event, the Marriott must use a BEO.

Part 3, from price to the date, is also information primarily needed by the banquet office. This part can only be completed after the client and banquet manager have agreed upon all items desired for the event. The banquet manager completes this area by filling in the price, signing, and dating it. Then it is sent to the client to be signed.

Part 2 of the BEO is the key to the success of the event; that is where all the information about the event is recorded. In effect, this part of the BEO becomes a work order for the event.

Part 1 of the Banquet Event Order

Figure 12–4 illustrates Part 1 of the BEO, as filled in for Mr. Lockwood's daughter's wedding.

Notice that the date includes the day of the week. This will avoid any confusion by you, the client, or the staff. People often get confused about what day of the week a date falls on. The banquet manager needs to put the day of the week on the BEO to avoid any confusion.

Usually, there are so many departments involved with a large event such as the Lockwood wedding that everyone knows what day of the week August 3 falls on. However, mistakes are more likely to occur for small functions—groups of 10 to 20—because fewer employees are scheduled to work the event. A party of 20 may be served by the staff on duty, rather than having a separate banquet staff.

Sweet or Sour?

Once a party was scheduled for 20 guests. The BEO was completed and distributed. At noon, the guests arrived for the luncheon; no food was prepared, nor was the room set up. Both the waiter and the cook misread the date on the BEO, which said July 1. Fortunately, it was the New York State Chiefs of Police Organization, regular guests of the hotel, who were most understanding of the problem. They conducted their meeting while the staff set up the room and prepared the food. But from that day on, the day of the week *always* went on the BEO.

FIGURE 12–4

Part 1 of the BEO, which covers information that is obtained at the time of the booking.

PART 1—BANQUET EVENT ORDER	
Event Date Saturday, August 3	Payment Arrangement Cash
Organization Lockwood-Jones Wedding	Business Phone 555-0978
Address 7 Lark Ave	Home Phone 555-0878
Cranston, RI 02907	
Person in Charge Jim Lockwood	
Estimated Number 200	

The rest of Part 1 of the BEO is straightforward information. The banquet manager should always obtain both the client's business and home phone numbers in case a question arises concerning the event. By having both phone numbers, the banquet manager can contact the client with relative ease. Information in Part 1 should be filled in completely and be verified as correct by reading it back to the client.

T I P $

TO INSURE PROPER SERVICE

Always check on the client's ability to pay before providing services.

Manager's Message

(*Courtesy of* ANGELO MAZZONE, OWNER, MAZZONE MANAGEMENT GROUP, SCOTIA, NEW YORK)

"Our mission is to continue to provide outstanding food, beverage, and hospitality to the people of the Capital District, while providing opportunities for the professional growth of our staff, improvements to our physical plant, and profits to the corporation. Our goal is to improve on the negative and always exceed the expectations of the guests. I challenge my staff to make the best better, the difficult simple, and the impossible possible."

"Everyone in the catering business should always ask their guests a simple, but very basic question: 'How may I help you?' The continued growth of our catering division is because we create benchmarks and then surpass them. We have taken our service to an entirely new standard. If a guest is not happy with their meal or catered event, I empower my employees to make them happy. Every customer who has a banquet or an off-premise catered event is sent a questionnaire asking them to rate the event from below average to excellent. If the event was not rated excellent, we ask why. Our company policy stresses being receptive to our fellow associates' criticisms and observations. We keep the focus on solutions, rather than mistakes and blame."

—*Angelo Mazzone*

(continues)

Manager's Message

(continued)

Mr. Mazzone began, in 1988, by purchasing the original Glen Sanders Mansion, one of America's oldest historic dwellings, dating back to 1658. Construction to attach a riverfront ballroom and kitchen to the structure began immediately. In 1989 the Mansion Restaurant opened to the public in the original Great Room of the mansion, along with the Riverfront Ballroom.

In 1995 Glen Sanders Mansion became a full-service facility by adding a 22-room inn. Angelo has earned the title "Caterer to the Stars" because his company performs all of the backstage catering for the stars that perform at the Saratoga Performing Arts Center and caters many events that take place at Proctor's Theater in Schenectady, New York. His business also operates the Hall of Springs Banquet and Restaurant facility at the Saratoga Performing Arts Center. Patrons of the Saratoga Performing Arts Center dine at the Hall of Springs before performances of the New York City Ballet, Philadelphia Orchestra, and other cultural events. In addition, his off-premise catering division complements the banquets that are held at the Glen Sanders Mansion and the Hall of Springs. The off-premise division has catered events throughout upstate New York and into Vermont. Angelo also runs the upscale steakhouse, Angelo's 677 Prime, which is located in the hub of Albany, NY's downtown theater district. The success of Angelo's business over the last decade can be summed up by restating his quote, "I challenge my staff to make the best better, the difficult simple, and the impossible possible."

Sweet or Sour?

At one party, the host guaranteed 100 people for breakfast for an organization whose goal was to legalize marijuana. Only 25 of the invited state legislators attended. At the end of the event, the head waiter gave the host the check for 100 breakfasts. The guest signed it and was billed directly for the event. A few days later, the bill was returned with the words, "addressee unknown." A call was made to the one phone number listed in the function book and on the BEO. It was the number of a billiards hall in a large city. They had never heard of the guest. The phone number and the address were never checked. No money was ever received for the party, and it ended up in the bad debt category.

The *estimated* number, shown on the BEO, is the number of guests that the client expects to attend the event. It is usually the number of people that will be invited. This number is almost always larger than the *guaranteed* number. For instance, at wedding receptions, the banquet manager can calculate that 20 percent of the invited guests—which is usually the estimated number—will refuse the invitation because of traveling distance or other commitments. Of course, sometimes the guarantee will exceed the estimate, but this number is always a general figure; the client is never responsible for paying for the estimated number of guests. Guarantee will be covered later in this chapter.

Part 2 of the BEO

This is the area of the BEO that is of utmost importance to the employees. In reality, it is their work order. For example, it specifies the exact time that all events are scheduled. The service staff can obtain the information needed to lay the place setting and cover from the BEO; the chef will be able to calculate how much food to order based upon the menu and estimated number of guests; the kitchen staff has an exact description of the food that must be cooked and served; and the bar knows what liquor the client has ordered and when to serve it. In short, everything about the function should be written on this sheet.

T I P $

TO INSURE PROPER SERVICE

Training your employees to fill out BEOs accurately and completely will avoid major problems and decrease the stress placed upon your staff.

However, before Part 2 can be completed, the banquet manager has to suggest and discuss different ideas with the client. Figure 12–5 is

FIGURE 12–5

Part 2 of the BEO. This part becomes the work order for the employees after the banquet manager determines the client's needs.

PART 2—BANQUET EVENT ORDER

Estimated Number 200   Guarantee _____   Set _____

Food   Program

Liquor

a blank Part 2 of the BEO. The following sections illustrate the step-by-step process that the banquet manager goes through with the client to obtain all the information needed to fill in the sheet.

Part 3 of the BEO

Figure 12–6 illustrates the last area of the BEO. This area is completed after all the information about the event has been received from the client.

FIGURE 12–6

Part 3 of the BEO. This part is filled in after all the plans have been made for the party.

PART 3—BANQUET EVENT ORDER

Price $50.00 + 20% grat and Sales tax   Booked by AJS

Guest Signature & Date

Notice that the price includes the gratuity and the sales tax. The price area should specify all the charges. Some banquet houses eliminate this section on the copy that goes to the staff.

The only thing left to be completed on the BEO is for the client to read, sign, and date it. At some establishments a separate contract is sent with the BEO. At other banquet facilities, the BEO is used as the contract between the client and the banquet establishment.

Purpose of the Event

The first thing that the banquet manager must determine about the event is its purpose. It will either be for a social or a business event.

Most of the time the main purpose of an event is not to consume a gourmet meal. The food, even though it is an important part of the success of the event, is secondary to the purpose of the event. The banquet manager has to plan the meal to serve the guests quickly and efficiently so that the client can begin the program.

When the client is having a social event, the purpose of the party is to honor someone or something. It could be celebrating a wedding or an anniversary. It may be a retirement party, or a company may have a banquet as a reward to honor its top sales producers.

Business meetings have many purposes. Some are held to introduce a new product. Others are held for the staff as a reward for a job well done. Other meetings serve as a sales meeting for the staff; still others are actually used to sell a product to a potential customer.

Once the banquet manager determines the purpose of the event, the room and meal can be chosen.

Menu Planning

Choosing a meal is important for both the client and the banquet manager. A meal must be chosen that can be served efficiently by the banquet establishment and also meets the needs of the client.

T I P $

TO INSURE PROPER SERVICE

At Marriott's Orlando World Center Resort and Convention Center, when the client has decided on specific food items, he or she is then invited to a tasting of the product. This is called the *Taste Panel*. Initiate your own taste panel at your banquet facility.

For instance, one client wanted his party served quickly. He stated that his guests had been up since 6:00 A.M. and did not want to spend a lot of time over a meal. The banquet house suggested having the appetizer placed on the table before the guests arrived. It is standard practice to present the appetizer. However, the client wanted not only the appetizer but the salad and dessert on the table before the guests arrived. The only item that was served was the main course. At another banquet, the meal was a stacked cold luncheon. At each place setting, three containers were stacked on top of each other. The top container contained the appetizer, the main course was in the middle, and the bottom container had the dessert.

The banquet manager and client have to agree upon a meal that will meet the nutritional needs of the guests, as well as the financial needs of the client.

The meal should look appealing on the plate. A boneless breast of chicken, with a white sauce served on a bed of rice with mashed potatoes looks bland. It has no color, and having two starches (potatoes and rice) is not nutritionally sound.

Menu planning also takes into account whether the client desires a heavy or light meal for the guests. This is determined by the purpose of the event. A lunch followed by a meeting should be light; but a dinner celebration may include hearty meats, wines, and even a decadent chocolate dessert buffet bar.

Other factors that determine the menu selection are the makeup of the guests who will be attending. For instance, at Italian weddings it is customary to serve a pasta course before the main course.

Once the menu has been set, the banquet manager and client can prepare for the event.

Planning the Details of the Event

The main part of the BEO is an open-ended area in which the banquet manager writes exactly what the client desires. All facets of the event must be included in this area: serving times for food and liquor; color of linen; a complete, detailed menu specifying everything that was promised to the client; liquor service; and special instructions. All this information must be included on Part 2 of the BEO. This is where the word *detail* takes on utmost importance for the success of the event.

Detail

Detail is defined in the *Random House Dictionary* as "attention to a subject's individual or minute parts."[1] That is how the banquet manager should approach running every event. The client wants the banquet manager to take care of all the little things that will make the party a success. Again, the premise of this section on banquet management is that the main job of the banquet manager is to *take the responsibility off of the client's shoulders and put it on his or her own shoulders*. Doing this will make the event a success and will result in repeat business for the banquet establishment.

Discussing the Details of the Party

The banquet manager needs to discuss every aspect regarding the event with the client. This is a must for obtaining all the information necessary for running the function. The banquet manager should always listen to what the client desires and then offer proper suggestions based upon the discussion. Once the client makes the decisions about the event, the BEO can be completed.

Because no two functions are alike, the following text will include discussions concerning different options that the client can have at banquets.

Types of Meals

Banquet houses offer three types of meals: the *cocktail reception*, serving drinks and finger foods; small plate food choices, usually eaten without utensils or with only a limited number of utensils, often referred to as *food station service*; the *sit-down, served meal*; and the *buffet meal*.

The cocktail reception is beneficial for the client who wants the guests to mingle with each other. There is usually a variety of food and drinks for the guests, located at set places in the room—called *stations*—or passed by the service staff, which is known as *butler service*.

Many times, a cocktail reception precedes a sit-down dinner. As a general rule, guests should be supplied approximately five hors d'oeuvres per person if the cocktail reception precedes a sit-down meal. If the cocktail reception is the only meal, the amount of food must be doubled. However, one fear almost all clients have is that they will not have enough food to serve all of their guests. Therefore, the banquet manager should find out from the client the makeup of the group of people who will be attending the event. The time of day and the type of event also influence the amount of food that will be consumed. The banquet manager can then suggest the correct amount of food based upon the information provided by the client. For example, younger guests may eat more food than senior citizens.

The sit-down meal is one of the most popular type to be served at a banquet. At this type of banquet, all guests receive the same meal, which is chosen by the host of the party. Many times a client will ask if the banquet establishment can offer the guests a choice of more than one main course. This will depend strictly on the capability of the kitchen and the serving staff.

Because the purpose of a banquet is to serve the meal quickly, limiting the number of choices is a wise idea for the banquet establishment. If the client insists that the guest have a choice of food, offer a choice only for the main course and limit it to two selections. The number of guests ordering each choice has to be given when the guarantee is called in to the establishment. The client will be responsible for identifying which guest gets which entree choice. The easiest way to do this is by having different colored tickets—red for beef, yellow for chicken—for the client to distribute. When two entrees are chosen (which usually becomes three, because of a vegetarian choice), the banquet establishment will charge the price of the most expensive entree for all three entrees. There is generally a minimum number of guests required to have two or more choices.

More banquet establishments are offering menus that have a combination of two items for the main course. These combination plates are designed to eliminate two or more entree choices. Some examples of the combination plate are chicken and shrimp, beef and shrimp, and beef and salmon.

In most cases, it is a bad idea to have the service staff take guest orders on how food—such as steaks—are to be cooked at a banquet. Taking individual orders takes too much time for the service person and too much time for the cook. Imagine serving steak for 200 guests!

If the client wants the guests to have many food choices, then the best meal selection is the buffet. Buffets offer guests an enormous choice of foods and a variety of serving options. The kitchen staff enjoys preparing buffets because they have the opportunity to present foods artistically.

Clients have three service styles of buffets from which to choose. The first is referred to as the *simple buffet* style, where guests serve themselves. Service staff is only needed to clear dirty dishes. The guest obtains all food, drinks, and utensils.

The second, called the *modified deluxe buffet*, has waitstaff set up tables with utensils, clear each course, and serve guests beverages. The guests obtain all additional food.

The third, the *deluxe buffet*, combines excellent service with the opportunity for the guest to have a wide variety of foods. The guests are served their appetizer, salad, beverage, and dessert. They obtain their main course from the buffet.

A banquet manager can tailor a buffet-type service to meet the needs of the client. The three types of buffets just described are only a guideline to the style of services for the buffets. The banquet manager can be creative and mix up the styles of service to create a new style to meet the needs of the client.

Once the client decides on the type of meal service desired for the guests, a menu may be chosen. Most banquet houses have preprinted menu selection choices. Figure 12–7 illustrates the dinner selection and Figure 12–8 illustrates the buffet menu that the host may choose from. Banquet houses usually have separate menus for each meal period, as well as a separate price list that includes the cost of all meals. Using a separate price list, the hotel only has to reprint one sheet of paper, rather than print up an entire set of menus when prices change.

DINNER

All Dinner Entrees will be Accompanied by:

Freshly Baked Rolls and Butter
Appetizer and Salad
served with Chef's Selection of Vegetable and Starch
Chef's Specialty Dessert
Freshly Brewed Coffee, Tea, Decaffeinated Coffee and Milk

BEEF

NEW YORK SIRLOIN STEAK $23.95
Grilled served with Three Peppercorn Demi Glaze
and topped with Crispy Onions

FILET MIGNON $28.95
Served with Wild Mushrooms
Finished with a Red Wine Sauce

BEEF WELLINGTON $24.95
Classically Prepared Tenderloin of Beef with a
Wild Mushroom Duxelle Roasted in Puff Pastry

COMBINATION DINNERS

BEEF AND SHRIMP $29.95
Tournedoes of Beef with Baked Stuffed Shrimp
Finished with a Lemon Beurre Blanc Sauce

BEEF AND SALMON $29.95
Sliced Tenderloin of Beef with Bordelaise Sauce and
Roasted Atlantic Salmon with Roasted Fennel and Dill

CHICKEN AND SHRIMP $25.95
Sauteed Breast of Chicken topped with Jumbo Shrimp
Complimented with a Lemon Garlic Sauce

All Prices Subject to 18% Taxable Service Charge and Applicable State Sales Tax

10/00

ALBANY Marriott.

189 Wolf Road, Albany, NY 12205 • (518) 458-8444

FIGURE 12–7

A preprinted dinner menu for a sit-down dinner banquet. (Courtesy of Albany Marriott)

DINNER BUFFETS
Available for Groups of 50 Guests or More
20-50 Guests add $2.50 per person

THE HUDSON BUFFET $26.50
Chef's Fresh Soup of the Day, Salad Bar,
Two Entrees, One Pasta,
Choice of Three Accompaniments and Three Desserts

THE EMPIRE STATE BUFFET $28.95
Chef's Fresh Soup of the Day, Salad Bar,
Two Entrees, Pasta, One Item from Extras
Choice of Three Accompaniments and Four Desserts

Buffets include Fresh Rolls, Breads and Butter
Coffee, Tea, Decaffeinated Coffee or Milk

ENTREES
Grilled Marinated Breast of Chicken,
Oriental Stir Fry of Beef or Chicken,
Beef Tenderloin Tips with Mushrooms,
Chicken Picatta, Roast Pork Loin Dijon,
Seared Salmon with Dill Sauce, Baked Boston Scrod

PASTAS
Stuffed Shells with Marinara Sauce, Baked Cheese Tortellini with a Pesto Cream Sauce,
Penne a la Vodka, Rigatonni Pomodoro, Pasta Primavera

ACCOMPANIMENTS
Rice Pilaf, Oven Roasted Redskin Potatoes, Baked Potato Bar
Garlic Mashed Potatoes, Green Beans Almondine, Honey Glazed Baby Carrots,
Grilled or Steamed Vegetable Medley and Stir Fry Vegetable Medley

EXTRAS
(One Extra included in The Empire State Buffet)
*Carved Top Round of Beef, *Carved Brisket of Corned Beef,
*Carved Country Smoked Ham, *Carved Roasted Turkey

These Items Require a Chef Attendant at a Fee of $75.00

DESSERTS
Carrot Cake, Chocolate Mousse, Fresh Fruit and Berries,
Mom's Apple Pie, Key Lime Pie,
Cherry Cobbler, Midnight Layer Cake, Cheesecake,
Assorted Mini Pastries, Strawberry Shortcake Bar

All Prices Subject to 18% Taxable Service Charge and Applicable State Sales Tax

10/00

ALBANY **Marriott**®

189 Wolf Road, Albany, NY 12205 • (518) 458-8444

FIGURE 12–8
A preprinted dinner menu for a sit-down dinner buffet. (Courtesy of Albany Marriott)

Alcoholic Beverage Service

Once the client has decided on what type of meal to have, the next item to discuss is what guests will drink.

There are two basic styles of **beverage service** used for functions. Guests can obtain their drinks from an **open bar**, where the client pays for all drinks consumed. The other option is for the client to have the banquet establishment set up a **cash bar**. At the cash bar, the guests have to pay individually for each drink that they consume. Of course, there are some functions where it will not be appropriate or practical to have a bar in the function room; so none is set up. At those functions, guests who desire an alcoholic beverage will purchase one from the bar open to the general public, in another part of the establishment.

Each establishment should explain the alcoholic beverage policies as required by state law on their policy sheet. The policy should clearly state the type of liquor license that the banquet establishment possesses and the rules that guests must obey to consume alcoholic beverages. For example, all alcoholic beverages must be purchased from the banquet establishment, and the establishment will staff all bars with their own bartenders. Another rule that should be clearly stated is that the establishment will refuse to serve alcohol to anyone who, in the establishment's judgment, appears intoxicated.

The policy sheet should also state the type of identification necessary for guests to purchase and consume alcoholic beverages. An example would be a driver's license with photo identification. The host of the party should also be informed that the banquet establishment will refuse to serve any person who is under the legal drinking age or who cannot produce proper identification.

Some establishments will limit the number of alcoholic drinks one guest may obtain at a time. Unfortunately, sometimes a person who is of legal age obtains alcoholic beverages from the bartender and gives them to a minor. When this occurs, the banquet manager must ask the host of the party to talk to the guest and demand that this practice cease. This information should be explained to the host before the banquet occurs. The authors know of banquets where the banquet manager was forced to close the bar because the host refused to stop such a practice.

Alcoholic Service Choices

Open bars have many different options for serving alcoholic beverages. Like the meal service, the banquet manager has to suggest the correct type of alcoholic service based upon the desires of the client.

The banquet manager should be able to estimate how much liquor the guests will consume. This should be based upon previous experience with parties of similar groups. For instance, the average consumption at an event used to be two-and-a-half drinks per person per hour. However, this number goes down significantly after food has been consumed, because the guests are full. Another reason for lower alcohol consumption after a meal is the public's awareness concerning drinking and driving.

Because alcohol laws differ state by state, the banquet manager must check the liquor laws in the state where the banquet establishment is located. The choices of service described next should only be used as a guideline. Each establishment must decide on its own policy of alcoholic beverage service based upon the laws of its state.

T I P $

TO INSURE PROPER SERVICE
Have soda and *mocktails*—nonalcoholic drinks—available for guests at all bars, open or cash.

Alcohol Placed on the Guests' Table

In this type of service, each table is provided with some type of alcoholic beverage. It may be pitchers of beer or bottles of wine. It could be two bottles of liquor with the appropriate mixers, called *setups*. The client is charged for the number of bottles that are placed on the tables. The guests serve themselves.

Open Bar

In this service, guests order a beverage at the bar and are served by a bartender. They may have whatever type of liquor the client has ordered. Generally, one bartender is needed for 50 guests at a cocktail party, and one for 100 guests after the meal has been served.

With this type of service, the client may be charged in a variety of methods. The first is that the client pays for all bottles of liquor that are opened. Another way is that the client is charged for only the amount of liquor that is used. Another method is to use the public bar and charge the client for the number of drinks that have been consumed. The method that most clients prefer is a per person charge. This way they know exactly how much money they will spend for the event. Another method involves providing the guests with tickets that are good for a drink.

À La Carte Drinks

At some events, the client wants the service staff to take individual drink orders and serve them to the guests. This may be done at an additional cost to the client if the banquet manager has to employ more staff to take and serve drink orders. The main job of the banquet staff should be to serve the food for the banquet, not to serve drink orders.

Cash Bars

This arrangement may cost the client nothing. The guests purchase their own drinks. Cash bars bring in less revenue than open bars. Therefore, most banquet houses have a minimum amount of liquor sales that must be attained. If the guests do not meet this minimum, the cost of the bartender has to be paid by the client.

The banquet manager should attempt to convince the client to have an open bar, if at all possible. Of course, the open bar increases the profits of the establishment. But more importantly, an open bar contributes to making the event a success. An open bar does not mean that all guests get drunk; but it does mean that the client is hospitable. Guests attending a wedding reception or any banquet are more likely to be in a positive state of mind when they are provided with drinks than when they have to purchase their own. This goes back to Maslow's theory, the love and belonging stage. The client has invited the guest to the banquet. Guests should be treated as if they were guests at the client's home.

T I P $

TO INSURE PROPER SERVICE
Have more than one kind of glassware to serve drinks. The glassware you select affects the perception of the quality of the drinks you serve.

Once the bar service has been decided, all the other details concerning the event must be determined. The next detail the banquet manager must attend to is determining the guarantee and set.

Guarantee and Set

The guarantee and set pertain to the number of guests that will attend the event. Both numbers are recorded on the BEO. The guarantee and set are filled in on the BEO in Figure 12–9.

PART 2—BANQUET EVENT ORDER

Estimated Number 200 Guarantee 198 Set 198

Food Program

Liquor

FIGURE 12–9
Part 2 of the BEO. This part covers the set and guarantee for the banquet.

Guarantee

The guarantee is the minimum number of guests that the client must pay for, even if fewer guests attend the event. Most banquet establishments request the guaranteed number of guests 72 business hours in advance of the event.

Most often this system works well. However, some establishments have found that clients play a dangerous game by underestimating their guarantee. They have 200 affirmative replies for the event; the client knows that the banquet facility will set up approximately 10 percent additional seats, so he or she only guarantees 180. This way, the client saves money if some guests do not attend. This creates a problem with seating arrangements, because many times all 200 guests show up. To solve this problem, some establishments have allowed the guarantee to go 10 percent in either direction. Therefore, if the host guarantees 200, a minimum of 180 will be charged; but the room is set for 220.

Set

Once the guarantee has been given, the banquet manager decides on how many extra seats to set in the banquet room. Oversetting generally ranges from 5 percent to 10 percent above the guarantee. As party sizes go up, the percentage of extra seats must diminish; otherwise, a banquet manager would be setting up 200 extra seats for banquets at large facilities. Therefore, many establishments state on their policy sheet the maximum number of seats that will be overset.

The reason for oversetting is that more guests may attend the banquet than had been guaranteed. Another, more common reason is that often guests are in groups of two or more and do not want to break up their group. Therefore, the banquet manager sets extra seats because it is easier to set them before the guests arrive. Banquets are staffed economically with service people. If a service person has to stop what he or she is doing and set up extra tables, chairs, and covers, it detracts from the event and almost always forces the staff to play a game of catch-up.

The only time the banquet room is not overset is when the client has seating arrangements. With seating arrangements, every guest is assigned a seat.

Setting Up the Time Schedule

Most clients want their guests to eat promptly and their program to start immediately. The banquet manager must be firm in allowing the service staff enough time to serve and clean up the meal. For American banquet service, it usually takes between one-and-a-half and two hours from the time that the guests are seated until the dessert and extra items are removed. For instance, if the party starts at 7:00 P.M., speeches should be scheduled for 9:00 P.M.

One of the most challenging events to plan for is the wedding reception. There may be a receiving line, pictures, blessing, toast, first dance, cake cutting, bouquet, and garter ceremonies. A wedding reception meal generally takes three hours from the time the guests sit down. Time must be planned for extra alcoholic beverage service if there are cocktails before the meal.

Once the client has decided on all the details of the event, this information must be placed onto the BEO. The information should appear on the BEO exactly as has been discussed with the client. There should be no surprises. Look at the completed BEO in Figure 12–10. This is a completed work order for the wedding that will take place in the Seville Room from 7:00 P.M. to 1:00 A.M.

As you may notice, the banquet manager has specified everything the client desires on this BEO. The reader can see exactly what time the cake is to be cut and what time each course is to be served. This BEO is set up thoroughly, even to the pink fan-folded napkins. Each function should have this type of BEO to keep mistakes to a minimum.

Confirming the Arrangements

Once the BEO is completed, the banquet manager must send a copy to the client. Along with the BEO, a cover letter must be included. Figure 12–11 is a sample cover letter for a wedding reception.

PART 2—BANQUET EVENT ORDER

Room: Seville   **Time: 7 P.M. – 1 A.M.**

Toast
  NV Moet Chandon   7:00 P.M.
Food
  1/2 Pineapple filled with fresh fruit in season
    (preset on table)
  Tossed Garden Fresh Salad, Italian Dressing   7:25 P.M.
  Prime Ribs of Beef, au jus   7:40 P.M.
  Baked Stuffed Potatoes
  Fresh Green Beans with Fresh Onions
  1961 Chateau Lafite Rothschild served with the meal
  Homemade Rolls and Butter served as soon as the guests
    are seated
  Coffee, Tea, and Decaffeinated Coffee served immediately
    after the Prime Rib has been served
  Wedding Cake served with SuperFudge Ice Cream   8:45 P.M.

Liquor Service
  Open Bar from 8 P.M. to 1 A.M.
  Three bars, four bartenders. Bars will open at 8 P.M.
  Seagrams VO; Dewars White Label; Smirnoff Vodka; Peach
    Schnapps; Molson Golden; 1961 Chateau Yquem available for
    after dinner wine.
  Fetzer Chardonnay & Chenin Blanc
  Iron Horse Cabernet Sauvignon (at least 10 years of age)

Program
  White tablecloths with pink napkins, fan-folded
  Head table skirted, with candelabras and fern
  Seating arrangements
  Cocktails from 5:45 P.M. to 6:45 P.M. at Pool (see attached BEO)
  7:00 P.M.—Announcement of Bride & Groom
  7:05 P.M.—Blessing by Father Fitzpatrick
  7:06 P.M.—Toast by Best Man
  7:10 P.M.—First Dance
  8:40 P.M.—Wedding Cake Ceremony
  Midnight—Bouquet & Garter

Band—Rhythm & Rain 555-3245 (obtained by the bride)
Cake—Chocolate with white frosting (we supply)

FIGURE 12–10

The completed Part 2 of the BEO. This provides everyone with complete information of what will be occurring at the wedding.

Scheduling Parties

Many banquet operations have more than one banquet room. Therefore, they may have more than one party occurring during a meal period. The banquet manager should not schedule two events to

SAMPLE COVER LETTER

Dear Mr. & Mrs. Lockwood,

We are pleased to enclose the banquet event order for Jill's wedding to be held in the Seville Room on Saturday, August 3, of this year.

Please examine the order carefully. If you are satisfied with the arrangements specified, please sign at the bottom, date it, and return it in the enclosed self-addressed stamped envelope. If you desire to change any item, please call me at 555-6211.

Our staff is proud of the job we do for our wedding receptions. We are excited to be able to share in your family's special day. A few weeks before the wedding, I will call you to set up a meeting with Chef Brown, Head Waiter Larkin, and Bar Manager Verrigni to review all the details of the wedding.

August 3 will be an exciting day for Jill. I am looking forward to sharing in the happiness of the day!

Sincerely yours,

Mr. Toby
Banquet Manager

FIGURE 12–11

A sample cover letter sent to the client with the BEO.

take place at the same time. Instead, try to stagger the times at 15-minute intervals.

It would be great for the banquet manager to sell the clients the same meal items. If it is impossible to sell them the same main course, at least give them the same accompaniments. This is another way to improve relations with the kitchen, and also it will make the parties run smoothly. American banquet style service is used for speed and profitability.

Distribution of the BEO

The banquet establishment should set up a policy regarding when to distribute the BEO to the department heads. This should be determined based on the amount of time needed to order the food and schedule the staff. Many establishments find that two weeks in advance of a party is a good time for each department to receive its own copy of the BEO.

Meeting with the Staff

In order for functions to run smoothly, there should be weekly staff meetings for the purpose of discussing events. Specifics about upcoming functions can be covered. The banquet manager will be able to explain any special requests that clients want for their event. Discussions can also take place on any problems that occurred at previous functions.

Many establishments use this meeting to have a dress rehearsal of the meal for the upcoming event. At this dress rehearsal, the kitchen prepares the meal for the staff meeting in order to work out any problems. After the food is prepared and eaten, the staff discusses any potential problems that may occur with the meal.

These weekly meetings alleviate problems and misunderstandings between the members of the staff.

T I P $

To Insure Proper Service

The day before a function, representatives from all service areas involved must attend a production meeting. All details about the event should be discussed.

Working with the Kitchen

The banquet manager must learn how to work effectively with the kitchen staff, and especially the chef. The secret is to treat them with respect and make them your allies.

To make the chef your ally, always ask him if it is possible to comply with a client's special request about a meal item before you promise it to the client. Include the chef in the planning for special menus for parties, and solicit the chef's input in planning events. Most importantly, introduce the chef to the client of the party.

The kitchen staff should always be told when the food is excellent, as well as when there is a problem. One of the most effective methods of encouraging the cooks to prepare excellent food is to bring the host of the party into the kitchen immediately after the meal. The cooks will look forward to this positive feedback. As a result, meals will always be prepared superbly.

Communication and respect will make it easy to work with the kitchen. If the banquet manager does not have an excellent working relationship with the kitchen, major problems will occur at functions.

Checking Details

The banquet manager should check with the client three or four days before the event. At this time, the guarantee must be obtained from the client. This is also a time when the banquet manager must verbally recheck every item, step-by-step, to make sure there will be no misunderstanding. The banquet manager must do this even though the client has signed the BEO; the client may not have read it well, if all.

If the client gives the banquet manager any changes, these must be communicated on all the BEOs. Whenever any written changes are made on the BEO, they must be initialed by the person who made the change, and the department head must be told verbally of the change.

TIP$

TO INSURE PROPER SERVICE
Contact the client three weeks in advance of the event to make sure plans are on track. This may help to avoid last minute surprises.

Seating Arrangements

The banquet manager is often asked to help plan seating arrangements for the party. The following is a step-by-step procedure for planning seating arrangements:

1. The guest estimate is received from the client. The client is given a tentative floor plan. The circled number is the number of guests to be seated at the table; the other number is the table number (see Figure 12–12).
2. As the client receives positive responses, guests are placed in groups the size of which correspond to the circled numbers.
3. The client assigns groups to tables.
4. After all guests have been assigned a table number, the client makes an alphabetized listing of the guests' names and table numbers.
5. The client makes out cards that read "Mr. Krishnappa, you are seated at table 7." The client does all the planning and writing of the names.
6. The client brings the alphabetized cards and list to the banquet establishment on the day of the party.
7. On the day of the party, the staff put table numbers on each table that correspond to the floor plan that the banquet manager has given the client.

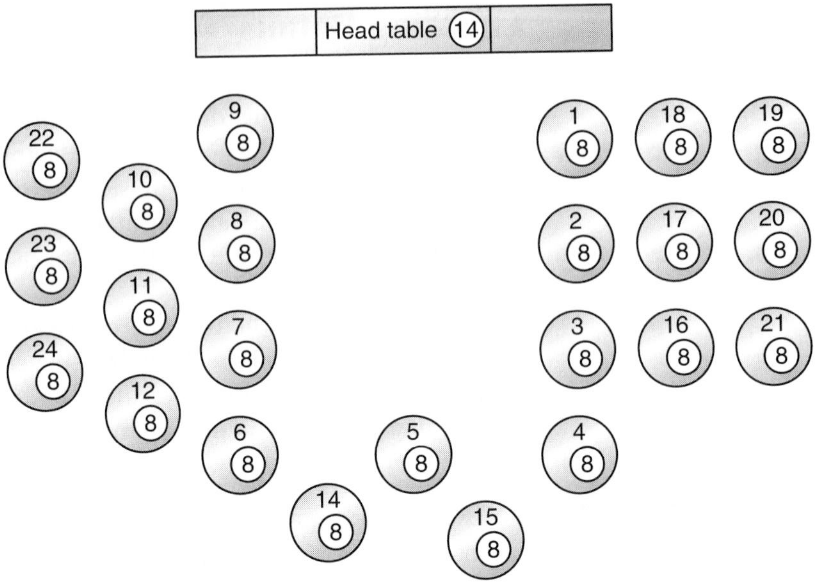

FIGURE 12–12

A tentative floor plan given to the client by the banquet manager to set up seating arrangements for a party. The number in the circle represents the number of guests that can be accommodated at that table. The other number is the table number.

8. On a table at the entrance to the banquet room, the cards are placed in alphabetical order. The guests find their names, read the cards, and proceed to the tables with the numbers that correspond to their cards.

9. The banquet manager should have the alphabetized list as a double check in case there is a problem with the cards.

TIPS

TO INSURE PROPER SERVICE

To set a positive tone for guests, start seating arrangements for events with table 10 instead of table 1. Always avoid using table 13 because of guests' superstitions.

The banquet manager now has all the information for the event on the BEO.

Weekly and Daily BEO

In order to let all the staff in the establishment know what events are happening, the banquet office uses two forms. One of these forms is a *weekly BEO*—distributed on the same day every week—which is given

DAILY BEO

Saturday, July 12

KILROY MANNERS SKILLS WORKSHOP
POD/Joan Starker/KS/525

7 A.M.	Regent Room	*ACCESS*, 3 6' registration tables, 3 chairs, 2 waste-paper baskets, water/glasses, have 10–13 of their boxes under this table by 7 A.M.
7 A.M.	5, 7, 9 Madison Room	*ACCESS*, Classroom f/300

No ashtrays/no smoking signs
8 × 12 stage 10' away from wall
6' table on left side of stage
4' table on right side of stage
Steps center of stage
Barstool center stage
Water station in back of room in addition to water on each table
Light colored linen (if available)
Flipchart w/ markers (at registration table)
8 × 8 screen (on stage)
Lavalier mic w/45 ft. cord

8:30 A.M.	Regent Room	Registration begins
8:30 A.M.–5 P.M.	5, 7, 9 Madison Room	Meeting

BILOXI/KING RECEPTION
POD/Kevin Biloxi/KS/

12 Noon–1 P.M.	Lancaster Gallery	Open bar f/75 Hors d'oeuvres
1–5 P.M.	24, 25 High Cafe	Dinner: set 75, GTD 71 (*SEE DIAGRAM*)

Headtable f/10 on risers
Predesignated seating
Placecard Table
Gift Table
Cake Table

JOHNSON/PEABODY RECEPTION
POD/Julea Johnson/KS/

1:30–2:30 P.M.	Lancaster Gallery	Open bar f/58 Hors d'oeuvres
2:30–6 P.M.	6, 8 Lancaster	Dinner: set 58, GTD 55 (*SEE DIAGRAM*)

Headtable f/6 on risers
Predesignated seating
Placecard Table
Gift Table
Cake Table
No ashtrays, even on request, send people into courtyard

FIGURE 12–13

A daily BEO. Each day, a sheet is distributed to all departments informing them of events taking place in the establishment.

to all departments. In addition, an updated *daily BEO* should be distributed. See Figure 12–13 for an example of a daily BEO.

Both of these sheets should have all the events taking place in the establishment, not just the food functions. This allows all staff to be in the information loop.

The daily BEO is simply an update of the weekly BEO. The guarantee, meaning the number of guests expected, is on the sheet.

Once all this information has been gathered, the banquet manager can proceed to run the party.

SUMMARY

1. A Banquet Event Order (BEO) is a detailed list of everything that will occur at the banquet from start to finish. It specifies every item that is requested for the function.
2. The banquet manager should realize that it is imperative to obtain accurate information concerning all details about an event. The banquet manager must really listen to understand exactly what the client requests. This information is specified on the BEO.
3. For most events, clients need guidance from the banquet manager to have a successful event. The banquet manager must use tact and diplomacy in making suggestions to convince the client that the suggestions will be beneficial for the success of the event.
4. To have a successful event, all information on a BEO must be complete. Nothing should be left for interpretation by any member of the staff.
5. For a meal function, clients have the option of a cocktail reception; a sit-down, served meal; or a buffet meal.
6. *Detail* in the banquet business can be described as attention to all the individual parts of the function.
7. The client at a banquet needs the banquet manager to tend to all of the details to make the event a success. The goal of the banquet manager should be to take the responsibility of that banquet off of the client's shoulders and put it on his or her own.
8. When guests are offered different meal choices at a banquet, the banquet establishment should provide the guests some form of identification to determine what guest is served what meal (e.g., a yellow card for chicken, a red card for beef). The banquet establishment should be set up to serve both meals at the same time. Waitstaff determine how many of each entree go to each table, and serve guests their different entrees.

9. The banquet manager and the chef must communicate continuously before and during the banquet to insure the success of the function. Technology has made it possible to communicate instantaneously.

10. The key to a successful banquet begins with the 5 *Ps* of planning—*Perfect Planning Prevents Poor Performance*. The banquet manager will have a successful event when the entire banquet—from preprepa-ration to cleanup—is planned, staffed, and organized effectively.

11. There are two general choices a client may make with regard to serv-ing alcoholic beverages at a banquet. In one, called a *cash bar*, guests have to pay for their own drinks. In the other, called an *open bar*, the host pays for all of the alcoholic beverages consumed. There are different variations of both cash and open bars.

12. Seating arrangements can be set up for any party. The banquet man-ager has to know how many guests are going to attend the banquet and how many guests can be seated at each table. From this infor-mation, a numbered table diagram of the banquet room will be developed. The host of the party determines where each guest will be seated. The host provides the banquet manager an alphabetized list of the guests with their table location.

REVIEW QUESTIONS

1. What is a BEO, and what is its purpose?
2. What important information should the banquet manager obtain from the host of the party? Why is that information important?
3. What does the term *detail* mean as it pertains to the banquet busi-ness? Why is it an important term?
4. How would a banquet manager serve more than one main course entree to the guests at a banquet? Explain the steps that a banquet manager would have to take to achieve this goal.
5. What is the difference between a cash bar and an open bar?
6. Explain the different options of open bars that a host can choose for the guests at a banquet.
7. Explain how seating arrangements are set up. Give a step-by-step explanation.

DISCUSSION QUESTIONS

1. Three days before a function, you contact the client for the guarantee. When checking the details of the event, you discover that the host has told the guests that they are going to receive sirloin steak for

their main course. The signed BEO clearly states that the meal will be top sirloin of beef. Because this is a retirement party of 150, and the guests have purchased their own tickets, you know a problem will develop. What would you do? Take into consideration the potential for repeat business in your answer.

2. Should Part 3 of the BEO be distributed to all employees? Or do you believe that Part 3 would be better left off the BEO? Explain your answer.

3. What problems would occur by having the service staff take individual orders for guests at a banquet? For instance, the staff is told to ask the guest how they want their filet mignons cooked: rare, medium, or well.

4. Refer to the section on *guarantee* in this chapter. Would you consider a guarantee of 10 percent in either direction as the book states? Explain your answer.

REFERENCE

1. *Random House Dictionary*. (New York: Ballantine Books, 1978), p. 248.

13

Managing the Function

OBJECTIVES At the completion of this chapter, the student should be able to:

1. Diagram the setup of a place setting from information provided on the Banquet Event Order (BEO).
2. Plan all equipment needed for the banquet service based upon information contained on the BEO.
3. List the four styles of service for serving a sit-down banquet.
4. Illustrate the quickest way to serve food from the kitchen to the banquet room.
5. Explain the methods for staffing and ending bar service correctly at a banquet.
6. Describe the proper sequence for setting up and serving a banquet room.
7. Explain the methods for controlling the amount of canapés and hors d'oeuvres at a party.
8. Illustrate the proper method for setting up a buffet and controlling traffic flow.
9. Describe how to clean up a meeting room and how to provide the guests with water, paper, and pencils.

KEY WORDS

back of the house
Banquet Event Order
(BEO)

butler style
combination method
condiments

follow-up method
station method
sweep method

Preparing for the Function

As was stated in the preceding chapter, three days before the event is to be held, the banquet manager obtains the guaranteed number of guests from the host. Now the banquet manager's most critical part of the job begins.

The banquet manager must plan and organize the minute details of the function to make it a success. *The banquet manager takes the responsibility for the event off of the client's shoulders and puts it on his or her own shoulders.* Great service will be made up of many moments of truth that the banquet manager must control. If the banquet manager successfully attends to the details of planning, organizing, and managing the function, the event will be successful.

The BEO from the Lockwood wedding, Figure 13–1, will help illustrate the type of details that the banquet manager's job encompasses.

Banquet Event Order

The banquet manager must use the information on the **Banquet Event Order (BEO)** to organize, plan, and manage the event. The BEO has been distributed to the department heads. Using this, the department heads have scheduled employees and obtained the food and beverages needed for the event. The banquet manager will make any last minute changes on the BEO and forward them to all the department heads, highlighting the changes. These were obtained when the guarantee was obtained from the client.

Staffing the Wedding

The first job the banquet manager has to perform after the guarantee is received is to make certain there are the proper number of employees to serve the party. The banquet manager should be concerned with not only the service staff needed but also the bar and kitchen staff. The banquet manager is the one ultimately responsible for the service of the banquet. Having too few bartenders or kitchen staff results in slow service for the guests. Once again a reminder: American banquet service must be fast.

BANQUET EVENT ORDER

Event Date Saturday, August 3 Payment Arrangement Cash

Organization Lockwood-Jones Wedding Business Phone 555-0978

Address 7 Lark Avenue Home Phone 555-0878

Cranston, RI 02972

Person in Charge Jim Lockwood

Estimated Number 200 Guarantee 198 Set 198

Room Seville Time 7 P.M.–1 A.M.

Toast
NV Moet Chandon 7:00 P.M.

Food
1/2 Pineapple filled with Fresh Fruit in season Preset on Table
Tossed Garden Fresh Salad, Italian Dressing 7:25 P.M.
Prime Ribs of Beef, Au Jus 7:40 P.M.
Baked Stuffed Potatoes
Fresh Green Beans with Fresh Onions
1961 Chateau Lafite Rothschild served with the meal
Homemade Rolls and Butter served as soon as the
guests are seated
Coffee, Tea, and Decaffeinated Coffee served
immediately after the Prime Rib has been served
Wedding Cake served with SuperFudge Ice Cream 8:45 P.M.

Liquor Service
Open Bar from 8:00 P.M. to 1:00 A.M.
Three bars, four bartenders Bars will open at: 8:00 P.M.
Fetzer Chardonnay & Chenin Blanc
Iron Horse Cabernet Sauvigon (at least 10 years old)

Program
White tablecloths with pink napkins fan-folded
Head table skirted, candelabras and fern
Seating arrangements
Cocktails from 5:45 P.M. to 6:45 P.M. at Pool
7:00 P.M.–Introduction of Wedding Party
7:05 P.M.–Blessing by Father Fitzpatrick
7:06 P.M.–Toast by Best Man
7:15 P.M.–First Dance after first course has been eaten
8:40 P.M.–Wedding Cake Ceremony
Midnight–Bouquet & Garter
Band–Misty Rain 555-3425 (obtained by the bride)
Cake–Chocolate with white frosting (from L & G Goodies, we obtain)
Food Price $50.00 + 20% grat and Sales tax Booked by AJS

Guest Signature & Date

FIGURE 13–1

The BEO for the Lockwood-Jones wedding reception. The banquet manager uses the information on the BEO to make the wedding a success.

Service Staff Needed

The staff scheduled by banquet establishments varies depending upon the number of guests at a table, the competency of the staff, and whether the staff is covered by union representation (in the case of union representation, the staff required is clearly stated in the contract). Figure 13–2 can be used as a guideline for staffing service personnel and bartenders. Generally, one service person can serve between 16 and 24 guests efficiently. Using this figure, one service person should be scheduled to serve two or three tables, depending on how many guests are seated at each table. For a food station, buffet, or cocktail party with butler service, one service person is needed for 35 guests. At a cocktail party without butler service, one server is needed for every 50 guests.

At the Lockwood wedding, 10 service personnel should be scheduled. Each person will serve approximately 20 guests. Because the cocktail party is before the main meal, some of the same staff can be used to pass the food butler-style during the cocktail reception.

Bar Staff Needed

At a cocktail reception—either before dinner or by itself—one bartender is normally needed for every 50 guests; after dinner, one bartender is needed for every 100 guests. This applies to both cash and open bars.

Often extra bartenders are needed only for the cocktail reception. Since they are only needed for a short time, it becomes expensive to employ them for the entire night or for the minimum required by some state laws. One way to alleviate this problem is to have service people act as bartenders. Another method is to schedule bartenders from a previous party to work one or two hours overtime. For instance, if a bartender is scheduled to work from 10:00 A.M. to 6:00 P.M., have the bartender stay for two hours of overtime. From 6:00 P.M. to 8:00 P.M., the bartender can set up the bar and serve the guests at the cocktail party. When the cocktail party is finished, the bartender is done working.

Sweet or Sour?

As guests arrived at a wedding reception, a service person was greeting them with a tray of champagne. To the left, on the bar, were glasses of merlot red wine, chardonnay white wine, and more champagne. Behind the bar a server was pouring extra wine so that no guests had to wait for their wine as they walked into the reception. This was an impressive sight and a fantastic way to begin the reception.

STAFFING TABLE		
Position	**Meal**	**One Employee Can Usually Serve**
Service person	Lunch or Dinner	16–24 guests
Service person	Breakfast	24 guests
Service person	Buffet or Food Station	35 guests
Service person	Butler Service	35 guests
Service person	Cocktail Reception	50 guests
Bartender	Cocktail Reception	50 guests
Bartender	Bar after Meal	100 guests

FIGURE 13–2

A staffing table for banquets using American banquet service.

At the Lockwood wedding there is a special request to have four bartenders throughout the evening. Because most guests remain at their table when the meal is being served, three bartenders are employed opening and serving wine during the meal. The other one will get the bar prepared for service after dinner.

TIP$

To Insure Proper Service

"The customer and food are what we're here for. They're the most important part of any restaurant," says Anthony Bommarito, owner of Anthony's in St. Louis. "The service staff should be there when you need them and remain in the background when you don't."[1]

Kitchen Staff

The staffing of the kitchen is something most banquet managers do not give proper consideration. At a banquet it is extremely important to serve the food as quickly as possible from the kitchen to the guests. To do this, the kitchen must be organized. If this has been delegated to a proven knowledgeable chef, your worries are over. If you have not worked with each other, you ought to work together to get the food plated efficiently and quickly.

There are many methods for serving that work well. All methods require teamwork to serve the meal quickly. Only one skilled culinary person is needed at each serving line. The other employees put the food on the plate and have to be able to work quickly. All systems work fastest when the meat has been sauced before being placed on the plate.

One method, which was used at The DeWitt Clinton Hotel, is shown in Figure 13–3. This requires four people at each station to serve the food. Each person has a specific item to put on the plate.

SERVING FOOD FROM THE KITCHEN AT A BANQUET

FIGURE 13–3

The DeWitt Clinton method of serving a banquet. This requires four people at each station to serve the food. Each person has a specific item to put on the plate. There are two piles of plates. Employee 2, the skilled employee, serves the main course; employees 3 and 4 serve the potato and vegetable.

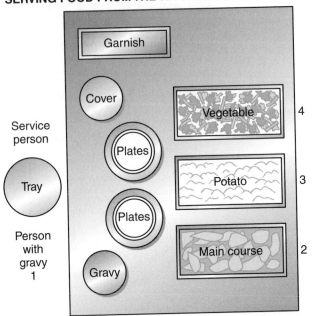

There are two piles of plates. Employee 2, the skilled employee, puts on the main course; employees 3 and 4 put on the potato and vegetable. Very quickly, they develop a rhythm to avoid crashes. The plate never moves until employee 1 removes it and puts the sauce on the meat, if needed. The service person garnishes the plate, covers it, and takes it out of the kitchen.

Another method, just as effective, is shown in Figure 13–4. This method, used at the Hall of Springs in Saratoga, New York, is similar to the DeWitt Clinton method. Three piles of plates are set up on a rectangular table. Employee 1 puts the main course item on plates from any one of the three piles. Employees 2 and 3 put on the potato and vegetable. Both employees—2 with the left hand, 3 with the right hand—pull the plates from the pile when the dish is complete. They place them on the table, and a service person garnishes the plates, covers them, and brings them out into the dining room.

Large banquet establishments have conveyor belts that move the plates in an assembly-line fashion. Only two people handle the plates. The first person puts the plate on the conveyor belt. The second person is at the end of the line and takes the completed plate off the belt and puts it onto the waitperson's tray. As the plates are being moved down the conveyor belt, the culinary staff places the food on the plates.

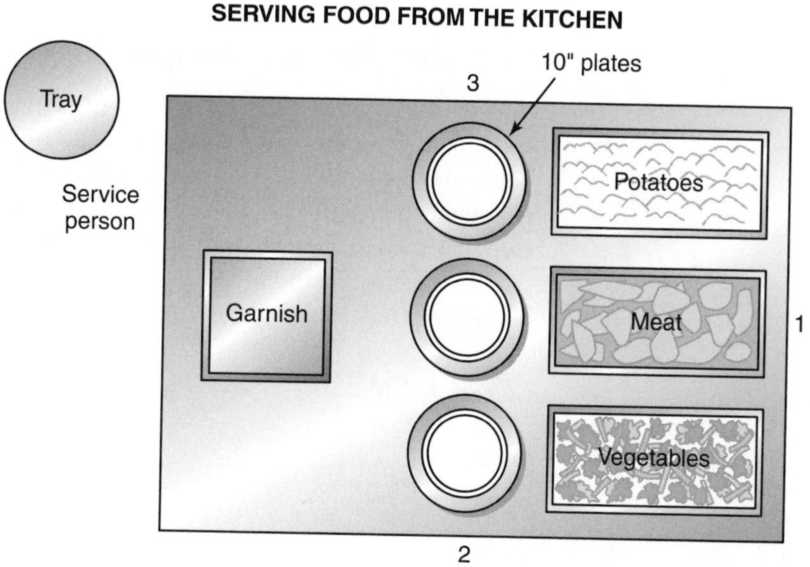

FIGURE 13–4

The Hall of Springs method of serving a banquet. Three piles of plates are set up on a rectangular table. Employee 1 serves the main course item on any one of the three piles of plates. Employees 2 and 3 serve the potato and vegetable. Both employees—2 with the left hand, 3 with the right hand—pull plates from the pile when the dish is complete. They place them on the table and a service person garnishes the plates, covers them, and brings them out into the dining room.

SERVING FOOD FROM THE KITCHEN

Other banquet establishments use some type of "hot boxes" that either plug in or are heated with sterno. Some newer methods will in effect reheat the food, which allows food to be plated up during the nonpeak meal periods. These methods work on the same principle: The culinary staff will plate up meals in advance of the serving time and hold them in the hot boxes. They are then transported to the area where the banquet is to be served. The plates are removed from the hot boxes and finished off with a sauce and garnish.

For the Lockwood wedding, there must be two serving stations for the 198 guests. A few days before the wedding, the banquet manager confers with the chef to develop a plan to serve the function. This plan has the names of the employees who will be serving the food; for example, Anne puts on the potatoes, Julio the prime ribs, and so on. In a nonunion establishment, the extra bartenders, service people, or even dishwashers may help with the planning of the meal.

All systems described here are workable. The key is to plate the food quickly. Plates should be handled by a minimum number of culinary staff. Too many people handling the plates will slow up the service. Using any system, an industry guideline is to serve one course to 100 guests in a maximum of 10 minutes. The time should always be the same regardless of the size of the party, since the number of serving stations are increased proportionately.

With staffing planned, the banquet manager can finalize the equipment that is needed for the event.

Planning for the Equipment

Information required for the planning of equipment that is needed for the function is obtained directly from the BEO. The banquet manager determines exactly what plates and utensils are needed to consume the meal. Using the Lockwood wedding BEO, the banquet manager can plan the equipment that will be needed.

It is best to list the menu item along with the equipment that will be needed to consume it.

ITEM	EQUIPMENT NEEDED
Toast	
NV Moet Chardon	Champagne Glass
Food	
1/2 Pineapple filled with Fresh fruit in season (preset on table)	Spoon, 7" Plate
Tossed Garden Fresh Salad, Italian Dressing	Fork, Salad Plate
Prime Ribs of Beef, au jus	Fork, Steak Knife, Dinner Plate
Baked Stuffed Potatoes	Served on Dinner Plate
Fresh Green Beans with Fresh Onions	Served on Dinner Plate
1961 Chateau Lafite Rothschild, served with the meal	Red Wine Glass
Homemade Rolls and Butter, served as soon as the guests are served	Butter Knife, Bread-and-Butter Plate
Coffee, Tea, and Decaffeinated Coffee, served immediately after the Prime Rib has been served	Coffee Cup, Saucer, Coffee Spoon
Wedding Cake, served with SuperFudge Ice Cream	Spoon, Fork, 7" Plate

From this information, the banquet manager can now plan how much equipment is needed by multiplying the amount of each item

BANQUET CHECKLIST FORM

Tables

_____ 6-Foot

_____ 8-Foot

_____ 72" Round

_____ 60" Round

_____ 8-Foot by 1½ feet

Linen

_____ 72 × 72

_____ Napkins

_____ 81 × 81

_____ 120 × 48

_____ 84 × 48

Flatware

_____ Teaspoons

_____ Soup spoons

_____ Cocktail Forks

_____ Dinner Forks

_____ Bread-and-Butter
           Knives

_____ Dinner Forks

_____ Steak Knives

_____ Ice Tea Spoons

Plates

_____ Bread and Butter

_____ Dinner

_____ Saucers

_____ Soup Cups

_____ Monkey Dish

_____ Coffee Cups

_____ Roll Basket

_____ Bread Board

_____ Ashtrays

_____ Sets of Salt and
           Pepper

_____ Sugar

_____ Cream Pitchers

_____ Salad Bowls

_____ Parfait

_____ Water

_____ Punch

_____ Water Pitchers

_____ Coffee Pots

_____ Tea Pots

_____ Ice Tea Glasses

_____ Table Number

_____ Candles

_____ Bud Vases

FIGURE 13–5

A banquet checklist helps the banquet manager organize the needed supplies.

by the set number (198) on the BEO. For instance, 198 coffee cups and saucers are needed; and each guest requires 3 forks, for a total of 594.

It is helpful to have a document such as the banquet checklist shown in Figure 13–5.

Using the banquet checklist, complete the planning of equipment for the Lockwood wedding.

T I P $

To Insure Proper Service

Rather than have everyone try to figure out how much equipment is needed, it is better to have one person make a list and obtain all the equipment for the party before the waitstaff comes in to set up the banquet.

Planning for Extra Equipment

In addition to figuring out how much equipment is needed for the guests, there are other items the banquet manager must make sure are available. These include salt and pepper shakers, butter dishes, sugars, roll baskets, and cream containers. Figure 13–6 is a guideline for equipment that should be placed on the guest tables.

Having the correct amount of this equipment adds to the success of the event. The next time you attend a banquet, notice how many sets of salt and pepper shakers are on the tables. Most banquet houses

FIGURE 13–6

A guideline for equipment to be placed on guests' tables.

EQUIPMENT NEEDED FOR TABLE SERVICE		
Item	**Head**	**Round or Oblong**
Whipped Butter	1 for 2	1 for 4 people
Butter Pats	2 pats on each Bread-and-Butter Plate	
Salt and Pepper Sets	1 set for every 2 people	
Sugar, Ashtrays	1 for 2	1 for 4
Cream	1 for 2	1 for 4
Amount of Cream	3 oz.	5 oz.
Roll Basket	1 for 3	1 for 4

Figure 1½ rolls per person. Rolls go on table with salad course.
All sugar, cream, and butter are placed on underliners.

LINEN	
Size	**For What Table?**
45 × 45	Deuces
54 × 54	4-tops
72 × 72	60-inch Rounds, Head, and Buffet
54 × 90	6-Foot by 3-Foot
54 × 108	8-Foot by 3-Foot

NOTE: Place a napkin in the center of the table, to place sugar, cream, etc., on. Only do this if the napkin is a different color from the tablecloth.

provide one for a table of eight guests, but it makes more sense to have a set for every two people. When the main course is served, the guests do not have to wait for the salt and pepper to be used by the other seven people at the table. While they are waiting to use the shakers, their food gets cold. Remember, it is the job of the banquet house to make sure guests have a pleasurable experience. Catering to that experience is having everything run so well that the guests never have to ask for any item. The guests should leave feeling great about the event, but without noticing how the banquet establishment accomplished it.

The same provisions should be made for the other items. All the items should be placed within easy reach of the guests. Try it yourself. Sit at a table like the one your guests and try to reach the items. This little experiment will give you a good idea of what your guests have to go through to obtain them.

There should be one sugar and creamer for every four people. The rolls should be served hot, in a bread basket. The banquet manager should plan on having one and a half rolls for each guest.

In addition, the banquet manager has to order extra napkins for use as sidetowels and for use in the center of the banquet table. These napkins are usually a contrasting color from the tablecloth, but the same color as the guest napkins. On the napkin will be placed the ashtrays (if needed), rolls, salt and pepper shakers, and other items that the guest needs to enjoy the meal. Extra bread-and-butter plates to be used as coffee shields must also be ordered.

Once all this equipment has been calculated, the banquet checklist can be completed. The equipment can be obtained by a dishwasher or banquet steward before service staff arrive. Everything should be ready for the service staff to set up the tables when they arrive. Obviously, if some equipment is not available, the banquet manager will know beforehand and can make adjustments.

Many times it becomes impractical to have all the plates and utensils that are needed to serve the party. The banquet establishment simply may not have a sufficient inventory to have three forks for each guest. If a caterer is renting the equipment, the cost may be prohibitive to rent an additional 200 forks.

The banquet manager has a couple of choices. First, the guest can use the same fork for the salad and main course. The service staff are instructed to leave the fork at the place setting when picking up the salad course. This is not proper service, but it is done.

The best method is to determine what items can be washed and used for another course. For example, at the Lockwood wedding, the plate that is used for the pineapple can be washed, dried, and used for the cake course. The guests would have no idea that they are eating off the same plates that contained the pineapple.

Organizing the Jobs for the Service Staff

When the service staff report to work, there should be a detailed work schedule for them. The banquet manager makes a job duty roster, which should be posted in the same location for each banquet. The service staff are usually scheduled to report to work two hours in advance of the function or at a time determined by the banquet manager. Once the banquet manager masters this system, the amount of time needed to set up the function room is reduced. This is valuable if the establishment is paying the service staff by the hour. For instance, if a service person gets paid $15 per hour, eliminating one hour's work for 10 staff members is a savings of $150. Over the course of a year, it would be a great savings.

When the service staff arrive for work, the roster will be posted on the wall. Figure 13–7 is the job duty roster for the Lockwood wedding. Notice that there are three columns: The first is the time by which the job must be completed; the second is who is responsible for doing the job; and the third is the specific job to be done. This duty roster should be completed for all banquets.

By having this roster, the banquet manager has an organized plan of attack. If the banquet manager has to leave the room, the staff know exactly what they need to do to set up. Notice also that the banquet room is set up on a team system, using an assembly-line method.

The first item on the duty roster is a meeting. Any special instructions about the event can be explained at this time. For instance, Naieem and Sam will be told that their primary responsibility before the main meal is to take care of the food at the cocktail party.

By using a duty roster, the banquet manager can easily make changes and correct the situation if there is a problem.

The First Job of the Day

When the banquet manager arrives at the establishment, the banquet room is the first thing checked to see that it has been physically set up. If it has not been, then it must be done. Yes, the banquet manager may have to move tables and chairs into their proper place.

Once it has been determined that the room has been set up properly, the banquet doors that the guests enter through are locked. This prevents guests from entering the room before it is set up.

		LOCKWOOD DUTY ROSTER
Time Completed By	**Staff**	**Job**
7:00 P.M.	All	Room completely set up
	All	Champagne poured (head table poured last)
6:50	All	Assignments given out
6:40	Mona, Jane Beth, Sue	Water poured at tables
	Jim, John Tom, Gerri	Pineapple preset at tables
6:20	Mona, Jane Beth, Sue Tom, Gerri	Head Table skirted
	Jim, John	30 Butters on tables, 30 Creamers in walk-in
6:00	Mona, Jane	Water glasses
	Beth, Sue	Wine glasses
	Tom, Gerri	Champagne glasses
	Jim, John	Salt & Peppers, Sugars on each table
	Naieem, Sam	Cocktail Party room set up
5:45	Mona, Jane	Coffee cups & Saucers
	Beth, Sue	Bread-and-Butter Plates
	Tom	Dessert Fork
	Gerri	Dessert Spoon
	Jim & John	Bread-and-Butter Knives (follow Beth and Sue)
5:30	Naieem, Sam	Chafing Dishes set up
	Mona, Jane	Knives
	Beth, Sue	Forks
	Tom, Gerri	Spoons
	Jim, John	Table Numbers & Napkins for center of table
	Jim, John	Tablecloths on tables
5:15	All staff	Meeting concerning function
5:00	All staff report	

FIGURE 13–7

A job duty roster for the Lockwood wedding. This form makes it easy for the staff and the banquet manager to have a successful banquet.

TO INSURE PROPER SERVICE

According to Elsie Panza, whose family has operated banquet establishments on both the East and West Coasts of the United States, there is one piece of equipment a banquet manager should always have at hand to assist in the smooth operation of wedding receptions: a roll of cellophane tape. Elsie uses it all the time to tape loose envelopes onto gifts so that the bride and groom know who gave them what gift. It is a small detail, but that is the key to the banquet business. No bride or groom ever has to wonder, "Who did this gift come from?"

Planning the Place Setting and Cover

The banquet manager also plans the place setting and cover for the banquet. This information is also obtained from the notes the banquet manager made for the equipment needed. Figure 13–8 is the place setting for the Lockwood wedding. One setting is set on one table in the banquet room before the staff arrive. It is called the *sample setting*.

For the Lockwood wedding, the banquet manager has decided to use a variation of the Russian banquet setting. The dessert spoon and fork are placed above the starter plate. The coffee cup is already in place. All this is done to save time. If this were Russian banquet service, the coffee cup would be brought when the coffee was served. It would not be preset. In American banquet service, however, the coffee cup is preset. The napkin will be folded in the shape of a candle and placed in the red wine glass.

Setting up a sample place setting eliminates any questions the service staff may have.

Direction of Setting Up the Room

The proper way to set up a banquet room is to set the tables farthest from the kitchen first and work back toward the kitchen. If, for some reason, the tables are not completely set up when the guests arrive, the service staff do not have to carry items through the guests to the tables in the farthest part of the room, but can continue to work their way back toward the kitchen.

Serving the Party

Once the banquet manager has the event organized and the service staff are aware of their pre-party assignments, a decision will be made concerning the best method to serve the food to the guests.

LOCKWOOD PLACE SETTING

FIGURE 13–8

A diagram of the place setting for the Lockwood wedding. The service staff will use this guide when setting up the dining room. A sample place setting is situated on one table to guide the service staff. A–bread-and-butter knife; B–bread-and-butter plate; C–salad fork; D–main course fork; E–plate for pineapple; F–serrated steak knife; G–fruit spoon; H–saucer and coffee cup (with handle at 5 o'clock); I–champagne glass; J–red wine glass; K–water glass; L–dessert fork; M–dessert spoon; N–napkin folded in candle fold, placed in wine glass; O–coffee spoon.

There are four styles of service used in American banquet service to serve a party. The first is referred to as the *station method*; the second is the *follow-up method*; the third is called the *combination method*; and the last is the *sweep method*.

The Station Method

In the **station method**, each service person is assigned two tables of either 8 or 10 guests, for a total of between 16 and 20 people. The service person is solely responsible for the service at those two tables. This system is best used when a large staff of temporary workers are hired to serve a large party. The advantage of this system is that the banquet manager knows who is responsible for service at all the tables.

This system has two main disadvantages. It is the slowest type of American banquet service. Also, guest tables usually will not be served in the proper order. For example, if Mona had tables 1 and 2, she would serve the guests at table 1 their food. Then she must return to the kitchen to obtain the food for table 2. In the meantime, the service person who has table 3 has already served that table. Table 3 is served before table 2, which is shown in Figure 13–9.

Another potential problem with using the station method is that service people will only set up their own tables. They will not assist in the setting up of the total banquet room. To avoid this problem, the banquet manager must not give out station assignments until the room is set up. Then the service people should be brought to the tables for which they are responsible so that there will be no mix-up concerning which table should be served by whom.

The Follow-Up Method

The **follow-up method** is one of the most efficient methods and quickest services if the staff can master the system. It takes planning, cooperation, and leadership by the banquet manager, the head service people, and the remaining service staff.

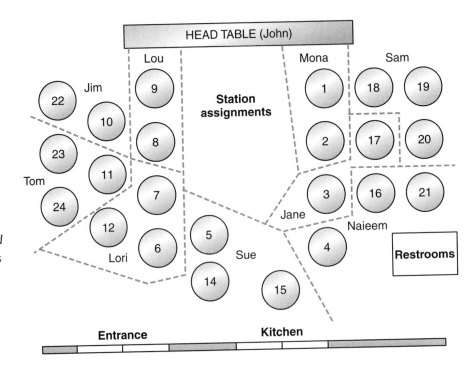

FIGURE 13–9

Service stations for an American-style banquet. This system is bad because the tables are not served in order. Table 18 will be served before Mona can serve table 2.

For the Lockwood wedding, the staff would be broken up into two teams of five. The responsibility of serving the food and removing the dirty dishes in the banquet room would be divided in half, as shown in Figure 13–10. Each group would have a head service person to supervise its side of the room. Three members of the team would carry the food into the banquet room. The other two—including the head service person—would serve the food to the guests. The head service person would instruct the other server in the correct order of service. Each team would obtain its food from an assigned plating area in the kitchen.

When it is time to clear the dirty dishes, all five members of the team work together in removing them. They work from the head table backwards toward the kitchen doors. The banquet manager should be in the banquet room making sure that all the guests get served and that the service is done correctly.

The advantages of this type of service are that it is fast and that all the guests are served in proper order. This is considered one of the best serving systems from the kitchen's point of view, because the food is picked up quickly.

The main disadvantage is that it is difficult to teach temporary workers to use this system. They generally lack the organization and teamwork it requires.

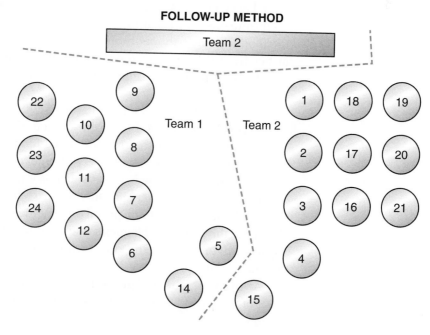

FIGURE 13–10

The follow-up method for serving a banquet is one of the most efficient methods and quickest services. The tables served first are closest to the head table.

The Combination Method

The **combination method** combines the best features of the follow-up and station methods. Serving the food is done by the team system; however, clearing dirty dishes and serving beverages is the responsibility of a service person who is assigned a station.

The advantage of this system is that it can be used with either permanent or temporary service staff. The only key people who must be employed are head service people. Another advantage is that tables are served in the proper order. Finally, confusion on the part of the service staff (Did we clear the dishes from table 14?) is eliminated.

The only disadvantage is that it is slower than the follow-up method.

The Sweep Method

The **sweep method** is best used when there is one entree choice. The sweep method utilizes speed and organization to enable the guests to be served and have the dishes removed quickly. Like the follow-up method, it takes planning, cooperation, and leadership by the banquet manager, the banquet supervisors, and the remaining service staff to make it work successfully. A great deal of communication has to occur between the banquet manager, waitstaff, chef, and culinary team to make this system work successfully.

The banquet room is divided into sections. Each section has a banquet supervisor. A few of the waitstaff are assigned stations to serve beverages; including wine, but most of the waitstaff are divided up into teams. Each team has members—called *luggers*—who carry the food into the banquet room from the kitchen and carry the dirty dishes from the banquet room to the dishwashing area. The other members of the team—called *servers*—serve the food and clear the dirty dishes.

The banquet supervisor is positioned in the front of the section. As the luggers bring the food from the kitchen, they locate the banquet supervisor and deliver the trays of plated food to the traystand near the banquet supervisor. The servers then take the plates off the tray and serve the guests. The banquet supervisor points out to the servers where the food is to be served. Only when a table is completely served will the banquet supervisor proceed to the next table. As the servers distribute the plates to the guests, the banquet supervisor keeps moving toward the tables of the guests who have not been served, moving the tray stands along.

At this time, the banquet supervisor and the team return to the front of the section and start removing the finished plates of the guests who were served first. This method differs from the other three because staff do not wait until all guests are finished eating to remove the dirty plates. Because staff are removing the plates of the people served first, this speeds up the service of the banquet. Now the servers are removing the finished plates from the guests and the luggers are carrying the trays of dirty plates to the dishwashing area. As soon as all plates have been cleared, the next course will be brought into the banquet room by the luggers.

The sweep method offers another option. This method is ideal to use when the host of the party is concerned with the banquet taking too much time. The sweep method is often used at a fund-raising event in the middle of the week. Because the purpose of these fund-raisers is to raise money for charity, many of the guests do not want to attend a banquet that will last longer than three hours, which includes the cocktail hour, dinner, and speeches.

The banquet manager should decide which of these systems to use based on the capabilities of the staff and the organizational qualities of the manager. In addition to the mentioned styles of services, there are other variations of the styles that banquet establishments use. For example, a variation of the station method is to have two service people responsible for four tables, but have them work as a team. One would carry the food from the kitchen, while the other would serve the food. Regardless of the system the banquet manager decides to use, the main factor in choosing one over the other must be guest satisfaction.

Whichever method is used, the banquet manager must be in the dining room when the food is being served and when dirty dishes are being cleared. It is the manager's job to correct mistakes and oversee service.

Proper Order of Serving the Party

The banquet manager has to know the correct order in which to serve the guests at a banquet. The head table is always the first table served. Next served are the tables in front of the head table. The service of the rest of the dining room would follow in a logical manner, going from the head table to the back of the room.

Figure 13–11 illustrates the floor plan for the Lockwood wedding. This is the way the guests should be served. The head table is served first, then tables 1 and 9; 2 and 8; 3 and 7; 5, 6, and 4; 18, 10, 17, 11, 16, 12, 19, 22, 20, 23, 21, 24, 14, and 15.

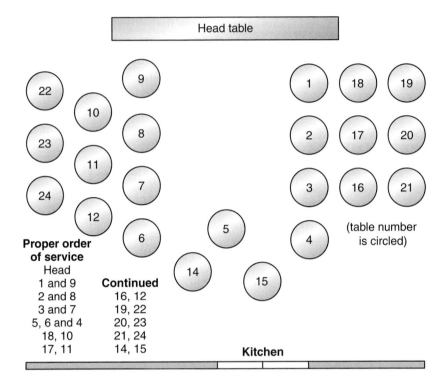

FIGURE 13–11

The proper sequence to serve the Lockwood wedding. The head table is served first, followed by tables 1 and 9; 2 and 8; 3 and 7; 5, 6, and 4; 18, 10, 17, 11, 16, 12, 19, 22, 20, 23, 21, 24, 14, and 15.

Often guests farthest from the head table receive their food before guests nearest the head table at a banquet. This should never happen.

The banquet manager has to inform the service of proper serving order. This information may be put on the duty roster; however, it works better when the banquet manager verbally communicates the correct order to the key staff.

Serving Cocktail Parties

Many times the guest receives their first impression of the banquet establishment during the cocktail reception. For this reason, both liquor and food service must be accomplished professionally and with dignity.

The bar manager is responsible for the performance of the bartenders, as the chef is for the cooks. A duty roster sheet, which the bar manager completes, should also be provided for the bar staff.

When the client arrives, the banquet manager should introduce the client to the bar manager. It is also an excellent idea to introduce the client to the bartenders. This is done to eliminate potential problems during the reception. For instance, if a guest desires a brand of liquor or drink different from those that have been ordered, the bartenders know who has the authority to approve changes.

The food being served at the cocktail party should be ample to provide the guests with the appetizers before the meal, but not so abundant as to spoil their appetite for the main meal. It should be presented attractively.

When the client requests that service staff pass out hors d'oeuvres and drinks, it is called **butler style**. The staff serves the food carried on trays. They will have with them cocktail napkins, which are offered to the guests when an hors d'oeuvre is taken. Staff have to be knowledgeable about all items on their trays and be able to explain these items to the guests. Throughout the cocktail party, staff are circulating throughout the room picking up dirty glasses and plates, changing ashtrays (if smoking is allowed), and replenishing the food.

Tips about Cocktail Parties

Always position bars away from entrances to the room and away from food tables.

Plan on staggering the service of hors d'oeuvres. For example, at a cocktail hour, do not serve them all within the first 15 minutes of the event. Plan to serve the food on small trays staggering the amount of food throughout the cocktail hour. Butler-style service, combined with hot and cold food displays, is always the most elegant type of service. This type of service keeps the food looking attractive and stops the guests from crowding around food displays.

The more food that is put out during the cocktail hour, the more food the guests will eat. Guests very seldom will take the last hors d'oeuvre. Instead they will wait until more food is brought out. Therefore, if you have to make food last, don't be too quick to bring out more food.

Plan on about five pieces of food per person at a cocktail party before a meal. Supplement the food with a bread and cheese table.

Tip Cups

A controversial issue is tip cups for bartenders. Tip cups are placed on the bars to allow the guests to give extra money—*to insure prompt service*—to the bartenders.

Ending the Cocktail Reception

The banquet manager needs to have a method to end the cocktail party. It must be done without offending the guests or the host. This involves tact and diplomacy.

About 10 minutes before the cocktail party is scheduled to end, the banquet manager locates the client and informs him or her of the exact time that the cocktail party will end. If a dinner follows the reception, it is critical that the party be ended on time; otherwise the food may be ruined. If no other meal is planned, the client can either end the party or extend it, depending on the policies of the establishment, which were set forth in the policy sheet.

If a meal follows the reception, the banquet manager would then circulate around the room informing the guests that dinner will be served shortly. The guests are asked to proceed to the dining room. Often this information is conveyed by making an announcement via a microphone.

Once the host agrees to end the party, the bars have to be shut down quickly. This is a critical moment in a party. The best way of closing bars is to have a prearranged sign with the bartenders. When the sign is given, the bartenders should finish serving the drinks they are serving, inform the guests that the bar is closed, and walk away from the bar.

Running the Banquet Party

When the doors to the banquet room are unlocked to allow guests in, the room has to be completely set to receive them. All food that should be present should be in place, and service staff should be ready to serve the party.

The main responsibility of the banquet manager now is to get all the guests seated and get the meal served. If the client has arranged seating for the guests, everyone will have a seat and the meal can commence. However, if there are no seating arrangements, the banquet manager must see that every guest has a seat. This may involve breaking up groups of four or six people and having them sit with guests they do not know.

There is a way to avoid having this problem. When the party does not have seating arrangements, select the table that is the worst location—farthest from the head table, next to the kitchen—and place a reserved sign on it. That way no guests will sit at that table.

The establishment should have the extra table because a banquet establishment usually oversets by 10 percent. Guests coming in early will generally fill up all the other seats. When the latecomers arrive, there is a table left for them. If they do not show up, there is one less table to serve. It works every time!

Serving and Clearing the Meal

Once all the guests have been seated and the introductions, blessings, or toasts have been given, the service staff can serve the meal.

Communication between the banquet manager in the front of the house and the chef in the **back of the house** is the key factor in having a successful banquet. More banquet managers are using headset microphones and earpiece receivers to communicate with the kitchen. The chef may also use a headset microphone, but instead of having a receiver that only he or she can hear, a speaker is turned on in the kitchen for the entire staff to hear the progress of the banquet. Using this system provides for instant communication between the banquet manager and the chef.

The banquet manager can instantaneously inform the service staff, as well as the kitchen staff, when to serve the meal. No one should serve any food, beverages, or rolls without being told by the banquet manager.

The same is true of clearing the dirty dishes. No service person should clear any dirty dishes without authorization from the banquet manager.

The objective in having the banquet manager tell the service staff when to serve and clear is to ensure that all the guests are served at approximately the same time.

Giving the Number to the Chef

One of the ways the banquet manager ensures a good working relationship with the kitchen is to keep the chef informed about the progress of the party. In order to have a successful banquet, the banquet manager and head service people should count the number of guests that are seated. Once the number of guests has been verified, the banquet manager should communicate that number to the chef. If there are more or less than the chef planned, adjustments can be made at that time. When late guests arrive, the chef should be informed immediately.

Obtaining Guest Preference from the Main Course Choices Offered

Some banquet establishments allow guests more than one entree choice. With a vegetarian selection, there may be as many as four choices. Other banquet facilities are limiting the choices to a combination plate and a vegetarian selection.

To facilitate the serving of the main course to the guests, the banquet manager should request that the guests place a colored ticket at their place setting. Each colored ticket represents a particular entree choice. The service people collect the tickets and record which and how many guests are having each item.

When the service people go into the kitchen to pick up the meals, they obtain the correct number of each item for each table. When a follow-up system is used, this requires much more organization from the staff. Again a reminder: All guests at the table should be served at approximately the same time. A banquet house should not serve all the chicken meals and then serve all the beef meals; but each table should receive the correct number of beef and chicken meals simultaneously.

Sweet or Sour?

At the Golden Anniversary of a large corporation, there was a choice of fish, chicken, or beef. Approximately 80 guests were in attendance. This was a great lesson in how not to serve a banquet. The guests made their meal choices when they RSVPed. However, the service staff did not ask who gets what entree. There were no colored tickets; they simply brought out the main courses. They were short one meal, and the result: the president of the corporation finally got his meal after everyone else had almost finished theirs!

At a wedding reception for 300 guests, there were two options: either beef or chicken. The waitstaff asked each guest at each table what they had ordered. They took the orders and served everyone at once.

The difference between the parties: A supervisor was in the room at all times during the wedding reception.

Controlling the Function

Some clients will only pay their bill based upon the number of meal tickets that are collected. Under these conditions, the banquet manager should have a person in the kitchen collecting tickets from the service people. For example, when the service person picks up 10 meals, that person should give 10 tickets to the collector. At a buffet, a service person is stationed at the beginning of the buffet line to collect tickets.

The service person should be taught that if a guest does not have a ticket, the banquet manager is to be summoned immediately. The banquet manager then checks with the client of the party to determine if the person is really a guest or a crasher of the party, which happens often at conventions and weddings.

As soon as the meal has been served, the banquet manager informs the client of the number of guests that the banquet house has served. If there is a discrepancy, the client and the banquet manager can count the number of guests and solve the problem.

Buffets

When the client chooses the option of having a buffet, the banquet manager is responsible for having it set up and ready for the guests at the scheduled time.

All buffets have a few basic principles. It goes without saying that all hot food must be served hot and all cold food must be served cold. Buffet lines are arranged so that guests will not have to stand in a long line waiting for food. The buffet has to look neat, and the food must be appetizing (see Figure 13–12).

Use of Buffets

Buffets are great for clients who want their guests to have a choice of meal items. Buffets are also great for serving a meal in a room that is located a distance from the kitchen. For instance, having a buffet at a pool is an ideal way to increase the use of the area around the pool, which in turn increases the revenue of an establishment.

Buffets are a lifesaver when the establishment has a limited number of function rooms. For example, a group would like to have an all-day meeting with lunch. The banquet house has only one room that will accommodate the guests. The solution is to have the meeting set up using tables. The client and banquet manager schedule a 30- to 45-minute break before lunch is served. By using a buffet, the establishment can serve the guests lunch. The service people will not have to set up their utensils and food from the buffet. As with all banquet functions, this service option requires much organization by the banquet manager to make it a success.

FIGURE 13–12

An attractive, tropical buffet. (Photograph by Randall Perry)

Other banquet establishments have buffet tables on wheels that can be rolled into a banquet room when it is time for the guests to eat. These tables are prepared with the buffet food in advance of the service time and brought either into the room where the meeting is taking place or to a location immediately outside of the meeting room. This saves time and allows the group to continue with a working meal.

Flow and Layout of the Buffet

If at all possible it is best to have separate islands for the different parts of the meal. There can be a separate table for beverages, one for appetizers and salads, one for main courses, and another for dessert.

One buffet line is needed to serve every 100 guests. The establishment can use ice carvings to keep food cold and chafing dishes or heating units to keep food warm. Food can be displayed on mirrors, in ice carvings, or in edible bread items.

All **condiments** are to be placed in front of or next to the food they accompany. For example, next to the ham would be mustard. It is recommended that the condiments be placed in monkey dishes—small cup-like dishes—which should have underliners beneath them. The proper utensils to use for the condiments should be placed on the underliner.

Sweet or Sour?

ⓐⓑⓒ

At a buffet, the first item was the plates for the food; the next item was the salad dressings; the third item, the salad. The guests were having to skip the salad dressings, put the salads on their plates, and then go backwards to put on the salad dressing: this was awkward and a time waster.

The Setup of the Buffet

Figure 13–13 and Figure 13–14 illustrate the setup of a buffet. The first item at the beginning of the buffet line should be clean plates. The banquet manager instructs the service people to check not only the top of the plates but also the bottoms for cleanliness.

The buffet is usually arranged in the same manner as a meal would be served: Appetizers are placed first on the buffet line, followed by salads, then the main course items, along with the starches and vegetables.

The rolls, butter, utensils, and beverages generally are the last items on the buffet line. Ideally, they should be on a separate table. By placing them at the end of the buffet line, it becomes easier for the guests to select the food and carry their plates without having to balance their utensils with their food. Of course, if the banquet establishment wants the guests to take less of the main course items, they will position the rolls and butter, along with the utensils, immediately after the plates.

FIGURE 13–13

The buffet is usually arranged in the same manner as a meal would be served. Appetizers are placed first on the buffet line, followed by salads, and then the main course items, along with the starches and vegetables.

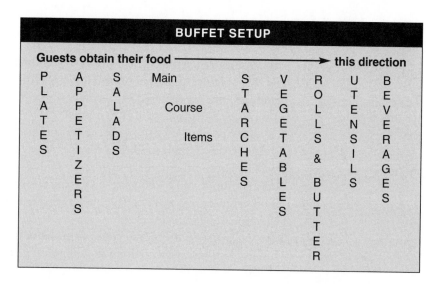

BUFFET SETUP								
Guests obtain their food ⟶						this direction		
PLATES	APPETIZERS	SALADS	Main Course Items	STARCHES	VEGETABLES	ROLLS & BUTTER	UTENSILS	BEVERAGES

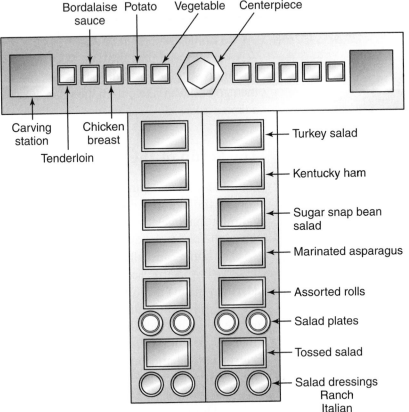

**TURF CLUB BALCONY BUFFET
"T" FORMAT WITH DOUBLE STEM**

FIGURE 13–14

A planned buffet setup using a "T" format with a double stem. The chef has planned where each item on the buffet table will be placed.

Service Staff Jobs at a Buffet

The amount of service assistance is limited by the service staff at a buffet. The service depends on the style of buffet that is chosen by the client. There are some jobs that have to be performed at a buffet that are not performed at a sit-down meal.

Service people will be positioned behind the buffet line to assist the guests with their food. The service people will portion out the food for the guests; they will also answer questions about the food, clean up any food spills, keep the buffet line moving, and replenish the food. Their job is to keep the buffet line looking neat and clean and the food appetizing.

One of the problems the banquet manager wants to avoid is having the guests wait for food. Service persons are instructed to replenish food when there is between one-third and one-fourth remaining on the tray or in the pan. The banquet manager assigns an employee to act as a runner. It is the job of the runner to obtain food from the kitchen and bring it back to the buffet line when told to do so by the service person. More food is obtained from the kitchen in a clean tray or pan called an *insert*. The runner brings the new tray of food; the food is not transferred from one tray to another. The remaining food is brought back into the kitchen. There the tray is replenished and garnished to be used again.

Some establishments place signs near the food, which explain the item. This is recommended; however, it is more effective to have knowledgeable service staff explaining the food items. If the signs have only the name of the item, the guests may have to ask questions about the food.

Controlling the Traffic Flow

Another problem that must be avoided is having all the guests rush up to the buffet table at once to obtain their food. The banquet manager has to see that guests proceed to the buffet table in an organized fashion.

When it is time to serve, the banquet manager announces that the guests may proceed to the buffet when their table is called. Informing the guests that they will be called to the buffet alleviates their fears about the establishment running out of food, even if they are the last table to be called. This system allows for a more controlled and civilized manner of serving a buffet.

Sweet or Sour?

One of the most effective methods of calling guests up to a buffet line was found by a DJ at a wedding. Instead of saying "Table 5, please go up to the buffet now," he played a trivia game. He asked a question and the guests at the table who yelled out the correct answer got to go up to the buffet line. Using this method made the time go by quickly. The guests had a great time, and the buffet establishment had the DJ controlling the guests going up to the buffet. A word of caution: the banquet establishment must have a professional DJ who can control the crowd.

The first person to have the honor of seeing and choosing the food at the buffet is the client. The banquet manager invites the host's table up to preview the buffet before anyone takes food. After guests at the client's table take their food, the banquet manager invites other tables up to obtain food from the buffet. To keep everyone calm, the banquet manager circulates among the guests telling them when it will be their turn. The next table is invited to proceed to the buffet when there are three or four people waiting in line to obtain their plates. This method eliminates many problems associated with buffets.

If during the preplanning for the event, the client informs you that the buffet must be served quickly, more buffet lines should be set up. Arranging buffet tables so that guests may go on both sides of the table works extremely well.

Chafing Dishes

Chafing dishes are used to keep food hot on a buffet. All employees need to know how they work and how to set them up.

The chafing dish consists of a frame, two pans, and a top. The top pan fits into the bottom pan, leaving two to three inches of space between the two pans. The bottom pan should be filled with about one inch of hot water.

Underneath the bottom pan, there are one or two containers that hold a can of jellied liquid that will burn for about an hour. This is referred to as *canned heat*. Sometimes, through careless handling and misuse, the container that holds the canned heat is lost. To solve the problem, an inverted bread-and-butter dish can be used as a substitute for the container. One problem to avoid is that of placing the canned heat too close to the bottom of the pan. When that occurs, the flame from the canned heat will be smothered and it will go out, resulting in cold food. Also, avoid placing the canned heat directly on table surfaces. This canned heat will get very hot and can harm the table.

Approximately 10 minutes before the function starts, the service person should light the canned heat, so the flame will heat up the water. When the water is heated, the top pan of food may be put into the chafing dish. Cover the food in the pan using the chafing dish top to keep the food hot. The chafing dish will act like a steam table: the heated water creates steam; the top pan does not let the steam out of the chafing dish; and the food stays hot. During the buffet, the service staff check to make sure that the canned heat does not go out. If it does, it is replaced. The service staff have to be careful to avoid being burned when taking off the covers or replacing a pan of food in the chafing dish.

T I P $

TO INSURE PROPER SERVICE

On a buffet line, keep all hot foods hot—above 165 degrees Fahrenheit. Keep all cold foods cold—below 40 degrees Fahrenheit.

Carvers

When serving buffets or a station type of service, clients request a culinary person to carve food. Banquet establishments will provide carvers to slice beef, turkey, and the like at a fee. The fee, per carver, should be clearly stated on the banquet establishment's policy sheet.

Final Tip on Buffet Setups

The buffet should look as appetizing as possible. Many times even though the food is spectacular, a buffet looks boring. This is because the food is not displayed with any imagination.

Platters of food can be raised by using an inverted bread-and-butter plate. Additionally, height may be created on the buffet table by using crates or boxes covered with linen. Flowers or food items are placed on these covered crates. Dishes with pedestals also add interest and height to a table.

Finally, stand back and look at the buffet. Then make adjustments to the items on the buffet table. These adjustments should be made based on the texture of the dishes, the color of the food, and the position of the items. The banquet manager may position an item away from its normal place to make the buffet more appealing.

Keeping Food Hot

Besides using chafing dishes to keep food hot on a buffet, the banquet manager must know how to serve food hot at a sit-down meal. When the banquet manager has to serve a banquet in a room that is adjacent to the kitchen, a detailed plan, as you read about earlier in this chapter, must be set up with the chef. In addition, all plates should be heated before the food is placed on them. Some establishments have special heating cabinets, others put the plates in the oven. If the food is placed on a cold plate, it will get cold.

When the banquet is served in a room distant from the kitchen, the food is generally transported in hot carts. Some are electrically heated; others use a form of canned heat to keep the food warm. Again, the key to keeping food hot is to preheat the cart. Once the food arrives at the location, a cook assists in taking the food out of the carts. This cook is responsible for the appearance and quality of the plates. Often, if the menu item requires a sauce, the cook puts it on at this area, which is called the *staging area*.

Timing is critical in making sure the food is available to be served to the guests when it is scheduled. If the party is to be served at noon, the banquet manager has to plan how long it will take to plate the food in the kitchen, transport it, and serve it so that the guests will obtain their meal at noon.

The Sequence of Service for a Sit-Down Meal

Using the Lockwood wedding as the guide, the sequence of service will be explained. The first three steps contain a reminder of proper service using American banquet service.

1. The appetizer course is served from the guest's left side with the service person's left hand. It may be set as a part of the guest's place setting, as was the pineapple.
2. Two roll baskets are served. They are placed in the center of the table by the service person, using the left hand. The rolls should be put in a location that is easy for all the guests to reach. (A tip: rolls and coffee are a lifesaver when the food is not ready to be served on time. Have the service person serve them to the guests and keep replenishing them. It gives the guests something to eat and drink, but more importantly, it shows them that everything is under control. If the guests were not being served some item, they would be wondering when the food will arrive.)
3. The plate, spoon, and pineapple are removed by the service person using the right hand, from the guest's right side.
4. The salad is served. At times, the salad can be preset on the table. It should be placed to the left of the salad fork.
5. The salad plate and fork are removed. The champagne glass should also be removed. If the guests have not finished their champagne or salad, instruct the service person to ask before taking these away. If the answer is negative, the service person should move the salad out of the center of the place setting and put it to the left of the guest's setting. The service person should also check to see if water glasses and roll baskets need refilling. If they do, the

service person should take the roll baskets back to the kitchen and bring them out with the next course. If time allows, the service person can refill the water glasses from water pitchers. Ashtrays should be changed, if needed. Water pitchers, ashtrays, extra utensils, and napkins should be set up at strategically located service stations in advance of the banquet so that service staff do not have to waste time obtaining these items.

6. The main course is served. Meat is positioned in front of the guests so that the first cut made by the guest is into the tenderest part. Remember: Serve all the guests at one table before serving another table. If the banquet establishment is using a station service setup and the service person cannot carry out 10 dinners on the tray, have another service person carry out the remaining dinners so that all the guests at the table are served at approximately the same time.

7. Red wine should be poured by the bartenders. When the service person places a prime rib meal, the bartender should follow by pouring red wine to the guest.

8. The coffee course is served. The service person must use a coffee shield. Tea should be placed in an individual pot above the coffee cup. A wedge of lemon should be served with the tea. At times, the banquet manager can have the service staff put a whole pot of coffee on each table, so the guests can pour the beverage themselves. This method is used especially for breakfast meals or when the client is on a limited time schedule.

9. The main course dishes are removed, along with utensils, red wine glasses, bread-and-butter plates, salt and pepper shakers, and rolls and butter. The only items left on the table are the utensils for dessert, cream, sugar, water glasses, and ashtrays.

10. Dessert is served, along with more coffee.

11. Dessert dishes, water glasses, utensils, and any items guests are finished with are removed. The banquet manager should also have an organized system for putting away items when they are returned to the kitchen. For example, the salt and pepper shakers should always be placed in the same location when they are cleared from the tables.

The banquet manager must be flexible when serving a meal. There are many parts to the meal. Some things may happen that the banquet manager has no control over. The ability to be flexible and to think quickly enough to use whatever items are necessary to keep the guests pleased is critical for the banquet manager. What has just been presented is simply a suggested serving sequence. Adjustments may have to be made in the sequence to satisfy the needs of the guests.

The Problem with Latecomers and Guests Who Leave Early

At many parties, guests will arrive after a few courses have been served. When this occurs, the banquet manager approaches the table and asks the guests if they would like to eat. If the answer is affirmative, the guests are served—as quickly as possible—whatever courses they desire. This may involve bringing out the pineapple course and salad course together.

You may also encounter guests who must leave in a hurry, before the meal is completely served. Try to accommodate this type of guest also. This can be done by serving the guest the main course before or while other guests are eating their salad.

Both of these types of guests create a challenge for the banquet manager. Using tact and diplomacy, the banquet manager can please the client and the guest by accommodating these individuals.

Banquet Checkbacks

To be a truly effective banquet manager, it is imperative to check the satisfaction of all the guest tables after the main course has been served to see whether the meal and service were satisfactory.

An experienced banquet manger will know whether the food has been satisfactory by observing the guest's plates. The type of inquiry the banquet manager makes will be determined by the situation that is observed. For instance, if guests have not eaten their meal, inquire if they would like another choice if such is possible. It is important to remember that influencing one guest at a banquet has the potential to sell an additional banquet for many guests. It is easier to obtain business from people who have experienced your operation than to create a whole new market.

When the opportunity arises that the banquet manager can be introduced to the guests, take advantage of this situation. It will be beneficial for future business.

Throughout the event, the banquet manager should be constantly communicating with the client. The client has to be informed of what will happen next, such as the cake cutting ceremony. The banquet manager continues to inquire whether everything meets the client's satisfaction.

Sweet or Sour?

A banquet was planned to honor a businessperson for all of his philanthropic works and his support of the community. When the committee was formed, they approached a banquet establishment and booked the party. The committee was in constant communication with the banquet manager before the party. The banquet was planned, including a cocktail hour with hors d'oeuvres and an open bar, which was to be followed by a meal consisting of two choices: beef or chicken.

When the committee realized that the event was going to be a sell-out, they contacted the banquet manager. At no time did the banquet manager indicate that there would be any problem with the number of guests or with any menu selections. The committee was comfortable and secure in the belief that staffing for all aspects of the evening would be performed professionally, because they felt they were dealing with professionals and the banquet establishment was noted for the successful operation of its banquet business.

The night of the banquet arrived, and the committee felt comfortable with all the arrangements. The guarantee had been given, along with the number of beef and chicken meals.

The problems started when the committee arrived. When they checked the dining room, they saw cardboard salt and pepper shakers on some tables. At other tables they saw an adequate number of chairs with an inadequate number of place settings or vice versa. Candles were lacking at some tables.

During the open bar cocktail hour, guests had an impossible wait to obtain a drink. There were an insufficient number of bartenders, including one who was completely inexperienced, which caused long lines. Complaints ranged from no liquor in some drinks, to shortages of white wine and ice, to "bad" beer—for those who were even successful in obtaining a drink. The committee sought out the banquet manager and demanded an additional half hour of open bar. This was agreed upon by the banquet manager, but he did not communicate this to the bartenders.

The food was another sad story. After the event, the committee members found that the hors d'oeuvres were unwrapped for serving when the cocktail hour started; not before it. Two and a half hours after the guests were seated for the meal, some guests had yet to be served dinner. When they were finally served, guests were told, "We're out of chicken, you will have to have beef."

The committee felt that the absence of controls to properly plan and provide for staffing and accommodations made the evening an embarrassment.

Manager's Message

(Courtesy of
PAUL WIXTED,
FOOD AND
BEVERAGE
OPERATIONS
MANAGER,
DISNEY'S GRAND
FLORIDIAN RESORT &
SPA CONVENTION
CENTER,
WALT DISNEY
WORLD,
LAKE BUENA VISTA,
FLORIDA)

"At the Grand Floridian Resort and Spa' once a contract has been signed for a banquet or a convention, the event is turned over to a service manager. It is the service manager's responsibility to be the contact person representing the Resort with the client. Everything concerning the event, from the menu to the flowers, is handled by the service manager. He or she has the responsibility to communicate all information required by the client to all of the operators involved with the event—kitchen, front desk, bus operations, florist, entertainment, et cetera. It is the responsibility of the service manager to make the event perfect for the client."

"I believe that in an à la carte restaurant great service will overcome poor food. Because when guests dine in an à la carte restaurant, that is their night out—their entertainment. A great server can save a poor meal. But in banquet service, you only have the guest captive for about 90 minutes. The meal is only one small part of the entire night. It is hard for a server to recover a bad meal. That is why attention to details is important for our service managers."

"For example, the weddings held at our Wedding Pavilion at the Resort must be magical. We do hundreds of weddings a year. But for the bride and groom, their wedding is the only wedding we do. So our service manager will go over all the details of the event and take copious notes. When we have our tasting menu, we will take pictures of how the food is plated. We even give the bride and groom their choice of napkin folds. It may not sound like a big thing, but this lets the bride and groom

(continues)

Keep in mind that musicians and photographers love to work at an establishment where the banquet manager informs them of the time and location of events at the function. If the banquet manager makes it easy for these individuals to do their job, it will benefit the establishment, because they will recommend the establishment to potential clients.

Managing the Meeting Room Business

Another type of business that the banquet manager may have concerns is meeting rooms. Knowing the correct way to set up the rooms is important, but just as important is knowing how to manage the meeting room business.

Manager's Message
(continued)

determine how the table setting and room will look for their wedding. So on their wedding day the detailed notes that the service manager took at the planning meetings will make their wedding perfect."

—*Paul Wixted*

Mr. Wixted is responsible for all food and beverage operations at the crown jewel of the Walt Disney World Resorts. In his role as food and beverage operations manager, Mr. Wixted oversees more than 15 different food and beverage operations at this hotel, which has 901 guest rooms and suites. Banquets can be held for up to 1,200 people in the convention center. There are four full-service restaurants for his guests to choose from: Victoria and Albert's, which has been awarded the highest rating by the American Automobile Association (five diamonds); a seafood restaurant, called Narcoossee's; Citrico's, a restaurant that features American Cuisine with flavors from Tuscany, Southern Provence, and the Spanish Riviera; and the Grand Floridian Café, which serves breakfast, lunch, and dinner.

Paul is also responsible for the mini-bars and private dining (room service) that is available 24 hours a day. The other 24-hour operation is Gasparilla's Grille and Games, a quick service food and beverage outlet.

Other unique food operations that Mr. Wixted is responsible for are the character experience buffets, which are held in the 1900 Park Fare restaurant at breakfast and dinner. Also, a high tea is served in the Garden View Tea Room.

All baking, stewarding, and the commissary kitchen come under Paul's direction. Rounding out his operations are two pool bars and a cocktail lounge called Mizner's.

Coffee breaks are often scheduled in the meeting rooms that the banquet establishment has to set up. As in other types of banquet management, the key to having repeat conference business is to make sure all items are in place and the room is correctly set up for the guests before they arrive.

Items such as water, glasses, pads, pencils, and ashtrays (if they are desired) should be on the tables. One water pitcher should be available for four guests. When the coffee break is scheduled for a specific time, make certain that the coffee and food arrive on time.

The timing is critical, but just as important is what happens while the guests are having their coffee break. During the break, the banquet manager should have a member of the staff in the meeting room, replenishing the water, cleaning ashtrays, and freshening up the room for the remainder of the meeting.

Again, organization is the key to successful meeting room business. All the equipment needed to freshen up the room should be set up outside in advance of the coffee break. At break time, the staff simply enter the room and replace, for example, the empty water pitchers with full ones.

Presenting the Bill to the Host and Rebooking the Party

The banquet manager's last job on the day of the function should be to present and explain the bill to the client. Payment should be obtained and the client should be thanked for holding the function at the establishment.

Finally, if the function is an annual event, ask the client if it may be rebooked for the following year. If the function was a wedding reception, ask the client to recommend your establishment to any future bride and groom.

And once again, thank the client for the opportunity to serve. Of course, in a few days, you will send the client a handwritten thank you note.

Breakdown of the Function

When it is time for the party to end, inform the client. As the guests and client are leaving the banquet, assist the client with any presents, the top of the wedding cake, or any other items with which assistance is needed.

Once the guests have departed, there is still work to be done. The banquet manager should have a system for cleaning up the dining room. The dirty dishes and equipment must be brought into the kitchen in an organized fashion. For instance, the staff should go into the dining room with big pots and glass racks. Glasses on the tables should have their contents dumped into the pots. The glasses can then be put into the racks, ready to be washed. Using a system like this eliminates confusion and breakage in the kitchen.

Finally, when the banquet room and kitchen are cleaned to your satisfaction, the employees should be thanked and dismissed. And you, the banquet manager, should feel proud that you have just completed another successful function.

T I P $

TO INSURE PROPER SERVICE
Always conduct a meeting with the staff after a banquet to determine what went right and what went wrong and what improvements can be made for future events.

Lawsuits and the Restaurant or Banquet Manager

The food service industry has been sued by an increasing number of guests who claim they fell at the restaurant or received chipped teeth or something caused their bridgework to fail. These are among the most common complaints that spark threats of legal action against food service establishments.

No case has received as much publicity as the one that resulted in a $2.9 million jury verdict against McDonald's Corporation. This resulted from the spilling of a 49-cent cup of coffee onto an elderly woman. The jury ruled in favor of the woman, because they learned that McDonald's had settled more than 700 hot-beverage injury claims for more than half a million dollars over the previous 10 years. Yet, the company had never considered lowering its standard coffee-holding temperature of 180 degrees, which is known to cause third-degree burns. Because coffee is not drinkable at 180 degrees, jury members said it constituted a defective product under New Mexico state law.

Running a food service operation leaves a business open to some strange legal cases. Managers should be aware of the types of cases that have been filed and what advice experts have given on how to avoid these lawsuits.

Sizzler International was sued by the mother of an employee who cut himself with a knife in a California-based unit. The suit contended that the knife should have carried some type of warning.

The Rainbow Room in New York was hit with a lawsuit a couple of weeks after a honeymooning couple spent an evening dining and dancing. They left without mentioning any problems. However, they sued the restaurant for $1 million claiming the lingering cigarette and cigar smoke "upset their right to conjugal happiness." The case never went to court.

A Muslim family in Houston sued On the Border Cafes for $600,000 after learning from a cook that the beef tacos they had eaten contained pork, a food strictly forbidden by Muslim dietary laws.

The Los Angeles City Attorney, on behalf of only two complaining customers, sued Gladstone's 4 Fish. The reason: Gladstone's ran out of

$9.95-a-pound Maine lobster in a promotion that fed 8,000 customers. The settlement: Gladstone's had to pay fines and fees totaling $30,000 and had to repeat the dinner offer for four weeks at the promotional price.

Foodmaker had to pay $100 million resulting from wrongful-death lawsuits after four children on the West Coast died from eating bacteria-laden, undercooked Jack in the Box hamburgers. In addition, Foodmaker lost over $137 million worth of business from the resulting negative publicity.

Johnson and Wales University paid $434,000 to the family of former student James Brown, Jr., 27, of Williston, South Carolina. Brown died in 1992, after having an allergic reaction to shrimp that he had been served at a school dining hall.

Since the Americans with Disabilities Act passed in the 1990s provides that guests be served with reasonable accommodations, a deaf woman from Santa Monica, California, sued Burger King after her handwritten drive-thru order was rejected by a worker. The settlement: Burger King agreed to revamp training policies, test visual electronic ordering devices, and offer order forms for customers with speech or hearing disabilities.

The manager is the person who can stop many of these lawsuits from getting beyond a complaint. Many, if not most, lawsuits can be prevented through good management practices. Additional benefits are lower insurance rates, increased productivity, and enhanced loyalty from guests and employees.

Attorneys and food service professionals indicate that detailed hiring and firing guidelines are a must. Preemployment screening is needed to eliminate potentially violent or otherwise undesirable job candidates. Regularly updated and widely posted written policies against discrimination or harassment of any kind are also recommended. Managers must be aware of and adhere to prevailing wage and hour laws. The maintenance of safe work areas and safe public areas is required. Finally, ongoing worker education related to safely preparing and handling food is recommended.

Robert Spivk, president and chief executive of Grill Concepts in Los Angeles, advises, "Just be humble." Give away lots of free meals and be sympathetic to appease disgruntled patrons and discourage lawsuits.

"Make sure that the guest knows that you care," said Spivk. If there is any problem, his restaurants always send follow-up phone calls and letters to assure guests of management's concern for their satisfaction. He always insists that his managers avoid arguing with lawsuit-minded guests. He estimates that costs for the free food run "one-tenth of 1 percent" of the legal bills that could result from adversarial responses to patrons' gripes. Grill Concepts also increased its training for risk-reduction efforts such as safety education for employees.

All establishments should have a lawyer available to handle their legal problems. This part of the chapter only illustrates possibilities and should serve as a guideline for managers.[2-7]

A Final Tip

Throughout this book there have been a series of To Insure Proper Service tips for the reader. The last one has to do with the practice of tipping. The practice of tipping in à la carte restaurants will very likely continue into the twenty-first century. There are many reasons for this.

At the DeWitt Clinton Hotel, in Albany, New York, one could witness the end of the tipping at banquets. In 1968, the guests still tipped the waitstaff by passing the basket after a meal. Today, no banquet facility has a pass-the-basket tip system. All banquets have a set fee added to the price of the meal. In some places, it is called a *gratuity*, but in New York state recent rulings have stated that a gratuity must go to the waitstaff serving the party. Therefore, banquet operators in New York state have changed the fee to a "service charge." This allows them to use the monies collected for any expense in the business. More and more banquet facilities are now paying their service staff a flat fee—$150.00 per function, $15.00 per hour, or something similar—for working.

The à la carte tipping in restaurants will soon follow this type of payment. Service staff will no longer be compensated by tipping as we know it today: Servers will be paid by the hour. Already some resorts—The Sagamore in Lake George, New York, some Walt Disney World packages, the Grand Hotel at Mackinac Island, Michigan—have a service charge automatically added on to the guests' à la carte bills. Most restaurant menus state: "Parties of six or more will have a 15 percent service charge added to the final bill." The Perry Restaurant Group of Vermont has a tip-pool policy that affects the front of the house staff. All tips are pooled. The tips are then distributed as wages based on a half-tip or full-tip criteria.

The final reason is the Internal Revenue Service. In 1995, the IRS started the Tip Reporting Alternative Commitment or TRAC. This program offers food service employers protection from IRS audits in exchange for their help in the tip tax education of employees and the collection of tip taxes.

TRAC requires employers to take an active role in educating and reeducating their employees, quarterly, about their tip reporting requirements. Employers must inform employees that they must keep a daily tip record. This will allow the employee to report their tips accurately to their employer. Employees must also be able to prove their tip income if their returns are ever questioned. TRAC has been extended to May 2005 with the possibility of it being extended even longer.[8] The idea is that employees will be well aware of their tax obligations under the law and will be forced to report a more accurate tip amount.

The Internal Revenue Service continues to update regulations concerning the required method of how tipped employees must document their income. The authors recommend that all individuals who receive tips or gratuities consult the Internal Revenue Service for the most current laws and regulations.

With all the pressure on the restaurant owner to keep track of the employees' tips, along with the changing attitudes toward service charges by guests, tipping as we know it will soon be replaced by the service charge. A service charge that has been added to a guest's bill is not considered a tip. Instead it is added to the employee's pay and treated as wages.[9]

SUMMARY

1. Based on information from the BEO, the banquet manager and staff will be able to diagram the setup of a place setting.
2. Based on information from the BEO, the banquet manager and staff will be able to plan for all equipment needed for an event.
3. The four methods of service for a sit-down banquet are the station, follow-up, combination, and sweep.
4. The quickest way to serve food from the kitchen to the banquet room will be determined by the equipment available and the skill of the service staff. For some establishments, it is using arm service; for others a tray method works.
5. Based on information from the BEO, the banquet manager and staff will be able to staff bars efficiently. Bar service should be ended through a system that informs the service staff to immediately cease serving drinks when signalled by the banquet manager.
6. A banquet room should be set up and served starting from the head table and systematically working back toward the kitchen or staging area.
7. To control the amount of canapés and hors d'oeuvres at a party, the banquet manager should plan enough food to tempt the appetite of

the guests but not overstuff them. These should be served staggered to make them last throughout the length of the party.

8. To control traffic flow, the banquet manager should invite guests up to the buffet table by table.

9. During a break in a meeting, the staff at the banquet establishment will take the participants' supplies on the tables and place them on chairs. The room will be freshened with clean tablecloths, water and glasses, paper, and pencils. The participants' supplies will be returned to their original location.

REVIEW QUESTIONS

1. Using the banquet function sheet, complete the banquet checklist form by filling in how much equipment would be needed to serve the Lockwood wedding.

2. Using the banquet function sheet, state what utensils can be used over again and how you would accomplish it if you were a banquet manager.

3. What is a chafing dish? How is it set up, and what is its purpose?

4. When should a buffet be used for a party? What are the advantages and disadvantages to a host in using a buffet?

5. What is the first and the last thing a banquet manager has to do on the day of a function? Why are both of these jobs important?

6. What is a duty roster and why is it important? How does it help the banquet manager?

DISCUSSION QUESTIONS

1. You have a doubleheader booked (two parties, one after another) in the same room. The first one is for 300 guests, followed by a party for 150 guests. You only have an hour between the two parties. At the end of the first wedding reception, the father of the bride sees that everyone is having a good time. He tells the band to play an extra hour. What problems do you anticipate, and how could this situation have been avoided?

2. Do you think that tip cups should be allowed at the Lockwood wedding? Should they be allowed at other events?

3. A group of eight guests were drinking and talking at the cocktail party and have just arrived in the room. All the other guests have been seated. There are enough seats to accommodate the eight guests; however, they must split their group up. Two people have to

sit at one table, four at another, and two at a third table. They refuse, because they want to sit together. What do you do to solve their problem?

4. The client has a party of 400, which must be served within 15 minutes. Your room can physically hold only enough tables for two buffet lines. How would you solve this problem?

5. Refer to the section in this chapter on planning for the needed extra equipment. After reading this section, can you discover any other uses of equipment for the Lockwood banquet?

REFERENCES

1. *Nation's Restaurant News* (May 4, 1987): F4.
2. Robin Lee Allen, "IRS Unfurls New Tip-Tax Program," *Nation's Restaurant News* 29, No. 25 (June 19, 1995): 1, 123.
3. "Food Court Litigation & Food Service," *Nation's Restaurant News* 28, No. 39 (October 9, 1995): 101–150.
4. Alan Liddle, "Lawsuit Prevention: Strategies Focus on Safety, Education, Compliance with Laws and Regulations," *Nation's Restaurant News* 28, No. 39 (October 9, 1995): 146–150.
5. Richard Martin, "Consumer Lawsuits: Wary Restauranteurs Seek Relief from Litigious Patrons' Reprisals," *Nation's Restaurant News* 28, No. 39 (October 9, 1995): 104–108.
6. "Holding Down the Tort: Reform Bills Spell Relief for Operators," *Nation's Restaurant News* 29, No. 14 (April 2, 1995): 51.
7. "J&W to Pay $434K to Student's Family," *Nation's Restaurant News* 29, No. 25 (June 19, 1995): 87.
8. IRS Simplifies Tip Reporting Agreement to Ease Burdens on Restaurant Industry and Improve Tax Compliance. National Society of Accountants. http://www.nsacct.org.
9. Publication 531, Reporting Tip Income; Keeping a Daily Tip Record. http://www.irs.ustreas.gov.

Appendix A

Eight Napkin Folds

The Tent

1. Lay the napkin out flat in front of you.
2. Fold the napkin in half.
3. Fold the napkin in quarters.
4. Fold the napkin into a triangle.
5. Fold the napkin into a triangle again.
6. Place the open end of the triangle facing the guest's seat.

FIGURE A–1

The Tent. An easy fan fold to learn.

The Cuffed Roll

1. Lay the napkin out flat in front of you.
2. Fold the napkin in half.
3. Fold the base of the napkin up approximately by 3 inches.
4. Turn the napkin over.
5. Going from left to right, make three even folds.
6. Place the silverware in the pocket.

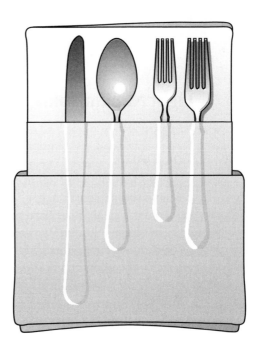

FIGURE A–2

The Cuffed Roll. An ideal fold for buffet service.

The Candle

1. Lay the napkin out flat in front of you in a diamond shape.
2. As if the napkin were a clock, fold the 6 o'clock point up to the 12 o'clock point to form a triangle.
3. Fold the base of the triangle up 2 inches so that it looks like a pirate's hat.
4. Turn the napkin over to hide the fold. The shape should still be a triangle.
5. Roll the napkin evenly from right to left, forming a candle.
6. Tuck the tail into the cuff formed by the fold.
7. Stand the candle in a wine glass at the place setting.

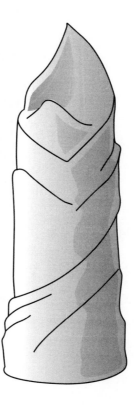

FIGURE A–3

The Candle. A great fold to give the impression of height.

The Lilly

1. Lay the napkin out flat in front of you.
2. Fold the napkin in quarters.
3. Fold the napkin into a triangle, so that the solid base is in front of you.
4. Make sure there are five ends at the top of the triangle.
5. Starting with the left base, accordion pleat the napkin from left to right.
6. Place in a wine glass at the place setting.
7. Separate out the five ends.

FIGURE A–4

The Lilly. This fold can be either placed at the cover or in a wine glass.

The Crown

1. Lay the napkin out flat in front of you in a diamond shape.
2. Fold the napkin into a triangle, with the points at the top and the base facing you.
3. Take the 3 o'clock and 9 o'clock points and fold them up to the 12 o'clock point.
5. Crease the base of the napkin.
6. Still holding onto the 6 o'clock point, fold the point down to base.
7. Turn napkin over.
8. Place three or four fingers at the base of the napkin in the center of the napkin.
9. Wrap the right side around your fingers and tuck it under them.
10. Take the left side and fold it so that you can tuck the left side into the pocket made by the first fold.
11. Stand the napkin up and face it toward you.
12. Peel the two outside "wings" of the napkin down.

FIGURE A–5

The Crown. An excellent fold to use either at the cover or on a cover plate.

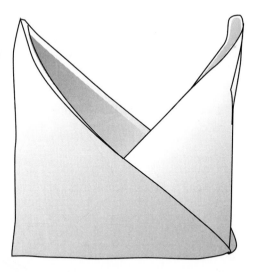

The Easy Cone

1. Lay the napkin out flat in front of you in a diamond shape.
2. Fold the napkin into a triangle, with the points at the top and the base facing you.
3. Take the 3 o'clock and 9 o'clock points and fold them up the 12 o'clock point.
4. Turn the napkin over.
5. Take the 6 o'clock point and fold it up one-quarter of the way toward the 12 o'clock point.
6. Turn the napkin over.
7. Place three fingers at the base of the napkin in the center of the napkin.
8. Wrap the right side around your fingers and tuck it under them.
9. Take the left side and fold it so that you can tuck the left side into the pocket made by the first fold.
10. Turn the napkin over and place it in the center of the place setting.

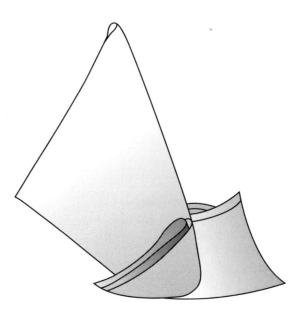

FIGURE A–6

The Easy Cone. As its name implies, an easy fold for the service staff to accomplish.

The Cock's Comb

1. Lay the napkin out flat in front of you.
2. Fold the napkin in quarters.
3. Fold the napkin into a triangle so that the base is in front of you and the points of the napkin are at 12 o'clock.
4. Make sure that the five ends are in the 12 o'clock position.
5. Take the 3 o'clock and 9 o'clock points and fold them so that the sides of the triangle meet in a parallel line leaving a cone-shaped triangle.
6. Take the bottom of the cone (3 o'clock and 9 o'clock points) and fold under the base of the napkin to form a triangle.
7. Crease the napkin with your right hand while holding it in your left hand. The napkin is not lengthwise.
8. Place the napkin lengthwise and separate the top four ends.

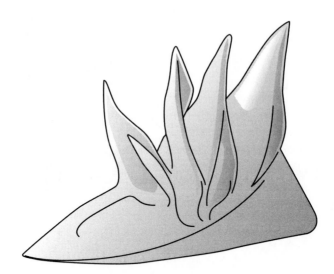

FIGURE A–7

The Cock's Comb. A fold that adds intrigue to the place setting.

The Fan

1. Fold the napkin in half.
2. Arrange the napkin so that it is lengthwise in front of you.
3. Working up from the bottom, accordion pleat the napkin three-quarters of the way to the top.
4. Holding the pleated end in your right hand, fold the napkin in half so that the pleats are on the outside of the fold.
5. The pleated part is now at the right-hand side of the napkin.
6. Take the bottom of the unpleated part with your left hand and fold it into a triangle so that the triangle forms a base for the fan. Tuck the triangle into the pleats.
7. At this point, a rubber band can be placed on the napkin and the napkins can be used when needed. (This is an optional step.)
8. Stand the napkin up on the triangle base. The napkin will fan out.

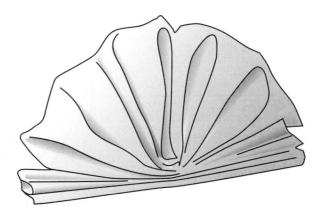

FIGURE A–8

The Fan. A favorite of many banquet houses, as fan-folded napkins can be done in advance.

Appendix B

American Place Setting

A Bread-and-butter plate   E Coffee spoon
B Salad fork   F Soup spoon
C Main course fork   G Wine glass
D Main course knife   H Water glass

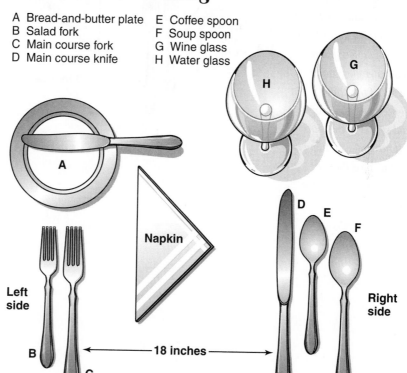

FIGURE B–1

The traditional American place setting includes a soup and salad course. Forks are on the left side of the guest; knives and spoons are on the right. Water and wine glasses are placed at the tips of the knife and spoon.

Basic American Place Setting

FIGURE B–2

The proper diagram for a basic à la carte place setting. On the left side of the napkin is the bread-and-butter plate, the salad fork, and the main-course fork. In the center of the place setting is the napkin. To the right of the napkin is the dinner knife (with the edge pointed toward the napkin), coffee spoon, and water glass above the tip of the knife. Notice there is no cup and saucer in this basic setting. However, there is a wine glass that is placed right next to the water glass.

A bread-and-butter plate
B salad fork
C main course fork
D dinner knife
E teaspoon
F soup spoon
G wine glass
H water glass

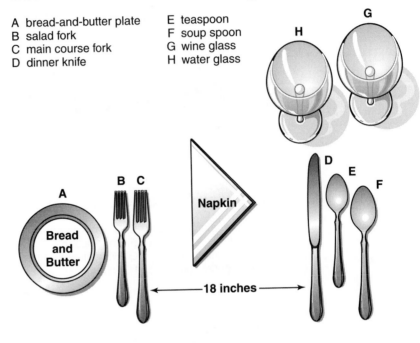

Staggered Pattern of Setting Utensils

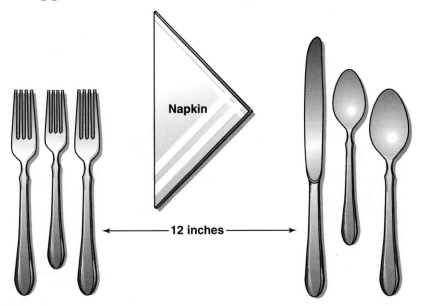

FIGURE B–3

Flatware placed in a staggered pattern makes for a more attractive place setting.

Napkin

12 inches

Coffee Cup Placement

FIGURE B–4

The handle on a coffee cup should be placed at a position that corresponds to 5 o'clock on a watch.

5 o'clock

Saucer

Coffee cup handle at 5 o'clock position

Russian/French Place Setting

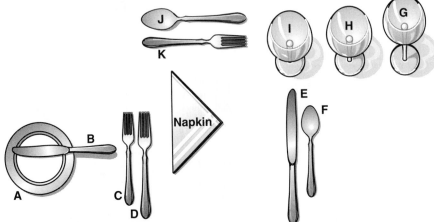

FIGURE B–5

Russian and French place settings are identical. The setting is basically the same as American style, except for a dessert spoon and dessert fork placed above the center of the place setting.

A bread-and-butter plate
B bread-and-butter knife
C salad fork
D main course fork
E dinner knife
F coffee spoon

GLASSES
G white wine glass
H red wine glass
 I water glass
J dessert spoon
K dessert fork

Space Requirements for American Banquet Service

FIGURE B–6

Space requirements for American banquet service. Each guest needs 24 linear inches. This table is 8 feet long by 3 feet wide. It can seat four guests on each side of the table.

24" ① 24" ② 24" ③ 24" ④

15"

6"

15"

3 feet
36"

⑤ ⑥ ⑦ ⑧

8 feet/96"

8 guests ((#)) have 2 feet/24" of space each

FIGURE B–7

The menu for a typical banquet, with the utensils needed to serve one guest. Two forks, three spoons, and two knives are needed. A bread-and-butter plate, cup and saucer, napkin, and water glass are needed as well.

TYPICAL BANQUET MENU	
Item	**Utensil Needed**
Fresh Fruit Cup	Teaspoon
Salad, House Dressing	Fork
Prime Ribs	Knife to cut, fork to eat
Baked Potato, Green Broccoli	
Rolls and Butter	Butter spreader
Chocolate Mousse	Teaspoon
Coffee	Teaspoon

American Banquet Place Setting

A coffee cup
B fruit spoon
C coffee spoon
D dessert spoon
E dinner knife

F main course fork
G salad fork
H bread-and-butter plate
I water glass

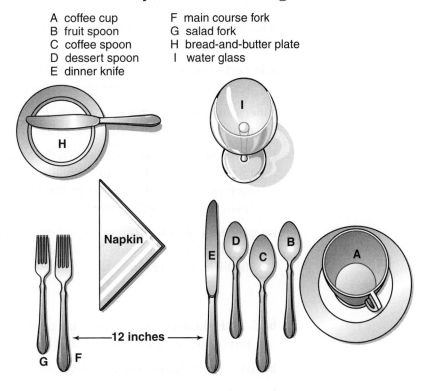

FIGURE B–8

An American banquet place setting.

Glossary

Aid: The member of the team (in the team system of service) who acts as a busperson, picks up dinners from the kitchen, and serves them to the guests.

à la carte restaurant: A business that serves guests individual meals on demand.

à la carte service: Service person takes individual guest food and beverage orders and serves them to the guests in American service.

American banquet service: Service in which the guest's food is all placed on one plate. Often known as "on the plate, no wait."

American service: Service in which the food and beverage is served to the guest by either an individual service person or a team method. The food is plated in the kitchen. Also referred to as "plate" or "German" service.

anaphylactic shock: The severest form of shock which may cause death. This shock could be caused by allergic reactions to nuts, shellfish, or other foods.

back of the house: A term referring to employees who do not come into contact with the guest in their normal line of duty.

baked: Food that is cooked by dry, continuous heat in an oven.

banquet: A meal with a menu that is preselected by the host for all of the guests attending the event.

banquet captain: The person responsible for service in a section of the banquet room.

banquet event order (BEO): A form prepared by the banquet office that lists in detail everything that the host desires for the banquet.

banquet facility: A business that serves groups of guests the same meal, at the same time.

banquet manager: The individual responsible for planning, organizing, and running banquets.

beverage service: The type of alcoholic or nonalcoholic drinks requested by the host at a banquet function.

blocking: Reserving a certain table at a certain time for a guest.

buffet: A banquet meal at which guests obtain a portion or all of their food by serving themselves from buffet tables.

buffett, deluxe: The guests are served the first and second course as well as their beverages and dessert. They obtain their main course from an elegant buffet.

buffet, modified deluxe: Guest tables are set with utensils and guests are served coffee, and perhaps desert by the service person.

buffet, simple: Guests obtain all their own food and drinks.

busperson: A restaurant employee who is responsible for assisting the service person.

busy bees: Guests who patronize the restaurant who are too busy with work and/or family responsibilities to find time to cook.

butler style: A type of service used in cocktail parties, in which the staff circulate among the guests serving food (usually hors d'oeuvres) on trays.

call-ahead seating: Also called priority seating. A system used in restaurants that do not accept reservations, in which patrons can call ahead to be placed on a waitlist.

captain: A restaurant employee who is responsible for an area of the dining room.

cash bar: At a banquet, an arrangement by which guests are required to buy their own drinks, both alcoholic and nonalcoholic.

cater-to-mes: Guests who patronize the restaurant because they are not in the mood to cook.

celebrators: Guests who patronize the restaurant who are on vacation or are celebrating a birthday, wedding anniversary, graduation, or some other special occasion.

checkoff method: A method of blocking reservations used in a large restaurant.

chef de rang: An individual in French service who finishes off the food tableside.

chef's creation: An additional item added to the regular menu.

combination method: A type of service in which the waitstaff use the station and follow-up method to serve the banquet.

commis de rang: An individual in French service who assists the chef de rang in the service of the meal.

competency: Serving food and drinks in the correct manner to the guest.

condiments: Food items that complement main course selections, like mustard and ketchup.

consumer orientation: The act of viewing your business from the perspective of your guests.

cover: The area or space for all utensils (including salt, pepper, and ashtrays) needed for each guest.

cross-contamination: The transfer of harmful microorganisms from one item of food to another by means of a nonfood contact surface (human hands, utensils, equipment), or directly from a raw food to a cooked one.

deluxe buffet: The most elegant kind of buffet service, in which guests obtain only their main course from a buffet, and are served everything else.

dependent needs: A part of Maslow's Hierarchy. They are needs that can only be met by someone else, not oneself. The first four needs of the hierarchy are dependent.

deuces: Tables that seat two guests.

deuxième maître d'hôtel: The French term for the person who has the responsibility for one dining room.

diplomacy: The ability to act tactfully with the guest.

directeur du restaurant: The French term for the person who has the responsibility for the total restaurant operation.

dupes: Stands for duplicate guest check. A copy of the original guest check turned into the kitchen or bar to obtain orders.

86:   A term used to signify that a restaurant is out of an item.

80/20 rule: Eighty percent of your business is obtained from 20 percent of your guests.

esteem needs: The fourth in Maslow's Hierarchy of needs. Esteem is the way in which people perceive the individual, which in turn affects the individual's ego.

est. wait time (estimated wait time):   The amount of time the host has estimated that the guest will have to wait for a table.

firm booking: A client reserves a room with a deposit.

first available seating: Guests reserve a table for a specified time, e.g. 6 p.m. The guest will be seated when the first available table is vacant. It may be at 6 or 6:02 or 6:05 p.m.

five Ps of management: Prior Planning Prevents Poor Performance: A method that, when followed, contributes to a successful event.

flambé: Food served flaming in ignited liquor, usually prepared at the guest's table by the chef de rang in French service.

follow-up: The member of the team (in the team system of service) who makes sure guests are satisfied, solves any problems, clears dishes, suggests and sells dessert, presents the check, and collects the money.

follow-up method: A style of service that has waitstaff serve a banquet from the front of room to the back of the room working as a team.

food stations or gazing service: A type of banquet service that allows guests to obtain food from individual tables strategically placed around the banquet room.

forecasting: Planning for anticipated business based upon previous history of the restaurant, reservations, and events that are planned for the community that will affect the business.

4-top: Also four-top. A table that seats four.

French service: A style of service in which final preparation of food is done at the guest's table with flourish and fanfare.

friendliness: A way in which individuals make their guests feel important by talking to them, and by using Maslow's theory to make them feel comfortable in the restaurant.

front of the house: A term referring to employees who work in direct contact with guests.

function: Any use of banquet facilities.

function book: A constantly updated list of the rooms that the establishment has to rent on a daily basis, and the functions booked into those rooms.

function sheet (also called banquet event order [BEO]): A form, prepared by the banquet office, that lists in detail everything that the host desires for the event.

grazing service: A type of banquet service that allows guests to obtain food from different locations throughout the room or rooms.

Gretzky service: A term that refers to service people's ability to anticipate their guest's needs and satisfy them before they even realize they have a need (refilling wine and water glasses, obtaining more bread, etc.).

guarantee: A host's promise regarding the minimum number of guests that the host will have to pay for at a banquet.

guéridon: A cart used in French service.

HACCP (Hazard Analysis Critical Control Point): A system that enables an operation to identify the foods and procedures most likely to cause illness.

head banquet waiter: A person responsible for the success of the party in the room in which he or she is supervising.

health department: An agency that issues permits for operation of food service establishments and monitors the cleanliness of the establishments.

host: The person who greets guests in a dining room, seats them, and handles any problems that might arise during the course of their dinner.

impulsives: Guests who patronize the restaurant who crave a menu item or are not in the mood to cook a meal.

"in the weeds":   A slang term used to describe an employee who has too many people to serve at once.

Lead: The member of the team (in the team system of service) who greets guests, takes dinner orders, sells and serves drinks and wine, turns dinner orders into the kitchen and times the dinners, and sets the pace for the team.

logbook: A document kept at the establishment's host desk. Information included in the book concerns the number of meals served, the weather for the day, any special events, the money generated per hour, and the money per meal period. A section is reserved for messages between the day and night hosts.

love and belonging needs: The third in Maslow's Hierarchy of needs. This need deals with the fact that individuals must belong or be accepted by their peers.

maître d'hôtel: The French term for the person responsible for all of the dining rooms in a hotel.

maître d'hôtel de carré: The French term for the person responsible for one section of the dining room.

Maslow's Hierarchy: A series of five needs that humans must satisfy. Before moving to a higher need, the lower need must be satisfied.

MBWA: Management by wandering around.

MICROS: A brand name for a point of sales system.

modified deluxe buffet: A kind of buffet service in which tables are set and guests are served coffee and perhaps dessert at their tables, but obtain the rest of their food from a buffet.

no-shows: Guests who do not show up for their reservations.

occupancy rate: A figure used in a lodging establishment to anticipate the number of guests who will be staying in the establishment on a certain night.

off-premise catering: Providing food, service, staff, and cleanup at the guest's location.

open bar: At a banquet, an arrangement by which the host pays for all drinks consumed by the guests.

open seating: The practice of allowing guests to reserve tables for any time that the restaurant is open.

overbooking: The practice of taking more reservations than the restaurant can accommodate.

physiological need: The first in Maslow's Hierarchy of needs. Physiological needs deal with food, water, sex, and sleep.

place setting: All the utensils, linens, plates, and glasses needed by one guest to consume the meal, arranged in the proper sequence.

point of sale (POS):   A computerized system that allows a waitperson to order food directly from a computer terminal, either hand held or stationary.

policy sheet: A sheet printed by banquet facilities that lists their specific policies on costs, deposits, guarantees, and contracts, among other things.

priority seating: Also called call-ahead seating. A system used in restaurants that do not accept reservations, in which patrons can call ahead to be placed on a waitlist.

QSC: An acronym for the standards of business at McDonald's. *Q* stands for quality; *S* for service; and *C* for cleanliness.

qualify: To determine how much money the client will spend at a banquet and if the client can pay for the banquet.

réchaud: A small heating utensil used in French service.

reservation: A promise for a table in a restaurant.

reservation manager: A person whose sole job is to plan and organize reservations for the restaurant.

residence time: The time it takes a party of guests to eat its meal and pay its bill.

Russian banquet service: A style of service in which the service staff work as a team. All food is placed in silver trays in the kitchen, and the service staff work in teams of two.

Russian service: A style of service in which food is placed on silver trays in the kitchen and then transferred from the tray to the guest's plate by the service staff in the dining room.

safety: A need to feel secure that the restaurant patron will not be robbed and that the food will be prepared in a sanitary environment governed by health department requirements.

sanitation: The process of keeping the restaurant clean of filth and foodborne diseases.

sautéed: Food that is browned or cooked in a small amount of hot fat.

seating: The tables in a restaurant used for one specific meal period.

self-actualization: The fifth of Maslow's Hierarchy of needs. Self-actualization comes from the individual, after the dependent needs have been met.

service: Competency and friendliness combined.

service person: The individual who has the responsibility of serving the guests their meals. Often this person is called a waitperson.

shadowing: A method in which a new employee follows a trainer around and observes how to do the job.

sidework: Tasks other than waiting on guests that the service staff have to complete, such as filling salt and pepper shakers and folding napkins.

silver service: Another term for Russian service, so called because food is served on silver trays.

6-top: Also six-top. A table that seats six.

socializers: Guests who patronize the restaurant who want to spend time with their family and or friends.

sommelier: A French term for wine steward, the restaurant employee responsible for suggesting and selling wines to guests to complement their meals.

standard abbreviations: A shortened form of words or part of words used to assist the hospitality staff communicate food and drink orders.

station: An area of the dining room, which usually consists of 12 to 24 seats.

station method: A type of service in which the waitstaff are assigned areas of the room to serve a banquet.

sub rosa: A term from Roman times, meaning confidentiality.

suggestive selling: The process in which waitpeople encourage guests to buy extra food or beverage items by using mouth-watering descriptions.

sweep method: A type of service in which the waitstaff work together to serve food and clear dirty dishes at a banquet.

table check: A form used to keep track of what point each table has reached in the course of its meal, enabling the host to know where and when he or she will be able to seat arriving guests.

table d'hôte: A complete meal served to all guests at a fixed price.

tact: The ability to say or do the correct thing so as not to offend the guest.

team system: A way of organizing a dining room for service, in which three people together serve a station of between 40 and 45 seats.

tentative booking: A client reserves a room without a deposit. The client will have first refusal if another guest would like the same room at the same time.

time in: The time that a guest entered into the restaurant.

time seated: The time that the guest has been seated at the table.

turning tables: Resetting the guest table for another party. The phrase is often used in conjunction with how many times a table is reset during the meal period. For example, "the tables were turned over three times" means that each table was used for three parties.

turnsheet: A form used to keep track of the number of guests that have been seated at a service person's station for a particular meal period.

ubiquitous: Everywhere at the same time.

underliner: A plate that goes beneath another plate to make it easier to serve food. For example, a saucer placed under a soup cup would be an underliner.

utensils: This refers to all forks, knives, and spoons used by the guests to eat their food.

waitlist: A form used by hosts that allows walk-ins to be seated in an organized manner.

walk-ins: These are guests who patronize the restaurant without making a reservation; in effect, they walk in the door expecting to obtain a table.

wine steward: The employee of the restaurant responsible for suggesting and selling wines to guests for their meals; also called the sommelier.

word of mouth: The most potent form of publicity; this occurs when people tell other people about their experiences (whether good or bad) with the business.

working the floor: Said of a host, it means circulating around the dining room talking to guests and assisting the service staff.

Index

Note: Page numbers in *italics* indicate figures.
Words in **boldface** are in French.